MEMORIALS OF HINDLEY.

BY JOHN LEYLAND,

OF

THE GRANGE.

PART FIRST.

"The river that by our door doth pass,
His first beginning is but small and shallow,
Yet, keeping on his course, grows to a sea."

SHAKESPEARE.

MANCHESTER:

JOHN HEYWOOD, 141 AND 143, DEANSGATE.

IN MEMORY

OF

ALFRED PENNINGTON,

A GREAT LOVER OF HINDLEY,

AND

A LIBERAL SUPPORTER OF ITS CHARITIES,

THIS VOLUME

IS AFFECTIONATELY INSCRIBED.

PREFACE.

THESE Memorials are not put forth as a History of Hindley. The Compiler, having for many years taken a great interest in the events of his native village, collected, as opportunity served, facts and dates bearing upon its history; and, unwilling for them to be lost, he has taken this means of ensuring their preservation.

THE GRANGE,
  December 31st, 1873.

MEMORIALS OF HINDLEY.

HISTORY, speaking in the general acceptation of the term, Hindley has none. No great event of war or politics has ever taken place within its boundaries, nor has it ever been distinguished as the birthplace or residence of any person of national celebrity. The Roman Road from Wigan to Manchester is known to have passed through it. This is supposed to have run in a direct line between the two places, its course having been traced at the back of Brook House and The Leylands, both of which houses are situate in Lord-street. The soil, when turned up by the plough, in this direction is said to be gravelly and of a different character to that of the adjoining land, and is supposed therefore to offer confirmatory evidence on the point. The late Rev. E. Sibson, incumbent of Ashton, a gentleman of considerable classic and antiquarian repu-tation, spent much time in investigating the course of the road, and his opinions coincide with the views here expressed.*

The soil has never yet yielded up any coins or pottery of that wonderful people. The history of the County Palatine and Duchy of Lancaster, written by the late

---

* Mr. Sibson was a man of eccentric habits. He was tall and robust, and a great pedestrian. His walks he often took in a direct line, letting neither ploughed field, nor hedge, nor ditch interrupt his course. A story is related of his Diocesan once paying him a visit. The bishop was accompanied by his chaplain, who began to prepare his lordship on the way for the sort of man he was about to call upon. After describing his personal appearance and peculiarities he ended by saying, "You will find him a diamond in the rough." On approaching the Parsonage Mr. Sibson was seen delving vigorously in his garden and flushed with the exercise, whereupon the bishop turned to his chaplain, and said, "You told me he was a diamond in the rough, but I call him a ruby."

Edward Baines, and edited by the late John Harland, contains the following notice of Hindley :—

"This township of Hindley is amongst the most populous and thriving districts in the parish of Wigan. A hill in this township, called Castle Hill, is supposed to have been the site of a watch tower, the existence of which is indicated by the remains of a moat or trench, the plough and the spade having destroyed all traces of the building. At the base of the hill is a pleasant valley called 'The Danes,' (? denes, *i.e.* dells). Swane, the son of Leofwine, a Saxon, in the time of Henry II., gave to Gospatric half a carucate of land in Hindele in free marriage, and Roger, the son of Gospatric, held that land of Thomas Burnhul in the reign of King Henry. Adam de Hindele held two bovates in Hindele of ancient feoffment; Robert, the father of Richard de Hindele, gave to the hospital thirty acres of that half carucate, in the time of King Henry; and the same Robert, in the time of King John, gave two acres and a half to the hospital, and six acres to the Abbey of Kokersand. Of this family was Hugh Hindley, of Hindley Hall, whose son Adam married Cecily, daughter of Henry Tildesley, of Wardley, and had a grandson, Robert, married in 8 Richard II. (1384-5) to Emma, one of the heiresses of Pemberton. Roger Hindley, about the age of Henry VIII., married Beatrix, daughter of Robert Molyneux of Melling, whose descendant, Robert Hindley, was living at the hall in 1613, having by his two wives four sons and three daughters. In 1664, Hindley Hall was the seat of James Duckenfield, Esquire, an utter barrister of Gray's Inn, younger son of Robert Duckenfield, of Duckenfield, Cheshire. Hindley Hall is now the property and residence of Roger Leigh, Esquire. An ancient residence of the Hindleys was called Oldfilde House in the reign of Philip and Mary. Hindley as a manor is a member of the barony of Newton. It was granted by Robert Banastre, the last baron of that name, to his kinsman Fulco Banastre, whose son Robert held it in the reign of Edward II., under John de Langeton and Alice his wife, the grand-daughter and heiress of Robert Banastre, by homage and fealty and the service of a pair of gilt spurs and the king's scutage. This property was alienated by the Banastres to Jordan de Workesley, whose daughter and heiress Margaret, with her husband, Thurstan de Tildesley contested the right to it unsuccessfully against Robert de Langeton, son and heir of John and Alice (who had had no power to alienate it). This Robert, and Margaret his wife, levied a fine at York in 1335 (9 Edward III.) of the third part of the manor of Langeton, in the county of Leicester, of a messuage and a carucate of land in Hendon, in the county of Middlesex, of a messuage and 38½ acres of land in Walton-le-Dale, and of the manor of Hyndleigh, and of half the manor of Goldburn, with appurtenances. An exemplification of this fine was granted by letters patent in 1391 (15 Ric. II.), on the requisition of John de Langeton, son of Robert, the second son of Robert and Margaret, and in the 19 Ric. II. a partition of deeds was made between him and his young cousin Ralph, baron of Newton, who had already in 1364 (3 of Edward III.) confirmed the settlement of the paternal estates in Leicestershire, of Hendon and of Hindley, on the junior branch of the family. The tenure of the manor of Hindley, as parcel of the Makerfeld fee, was in free soccage by a rent of three peppercorns yearly for all services. The Leicester-shire property continued in the Langtons until the time of Henry VIII. They were seated at Low Hall, in Hindley, now a farmhouse surrounded by a moat, until the eighteenth century, when Edward Langton, of Low dying without issue, the estate was inherited in 1733 by a nephew named William Pugh, whose nephew and heir, Edward Philip Pugh, of Coytmore, in Carnarvonshire, conveyed in 1765 the Low Hall estate in Hindley, the manor of Hindley, a certain reserved rent, and the mineral under Rigby's tene-ment, near Hindley Green, for a consideration of £6,650 to the Duke of Bridgewater, whose trustees now hold the lordship. An Irish family of Langton, seated at Kilkenny in the reign of Henry VII., claim descent from this line. Hindley was formerly subject to inundations, and hence two briefs were granted in this place, the one in 1795, and the other in 1802, to repair the damage suffered by the inhabitants; the former of which yielded £1,310, and the latter £1,002. Hindley Hall is in Aspull. The places of worship in this township are numerous. The Episcopal Chapel was originally built in 1641 by the Puritans, and so was not consecrated. In 1650 the inquisition returned Mr. William Williamson, 'an able, godly, and faithful minister,' as officiating and recommended that it should be made a separate parish. In 1662, the chapel was held by Mr. James Bradshaw, a Presbyterian, a moderate man, who had been removed from the rectory of Wigan by the Independents for not observing the fast in June, 1650. He was one who took a forward part in promoting the Restoration, but nevertheless he was ejected in 1662, and was imprisoned for some months in the attempt to silence him. Owing to the non-consecration of the building, disputes took place about it, the non-conforming party who had built it claiming it with its endowments; but finally they were defeated, and built the present Presbyterian Chapel, where, and at Ranford (? Rainford), Mr. Bradshaw preached. The church, All Saints', was consecrated in 1698, when it probably (says Canon Raines) obtained parochial rights. The living is now a vicarage; the Rev. C. H. Newbold (1863) is the present incumbent; patron, the rector of Wigan. A second church, St. Peter's, built in 1864, is also a perpetual curacy; the Rev. Peter Jones (1866) is the incumbent; patrons, the trustees. There is also a Catholic Chapel, built in 1788; a Presbyterian Chapel, built subsequent to 1662, for Mr. Bradshaw, the ejected minister of Hindley, but now used by the Unitarians; an Independent Chapel, built in 1815, and another built in 1830; and a Wesleyan Methodist Chapel, built in 1832. There are also Primitive Methodist and Baptist Chapels. The sanitary state of this township, which has increased considerably in population of late years, has recently excited considerable attention, owing to the frequent visitation of epidemic diseases. An effort to place the government of the town in the hands of a board constituted under the provisions of the Local Government Act has this year (1867) been successful, and already sewerage works have been commenced, and before long it is expected there will be a good water supply."

A phenomenon, known as the burning well, obtains this notice from the historian :—

" For nearly three hundred years the cannel of Haigh and the burning well of Hindley have attracted the attention of the curious. Leland, the itinerant, we have seen, mentions the former ; and the following curious description is given by the honourable Roger North, in his Life of Francis North, Baron Guildford, in the year 1676. In a circuit through the north of England the lord-keeper visited Lancaster, and his biographer says :—

"' In the return homewards from Lancaster his lordship took all the advantage he could of seeing great towns and places of note. He staid some days with Sir Roger Bradshaw, whose lordship is famous for yielding the canal (or candle) coal. It is so term'd, I guess, because the manufacturers in that country use no candle, but work by the light of their coal-fire. The property of it is to burn and flame till it is all consumed, without leaving any cinder. It is lighted by a candle like amber, and the grate stands, not against the back of a large chimney, as common coal grates ; but in the middle, where ballads are pasted round, and the folk sit about it, working or merry-making. His lordship saw the pits where vast piles of that coal were raised ; and it is a pity the place wants water carriage ; else London would be, in the better part, served with it. But the greatest wonder his lordship saw, was that which they call the Burning Well. The manner of it is this. First, in some place, where they know the

sulphurous vapour perspires (often in a ditch) they
dig up a turf, and clap it down in its place again; and
then they are ready for projection. When the shew
company are come, a man takes up the turf, and, after a
little puffing of a brown paper match gives fire, and
instantly the hole is filled with a blue spirituous flame
like brandy. It seem'd to waste, and I believe would
not have burnt in that manner long; but while it was
burning they put water in the hole, and the flame continued upon the water as if it had been spirits. And
some people said they used to boil eggs there. That
which seem'd most strange was that the vapour should
come through the water and burn, and no bubbling of
the water appear. It seems to infer that the vapour
permeates the body of the water, as water through
sands. But, I question, if the body were not fluid, but
rigid, as glass, whether the vapour would so easily pass
it; for the perpetual action of the fluid parts facilitates
the passage. And it is some demonstration how easily
the effluvia of a magnet may permeate glass, metals,
and every palpable substance we are acquainted with,
as we continually observe of them.'

" Other accounts of the burning well, which, a generation ago continued to attract visitors, but has now
long disappeared, are given in the *Philosophical Transactions*, and other publications, with some variations, and
with the details of a number of experiments, but they
all resolve themselves into the same phenomena. In
Mr. Stirling's account of the burning well, he speaks
of it as at one place only; and says that the water at
the boiling place boiled and rose up like water in a
pot upon the fire, though his hand put into it felt no
warmth. The flame rises in a cone-like form, with a
circular base about the circumference of a man's hat
at the brim. The burning well was in Derby Lane,
about a mile from Hindley Hall, and in 1835 was
described thus: 'The gas ascends out of a small
hole through a heap of clay, near a little rill, and
takes fire on the application of the flame of a candle,

the carbonated (carburetted) hydrogen, a black oily liquid, boiling up and bubbling continually at the bottom, while the flame ascends about half a yard high.' "

The burning wells of Hindley are now things of the past. For many years there were two in existence. The best known was in Derby Lane, on the margin of a deep ditch, of a few inches in diameter, and about as deep as wide, and is the one referred to in the foregoing extracts. The other was near the Dog Pool, or, as it is now called, Grange Brook. The latter was bricked round, two feet or more in diameter, and several feet in depth. Originally it was within the precincts of the garden of an old farmhouse which stood near the spot, and was doubtless sunk for domestic purposes. The gas passing into the well would render the water unfit for drinking, and cause it to be disused. It is still in existence, but covered up. The one in Derby Lane has been long since buried beneath cartloads of rubbish.

The area of the township is 2,610 acres, statute measure. The surface is for the most part flat. An eminence in the northern part, called the " Castle Hill," affords an extensive prospect. On the west side of this eminence lies a valley, called " The Danes," through which flows the Borsden Brook, which is not without its aspects of picturesque beauty. The soil in this neighbourhood, and up to the northern extremity of the township, is of a rich, loamy character; in all other parts it is thinner and near the clay.

POPULATION.

Year.	Population.
1841	5,458
1851	7,023
1861	8,477
1871	10,627

The number of inhabited houses is 2,159, and the present rateable value of the township is £49,950 0s. 8d.

The Tithes are commuted at £298 11s. 0½d.

A Local Board was formed for the government of the township in 1867, under the provisions of the Local Government Act 1858, consisting of twenty-one members, elected by the ratepayers for three years, one-third of whom retire annually. Sewerage works are now being carried out by the Board, which, when completed, will doubtless contribute materially to the health of the neighbourhood.

Places of Worship.

	Built.	No. of Sittings.
All Saints' Church*	1641	700
Presbyterian Chapel †	1700	250
St. Benedict's Roman Catholic Church‡	1788	450
St. Paul's Independent Chapel §	1815	480
Bridge Croft Independent Chapel	1838	200
Wesleyan Methodist Chapel, Frederick Street	1851	300
Primitive Methodist Chapel, Platt Bridge	1854	200
Particular Baptist Chapel, Market Street	1854	150
Brunswick Chapel, Hindley Green, United Methodist Free Church	1855	300
Primitive Methodist Chapel, Woodford Street, Castle Hill	1856	200
St. Peter's Church	1863-6	700
United Methodist Free Church, Hindley Common	1866	200
Independent Methodist Chapel, Lowe Green	1867	200
Wesleyan Methodist Chapel, Walthew Lane	1869-70	260

---

* Rebuilt, 1766.

† Rebuilt, 1788.

‡ Rebuilt, 1868-9. Before 1788 a chapel existed at Strangeways Hall, where service was performed, and before that again at the Lowe Hall.

§ The number of 480 includes the sittings in the galleries, which were not erected until some years after the building of the chapel.

The Lowe Mill was originally a corn mill, with a thatched roof, worked by water power. About 1780-1790, Mr. Richard Battersby, the then owner of the mill estate, added a cotton mill to the corn mill, and was the first to introduce factory labour into the township. Early in the present century the late Mr. John Pennington founded the cotton works known as Worthington Mills, which are still in the possession of his family, and have been growing in importance from that time until now, and in 1832 he became the proprietor, by purchase, of the Lowe Mills. The manufactories at present consist of the Lowe Mills, the Worthington Mills, the Borsden Mills, the Marsh Brook Mills, the Hindley Mill, and the Hindley Common Mills. Altogether, they are computed to have room for upwards of 130,000 spindles, and to give employment to from 1,400 to 1,500 hands. Power-loom weaving is carried on at the Worthington and at the Hindley Mills.

Seams of coal of great value lie under the entire township. They are worked by various proprietors, and afford employment to a large portion of the inhabitants.

The quantity of coal at present raised, I am informed by one of the coal proprietors, is estimated at 950,000 tons yearly, and employment is found at the various collieries for 2,350 persons.

There are no great estates in the immediate neighbourhood of Hindley. The land in the township itself, and for a mile or two round, has been broken up into a variety of small holdings. The manor of Newton, and fee of Mackerfield, which extends over the townships of Lowton, Golborne, Haydock, Ince, Pemberton, Billinge, Winstanley, Orrell, Hindley, Abram, Kenyon, Ashton, Southworth-with-Croft, Haughton, Middleton, and Arbury, Woolston-with-Martins-Croft, and Poulton-with-Fearnhead, was formerly owned by the Langton family, of Lowe Hall, and was sold by them to the Leghs of Lyme, in Cheshire, about 200 years ago, in whose possession it has remained ever since. The manorial rights of Hindley do not yet appear to be clearly defined. About forty years ago some of the freeholders were summoned by Mr. Legh to attend a court leet at Newton, which was then considered a new exaction, and similar summonses have been served at times subsequently. Other powers than these I never heard of being exercised.

THE LOWE HALL.

The Langtons were formerly the most influential people in the township. Their ancient residence was the Lowe Hall, where they appear to have been settled for several centuries. In 1733 Edward Langton died without issue, and the family was represented afterwards by his nephew, William Pugh, and *his* nephew, Edward Philip Pugh, sold the hall, with some surrounding land, in 1765, to the Duke of Bridgewater, whose representatives are the present owners. The greater part of the estate, however, had been sold piecemeal, farm by farm, previously.

The house is now nothing more than a farm house; the moat surrounding it, with the tall columns of a gateway, being the only remaining evidence of its former state. A few scattered trees on its western side, some dead, and others dying through the effects of the smoke and vapours of the neighbouring manufactories, mark where an ornamental plantation once stood. Some tapestry hangings were removed—in the memory of people recently living—to Worsley Hall.

The Langtons of Lowe Hall, and the Hindleys of Hindley Hall, are mentioned in several of the Herald's visitations.

HINDLEY HALL.

Hindley Hall, notwithstanding its name, is situate, as stated by the historian, not in Hindley, but in the adjoining township of Aspull. It never seems to have been a place of importance. If it was ever surrounded by a domain of any extent, it long since disappeared, as, less than a century ago, it was comprised within a score or two of acres immediately surrounding the house. The present estate was formed by the late Sir Robert Holt Leigh, Bart., the then proprietor, purchasing several of the contiguous farms.

In a volume issued by the Chetham Society in 1866, entitled " The Admission Register of Manchester School, with some Notices of the more Distinguished Scholars," edited by the Rev. Jeremiah Finch Smith, M.A., rector of Aldridge, Staffordshire, there is a notice of this gentleman.

"Sir Robert Holt Leigh, Bart., M.A. (date of admission unknown). He was the eldest son of Holt Leigh, Esq., of Hindley and Whitley Halls, Lancashire, by Mary, younger daughter and coheiress of Thomas Owen, Esq., of Upholland Abbey, in that county, and Margaret his wife, only daughter and heiress of Thomas Bispham, Esq., and was born at his father's town residence in Wigan, on Christmas day, 1762. He was descended from a highly-respectable line of ancestry, who had been for some centuries possessed of landed property in this part of the county. His grandfather, Alexander Leigh, Esq., of Bretherton, completed at his own expense the canal which extended from Wigan to the River Ribble, having obtained in 1720 an Act of Parliament for the purpose, thereby conferring great benefit upon Wigan and the neighbourhood. Robert Holt Leigh proceeded from the school to Christ Church, Oxford, and passed the requisite examinations ; but, strange to say, he did not take any degree till he was 70 years of age. When I was residing in Oxford as an Hulmian exhibitioner, I remember the baronet coming into residence at Christ Church for the requisite number of days before he could be admitted to the degree of B.A., which he took on the 26th October, 1837, and proceeded M.A. on the 30th of May in the year following. It was said at the time that he did so in order to secure a vote as a

member of convocation on those questions of deep
interest affecting the Church and the university which
then began to be publicly agitated. He was throughout
life a high Tory and firm Churchman, but strenuous
Protestant. He was first returned to Parliament in
1802, as member for Wigan, and continued to represent
his native borough to the year 1820, when he voluntarily
resigned, and was succeeded by Lord Lindsay, afterwards
Earl of Balcarres. Throughout his parliamentary career
he gave his hearty support to Mr. Pitt and Mr. Canning,
except on the question of the Roman Catholic claims,
on which he was opposed to them. On the accession of
Mr. Canning to office he was created a baronet, his
patent bearing date 23rd of May, 1815, with remainder
to the male issue of his father, none of whom, however,
survived to succeed to the title, and, the baronet dying
a bachelor, it became extinct. In the year 1798, when
the peace of the country was disturbed by a spirit of
discontent leading on to insurrection and riot, he became
commandant of a society of gentlemen at Wigan, called
the Wigan Arms Association, and distinguished himself
in various encounters with the mob. In the agitation
consequent upon the Reform question, in 1831, he
suffered severely from the violence of the mob at the
Wigan election, when he was the proposer of Mr. J. H.
Kearsley; and he used afterwards to tell an amusing
story how the Liberals of that day, when they got him
on the ground and were intent upon administering very
severe corporal punishment, even if they spared his life,
kicked each other's shins with their heavy clogs as they
hastily aimed at his prostrate body, to his amusement
and satisfaction alike. His brother, Mr. Roger Holt
Leigh, of Leeds, died on the 13th of May, in that year,
in consequence of the injuries which he received at this
election. Through life he interested himself in all
matters relating to the town of Wigan, and was a
trustee of the grammar school of that place, as well as
of the Manchester school, of which his high classical
attainments, quite as much as his rank in society, have

given him a place among her most distinguished alumni. He died at Hindley Hall, on the 21st of January, 1843, in his 81st year, a magistrate and deputy-lieutenant of the county. He left behind him a large property, and a valuable library, particularly rich in classical books, which not only ornamented his shelves, but were read and remembered, and readily and aptly quoted by him as occasion served. One of the great scholars of the age, Dr. Donnegan, in the preface to his Greek and English Lexicon, fourth edition, 1842, says : ' Among the advantages which I have derived from the publication of my ' Greek and English Lexicon,' there is none I deem more precious than its having procured me the acquaintance, and I may with just pride add, the friendship, of Sir R. H. Leigh, Bart., a gentleman who has improved his talents by refined, well-directed, and assiduous culture. Thoroughly acquainted with the best writers of the modern languages, and having attained a critical and profound knowledge of the Greek language and literature—the excellencies of which his peculiar turn of mind enables him to appreciate fully— he still devotes a considerable portion of his studious hours, with glowing enthusiasm and untiring ardour, to the poets and orators who have bequeathed to us such splendid and enduring monuments of Grecian genius. To the accomplishments of a scholar he has added the advantages of having visited the most interesting countries of Europe, surveyed their choicest specimens of art with a critical eye, and observed the characters of men and manners so truly, as to justify the application to him of the commendation bestowed upon Ulysses by the great poet. Sir Robert Holt Leigh occasionally attended the anniversary meetings of the old scholars, and was steward in 1796, as colleague to George Lloyd, Esq. The preceding brief notice of this distinguished scholar would be imperfectly true, unless it were added that over the latter years of his life it is better that a veil should be drawn. It is very sad to record folly and profligacy in the mature years of a life in which, otherwise, there is much to admire. By Sir Robert Holt Leigh's will the estates descended to his cousin, Thomas Pemberton, Esq., Q.C., for his life only, who thereupon assumed the additional title of Baron Kingsdown. To him I am indebted for a small photograph of the baronet, which is in the old school, and taken from a miniature, the only portrait in existence of this loyal subject and sound classical scholar. Sir R. H. Leigh was said to be the greatest snuff-taker in England, and carried snuff in his waistcoat pocket. He was also a great epicure, and generally tasted every dish on the dinner table. He rebuilt Hindley Hall from his own designs, and forgot to include a staircase! In affluence and readiness of classical quotations Sir Robert was perhaps unsurpassed by any scholar of his day.'"

ALL SAINTS' CHURCH.

The first church (or chapel, as it was originally called)
was built in 1641 on land given by Mr. George Green.*
Funds for the building were raised by subscription and
from the sale of pews.   An opinion prevails, and has
even found its way into the history of the county, that
it was built by the Puritans; but a Decree issued by
the Duchy Court of Lancaster, in 1669, gives particulars
of the early history of the chapel, and authoritatively
refutes this opinion.   As the document has special
relation to a portion of the endowment still enjoyed
by the church, I give it entire.   It was made
in Trinity Term, in the 21st year of King Charles
the Second, in a cause "Between Edward Green,
Peter Harrison, Wm. Crook, Wm. Dennys, John
Green, Nathaniel Molyneux, Jeremiah Harrison, Wm.
Chetam, and Ralph Prescot, Plaintiffs; Ellen Ranicars,
Pearce Ranicars, John Thomason, and Richard Hilton,
Defendants.   Whereas, the Plaintiffs did in or about
Easter Term, 1668, xhibit their Bill into this court
against the Defendants, thereby setting forth that
George Green, late of Hindley, in the county of Lancaster, deceased, about 30 years ago having a charitable
inclination to promote the erecting of a Chapel within
the Township of Hindley, where-in the word of God
and sacraments might be duly dispensed for the Ease
of the neighbourhood (being at a great distance from
their Parish Church of Wigan), by his Indenture or deed
lawfully executed, did give and convey to the plaintiffs,
together with some other persons, since deceased, and
their heirs, a parcel of land then marked, hedged out,
walled out, or divided from other of his lands, for the
erecting of a Chapel therein, and making and fitting of
a chapel yard thereunto, and whereupon, at the charge
of the plaintiffs, with other of the inhabitants, a Chapel

---

* Mr. George Green was the owner of the adjoining estate of Wood-daggers,
which continued in the possession of his family up to a recent period.

was afterwards erected, and a chapel yard made, wherein, since the erecting thereof, upon every Lord's day ordinarily the Word of God and prayers of the Church, by some orthodox Minister thereto ordained, have been duly preached and said; for the encouragement whereof and towards the maintenance of the Minister since the foundation of the Chapel, some charitable persons have contributed sundry sums, or other yearly benefit, and particularly one John Ranicars, late of Atherton, who, being seized of several messuages and Lands in Hindley, Westleigh, and Pennington, in Lancashire, by his last will dated in August, 1655, devised the messuages and lands unto John Stancliffe, alias Ranicars, and the heirs of his body, and for default thereof unto Pearce Ranicars, of Pennington, his nephew, and to the heirs of his body, chargeable that he the said Pearce Ranicars and his heirs should pay unto the executors of the said John Ranicars the annual rent of six pounds towards the maintenance of a Minister at the said Chapel, and to continue chargeable upon the said lands for ever, and named the Defendants, John Thomason and Richard Hilton, executors, and that shortly afterwards the said John Ranicars dyed, and the said John Stancliffe, by virtue of the devise to him, entered, and about December, 1666, also dyed, whereby the rent of six pounds was growing payable to the said Chapel. That Pearce Ranicars is also dead, and has left Pearce, the Defendant, his son and heir. That after his death the Defendant, Ellen Ranicars, mother of the Defendant Pearce, to whom these lands then remained (he being then an infant), or he the said Defendant, Pearce, entered upon the lands, and having the deeds and last will concerning the disposition of the lands and the rent, together with the other Defendants, take the profits to their own uses, and do not allow unto William Dennys, one of the Plaintiffs, being the present Minister of the said Chapel, the said rent, and that the Executors deny to intermeddle or sue for or receive this rent for the Minister, and to make any settlement thereof. And that the Defendants in their answers may set forth the will of Jno. Ranicars, and especially concerning the charging of the said rent for the use of the Chapel. And that the Defendants may be compelled to pay over the said rent, and the arrearages thereof, and that the said rent by the Decree of this Court may be secured and settled upon the plaintiff's Feoffees or Trustees, for the use of the Minister for the time being of this Chapel is the scope of the Bill. To which Bill, in or about Easter term last, the Defendants answered, and by their answers the said Defendants, Ellen Ranicars and Pearce Ranicars, say they believe that George Green, deceased, made and executed such conveyance of the parcel of Land in Hindley for the erecting and making of a Chapel and chapel yard, and for such use and intent as by the Bill, and confess that John Ranicars, deceased, by his last will, dated the 16th of August, 1655, did give all his messuages and lands in Hindley, Westleigh, and Pennington, unto John Stancliffe, alias Ranicars, his reputed son, and to the heirs of his body, and for default thereof to his nephew, Pearce Ranicars (now deceased), late husband of the Defendant Ellen, and late father to the Defendant Pearce, and to the heirs of his body, charged and chargeable that he, the said Pearce and his heirs, should pay to the Executors of the said John Ranicars and their heirs the annual rent of six pounds, for and towards the maintenance of a Minister at the Chapel of Hindley, out of the issues and profits thereof, to continue for ever for the use of the said Minister, and named the Defendants, John Thomason and Richard Hilton, and one John Withington (since deceased), his Executors, and shortly afterwards dyed, and that John Stancliffe, alias Ranicars, the first devisor, also dyed about the time in the Bill mentioned, without any issue of his body begotten. That since his death the Defendant, Ellen Ranicars, in right of the other Defendant, her son Pearce, did enter upon the said lands and received the profits, amounting to twenty pounds per annum, concerning which and the said yearly rent of six pounds given to the use of the Minister at Hindley, and the settlement thereof upon the complainants as Feoffees or Trustees for the use and benefit of the said Chapel, the Defendants submit to the order and decree of this Court. And the said other Defendants, John Thomason and Richard Hilton, do by their answers say that they do believe that George Green made such settlement upon the Plaintiffs for the use of the Chapel as in the Bill is set forth, and that John Ranicars, deceased, made such last will for the disposition of the six pounds per annum for the use of a Minister at the Chapel of Hindley as in the other Defendants' answers are set forth, and the other Defendants, Ellen and Pearce Ranicars, or the one of them, have entered upon the lands and take the profits thereof yearly, but deny that they at any time have received the said annual rent of six pounds so given by the will, or intermeddled therewith, albeit they are satisfied that it ought to be paid for the use in the will mentioned; and as to the settlement thereof upon the complainants as Feoffees or Trustees, for or on the behalf of the said Chapel and of a preaching Minister there, they, the said Defendants, submit to the discretion of this Court. And whereas it is ordered on the 12th of June instant, by consent, that the cause should be set down to be heard and determined in this Court upon Bill and answer this present day without notice to be given to the Defendants, or any of them. Now this day the same came to hearing accordingly. Upon opening the Plaintiff's Bill, by Mr. Lever, of the Plaintiff's counsel, and the Defendant's answer, by Mr. Holden, of the Defendant's counsel, it is this day finally ordered, adjudged, and decreed by the Right Honourable the Chancellor and Council of this Court, that the Defendants, Ellen Ranicars and Pearce Ranicars, or the one of them, and the heirs of the said Pearce, shall, from June to June, for ever hereafter, pay yearly unto the Plaintiffs, their heirs and assigns, the annual or yearly rent or sum of six pounds upon the feast days of Saint Michael the archangel, and the first day of May,

by equal portions, for the use and towards the maintenance of a preaching Minister at the Chapel of Hindley,
and that the messuages, lands, tenements, and here-
ditaments in and by the said last will of the said John
Ranicars, mentioned, given, and devised, shall from time
to time stand and be chargeable with the payment of
the said annual or yearly rent as aforesaid, and that
the other Defendants, John Thomason and Richard
Hilton, the Executors named in the said will, shall be
hereby discharged from the receipt of payment thereof.

"J. HEATH."

From this document it therefore clearly appears that
the building was destined from the first as a place of
worship for the Church of England. During the unsettled period which followed its erection it fell, like
other churches in the kingdom, for a time into the hands
of the Nonconformists, and a contest ultimately ensued
between one portion of the trustees who supported the
Church of England, and another who supported the
Nonconformists, for the possession of the building, when
it was finally decided that the latter had no valid claim
to it. From various causes, therefore, it was not until
the year 1698 that steps were taken for its consecration.

Copy of the Petition to the Bishop of Chester to Consecrate Hindley Chapel (1698.)

"To the Right Reverend Father in God Nicholas Lord
Bishop of Chester,—May it please your Lordship, we,
John Ranicars, Church Warden of the Parish Church of
Wigan, John Prescott, James Cheetham, Jonathan
Thomason, John Marsh, the Feoffees for the land
whereon the Chappell of Hindley is built, the said
Chappell and Chappell yard thereto belonging, and
we, Peter Worthington, John Prescott, and James
Cheetham, named and constituted Feoffees or Trustees
of several pious Devises, Gifts, and Legacies to ye use
of the said Chappell of Hindley, in the Parish of Wigan
and County of Lancaster, and the rest of the inhabitants

of ye Township of Hindley aforesaid, do, with united minds and desires, humbly represent unto your Lordship that our said Parish Church of Wigan being three miles distant from the greatest and most populous part of the said Township of Hindley, and George Green, of the said Township, Gentleman, having given and devoted a parcell of land to the end a Chappell might be built upon it, and the residue of the said parcell for a Chappell yard, a Chappell was thereupon erected, and a Chappell yard enclosed and fenced, in the year of our Lord God 1641, with the approbation and consent of Doctor Bridgman, ye then Lord Bishop of Chester and Rector of Wigan, at the contributions and charges of the Inhabitants of the said Township. That the said Chappell is regularly built, with a Chancell at the East end of it, distinguished from the body of the Chappell, having a communion table placed therein, and in ye Chappell a reading desk, pulpitt, seates, with other necessaries and ornaments. That, since the happy restoration of King Charles the Second and of the rights and privileges of the Church, several Benefactions and Legacies have been made and given to the endowment of ye said Chappell and the use and maintenance of an Orthodox and lawfull Minister of the said Chappell, so that the same do amount to the sum of Twenty Pounds per annum, or thereabouts. That some Dissenters from the Church of England (which God Almighty preserve) have (as your Lordship very well knows) by a long and obstinate suit attempted to seize ye said Chappell and to pervert it and the said gifts and devises from ye said uses to which they were piously devoted, and had probably succeeded had not your Lordship interposed as well your indefatigable pains, as your purse, in that cause wherein you have prevailed to have them restored and settled by definitive Decree in the Chancery of the Dutchy of Lancaster; and for your Lordship's affectionate and just vindication of the rights of the Church in general, and of the said Chappell in particular, we have reason to bless God and to hold your name and memory in veneration. And now for the reasons above mentioned we the said John Ranicars, John Prescott, James Cheetham, Peter Worthington, Jonathan Thomason, John Marsh, Feoffees and Trustees, and we the said Inhabitants, become humble and unanimous suitors to your Lordship as God's minister, the Bishop and Ordinary of this Diocese, to accept of this our free-will offering, and to Decree this Chappell and Chappell yard to be severed from all common and prophane uses, and so to sever them; and also by the Word of God and prayer, and other spirituall and religious duties, to dedicate and consecrate this Chappell to the sacred name of God, and to His service and worship only, and this Chappell yard to be a Cemetery or place of Christian buriall, wherein our bodies may be laid up until the day of the general Resurrection; promising that we will thenceforward ever hold this said Chappell as an Holy place, even as God's house, and this said Chappell yard as Holy ground, and use them accordingly; and that we will from time to time, and ever hereafter, as need shall be, see this Chappell conveniently repaired and decently furnished, and this yard conveniently repaired and fenced, in such sort as a Chappell and Cemetery or burying place ought to be; and we will (as occasion shall require) procure us some sufficient Clerke, being in Holy Orders, by your Lordship as Ordinary of this place, and by your successors, to be admitted and licensed, and to him to yield competent maintenance, to the end that he may take upon him the cure of the said Chappell, and duly say Divine Service in the same at times appointed, and perform all other such offices and duties as by the Canons of the Church and laws of the realm every Curate is bound to perform.

THE FEOFFEES.

Jno. Ranicars.	P. Worthington.
Jno. Prescott.	Jonathan Thomason.
James Cheetham.	Jon. Marsh.

THE INHABITANTS.

J. Hindley.
Jon. Bethell.
Wm. Taylor.
Jon. Morres.
Josep Skinner.
Wm. Aspull.
Thomas Lythgoe.
John Chadock.
Jon. Smethurst.
John Ashurst.
Wm. Needham.
Ralph Green
Richard Hindley.
Gilbert Lythgoe.
Peter Lythgoe.
Adam Johnson
Edward Marsh.
Jonathan Rothwell.
George Greene.
Matthew Smith.
Robert Rigby.
John Hodson.
John Farbrother.
Henry Walker.
George Jolly.
James Whittle.
Richard Yates.
Anthony Rigby.
Peter Greene.
John Adamson.
George Jolly, sen.
Jon. Rigbie.
Roger Aspull.
Christop. Thomason.
Joseph Southworth.
Jon. Alred.
Raph Ricroft.
George Sæpraef.
Wm. Bibby.

Rowland Meadow.
Ja. Bradshaw.
Henry Leyland.
John Hayes.
James Jolleyes.
John Leyland.
Thomas Partington.
John Lowe.
Thomas Hindley.
Richard Ince.
Jon. Duckworth.
Roger Ranicars.
Thomas Rigbys.
Giles Gregoreys.
Thomas Morris.
James Pennington.
James Haverson.
William Swift.
Oliver Rigbie.
Widow Snape.
Widow Donnall.
Gilbert Ounsworth.
John Swisft.
Jane Thomason, widow.
William Hampson.
Margt. Hart.
Jonathan Whalley.
Hugh Hyton.
Peter Smith.
Tho. Leyland.
John Hodson.
James Hodson.
Ralph Rigby.
William Raycroft.
Joseph Hoult.
Richard Cross."

Copy of the Deed of Consecration (1698).

"In the name of God, Amen. Since George Green, of Hindley, in the County of Lancaster and our Diocese of Chester, Gentleman, moved by a pious and religious devotion, has given and dedicated a parcel of land, or his field, that a Chapel or Oratory should be built in a part of the same, and that the rest of the same be consecrated as a place of burial, or Cemetery, for the use of the inhabitants of the village of Hindley aforesaid, within the Parish of Wigan, in the County of Lancaster and our Diocese of Chester as aforesaid. Since from that time foresaid inhabitants of the said village (the same village, or a part of it, being distant to the inhabitants more than three miles or thereabouts from the Parish Church of Wigan aforesaid) have built, raised up, and enclosed, in the year of our Lord 1641, this Chapel or Oratory (which, with the chancel, contains in itself, from east to west, 19 rods and four thumbs' breadth in length, and from north to south 8 rods 1 foot and five thumbs' breadth in width, or thereabouts ; also the land or surrounding place as a place of burial (with approbation and consent of the Revd. in Christ Father John Bridgeman, at that time Bishop of Chester, and rector of the rectory and Parish Church of Wigan aforesaid, our predecessor), and have decently and suitably provided ornaments, the said Chapel or Oratory with a reading desk or pulpit, a table adapted for the holy supper, convenient seats, and other necessaries. Since from that time many inhabitants of the said village, or the same neighbourhood, led on by a similar pious and religious devotion, have given, left, and devoted legacies, donations, and sums of money to the annual amount of £20, or exceeding, for the endowment of the said Chapel or Oratory, and for the use and support of a Minister lawfully sent, or to be sent, to serve the same curacy ; and since prudent and discreet men—John Ranicars, John Prescott, James Cheetham, Jonathan Thomason, and John Marsh, feoffees of the parcel of land or the aforesaid field or close, as also Peter Worthington and the said John Prescott and James Cheetham, feoffees of the said gifts, legacies, and sums of money, setting aside their right, title, and interest in the same, and giving up to us willingly and humbly their right, title, and interest for the following uses, have, together with the inhabitants of the foresaid village of Hindley, earnestly intreated, insomuch that we have vouchsafed to separate from common and profane uses, and by our ordinary and Episcopal authority, to dedicate and consecrate this House or Chapel for sacred and divine uses ; as also, the place or surrounding portion of land or foresaid field, for sacred uses, and as cemetery or place of burial for the inhabitants of the aforesaid village of Hindley, that the bodies of those dying there may be buried according to the Christian rite. Therefore, We, Nicholas, by the Divine permission Bishop of Chester, favouring in this respect the pious and religious wish of the same feofees and inhabitants, for the consecration of this House or Chapel erected and supplied with all requisites, and also of the aforementioned surrounding (as before mentioned) on this day, Wednesday, the feast of All Saints, that is to say the first day of November, 1698, instant, and having first humbly called upon the great and only God, Father, Son, and Holy Ghost, by our ordinary and Episcopal authority we separate this Chapel or Oratory and land aforementioned surrounding place, from all common and profane use ; and—according to the power vested in us, and we can by the canons of the Church, and the statutes of this Kingdom of England—we devote, dedicate, and consecrate, to the honour of God, this Chapel or Oratory raised for divine service, the celebration of sacred rites, for ministering the sacraments in the same, likewise for pouring out divine prayers to God, for preaching and expounding in the same the pure and sincere Word of God, for burying the dead inhabitants of the aforesaid village of Hindley, and for the performance of those other things that are done in

other chapels ; and we consecrate the said land or surrounding place for a cemetery or place of burial for the
bodies of those who die in the said village, that they
may be buried according to the Christian rite, and we
openly and publicly decree and declare that these same
ought in future to remain devoted, dedicated, and consecrated, without, notwithstanding, any prejudice, and
the right of the parochial and mother church of Wigan
aforesaid, being always preserved in all its tenths, privileges, and ecclesiastical profits whatsoever ; as likewise our rights and those of our successors, and the
dignity, jurisdiction, and honour of our cathedral church
of Chester being always preserved ; provided always that
all and each of the priests or ministers, about to take
from time to time the cure of souls in the said Chapel,
be examined, approved, and admitted by us and our
successors, according to the laws and canons of the
kingdom of England ; and that the forementioned
feofees and inhabitants, and their successors, maintain
and support the same priests or ministers thus
examined, approved, and admitted, and that they pay
to the same the annual stipend of £20 at least, and that
they keep the said Chapel sufficiently repaired, covered,
and decently furnished, and the cemetery or place of
burial sufficiently enclosed and fenced, without any
diminution or defalcation of the ecclesiastical rights, of
tenths, oblations, or gifts, belonging by right or custom
to the said parochial or mother church of Wigan aforesaid, or the Rector of the same for the time being. All
which and each, as far as lies in our power, we thus
decree and confirm for us and our successors by these
presents."

The chapel was built in 1641, and from that time up
to a recent period was called " the Parochial Chapel of
Hindley." The original building stood for 125 years,
when it was pulled down, having probably become
dilapidated and too small for the wants of the neighbourhood. The present church was erected in its place
in 1766, partly by a brief, partly by the sale of pews,

and partly by subscriptions. It is a plain brick structure, with arched windows, and is entirely destitute of architectural beauty. The property with which it was endowed was vested in trustees, and the patronage in the trustees and the best inhabitants of the township. The patronage was thus exercised without molestation for a considerable time, and there is no evidence of the transfer of the right. It is yet an undeniable fact that the rectors of Wigan claim, and now possess, the patronage. The trustees to whom George Green conveyed the land for the erection of the chapel are named in the Decree of the Duchy Court of Lancaster I have already quoted. The names of the trustees at other periods are subjoined.

A Trust Deed bears date the 28th and 29th of February, 1776. Thomas Needham, of Hindley, Yeoman, was the sole survivor of the former trustees.

The new trustees appointed therein were—

John Walmesley, the elder, of Preston, Esquire.
Ralph Peters, of Platt Bridge, Esquire.
Holt Leigh, of Wigan, Esquire.
James Eckersley, the elder, Hindley, Chapman.

John Birchall,	do.,	Yeoman.
Robert Ashton,	do.,	Shoemaker.
James Needham,	do.,	Weaver.
Henry Southworth,	do.,	Chapman.
James Woods,	do.,	Yeoman.
John Rigby,	do.,	do.
Hugh Stirrup,	Lowton,	Chapman.

The next Trust Deed is dated the 23rd and 24th of February, 1824. Of the former Trustees, John Walmesley, the elder, formerly of Preston, now of Bath, was the only survivor.

The new Trustees were—

John Walmesley, the younger, of Bath, Esquire.
Sir Robert Holt Leigh, Hindley Hall, Baronet.

Peter Ditchfield, Hindley, Gentleman.
John Pennington, Hindley, Cotton Spinner.
John Hargreaves, Westhoughton, Common Carrier.
Charles Ditchfield, Hindley, Gentleman.
Henry Battersby, do., Cotton Spinner.
Charles Battersby, do., do.
Richard Pennington, do., Cotton Manufacturer.

Another Trust Deed was executed on the 29th of October, 1853.

John Walmesley, John Hargreaves, and Richard Pennington, were the survivors of the preceding body.

The new Trustees were—
Alfred Pennington, of Hindley, Cotton Spinner.
Richard Spooner Bond, do., Cotton Spinner.
John Leyland, do., Gentleman.
John Jacson, do., Cotton Spinner.
Robert Rowbottom, do., Gentleman.
Richard Pennington, the younger, do., Cotton Spinner.

In the interval of little more than eight years from the date of the preceding Deed the deaths of two of the Trustees occurred, viz., John Walmesley and John Hargreaves, Esqrs., and the resignation of two others—Richard Spooner Bond and John Jacson, Esqrs.

A further Trust Deed became necessary in consequence, which bears date December 27th, 1861.

The remaining Trustees were therefore—
Richard Pennington, of Hindley, Esquire.
Alfred Pennington, do., Cotton Spinner.
John Leyland, do., Gentleman.
Robert Rowbottom, do., do.
Richard Pennington, the younger, do., Cotton Spinner.

To these were added—

Nathaniel Eckersley, of Wigan, Banker.
Charles Ducket Hargreaves, Bolton-le-Moors, Cotton Spinner.

Edward Grime, Hindley, Shopkeeper, and
Johnson Martin,   do.,   Gentleman.

A record of the early ministers of the Chapel has not
been preserved.   At the Restoration a Mr. Bradshaw
seems to have been the minister, but, on his refusing to
conform to the usages of the Church, he was ejected.
After this the chapel stood vacant until 1668, when the
Rev. William Dennys, the first regularly-constituted
minister, entered upon the office.   Various gentlemen
followed him in the few succeeding years, but it was not
until the appointment of the Rev. John Jackson, in
1698, that the names of the incumbents, and the dates
of their appointment, can be given with accuracy.   To
Mr. Jackson succeeded the Levers, father and son, who
together filled the office for the long period of 81 years.
The Rev. Thomas Lever was the last clergyman who
inhabited the old parsonage at the Hollins ; he died in
1789, and was followed by the Rev. John Croudson.
This gentleman was head-master of the Wigan Grammar
School, an office he retained all the time of his 22 years'
incumbency.   He died on the 24th December, 1810.
It was his custom to visit the village one day in each
week, accompanied by Mr. Ralph Peters, of Platt
Bridge (of whom I shall have to say more hereafter).
Regularly as the day came round the two gentlemen
might be seen entering the different houses of the
parishioners, inquiring after those who had been absent
from church the preceding Sunday, and carrying the
messages of the Gospel to the sick and to those who
from other causes were unable to attend public worship.

In 1813 the living was sequestrated, in consequence
of some impropriety, or alleged impropriety, on the part
of the then incumbent, the Rev. George Hendrick, and
the Rev. Hugh Evans was appointed curate in charge,
the duties of which office he continued to discharge
until Mr. Hendrick's death, in 1830.

Date of Institution.	Incumbents.	Cause of Vacancy.
Minister in 1668	William Dennys	———————
————	——— Atherton	———————
————	John Wood	———————
————	Richard Croston	———————
————	Robert Bradshaw	———————
————	Samuel Shaw...............	———————
————	James Shaw	———————
1698	John Jackson*	Died, 1708
1708	Samuel Lever†	Resigned, 1753
1753	Thomas Lever	Died, 1789
1789	John Croudson	Died, 1810
1811	Edward Grime	Resigned, 1811
1811	George Hendrick	Died, 1830
1830	Edward Hill	Died, 1853
1853	Peter Jones	Resigned, 1863
1863	Chas. Hutchison Newbold	

* Mr. Jackson was the first incumbent who kept registers. These records commence on the 24th of June, 1698. The first entries are as follow :—

CHRISTENINGS.
October, 1698.

16th. John and Alice, son and daughter of John Chadock, of Hindley, baptised.

MARRIAGES.
January, 1698-9.

5th. Thomas Rigby and Jane Hart, of Hindley.

BURIALS.
October, 1698.

17th. Nathanael, son of Roger Gregory.

† This gentleman appears to have been the first minister appointed by the rectors of Wigan.

The Table of Benefactions suspended inside the church preserves some historical facts.   On it we read: "This chapel and an house for the curate were built about the year 1641, by the inhabitants of Hindley, the ground being given by George and Edward Green."

Here follows a list of Benefactors and Benefactions since :—

	£	s.	d.
John Ranicar, of Atherton, gave a rent-charge upon Stone House for ever ...	6	0	0
Mrs. Frances Duckinfield, al's Croston, a rent-charge upon lands in Mobberley for ever	2	10	0
Humphry Platt, the yearly crop of hay and grass arising from 3 tofts lying in Low Meadows	0	15	0
Oliver Stopford, a legacy of	10	0	0
Thomas Aspul, do.	10	0	0
Edward Green do.	10	0	0
William Sale, sen., do.	3	0	0
William Sale, jun., do.	3	0	0
Randal Collier, houses and land in Hindley, to the yearly value of	10	7	0
Mary Collier, widow, and relict of the said Randal, a legacy of	50	0	0
Mr. Thomas Crooke, of Abram, gave an estate in Aulston and Whittingham to several pious uses, of which the Minister of Hindley's share is yearly, more or less	0	18	0
Improvements made by the Feoffies during several vacancies	114	0	0
Mr. Richard Wells, of Wigan, a legacy of	100	0	0
Thomas Lythgow, for a sermon every Saint Thomas' day, a legacy of	20	0	0
Mr. John Prescott, a rent-charge upon his lands in Hindley for ever............	0	10	0
Margaret Hart, a legacy of..................	5	0	0
James Pemberton, of Aspull, for an annual sermon on St. James' day	10	0	0

"Nehem. xiii., 14: Remember me, O my God, concerning this, and wipe not out my good deeds that I have done for the House of my God, and for the offices thereof."

The following extracts from the Churchwardens' Accounts may be found interesting :—

		£	s.	d.
1753-4.				
April 24.	P.^{d.} Visitation Court Fees ...	0	5	0
	Spent as Usual	0	2	0
	P.^{d.} Visitation Court Fees ...	0	4	0
	Spent upon that and some other of the Chapel Affairs ...	0	3	0
	P.^{d.} for Ale and Candles for th' Ringers on the 5th Novr.	0	2	1
	Spent among the Feoffes on New Year's Day	0	0	9
	Spent at Signing the Ley Book...	0	1	6
	P.^{d.} Clerk his Wages	2	0	0
	P.^{d.} for Cleaning Chapel, Dubing, Weeding, and Hanging Pulpit Cloths	0	4	6
	P.^{d.} Mr. Mort for Writing a Ley Book	0	1	6
1756-7.				
April 20.	P.^{d.} for an Act against Profane Swareing	0	0	6
1757.				
May 7.	P.^{d.} Samuel Hilton Bill for Chapel P.^{d.} Yate	0	5	7½
1758.				
March 27.	P.^{d.} to Samuel Hilton for Mending Chapel Yate	0	1	4
	P.^{d.} for a Form of Prayer for taking of Louisbourgh ...	0	0	8
	P.^{d.} for a Whip for Thomas Rycroft	0	0	2½
	P.^{d.} for a Notice for a Publick Fast	0	0	8

		£	s.	d.
	P^{d.} the Apparitor for a Form of Thanksgiving	0	0	8
	P^{d.} to the Singers towards Buying Dr. Green's Vol. of Anthems	1	1	0
	P^{d.} Thomas Rycroft in part of his Wages*	0	6	6
1759. May 18.	P^{d.} to Thomas Rycroft for a Hat	0	2	6
	P^{d.} for making Bier Cloth and Turning Pulpit Cloth	0	2	0
1759. May 18.	P^{d.} for Ale for Ringing for the Taking of Quebeck	0	1	0
	P^{d.} for a Proclamation for a General Fast	0	0	8
1760. May 18.	P^{d.} for a Form of Prayer for taking of Montreal	0	0	8
	P^{d.} for an Order of Councel for Praying for ye Royal Family	0	0	8
	P^{d.} for a Quarter of Cloth and Threed for Necking Surplice	0	0	6½
1762. April 13.	P^{d.} for 600 of Brick	0	6	0
	P^{d.} for an Anthem Book for the Singers	0	3	0
	P^{d.} for a Reed for the Bassoon	0	1	0
	Spent on the Coronation Day	0	5	0
	P^{d.} Mr. Finch for Binding Common Pray'r Book	0	5	0
	P^{d.} for Writing the Register†	0	2	0
1763. April 5.	P^{d.} to Robert Grime for 3 Reeds for the Bassoon promised by John Birchall whilst he was Chapel Warden	0	3	0

---

* As Sexton probably.

† A frequent charge in the accounts.

C

	£	s.	d.

P^{d.} Thomas Marsh for 16 Baskets of Coals and Leading for the Vestry 0 4 4

P^{d.} to John Hays for a Box to gather the Brief Money in... 0 0 6

P^{d.} Mr. Alcock's Bill when over concerning the Brief ... 2 12 6

P^{d.} for a Stamp 0 1 7

Spent at the same time at Mr. Wiggans 1 1 7½

P^{d.} to the Workmen for Enlarging the Chapel Yard and for Quick Woods 3 16 10

1764.

April 23. P^{d.} for a Form of Prayer for the Young Prince 0 0 8

P^{d.} for Cloth and Necking New Surplice, and Repairing the Old Ones 0 1 8

1765.

August 24. Gave the Sextones of Wigan for Finding us out a Bell Rope 0 0 2

Sept. 2. P^{d.} to some Strange Singers who came of Singing to the Chapel 0 2 0

1765.

Jan. 21. Sp^t at Wigan on some of the Trustees meeting to Sign a Draft on Mr. Byrd, of Stafford, for Payment of Part of the Brief Money, and some other business relating to the New Chapel 0 3 5½

At a Vestry held this 9th day of April, 1765, it is ordered by the inhabitants assembled that the Clerk's Wages for the future shall be encreased to the sum of £3 12s. per annum. And it is further agreed that the Sexton's Dues for Burials shall be as follows. That is to say :—

	£	s.	d.
For Making the Grave ...	0	0	8
For Carrying the Bier ...	0	0	4
For Tolling	0	0	2

1766.

June 26. P^{d.} for Box and Lead Weight to Ballance Chancel Door for clapping too with the wind as ordered at the last Vestry meeting 0 1 6

July 3. P^{d.} for a Book of Articles ... 0 0 8

March 29. P^{d.} for a Commission from Chester to Pull Down and Rebuild the Chapel by 5 2 4

1767.

April 21. P^{d.} for a Form of Prayer for the princess 0 0 8

Laid Down for a Brief 0 5 2½

Geave the Workmen when the first Stone of this Chapel was Laid 0 2 0

1767.

April 21. Divine Service was performed in this Chapel being the first time after its being rebuilt.

1768.

April 5. P^{d.} one half of the Expences when agreement was made with Edwd. Green for Exchanging some Land to be laid to the Chapel Yard, omitted last year 0 2 0

P^{d.} for Publishing two Meetings about Selling the New Seats, &c. 0 0 4

P^{d.} for mending the Pulpit Cushion 0 0 8

Oct. 9. P^{d.} for Gravelling the Chapel Yard, Mending the Horse Stone &c. 0 6 0

	£	s.	d.
Oct. 21. P^{d.} Mr. Dennil a Fee when consulted relating to the Singers obtaining consent from ye Court to Sing Anthems ...	0	5	0

Oct. 21.   P^{d.} Mr. Dennil a Fee when consulted relating to the Singers obtaining consent from ye Court to Sing Anthems ...   0 5 0

1767.

March 27. P^{d.} Richard Prescott for Platstones used about the Horse Stone 0 1 4

1771.

June 18.   P^{d.} for a Prayr for the Yong princess 0 0 8

March 23. P^{d.} Clerk for Candles for Ringers on Novr. 5th 0 0 1

1774.

P^{d.} William Blundell for Ale for the Ringers on Novr. 5th   0 3 0

March 18. P^{d.} Ralph Rylance for a New Chest for the Chapels use ...   3 9 5

Expended on the Chapel Warden and Singers in waiting of his Lordship the Bishop of Chester in Petitioning for to Sing Anthems 0 5 0

July 28.   P^{d.} for Cleaning Dialpost and painting 0 1 6

Oct. 21.   P^{d.} for Brief Money that was stolen 0 9 2½

Oct. 22.   P^{d.} for a Quarter of Cloath to Neck the Surplice 0 1 0

P^{d.} for Repairing Surplice   ...   0 0 8

P^{d.} for a Load of Cennel   ...   0 2 10

1776.

May 19.   P^{d.} to a Brief for Hail Storm in West Wycombe 0 4 2½

P^{d.} to a Brief for Bradshaw Chapel*0 2 7

---

* Such entries are numerous.

		£	s.	d.
Nov. 10.	P^{d.} to a Brief for Thornhill Church	0	2	5½
	P^{d.} for Assisting in puting up Kings Armes and the Commandments to two men ...	0	2	0
	P^{d.} to a Brief for Edenfield Chapel	0	2	8
1777.				
April 1.	P^{d.} for a Brief for Epston Church	0	2	2
	P^{d.} for a Brief for Boteswergoch Church	0	2	4
	P^{d.} for Ale on the Rejoicing of the Good News from America ...	0	3	6
	P^{d.} for Ale on the Rejoicing of the News from America ...	0	5	0
	P^{d.} for Writing these Accounts ...	0	0	6
1778.				
April 21.	P^{d.} to James Wielding for a Cheain and Pullies for the font and fixing them	0	11	0
	P^{d.} to Horwhich Church Briefe...	0	4	1
	P^{d.} to Butterton Church Brief ...	0	1	9
	P^{d.} to Ale for Ringers on Novr. 5th as usual	0	3	0
	P^{d.} to a Form of Prayer for Young princess	0	0	8
1778.				
April 21.	P^{d.} To a Book of Articles ...	0	0	8
	P^{d.} To Court fees	0	4	0
	P^{d.} To Attending Court ...	0	2	0
	P^{d.} To one Load of Cannel, and Leading	0	5	6
	P^{d.} To Robert Grimes, for Reeds, as usal	0	10	0
1780.				
March 28.	P^{d.} To Good New(s) from America for rejoiceing	0	2	0
	P^{d.} To Welling Church Brief ...	0	4	5
	P^{d.} To Holemford Chapel Brief	0	2	11
	P^{d.} To Weandworth Brief ...	0	4	7
	P^{d.} To Staponhill Brief ...	0	3	2

	£	s.	d.
P^{d.} To the King's Proclaimation for a general fast	0	1	4

1781.
April 17. P^{d.} for Alteration of ye prayer for Rebellion 0 0 8

P^{d.} for Rejoiceing for Taking of Charls Town in America ... 0 3 0

P^{d.} for Rejoicing for Taking St. Eustatia 0 1 0

P^{d.} for 2 Measuers of Lime for Building Chapel Horse Stone 0 1 0

P^{d.} for Brickwork and serving do. 0 2 0

1782.
Nov. 8. P^{d.} for Crying Seats 0 0 2

P^{d.} for Crying Vestery Meeting 0 0 2

1783.
May 16. P^{d.} for Rejoiceing for Rodneys Counquest over the French Fleet on the 12 of April ... 0 2 6

P^{d.} for Book of Thanksgiving ... 0 0 8

P^{d.} to Talk on ye hill fire Brief 0 1 2

P^{d.} for Handels and Purcels Tedeum for Singers ... 0 13 0

1784.
April 13. P^{d.} To a Stamp for Births and Burials 0 6 0

P^{d.} Mr. John Lever for Copying sev^{rl.} Deeds writing relating to Benefactions and Charities bestowed upon Hindley Chapel by Bill ... 3 13 6

1786.
April 18. P^{d.} to Mr. John Lever for Writings Betwixt the Feffees of this Chapel and George Hodkinson concerning personage house 1 0 6

1787.
April 10. Spent when looking for Donations 0 1 0

£   s.   d.

P^{d.} to Necking Surplice   ... 0   1   6

1787.

April 10. P^{d.} for a Box and Lock and
Key to put Duty Money in 0   1   6

At the proceedings of a Vestry Meeting held on Nov. 5th, 1789, we read : " At the same Time it was agreed y^{t.} the Communion Plate should be remov'd out of the Vestry to the House of Mr. Richard Battersby, and to be fetch'd by the Clerk every Time it is wanted : and y^{t.} a good strong Oak Box be provided for putting the same in, with a Lock to it.   Also y^{t.} 4 small Boxes be provided for collecting Alms.   At the same Time it was agreed y^{t.} two additional Locks of different form be provided with Keys, one Key of which to be in the Possession of the Minister, one of the Chapel Warden, and one be lodg'd with Robert Ashton.

" It was at the same Time further agreed that ten shillings a year be allow'd the Clerk for washing the Surplice and his Trouble of conveying the Communion Plate to Mr. Battersby's.

" And y^{t.} two Pounds two shillings a year be allowed the Sexton for ringing the Bell and keeping the Chapel Yard in decent Repair."

1791.

April 29. P^{d.} for a sequesteration 1 13   0

May 29. P^{d.} for a Umberello   1   2   0

Feb. 9. P^{d.} for 6 Black and White Pall
Bobs 2s. 0 12   0

1794.

April 2. Spent as Usal of Eeaster Tuesday 0   7   4

April 9. To ringing at Chapel for News ... 0   2   6

1795.

May 28. Gave for Ringing on the Duke
of York Victory   0   3   0

June 1. Gave for Ringing on account of
Lord Hows Victory 0   4   6

£   s.   d.

1796.

Feb. 29. To 100 Advertisements for prohibiting Shop-Keepers Sabbeth breaking 0 3 0

To 101 Sparrow heads 0 4 2½

1796.

March 21. To Thomas Huff for removing the Horse Stone and rebuilding it and lime 0 5 9

1798.

April 10. 28 Dozen and 11 Sparrow Heads 0 14 5½

1801.

Jan. 4. P$^{d.}$ for Sparrow heads 0 18 7½

1806.

April 16. To Sparrow Heads 2 17 0

1807.

March 31. P$^{d.}$ To Sparrow Heads 0 17 2

1814.

April 11. To the Reverend Hugh Evans Ordanition 0 10 0

To Violincelles Strings 0 3 6

"February 23, 1815.—At a public Vestry Meeting held this day, pursuant to public notice given on Sunday last in this Chapel, to consider the necessity of an application to the Lord Bishop of Chester for a faculty to empower the Chapel Warden, or his successors, to take down the East end of the said Chapel, and to rebuild it upon a larger plan, with power for Trustees to dispose of the seats. Also to fix what quantity of land shall be purchased from Mr. George Green to enlarge the said Chapel yard.

" We whose names are hereunto subscribed, being a majority of land owners and leaseholders there present, do agree and consider the Chapel as it now is is too small for the congregation to assemble, and that an enlargement of the said Chapel is necessary, and do appoint the Chapel Warden or his successor to apply for a faculty for the same, and that about forty falls of land be purchased to be laid to the aforesaid burial ground.

> " H. Evans, Minister. Peter Ditchfield.
> " Henry Southworth. Thomas Somner.
> " Jona^n Thomason. Tomas Cave.
> " George Green. H. Battersby."

The new Parsonage was built in 1810. The site chosen for it was on an estate called Rosbothams, purchased on the 23rd of October, 1779, from William Clayton, of Wigan, gentleman, for £400, in order to augment the living. £200 of this sum was contributed by the Governors of the Bounty of Queen Anne, and the remainder, with the expenses connected with the purchase, which amounted to £30, was raised by the Trustees and by the Incumbent giving up one half-year's salary. This estate is under the entire control of the Incumbent, and is the only part of the church property not vested in the Trustees.

The principal contributors to the new Parsonage were :—

	£	s.	d.
Ralph Peters, Esq.	100	0	0
The Marquis of Stafford	100	0	0
The Hon. & Rev. George Bridgeman	100	0	0
Robert Holt Leigh, Esq.	50	0	0
John Hopwood, Esq.	50	0	0
Edward Kearsley, Esq.	50	0	0
John Pennington, Esq.	30	0	0
The Rev. George Hendrick	20	0	0
Queen Anne's Bounty Office	300	0	0
Proceeds of Timber, &c.	52	8	9
	£852	8	9

Mr. Pennington, the subscriber in the above list of £30, was Chapel Warden at the time the Parsonage was erected. The cost of the building amounted to about £300 more than the subscriptions, a sum Mr. Pennington never succeeded in recovering.

The members of the choir were formerly great chapel functionaries, but since the erection of the organ, which was opened on Sunday, the 23rd of February, 1840, their importance has considerably declined. The well-known family of Grime, with whom musical genius seems to be hereditary, contributed several members. *
I have heard of an old Robert Grime and his wife Catherine, long before my time, always sitting up on Christmas Eve, with a bottle of good home-brewed ale for company, and as soon as the clock struck twelve, singing the Christmas Hymn.

Several persons named Eatock rendered valuable service also to the choir. Timothy Eatock, in my early days, was one of the most noted. He used to sing, alone, the first verse of the Easter Hymn :—

> " The Lord is risen ! He who came
>   To suffer death, and conquer, too,
> Is risen ! Let our songs proclaim
>   The praise to man's Redeemer due."

As he became old his voice grew shrill and querulous, but he sang the glorious words to the last. The only one of the body I was personally acquainted with was James Platt, the bassoon player. I took lessons from him in psalmody when I was a lad, and was intimately acquainted with him for a many years afterwards. He

---

*In 1788 the choir consisted of—

Robert Grime, and his wife, Catherine.	Ralph Pennington.
Richard Chisnal.	John Bethel.
Alexander Winward.	John Jenkinson.
Thomas Oakes.	Timothy Eatock.
Christopher Meadow.	Richard Hunter.
John Bullow.	John Lathwate.
James Isherwood.	James Bullow.
James Rigby.	Betty Grime.
William Grime.	Molly Eatock, and
	Ann Grime.

William Grime died in 1825, after being a member of the choir for fifty-three years, and leader of the choir for forty years.

had an invaluable helpmate in his wife, who kept her house a pattern of neatness and order. Both died before old age overtook them, and within a year or two of each other. They were as worthy a couple as ever lived. One of their sons was also a bassoon player, and a story is told of the odd use he once made of his instrument. Along with some others, he had been invited by a son of the farmer at Lowe Hall, in his father's absence, to join an evening musical party; and when the assembled guests were in the midst of their harmony the master of the house unexpectedly returned, and not only expressed strong disapprobation at the visit, but dismissed them summarily, saying he would have no *consorts* there. The visitors had therefore to beat a precipitate retreat. But a moat surrounded the house and interposed a difficulty to a hasty exit, and young Platt used the bassoon to probe the depth of the water, and was thus enabled to choose a shallow place to cross over.

The choir had a tier of pews allotted to their use in the west gallery of the chapel, and the front pew was occupied by the bass singers. One, Aaron Bullough, a short stout man, played the violoncello, and sat in this pew. Towards the end of his days he grew deaf, and led his colleagues one Sunday forenoon into an unpleasant dilemma. Somehow or other he mistook the tune which had been selected for one of the psalms, and began playing a wrong tune. The other members of the choir were put out in consequence, and came to a dead stop. Again they started; Bullough's deafness preventing him from discovering what he was doing. This time he played louder than before, thinking that the discordance in the ranks behind him might be overcome by his own resolution; just as the captain of some host, on seeing his followers hesitate in battle, endeavours to infuse fresh courage into them by the display of his own personal valour. The singers were again brought to a standstill, when he turned round and indignantly cried "Shame, shame." The instrumental part of the choir consisted ordinarily of a violoncello, bassoon, and clarionet; but on great occasions, such as a charity sermon, or one of the Church festivals, fiddles, hautboys, French horns, and I don't know what besides, were put in requisition. On a grand muster like this the congregation were generally treated to an anthem, which used to inspire me, when very young, with feelings of deep admiration. The hymns for Advent, Christmas, and Easter had each its own peculiar tune, and were very popular. To have sung a new tune to any one of them would have stirred up as great a commotion in the congregation as the suspension of Habeas Corpus or trial by jury would among the people of Great Britain. The services of the choir were gratuitous, their only remuneration being at Christmas, when they went the round of the houses of the principal members of the congregation, and received a present according to the means of the various families. *

For the long period of forty years there was connected with the chapel, first as sexton and afterwards as clerk, one Joseph Oakes. In the first capacity he kept, for the twenty-three years ending in 1839, the chapel and chapel-yard in a state of commendable cleanliness and order; and his staid, reverend look, and his grave manner of reading the responses, enabled him, for the seventeen following years, to fill admirably the latter office. Two anecdotes may serve to give the social aspect of his character. During the time he officiated as sexton there was a funeral at the chapel one Sunday afternoon, and the funeral party adjourned, according to a custom among the operative

---

* About a century ago there was an officer attached to the chapel called a "Bobber," whose duty was to perambulate the aisles during service with a short staff, and if he saw any of the congregation giving way to sleep, to touch or "bob" them on the head with his staff. Correction in this public manner usually gave considerable annoyance, and emphatic protestations were often heard from the reproved persons at the conclusion of the service, that they were as wide awake as the "Bobber" himself.

class, accompanied by Joseph, to the Hand and Banner—a public-house in the immediate neighbourhood—after the interment. It not unfrequently happens on such occasions that excesses are indulged in, and that mirth and revelry follow quickly on the heels of sorrow and mourning. From the sequel it would appear to have been the case in the present instance. The evening had advanced to a late hour, when the conversation turned upon the courage necessary to go alone at that time of night into the chapel. The scene that ensued may be easily imagined. First one and then another would boast of possessing sufficient courage for the exploit, until some person would be dared to undertake it. At last a female volunteer stood forth. To guard against false play, and to prove that she had really been inside the chapel, it was arranged that she should ring the bell; and, woman as she was, she went boldly through the undertaking. Results often follow pranks of this nature which are at the time little anticipated. The bell was heard by the assembled company it is true, but, unluckily, it was heard by others as well, and created considerable alarm in the neighbourhood. Inquiries were made as to the reason of such an unusual proceeding, when the whole affair became public, and Joseph was summoned before the authorities. In his defence he said the keys of the chapel had been stolen from his pocket, and that he was perfectly innocent in the affair; but he failed to convince his judges that he was less guilty than the more active offender, and got suspended for a year from his office.

The other anecdote is this: One Friday, on his return, at a late hour, from Wigan market, Joseph was set upon by robbers, who took away his watch and some money he had upon him. Soon after, a person was taken up on suspicion of being concerned in the robbery, and brought before the magistrates. At the examination the legal gentleman who defended the prisoner thought proper to question Joseph closely as to the state he was in at the time of the robbery. Joseph maintained stoutly that he was sober, but admitted to being *market merry*, a term he had some difficulty in explaining, and which caused considerable amusement in court.*

The church contains several mural tablets, the inscriptions on which I subjoin :—

ON THE SOUTH WALL OF THE CHANCEL.

In the Vault underneath
the adjoining Communion Table
are interred the remains of
ELIZABETH the Wife of RALPH PETERS
of Platbridge, in the Parish of Wigan, Esquire,
who died the 5th day of September, 1801,
Aged 70 years.

And of the same RALPH PETERS,
who died the 12th day of July 1807,
Aged 78 years.

They lived beloved and died respected
and in memory of them this tribute is erected
by their affectionate Son, RALPH PETERS.

ON THE NORTH WALL OF THE CHANCEL.

In a Vault underneath lieth the Body
of R. Peters, Esquire,
Late of Plat Bridge Hall in this County
who departed this life the 3rd of December, 1838,
Aged 63 years.

Sacred be the Tablet which the gratitude and affection
of his bereaved Family have erected to the memory
of a beloved and affectionate father.

Also Frances, relict of the above Ralph Peters,
who departed this life 3rd December, 1845, aged 61 years.

---

* Among the clerks of the chapel I find the name of James Chisnal, in 1760, and that of his son, William Chisnal, in 1788. Father and son filled the office, one after the other, for more than sixty-eight years. Robert Grime was clerk from the 8th of April, 1819, to his death, on the 7th of January, 1839.

AT THE EAST END OF THE SOUTH GALLERY.

To the Memory of
Lieut. Colnl. Nathaniel Eckersley, K.H.,
Son of James and Mary Eckersley of Hindley,
who died at his residence in this township
on the 12th of November 1837,
Aged 58 years,
and was interred in the Cemetery of this Chapel.
He enlisted into the 10th Regiment of Light Dragoons,
as a private, in the year 1795, and was in active service
under the Command of the Duke of Wellington,
during the Peninsular War.
He was stationed in Manchester 8 years
from 1819 to 1827,
as Brigade Major of the District,
and was afterwards 6 years at Barbadoes
as Deputy Quarter Master General of the Forces
in the Windward and Leeward Islands, West Indies.

ON THE SOUTH WALL OF THE SOUTH GALLERY.

In a Vault
in the
Yard of this Church
lie the remains of
John Leyland
of
Hindley,
who died in February, 1811,
in the 84th year of his age.
"*THOU SHALT COME TO THY GRAVE IN A
FULL AGE, LIKE AS A SHOCK OF CORN
COMETH IN IN HIS SEASON.*"
He married Alice,
daughter of
John and Mary Bradford,
of Kingsley,
in the County of Chester;
who survived him until the year 1817,
and was interred at Winwick,
in this County;
the Burial Place,
for several generations,
of the
Leyland Family.

ALSO ON THE SOUTH WALL OF THE SOUTH GALLERY.

IN MEMORY
OF

WILLIAM LEYLAND	MATTHEW SEDDON
OF	OF
HINDLEY,	HINDLEY
WHO DIED AUGUST 9TH 1830	WHO DIED MARCH 3RD 1804
AGED 56 YEARS ;	AGED 70 YEARS ;
AND OF	AND OF
CATHARINE HIS WIFE (DAUGHTER OF MATTHEW AND ISABEL SEDDON) WHO DIED JULY 10TH 1847 AGED 72 YEARS :	ISABEL HIS WIFE (DAUGHTER OF RICHARD & CATHARINE BATTERSBY) WHO DIED DECEMBER 29TH 1804 AGED 68 YEARS :
ALSO OF	ALSO OF
SARAH THEIR DAUGHTER, WHO DIED JAN. 4TH 1825 AGED 14 YEARS.	ELIZABETH THEIR DAUGHTER, WHO DIED JANUARY 22ND, 1837, AGED 65 YEARS.

THEIR REMAINS ARE INTERRED IN A VAULT IN THE YARD OF THIS CHURCH.
"FOR AS IN ADAM ALL DIE, EVEN SO IN CHRIST SHALL ALL BE MADE ALIVE."

On the external south wall of the vestry there is a brass plate embedded in a framework of stone, inscribed—

IN HOPES of a GLORIOUS RESURRECTION
In this
VAULT
are deposited the
REMAINS
of the late REV^{D.} JOHN CROUDSON,
22 years MINISTER of this CHAPELRY, and
36 years Head Master of the Free Gram^{r.} School, Wigan.
HE DIED 24TH DECEMBER, 1810, AGED 62.
Leaving to the World an Example Worthy Imitation.
Also
Mary his Wife
who died 19th September, 1806, aged 47.
Likewise
MARTHA,
the beloved wife of WILLIAM, son of the above,
Cut off in the Bloom of Life by that fell Despoiler of Beauty,
CONSUMPTION,
on the 13th September, 1814, aged 26.
This short MEMORIAL, a tribute of GRATITUDE,
is Inscribed by AN AFFECTIONATE SON
A FOND HUSBAND.

A stone slab placed immediately underneath the above contains a further record of this family :—

SACRED
TO THE MEMORY OF
WILLIAM CROUDSON, OF WIGAN,
eldest son of the Revd. John Croudson,
Who died 15th January, 1854,
Aged 70 years.

Also of
MARY ANN, his second wife,
Who died 9th January, 1826,
Aged 28 years.
And of their only son,
WILLIAM MELLOR,
Who died 17th May, 1840,
Aged 16 years.
Also of ELIZABETH HARDING, SISTER
of Mary Ann Croudson, who died
1st September, 1859,
Aged 73 years.
"Blessed are the dead which
die in the Lord."

The yard appears to have been enlarged about 1763, to a small extent. Half a century later, we gather from an extract given from the Wardens' Books, in the foregoing pages, that public attention was drawn to the necessity for enlarging both the chapel and yard. The project, so far as the chapel was concerned, was never carried out; but the want of additional burying ground became so urgent that a considerable enlargement was made to the yard in 1837 and 1838, the funds for which (£350 12s. 11d.) were raised by subscription. The old yard was surrounded by lime trees, planted, it is said, by Madame Walmesley. Some of these are still standing, and suffice to mark the boundaries of the old yard; others were cut down when the yard was enlarged.

A statement of the income of the Church, given in a book kept in the Church chest, dated November 30th, 1699, enables us to compare it with that of the present time.

D

"A true and perfect account of all the Donations belonging to the Chapel of Hindley, together with the Names of the Benefactors, as they stand this 30th day of November, Anno Domini 1699 :—

	£	s.	d.
John Ranicars, of Atherton, gave the yearly sum of	6	0	0
Mrs. Frances Duckenfield, of Abram, per annum	2	10	0
Humphrey Platt, of Hindley, the yearly growth or crop of hay-grass arising off three-quarters of an acre of land lying within the Low Meadows, amounting to the yearly sum of	0	15	0
Oliver Stopford, of Hindley, per annum	0	10	0
Thomas Aspul, of the same, per annum	0	10	0
Edward Green, of the same, per annum	1	4	0
William Sale, jun., of the same, per annum	0	3	0
William Sale, sen., of the same, per annum	0	3	0
Randle Collier, of the same, in land in present possession, to the clear yearly value of	6	0	0
More in land in reversion, not yet fallen, to the clear yearly value of	6	0	0
Mary Collier, relict of the said Randle, per annum	2	10	0
Thomas Crook, of Abram, Gent., per annum	1	0	0
The improvement of the arrears, as in the page foregoing, per annum*	6	16	0
Mr. Jno. Prescott, a rent-charge, per annum	0	10	0
Mr. Wells, legacy of £100	5	0	0
Thos. Lythgoe's legacy, per annum	1	0	0
	£40	11	0

Particulars of the Yearly Income of the Parochial Chapelry of Hindley, now called All Saints' Church— 1873 :—

---

* Taken from a book deposited in the Church chest.

	£	s.	d.
Sundry small farms	69	8	0
Do. chief rents	59	18	2
Stipulated rent of mines under the Trust Lands leased by the Trustees to the Wigan Coal and Iron Company Limited, at £200 per annum—one-fourth of this sum being paid to the Incumbent, and the remaining three-fourths being invested. The interest on the sums invested (£1,981 4s. 8d.) is also paid to the Incumbent	50	0	0
Wigan Coal and Iron Company, for Coal Way-leave	10	0	0
Interest on proceeds of mines (£1981 4s. 8d.) invested in 3 per cent Consols	64	5	0
Interest on balance of mine rents (£327 4s. 8d.) lying in the Bank of Messrs. Woodcock, Sons, and Eckersley, about	5	0	0
	£258	11	2

The above are the gross sums paid to the Trustees, and are subject to property-tax and charges for repairs.

The following sums are paid to the Incumbent direct :—

	£	s.	d.
Rent-charge, devised by John Ranicars, on Stone House Farm, in Hindley............	6	0	0
Rent-charge, devised by Mrs. Frances Duckenfield, on lands in Mobberly, Cheshire	2	10	0
Rent-charge, devised by Thomas Crook, on lands in Alston and Whittingham	1	0	0
The Bridgewater Trustees pay Humphrey Platt's bequest of Hay-grass, on land lying in the Lowe Meadows	0	15	0

	£	s.	d.
Pew Rents, which William Bavington, the Collector for many years past, states, produced during Mr. Jones's Incumbency in March of each year, £12 16s., and in September of each year, £3 12s.—together, £16 8s.—produced only in September, 1872, £2 18s. ; and in March, 1873, £7 2s. 6d.	10	0	6
The value of the Parsonage or Vicarage House is estimated at........................	25	0	0
The land surrounding the Parsonage or Vicarage House, is leased to Mr. Edward Grime for a term of six years, from May 12th, 1873—the first year's rent to be £30, the remaining five years to be £32 10s.	30	0	0
The surplice fees are estimated at.............	70	0	0
The Grant from the Ecclesiastical Commissioners is	104	0	0
	£507	16	8

All Saints' Church Sunday Schools.

In the last generation a gentleman named Peters (to whom I have already referred) was deservedly held in great honour and esteem by the inhabitants of Hindley. By profession he was a barrister, and filled the office of Recorder of Liverpool, in which town he resided a part of every year. At other times he lived at his house at Platt Bridge, on the borders of Hindley. Through his indefatigable zeal, Sunday schools were opened in the township two years only after they were first established by Robert Raikes at Gloucester. The first school was held in the Danesgate, under the superintendence of a Mr. Eccles. A second was soon after opened at Hindley Common, and conducted by one Adam Rigby.[*] Three years afterwards a school was erected for girls in Mill Lane, and another for boys at Chapel Green. The cost of the school in Mill Lane was defrayed entirely by Mr. Peters. To the fund for the erection of a Boys' School, and for the permanent endowment of both schools, Mr. Peters also contributed liberally. The Boys' School was erected on land at Chapel Green given by the Duke of Bridgewater, in extent far beyond the requirements of the school. Subsequently a number of cottages were built on the land out of funds raised for the endowment.

In the articles of agreement dated the 18th of February, 1788, between the subscribers and the Trustees, the names of the subscribers are given. They are—

	£	s.	d.
Ralph Peters	109	0	0
Rev. Thomas Lever	21	0	0
Benjamin Eckersley	10	10	0
John Leyland	6	6	0
William Blundell	4	0	0
John Hargreaves	10	10	0
Jonathan Thomason, jun....	4	4	0
Richard Battersby	3	3	0

---

[*] The jubilee of the schools was celebrated on the 7th of September, 1834.

Peter Ditchfield	...	...	...	...	£2	2	0
Rev. Joⁿ Hodgkinson	..	...	...		2	2	0
James Needham	...	...	...	...	1	1	0
Edward Prescott	...	...	...	(no sum stated)			
John Watmough	...	...	...	...	1	0	0
Peter Gaskell	...	...	...	...	..	1	0	0
Francis Heyes	...	...	...	...	...	1	0	0
William Bullough	...	...	...	...	0	5	0

The subscribers who signed the deed are—Thomas Lever, minister, of Hindley, R. Peters, Benjamin Eckersley, Jonathan Thomason, Richard Battersby, and James Needham. Ralph Peters and Thomas Lever were appointed Visitors, and Ralph Peters Secretary.

A Lease and Release, bearing date respectively the 24th and 25th of October, 1788, convey the property to the following Trustees :—

Ralph Peters, the elder, Esquire.

Ralph Peters, the younger, Esquire.

The Rev. Croxton Johnson, Rector of Wilmslow, Cheshire.

John Gilbert, the younger, of Worsley, Esquire.

James Kearsley, of Hulton, Esquire.

Edward Kearsley, of Hindley, Esquire.

John Lever, of Wigan, Gentleman.

Ralph Peters, the younger, was the sole survivor of his colleagues. He died on the 3rd of December, 1838, without having appointed successors, and it therefore devolved upon Thomas Batty Addison, Esq , the surviving devisee in trust named in his will, to discharge that duty.

On the 29th of November, 1851, a new Trust Deed was executed by Mr. Addison, appointing the following gentlemen Trustees :—

The Rev. Thomas Peters, Clerk, Rector of Eastington, in the County of Gloucester.

Alfred Pennington, of Hindley, Cotton Spinner.

John Leyland, do., Gentleman.

Richard Pennington, do., Cotton Spinner.

Richard Pennington, the younger,	of Hindley, Cotton Spinner.	
John Scowcroft,	do.,	Collier.
Rev. Edward Hill,	do.,	Clerk.
John Grime,	do.,	Farmer.

The first sermon on behalf of the schools was preached on Sunday, the 15th of October, 1786, by a Mr. Bennett, and the hymns were sung by children belonging to the Sunday school in the district of St. Mary's, Manchester.* It was the first celebration of the kind in the neighbourhood, and excited much interest. People flocked thither far and near, and so dense was the crowd round the chapel, as the time of divine service approached, that the preacher had some difficulty in forcing his way through. Even at the present day the anniversary sermons draw a large concourse of visitors. Of late years the day has been known as " the wakes."

The present schools were erected in 1828, at a cost of £220, chiefly raised by subscription. In aid of the building fund a ball was held, on the 13th February, 1829, at the house (then untenanted) which Mr. Alfred Pennington gave, in 1870, to the trustees of St. Peter's Church, in order that the site might be added to the churchyard, and which has since been pulled down. The ball was eminently successful ; the arrangements were excellent, and the enjoyment among the guests was general. A circumstance connected with it caused a good deal of amusement at the time. The managers, wishing the proceeds to be as large as possible called on the principal inhabitants a day or two before the ball took place, to solicit gifts of wine, which was responded to so liberally that not a penny had to be expended on that score. Some wag informed the newspapers, and a paragraph appeared in the next publication of a Wigan newspaper, headed " Economy Extraordinary," setting forth that, at the recent ball at Hindley, the company lacking some exhilarating beve-

---

* A copy of the hymns sung on the occasion is in my possession.

rage, the managers went out to beg wine in the neighbourhood; making it appear as if it was done at the very time the ball was being held. The schools were considerably enlarged in 1842, and class-rooms were added in 1866.

The endowment now consists of eight cottages and a chief rent, the gross yearly income of which amounts to £59 17s. 10d.

Mr. Peters had a worthy coadjutor in his benevolent schemes in the person of his wife. Among other good deeds, she dispensed medicines one day in each week to the poor gratis. The Peters family were the first to use umbrellas at Hindley, and probably soon after they were introduced into the metropolis by the celebrated Jonas Hanway. I have heard a lady, who was an eye-witness, describe the surprise she experienced, when quite a girl, on seeing Mrs. Peters's servant carry one over his mistress's head for the first time from her carriage to the chapel door. A skeleton of one of the earliest of these now indispensable articles, which belonged to my grandfather, lay for a long time in a lumber room at our house. It was large and heavy; the whalebones were of great strength, and two strong brass wires stretched from each whalebone to the stick; the covering had been of oilcloth. Its general appearance was not very unlike, though smaller in size, a modern gig umbrella, and presented a strong contrast to the neat and light article of the present day.

Mr. Peters and his lady lived to a good old age, revered by their neighbours, and died universally lamented. Their son, some years afterwards, sold the family property, and moved to another part of the country.

St. Peter's Church.

The foundation-stone of this church was laid on the 19th of October, 1863, by Richard Pennington, Esq., of Westfield House, Rugby,* and three years afterwards, on the 15th of October, 1866, the church was consecrated by Dr. Jacobson, Bishop of Chester. It is built of stone in the decorated style of pointed architecture, and consists of a nave of fine bays, with side aisles, and choir. The cost of the fabric and the site, including £1,100 paid to the Ecclesiastical Commissioners towards the endowment, and £200 set aside for a Repair Fund, amounted to £9,506 13s. 1d. This money was raised by subscription, the principal portion being given by the Pennington family, the late Mr. Alfred Pennington alone contributing £3,781. In addition to this munificent subscription, Mr. Alfred Pennington presented the church with an oak reading-desk, a stone pulpit, and a peal of eight bells. Mrs. Jane Pennington, of Westfield, Rugby, gave the font. The church was placed behind a pile of buildings, which stood on its north-western side, between it and the public road. Mr. Alfred Pennington owned these buildings, and generously gave them to the church in 1870, on the condition that they should be pulled down, and the site added to the church-yard. The public road was widened some little out of the land, and the church was thus opened to the view of the principal thoroughfare.

The Rector of Wigan being the owner of the Tithes of Hindley, which are commuted at £298 11s. 0½d. the year, for which he returns no service to the township, the Building Committee applied to him, and to the Earl of Bradford, the Patron of the Wigan Rectory, to endow the church with some portion of the amount. Lord

---

* At the ceremony of laying the foundation-stone a silver trowel was presented to Mr. Pennington, bearing an appropriate inscription. By some mischance the box containing the trowel was lost on Mr. Pennington's journey homewards. The trowel was naturally much valued by him, and its mysterious disappearance was a source of considerable regret. After the lapse of nearly three years, and when the hope of its recovery had been given up, it was found in the lost luggage office, Euston Station, London.

Bradford, after communicating with Mr. Gunning, the then Rector, offered to endow the church with £50 per annum on the condition that the patronage should either be vested in five trustees, of which number himself and Mr. Gunning were to be two, or that it should be vested in the Rector, and any trustees the committee might appoint, with alternate presentation. The latter stipulation was accepted, and it was arranged that the first appointment should be exercised by the trustees. Messrs. Richard Pennington, of Rugby; Alfred Pennington and Richard Pennington, jun., of Hindley; Nathaniel Eckersley, of Wigan; and John Leyland, of Hindley, were the trustees appointed by the Building Committee.

The income of All Saints' Church having for some years increased, owing to the leasing of the mines, the Rev. P. Jones, the incumbent, offered, as the new church took away a portion of his district, to endow it with £25 a year out of his living. Fifty pounds having thus been promised by the Rector of Wigan, and £25 by the Incumbent of Hindley, the committee entered into communication with the Ecclesiastical Commissioners, who agreed to raise the income to £150, provided the committee handed over to them the sum of £1,300. The committee agreed to do this, and, at the appointed time, paid the money. At this juncture Lord Bradford unfortunately became incapacitated for business, Mr. Gunning resigned the Rectory of Wigan, and Mr. Jones resigned the Incumbency of Hindley—a combination of circumstances which caused much trouble and anxiety to the committee. The Honourable and Reverend G. T. O. Bridgeman, son of the Earl of Bradford, was appointed Rector of Wigan, and the Rev. C. H. Newbold Incumbent of Hindley. Mr. Bridgeman refused to carry out the promise made by his own father and his predecessor, unless he had the whole and undivided patronage—a demand to which the committee very properly refused their consent; and Mr. Newbold never could be induced to pay one farthing of the £25. The arrangement with the Ecclesiastical Commissioners, therefore, fell to the ground, and all that was left for the endowment was the interest on £1,000, a portion of the money paid by the committee to the Ecclesiastical Commissioners, and a grant of income to meet the remaining sum which was treated as a Benefaction ; so that the endowment at the present time amounts only to £58 17s. 4d.*

Much credit is due to the Rev. Peter Jones for his exertions on behalf of the church. The idea originated with him, and from the first meeting of the committee, which was held on the 7th of January, 1856, to the time of his resignation of the living of All Saints', in 1863, he laboured indefatigably in furthering its interests. So much were his services valued that the majority of the trustees, with many others, were anxious for him to fill the office of incumbent to the new church; and although he at first declined the offer when it was made to him, he was ultimately induced to accept it.

An organ built by the celebrated builder, Schulze, of Germany, was opened on the 18th of February, 1873, the cost of which was wholly defrayed by the representatives of the late Mr. Alfred Pennington, in conformity with his expressed wish. It remains yet without a case, but the efforts now being made to supply this want will, no doubt, shortly be crowned with success. A brass plate has been placed in the north wall of the church, near to the font, inscribed thus :—

ST. PETER'S CHURCH, HINDLEY.

The Foundation Stone of this Church was laid on the 19th of October, 1863, by Richard Pennington, J.P , of Westfield House, Rugby, formerly of Hindley. The Church was consecrated on the 15th of October, 1866, by the Right Reverend William Jacobson, D.D., Lord Bishop of Chester.
The entire cost (including £1,100, towards the endowment, and £260 for the repair fund) was £9,506 18s. 1d. This sum was raised by voluntary contributions, assisted by the Incorporated and Diocesan Church Building Societies.
the principal contributor being Alfred Pennington, of Hindley, who was also the donor of the Peel of Bells and of the Pulpit.
Peter Jones, M.A., First Incumbent. Edward G. Paley, Architect.
James Neill, Builder.

Alfred Pennington, } First Wardens.
John Leyland,

This plate was erected by Richard Pennington, jun., J.P., of Hindley Lodge, July, 1872.

---

* On the failure of the agreement with the Ecclesiastical Commissioners £200 of the £1,300 paid was set aside by them for a repair fund.

Handsome schools are now (1873) in course of erection near to the church, by the Pennington family, as a memorial to the late John Pennington and his son Alfred. The foundation stone was laid on the 26th of April, 1873, by Richard Pennington, jun., J.P., of Hindley Lodge.

Another school is likewise being erected at Lowe Green, in St. Peter's district, the foundation stone of which was also laid by Mr. Richard Pennington, jun., on the same day as that of the schools near to the church. The site for the Lowe Green Schools was given by the Bridgewater Trustees, and the cost of the building is estimated at £1,800 or £1,900. The greater part of the sum has been raised by subscriptions, but several hundred pounds are still wanting to complete the amount.

St. Benedict's Catholic Chapel.

The Fathers of the English Congregation of St. Benedict were chaplains to the Langton family of Lowe Hall; and it was in a chapel under the roof of the Hall that the members of the Catholic faith formerly met in the township for public worship. The Langtons embraced the Reformed religion soon after the middle of the eighteenth century, upon the occurrence of which event the Trafford family gave the Benedictine Fathers an asylum at Strangeways Hall, and the congregation continued to meet there until 1789, when a chapel in the Mill Lane, now Market Street, was opened for public worship, which had been erected in the preceding year, 1788. The funds for the building were raised by subscription, and through the exertions of the Rev. Edmund Ducket.

The Chaplains at Lowe were :—

Father Placid Acton, who died there in ...			1727
Father Edward Houghton, who also died there in			1751
The Congregation was probably served from Standish until			1758
Father Anslem Eastham next followed, in whose time the chapel was removed to Strangeways, and who left in			1773
Father Edmund Ducket succeeded, and removed to Hindley in 1789, where he died in			1792
Father Placid Bennet, the next in order, left in			1792
,, Bernard Ryding	do.	do.	1797
,, Dunstan Webb	do.	do.	1801
,, Laurence Forshaw	do.	do.	1805
,, Richard Marsh	do.	do.	1806
,, Anselm Appleton	do.	do.	1836
,, Placid Corlett	do.	do.	1862
,, Cyprian Tyrer	do.	do.	1864
,, Ignatius Stuart	do.	do.	1864
,, Augustine Bury	do.	do.	1870
,, Ildefonsus Brown	do.	do.	1872
,, Cuthbert Murphy			

The church was rebuilt in 1868-9, after designs by Joseph Hansom, of London, Esq., in the early English style of architecture, at a cost of £3,500. The foundation stone was laid by Dr. Goss, the Catholic Bishop of Liverpool, on Sunday, April 26th, 1868, and was opened by the same prelate on Sunday, October 10th, 1869. A tower, which formed part of the plan of the building, has not yet been erected.

The foundation stone of new and commodious schools was also laid by Bishop Goss some years previously, viz., on the 10th of June, 1861. They are calculated to hold 250 children, and the cost was about £1,700.

The earliest officiating priest, in my recollection, was the Rev. Thomas Appleton, a gentleman noted in the neighbourhood for his eccentricities. Although of the most uncouth appearance, he was a well-informed man, a good classic scholar, and intelligent and agreeable in conversation, so long, at least, as he steered clear of religion and politics. That he should be a strenuous supporter of his church, and defend it warmly against attack, was what might naturally have been expected, but he was apt to lose his temper in argument, and to give way to violent language. Returning from Manchester on one occasion by the stage coach, he entered into a dispute with a fellow-passenger of different politics, and got so excited that he actually spat in his face. How I first gained his acquaintance I cannot tell, but gain it I did somehow or other. The recollection of a *rencontre* I had with him one day when I was quite a lad, has often amused me. I was walking up the Castle Hill reading Mrs. Radcliffe's novel of "The Italian." Happening to look from the page, I saw him approaching, and involuntarily shut the book and put it in my pocket. When he came up to me he stopped, planted his stick firmly on the ground before him, for he had a curious halt in walking, and always used one, and said very fiercely, " What is that book you are so solicitous to hide ? " Cowed by his sternness, I instantly produced the book. " Ay," he said, turning over the pages, "it is a bad book, a very bad book; there is not one of these books fit to read, excepting the Vicar of Wakefield, and even that is not without its faults." The book contained wood engravings of the incidents of the story, one of which represented the Monk Schedoni in the open country, which he mistook for a nun, for he said, " Here is a nun ; now the nuns are never allowed to go out. Go home, boy, and burn the book ; it is a very bad book."

Some years after this a Conservative society, called " The True Blue Club," was established in the village, of which I became secretary. On meeting him one day about this time, he said to me very contemptuously, " You young sprig, I hear of your doings." The club, on one occasion, had a public dinner, and shortly before it took place, I met him in company with one of the most prominent members, who asked him, by way of joke, if he would join us at dinner, to which he replied, with great vehemence, " I would as soon dine with Lucifer in Pandemonium." Mr. Appleton rented a few acres of land from the Trafford family, which he cultivated in a great measure with his own hands. Often he might be seen going backwards and forwards between the fields and his own house, with a spade on his shoulder, dressed as a common labourer, and sometimes driving his cows. His sister, a lady of great amiability, who bore his rough humours with the utmost meekness, kept his house. She dressed in the coarsest manner, and it was said by his express orders. I was once inside his house, along with my neighbour, Thomas Gaskell, who asked me to accompany him on some little business he had to transact. Soon after we were seated, he called in fierce tones to his sister, " Woman, bring a tankard of ale ; " and the good lady, without a word of expostulation at his uncourteous address, obeyed, and placed a brimming tankard on the table, with three glasses. Such was Priest Appleton. I have yet heard several instances of his charity related at different times, which show that, with all his roughness of manners, he had a kind and feeling heart.

The Presbyterian Chapel.

Presbyterianism struck deep roots in Lancashire during the period of the Commonwealth. Very many of the Episcopalian pulpits were filled by Presbyterian ministers, and a great number of chapels were erected for the ejected ministers, after the Restoration, by such of the people as had become attached to the Presbyterian form of worship. *

Misconception seems to exist respecting the foundation of this chapel as well as that of All Saints' Church. According to the county historian it was erected for

* A scarce tract, "Printed for Edward Husbands, Printer to the Honourable House of Commons, 1646," contains some curious information relative to the Presbyterians of Lancashire. I quote only so much of it as relates to this immediate neighbourhood :—

" Die Veneris 2° Octobris 1646

" The County Palatine of Lancaster, is divided into nine Classicall Presbyteries following."

"The fourth Classis to contain Warrington Parish, Winwike Parish, Leigh Parish, Wigan Parish, Holland Parish, Prescot Parish.

"The ministers fit to be of the fourth Classis. Master Charles Herle of Winwick. M. Thomas Norman of Newton. M. James Wood of Ashton. M. William Leigh of Newchurch. M. Henry Atherton of Hollinkaire. M. Bradley Hayhurst of Leigh. M. Thomas Crompton of Astley. M. James Bradshaw of Wigan. M. Thomas Tonge of Hindley. M. Henry Shaw of Holland. M. William Plant of Farnworth. M. Richard Modesley of Ellins. M. Timothy Smith of Rainsforth. M. John Wright of Billing.

"Others fit to be of the fourth Classis. William Ashhurst of Ashhurst, Esqre. ; Peter Brook of Sankie, Esqre. William Vernon of Shakerley, Gent. ; John Dunbabin of Warrington, Gent. ; Thomas Risley of Warrington, Gent. ; Robert Watmough of Winwick, Gent. ; Gilbert Eden of Winwicke, Gent. ; John Ashton of Newton, Gent. ; George Aynsworth of Newton, Yeoman ; James Pilkington of Ashton, Gent. ; Arthur Leech of Westleigh, Yeoman ; Peter Smith of Westleigh, Yeoman ; Richard Ashtley of Tildaley, Gent. ; Thomas Guest of Astley, Yeoman ; Henry Morrice of Atherton, Gent.; Alexander Tompson of Wigan, Gent. ; Peter Harrison of Hindley, Gent. ; Thomas Sephton of Skerndsdale, Gent. ; Jeffery Birchall of Orrell, Gent. ; John Lathom of Whiston, Gent. ; George Deane, of Rainhill, Yeoman ; William Barnes of Sankie, Gent. ; John Marsh of Bold, Gent. ; John Rylands of Sutton, Yeoman ; Thurstian Peak of Warrington, Gent. ; Ewan Heaton of Billing, Gent. ; Roger Toppoing of Dalton, Yeoman ; Peter Leyland of Haddock, Yeoman."

" Die Veneris 2° Octob. 1646.

" Resolved by the Lords and Commons assembled in Parliament,

" That they do approve of the Division of the County of *Lancaster* into the Nine Classicall Presbyteries, represented from the said county.

" Resolved, &c.

" That the said Houses do approve of the ministers and other persons represented from the County of *Lancaster*, as fit to be of the severall and respective Classis into which the said county is divided.

" Jo. Brown, Cler., Parliamentorum.
" Hen. Elsynge, Cler. Parl. D. Com."

the ejected minister, Mr. Bradshaw.   I do not find
that this gentleman had anything to do with the
building of the chapel.*   Documents in the possession
of the Trustees evidence that it was erected in the year
1700 by Mr. Richard Crook, of Abram.   An inscription
on the front of the gallery inside the chapel, also gives
this date.   It runs—

Anno Dom 1700,
Hœc
Capella fuit
fundata per
Richardum
Crook, de Abram.

The chapel remained Mr. Crook's private property
for the seventeen following years.   On the 16th of Nov.,
1717, a deed was executed by Mr. Crook conveying an
acre and a half of land, and the new edifice, oratory, or
chapel, lately built and known as Hindley New Chapel,
with the houses, barns, stables thereon, unto

Thomas Sargent, of	Ince,	Yeoman.
Roger Rycroft,	Westhoughton,	Yeoman.
Abell Aldred,	Westhoughton,	Naylor.
George Leigh,	Westhoughton,	Naylor.
Lambert Sale,	do.,	Chapman.
John Laithwait,	do.,	Husbandman.
William Hilton,	Hindley,	Yeoman.
Peter Fletcher,	do.,	Tanner.
Peter Astley,	do.,	Yeoman.
James Green,	Abram,	do.
John Walmesley, the younger,	Wigan,	Gentleman.
George Marsh,	Westhoughton,	Yeoman.

as Trustees.

On the 26th of February, 1725, a second Trust Deed
was executed.

---

* A congregation may have been formed to which Mr. Bradshaw might
minister in a temporary place of meeting.

E

The surviving Trustees were :—

Thomas Sargent,	Ince,	Yeoman.
Roger Ryecroft,	Westhoughton,	do.
John Laithwaite,	do.,	Husbandman.
Peter Fletcher,	Hindley,	Tanner.
James Green,	Abram,	Yeoman.
John Walmesley,	Wigan,	Gentleman.
George Marsh,	Westhoughton,	Yeoman.

The new Trustees were :—

John Parr,	Hindley,	Gentleman.
John Sargent,	do.,	Yeoman.
William Hilton,	do.,	do.
Thomas Sale,	Westhoughton,	Chapman.
Ralph Leigh,	do.,	Yeoman.

The third Trust Deed bears date the 8th of
August, 1744.

The surviving Trustees were :—

Roger Ryecroft,	Westhoughton,	Yeoman.
James Green,	Abram,	do.
Thomas Sale,	Westhoughton,	Chapman.
William Hilton,	Hindley,	Yeoman.
Ralph Leigh,	do.,	do.
John Sargent,	Ince,	Husbandman.

The new Trustees were :—

William Milligan,	Wigan,	Chapman.
George Leigh,	Westhoughton,	Yeoman.
John Naylor,	Abram,	Husbandman.
Robert Leigh,	Westhoughton,	Yeoman.
George Lyon,	Hindley,	do.
Peter Parr,	Westleigh,	do.

The fourth Trust Deed bears date September 30th, 1763.

The surviving Trustees were :—

Thomas Sale,	Westhoughton,	Chapman.

John Naylor,	Abram,	Husbandman.
George Lyon,	Hindley,	Yeoman.
Peter Parr,	Westleigh,	do.
George Leigh,	Bolton,	Chapman.

The new Trustees were :—

James Leyland,	Abram,	Yeoman.
Benjamin Aspinall,	Westhoughton,	Chapman.
Simon Sale,	Ince,	Yeoman.
Edmund Laithwait,	Hindley,	do.
Joseph Hatton,	do.	Chapman.
Richard Harrison,	Wigan,	Farmer.
Richard Sale,	Westhoughton,	Yeoman.
Henry Gaskell,	Hindley,	Chapman.
William Gordon,	Wigan,	do.
James Hilton,	Hindley,	Yeoman.

The fifth Trust Deed bears date December 2nd, 1785.

The surviving Trustees were :—

George Lyon,	Hindley,	Yeoman.
Edmund Laithwate,	do.,	Weaver.
Joseph Hatton,	Westhoughton,	Chapman.
Henry Gaskell,	{ Late of Hindley, now of Warrington, }	Warehouseman.
William Gordon,	Wigan,	Chapman.

The new Trustees were :—

Peter Gaskell,	Hindley,	Yeoman.
John Leyland, the elder,	do.,	Chapman.
John Leyland, the younger,	do.,	Yeoman.
John Lyon,	do.,	Weaver.
John Harrison,	Westhoughton,	Husbandman.
Richard Harrison,	Hindley,	do.
Edmund Manley,	Hindley,	Husbandman.
Peter Rosbotham,	do.,	Weaver.

Thomas Horridge,	Hindley,	Weaver.
James Marsh,	Aspull,	Husbandman.
Joseph Cundliffe,	Hindley,	Weaver.
Robert Horridge,	do.,	do.
Thomas Horridge, the younger,	do.,	do.
William Greenough,	Aspull,	Weaver.
James Greenough,	do.,	do.
Jonathan Pendlebury,	do.,	do.
Robert Rosbotham,	Hindley,	do.
John Laithwaite,	do.,	Yeoman.

The sixth Trust Deed bears date December 25th, 1812.

The surviving Trustees were :—

Peter Gaskell,	Hindley,	Yeoman.
Richard Harrison,	do.,	Husbandman.
Edmund Manley,	do.,	Yeoman.
Robert Horridge,	do.,	Weaver.
William Greenough,	Aspull,	do.
Jonathan Pendlebury,	do.,	do.
John Laithwaite,	Hindley,]	Yeoman.

The new Trustees were :—

Richard Barlow,	Hindley,	Yeoman.
Thomas Gaskell,	do.,	Husbandman.
Peter Gaskell, the younger,	do.,	do.
William Leyland,	do.,	Cotton Manufacturer.
Roger Eckersley,	do.,	Farmer.
James Manley,	do.,	Husbandman.
John Dorning,	do.,	Farmer.
James Lowe,	do.,	Wheelwright.
James Whittle,	Ince,	Yeoman.
Robert Longworth,	Aspull,	Farmer.
Hugh Gaskell,	Wigan,	Yeoman.
Henry Butterworth,	Hindley,	Farmer.
George Knowles,	do.	do.

| Samuel Lyon, | Hindley, | Weaver. |
| George Lyon, | do. | do. |

The seventh and last Trust Deed bears date June 2nd, 1862.

The only surviving Trustee was

| Thomas Gaskell, | Hindley, | Gentleman. |

The new Trustees appointed were :—

Samuel Lyon,	Westhoughton,	Weaver.
Abraham Hurst, the elder,	Hindley,	Farmer.
Abraham Hurst, the younger,	do.	do.
William Harrison, the elder,	do.	do.
Thomas Harrison,	do.	do.
Joseph Barwise,	Wigan,	Druggist.
John Holme,	Ince,	Weaver.
David Shaw,	{ Park Lane, near Wigan, }	Lock and Hinge Maker.

An endorsement was made on this deed on the 24th of December, 1862, in consequence of some of the property of the Trust having been omitted in the Recital of the property in the body of the deed; and in order to supply the omission a further endorsement was made on the 31st of October, 1867, appointing seven additional Trustees.

They were :—

John Jones,	Ince,	Colliery Clerk.
Robert Pearson,	Hindley,	do.
William Hotchkiss,	Ince,	Colliery Manager
Josiah Gaskell,	Park Lane,	Lock Manufactr.
Richard Harwood,	Bolton,	Esquire.
Joseph Gerrard,	do.,	Solicitor.
Frank Taylor,	do.,	Cotton Spinner.

Date of Institution.	Ministers.	Cause of Vacancy.
Minister in 1717	James Brownlow	————
1746	Joseph Bourne	Died, 1765
Minister in 1777 & '78	William Davenport* ...	Resigned, 1788
1779	Jonathan Hodgkinson..	Died, 1812
————	Abraham Manley	Resigned, 1818
1819	James Kay..............	Resigned, 1821
1822	John Ragland	Resigned, 1861 or 2
1862 or 3	George Hoade	Died, 1868
1868	Adam Rushton	

As already stated, Mr. Richard Crook gave an acre and a half of land, in 1717, with the chapel and other

---

* Differences sprung up in 1777 between Mr. Davenport and either the whole or a part of his congregation. The occasion of the dispute is not stated, but a tradition has been handed down that it arose from an attempt made by Mr. Davenport to carry the endowment to the Presbyterian Chapel in Wigan. Be that as it may, the quarrel grew serious. Mr. Davenport received an anonymous letter signed A B C, "informing him that if he did not immediately leave the chapelry he then held in Hindley, some very serious and disagreeable consequences would soon ensue, it being the intention of some part of his congregation speedily to execute them ; and that nothing but a direct resignation on his part would avert the stroke ; and telling him that a wise man would endeavour to keep himself secure, and a good shepherd would strive to for the love of his sheep, and that a word is sufficient to the wise."

On the night of the preceding 4th of September, Mr. Davenport was "assaulted, battered, and wounded" on his return from Wigan to Hindley, by some, as it was supposed, of his opponents. The quarrel was thus brought to a crisis, and it was ultimately agreed to refer the case to arbitration. Accordingly, Robert Taylor, of Bolton-le-Moors, gentleman, the Rev. Richard Godwin, of Gataker, minister, and the Rev. John Hughes, of Bury, minister, were appointed arbitrators in the dispute ; who, after careful inquiry, gave their decision in writing on the 1st of June, 1788, which was that Mr. Davenport should resign his office on the 1st of the following July, and that the trustees should pay him the sum of £31 19s. 9d. This decision was not to prejudice his claim to proceed by action-at-law against the writer of the letter, or the authors of the assault. The Rev. Wm. Davenport, Joseph Hatton, of Westhoughton, chapman, Wm. Gordon, of Wigan, chapman, Robert Cockran, of Wigan, shopkeeper, and Hugh Gaskell, of Wigan, chapman, by the desire of the said Wm. Davenport, of the one part, and George Lyon, Edmund Laithwaite, and James Leyland, of the other part, bound themselves by deed, dated the 4th of March, 1778, in a penalty of £100, to abide by the decision of the arbitrators. A clause in the award provided that the Rev. Philip Holland, of Bolton, should perform duty for two years from the 1st of April on every other Sunday.

buildings thereon. The estate on which the Parsonage now stands, called "Bethell's Tenement," was purchased by the Trustees in 1724, probably from funds arising from gifts or bequests, although there is no record of any such being made. In 1753 a Mrs. Alice Lawton, by her will, dated the 8th of January in that year, bequeathed £20 to the Trustees, the interest of which was to be appropriated to the support of the minister. The Lancashire and Yorkshire Railway passed through Bethell's Tenement, and the money received in compensation for the land they occupy was invested in the purchase of a small farm in Boggart House Lane, and a plot of land near to the Red Lion Inn. Since then the mines have been leased, under the land near the chapel and in Boggart House Lane, and several plots of land let for building purposes, so that the endowment has increased considerably in value.

The accounts for the year 1786-7, a copy of which I possess, show that the income received by the minister, the Rev. Jonathan Hodgkinson, amounted in that year to £29 19s. 1d.

Copy of the Accounts of the Trustees, for the year 1786—7.

1786.			£	s.	d.
Oct. 30.	Recd.	George Wellington's Interest	0	10	0
Nov. 26.	,,	Ralph Lyon's Half-years' Rent	1	11	6
Dec. 22.	,,	Richard Fairclough's do.	1	10	0
,, 25.	,,	Edward Fearnley's do.	2	10	0
,, ,,	,,	Edward Ramsdell's............	1	12	0
,, ,,	,,	Edmund Laithwaite's..........	6	6	8
,, 31.	,,	Rodger Mason's Legacy for 2 years	1	0	0
			£15	0	2

Received the above by me,

J. Hodgkinson.

<table>
<tr><td colspan="2">1787.</td><td>£</td><td>s.</td><td>d.</td></tr>
<tr><td>May 23.</td><td>Recd. Ralph Lyon sd. Half-year's rent. Leys and Repairs was 9/^{s.} ....</td><td>1</td><td>2</td><td>6</td></tr>
</table>

1787.		£	s.	d.
May 23.	Recd. Ralph Lyon sd. Half-year's rent. Leys and Repairs was 9/	1	2	6
„ „ „	Edward Fearnley sd. Half-year's rent. Allowed in part for a Stamp, 3 1 ...	2	6	11
„ 28. „	Rd. Fairclough sd. Half-year's rent. Leys was 8 5	1	1	7
„ 30. „	Mr. Mort, Interest	1	0	0
June 17. „	Edmund Ramsdel's sd. do. rent......................... Leys was 8 5 ; Repairs, 7	1	9	0
„ „ „	Edmund Laithwaite's sd. Half-year's rent ; do. in part, 4 10 6 ; in full, 1 15 5 ; 33 Sunday's Board, at 12 per, 1 13 0 ; Leys was 3 15 10 ; Repairs, 18 7...................	7	18	11
		£14	18	11
		15	0	2
		£29	19	1

Recd. the above by me,
J. Hodgkinson.

The Rev. Jonathan Hodgkinson and his family were well known and much esteemed by various members of my own family, and I have in consequence heard him and them often spoken of. He was a man of great amiability, and earned the love not only of the members of his own religious body, but of the entire neighbourhood. For some years after his appointment he kept a boarding-school at Birket Bank, two miles distant from Hindley, and used to ride on horseback on the Sunday to officiate, with his wife on a pillion behind him. " Now Bess," he would say to his mare as he rode along, " a little faster, Bess," and touch her at the same time gently with his whip. " A righteous man," Solomon says, " regardeth the life of his beast."

At this time there was no suitable residence for the minister belonging to the chapel. By much exertion Mr. Hodgkinson succeeded in obtaining funds, by subscription, for erecting a Parsonage-house, to which he removed as soon as it was ready for his reception. But he did not long enjoy it. After a short illness his end came, and he had to exchange it for the house appointed for all living. The Trustees of the chapel, in consideration of his exertions in building the house, very properly gave his widow a life interest in it, and she lived there until her death, many years after. I remember her well, and her only daughter, who became the wife of her cousin, Mr. Thomas Hibbert. The masters in her father's school afforded Miss Hodgkinson, when growing up, many advantages, and she was led to enter upon branches of study seldom pursued by ladies. Her acquisitions, however, sat well upon her. Of her it may be said, as was said of a distinguished French lady, that " to the graces peculiar to her own sex she added the accomplishments which are the ornaments of ours."* Sprightly in manner and conversation, and in her early days abounding in animal spirits, no society in the neighbourhood was more coveted than hers. Her mother was also a woman of great worth, and out of a not very liberal income the two contrived to bestow in charity as much as many people who had five times their means. On the death of Mrs. Hodgkinson Mrs. Hibbert removed with her family to Liverpool.

Three tablets adorn the chapel—two, the inscriptions on which next follow, are placed on the western wall,

---

* Mademoiselle de Joncourt. (See Pascal's Letters.)

and the last, in memory of the Rev. George Hoade, on the northern wall :—

SACRED
to the Memory of the
REV^{D.} JOSEPH BOURN,
Minister to this Society
Nineteen Years.
He died Feby. 17th, 1765,
Aged 52 Years.

SACRED to the MEMORY
of the REV^{D.} JONATHAN HODGKINSON, of BURKITT BANK,
near WIGAN, and Minister of the Congregation assembling in
this Chapel during a space of 33 Years.

His mild, frank, and unassuming manners endeared him to the society of his family and friends, and he discharged the duties of a Christian teacher with unaffected seriousness, simplicity, and candour.

From an early period of his life he devoted a considerable portion of his time to the education of Youth, and in this honourable employment, his assiduity and knowledge united with a temper distinguished by forbearance and lenity, rendered his exertions peculiarly successful.

His surviving pupils remembering with gratitude the days which they passed under his faithful and judicious care, have erected this Tablet as a testimony of affectionate esteem for their INSTRUCTOR and FRIEND.

He died 13th July, 1812.   Aged 68 years.

In Memory of
THE REVD. GEORGE HOADE,
FOR SIX YEARS MINISTER OF THIS CHAPEL,
WHO DEPARTED THIS LIFE FEBRUARY 14TH, 1868,
AGED 51 YEARS.

The Chapel is now in the possession of the Unitarians.

St. Paul's Independent Chapel.

St. Paul's Chapel was built by subscription in the year 1815, at a cost of over £700, on land given by the late Mr. John Aspinall.

A few persons supporting the doctrines and form of Church government, for which this building was provided, met about three years previously in a thatched cottage, since pulled down, adjoining the Lord Nelson Inn, who were ministered to by the Rev. William Roby, of Manchester. After a time their place of meeting was removed to a workshop belonging to Mr. William Livesey at the Three Lane Ends, and later on to a room over a warehouse in Mill Lane, then occupied by a Mr. Joseph Bullough. The Rev. Mr. Steele, of Wigan, ministered to the congregation which assembled in this room.

The members increasing, a permanent place of worship was thought desirable, and the present building was consequently erected.

The first Trust Deed of the chapel is dated the 1st of April, 1814, and the Trustees appointed therein were :—

John Aspinall,	Hindley,	Chapman.
Thomas Leyland,	do.,	Weaver.
William Livsey,	do.,	Joiner.
James Pierpoint,	do.,	Weaver.
John Sergeant,	do.,	do.
Richard Molyneux,	do.,	do.
John Bleasdale,	do.,	Coal Merchant.
Simon Marsh,	do.,	Weaver.
Richard Hodkinson,	do.,	do.
James Mort,	do.,	do.
Peter Appleton,	do.,	Dyer.
Archibald Stuart,	Wigan,	Linen Merchant.
Roger Atkinson,	do.,	Printer.
Peter Latham,	do.,	Cabinet Maker.
Aaron Stock,	do.,	Cotton Manufacturer.
James Glover,	do.,	Weaver.
Samuel Aspul,	do.,	Cooper.
Robert Brown,	Prescott,	Linen Manufacturer.

The chapel was opened on the 12th day of September, 1815, when the services were conducted by the Rev. Dr. Raffles, of Liverpool, and the Revs. Samuel Bradley and William Roby, of Manchester.

The Trustees having become reduced to four, new Trustees were appointed by a Deed dated April 23rd, 1855.

The names of the surviving Trustees were—John Bleasdale, Richard Hodkinson, Roger Atkinson, and Robert Brown.

The new Trustees were ten in number—

George Ormrod,	Hindley,	Corn Merchant.
Elisha Gregory,	do.,	Shopkeeper.
William Livsey,	do.,	do.
Thomas Downall,	do.,	Gentleman.
Ralph Rigby,	do.,	Shopkeeper.
William Marsh,	do.,	Delf Master.
William Grundy,	do.,	Loomer.
Thomas Heys,	do.,	Weaver.
James Rigby,	do.,	Bookseller.
James Lowe, sen.,	do.,	Shopkeeper.

Date of Institution.	Ministers.	Cause of Vacancy.
1815	— Brown, of Prescot ...	——————
	Daniel Atkin of Warrington, and others	——————
1822	William Turner (the first settled minister)	Resigned, 1831
1832	William Howe	Resigned, 1838
1839	John Jones.........	Resigned, 1841
	Vacancy	
1846	William Craig	Resigned, 1849
	Vacancy	
1857	Robert Berry................	Resigned, 1861
	Vacancy	
1865	Fenton Smith	Resigned, 1868
1869	Henry Banks................	——————

Bridge Croft Independent Chapel.

About the year 1830 differences arose in the congregation of St. Paul's Chapel between the Rev. William Turner, the then minister, and the majority of the congregation, which ended in Mr. Turner's resignation. His friends opened a temporary building for him to minister in in the Bridge Croft, near to Borsden Bridge. Here he performed divine service until 1838, when the present chapel was built, at a cost of £454 13s. 1½d.

Mr. Turner officiated to this congregation with an unobtrusive perseverance, which won for him general respect, from 1831 to 1862, when age and infirmities compelled him to resign. Since his resignation there has been no settled pastor, with the exception of the Rev. William Scott, who held the office from August, 1867, until December, 1868.

The chapel, in September, 1838, was vested in the following Trustees :—

The Rev. William Turner, Hindley.
James Jolley,   do.
Samuel Ormrod,   do.
Oliver Ormrod,   do.
George Ormrod,   do.
James Ormrod,   do.
William Kearsley,   do.
Edward Kearsley,   do.
Robert Elliott,   do.
Thomas Cook,   Wigan.
James Monks,   do.
James Platt,   Hindley.
John Platt,   do.
John Bethell,   do.
John Anderton,   do.
Thomas Green,   do.
William Robinson,   do.
James Parr,   do.

The Wesleyan Methodist Chapel, Frederick Street,

Was built in the year 1851; the cost, with the adjoining schools, was £850. The chapel affords accommodation for nearly 300 persons, and the schools are about as large as the chapel. The congregation has never had a resident minister. The land on which the chapel and schools are built was purchased in 1846, and vested in the following Trustees :—

The Rev. Thos. Adams, Wesleyan Minister, Wigan.
Joseph Meek, J.P., Wigan.
William Altham, Wigan.
William Brown, Wigan.
Thomas Taylor, Standish,
Richard Christopher, Ince.
William Melling, senr., Ince.
William Melling, jun., Ince.
George Royle, Hindley.
William Meadows, Hindley.
Thomas Ashton, Wigan.
William Whyte, Tranmere, Birkenhead.
Thomas Howarth, Wigan.
William Yeomans, (Scholes,) Wigan.
John Toft, (Lamberhead Green,) Pemberton.

The Ebenezer Particular Baptist Chapel, Mill Lane.

Like most buildings for public worship, the funds for this chapel were raised by subscription. It was built in 1854 on leasehold land, owned by the late Mr. Peter Bradshaw, at a cost of £750. It has accommodation for 150 worshippers. The schools adjoining the back of the chapel contain room for 80 or 90 scholars. Mr. Bradshaw died in 1857 without having conveyed the property to trustees, an omission followed by litigation, which lasted until 1871.

The Wesleyan Methodist Chapel, Walthew Lane,

Platt Bridge, built in 1869-70, cost £1,165, and contains 260 sittings.

THE UNITED METHODIST FREE CHURCH, Hindley Green (known as Brunswick Chapel), built in 1855, cost £475, and contains 300 sittings.

THE UNITED METHODIST FREE CHURCH, Hindley Green, built in 1866, estimated cost £300, and contains 200 sittings.

THE PRIMITIVE METHODISTS, Woodford Street, Castle Hill, built in 1856, cost £210, and contains 200 sittings.

THE PRIMITIVE METHODISTS, Platt Bridge, built in 1854, cost originally £100, but has since been considerably enlarged, and contains 200 sittings.

INDEPENDENT METHODISTS, Lowe Green, built in 1867, cost £220, and contains 200 sittings.

Hindley and Abram Grammar School.

A stone in front of the old school-house, at Lowe Green, records that—

"This School was built by the gift of Mrs. Mary Abram, Widow, whose soul I trust triumpheth now among the just.   Anno Domini 1632."

The documents in the possession of the Trustees of the school do not, however, verify the record of Mrs. Abram being the foundress.   The credit of being the first to take any steps to attain so desirable an object is unquestionably due to her, inasmuch as she gave the sum of £92 to Miles Gerrard, of Ince, Esq., towards the founding of a school for the children of Hindley and Abram.   The land, the most valuable portion of the school property, was the gift of Abraham Langton, Esq., of Lowe.   Even the money given by Mrs. Abram was insufficient for the building, as subscriptions were subsequently made by the inhabitants of Hindley for the purpose.   These facts are obtained from an agreement entered into, on the 23rd April, 1632, by Abraham Langton, of Hindley, Esq., and Adam Aspull, Richard Currie, and Richard Seddon, of Hindley, and Roger Culchoth, Richard Ashton, Richard Urmston, and Henrie Lithgoe, of Abram.

The document from which I quote relates further that the sum left by Mrs. Abram came into the possession of Philip, father of Abraham Langton, who had promised to give half an acre of land to set the school-house upon ; that the said Philip had bought timber and slate for erecting the school, but, because the building went not forward, he sold them again ; that Abraham Langton covenants with the above-named persons to hand over the money in his possession to Roger Culchoth and Richard Green, and that, instead of the half acre promised by his father, he would give one whole large acre of the Common either of Hindley or Lowe Green.

It thus appears that the site was not selected arbitrarily by any of the chief donors, but that it was probably fixed upon afterwards by the inhabitants of the neighbourhood as being at the time central and convenient.

A Decree of the Commissioners for Pious Uses of the County of Lancaster, dated at Bolton-le-Moors on the 25th September, 1632, after referring to the bequest of Mrs. Mary Abram, states that "the inhabitants of Hindley and Abram have several times assented and laid divers sums of money for the erecting of a school there, but some of them have since refused to pay their share, or load materials, and do other works towards that fabric as the rest of the inhabitants have done, and (after several entreaties of their neighbours and admonitions of the Commissioners of pious uses) have obstinately refused to contribute and do as the rest of their neighbours, alleging either that they have no children now to be taught, or that they care not for that benefit hereafter. It is now, therefore, ordered by us, the said Commissioners, that so many of the inhabitants of the said townships as shall peremptorily continue in that obstinacy, and will not contribute, load, or carry, and do such other acts as their neighbours, for and towards the building up of the said school, shall from henceforth be debarred from having their children and posterity (dwelling in their now habitation) taught freely in the said school, and, as a note of their unworthiness, shall have their names set up in the said school apprising the cause." The list of these delinquents has not, unfortunately, come down to us.

Other official records containing information relating to the school are :—

The Decree of an Inquisition, dated the 3rd Sept., 1656, taken at Prescot, in the County of Lancaster, on the 26th of August (the preceding month), by the Commissioners for Pious Uses.

A Decree of the Court of Chancery for the County Palatine of Lancaster, dated the 5th of June, 1657 ; and

F

A Decree of the same court, dated the 22nd of Oct., in the same year.

The three documents bear reference to the **same facts**. They set forth that Robert Hindley, of Hindley, gentleman, had a debt of £20 due to him by Thomas Ince, of Ince, gentleman, for which he held his bond, and that he would give the said debt to the free school at Hindley; but Mr. Ince refusing to pay, £10 was accepted by Mr. Langton, and other inhabitants of Hindley, in satisfaction of the full amount, rather than proceed to law.

They further inform us that Abraham Langton, of Lowe, and Abraham Lance, of Abram, gentleman, had each of them the sum of £50 in his possession belonging to the school, being in the whole £100; that Ann Aspull was owing £15 for the fine of an acre of land for 21 years; that according to a mutual agreement made by the inhabitants of Hindley and Abram, they appoint:

Robert Hindley, (before-mentioned), Matthew Green, William Peterson, and John Seddon, the younger, } of Hindley, Yeomen.

John Chadock and John Smethurst, } of Abram, do.

to be Feoffees. In these persons the property of the school was to be vested. That when four of their number die the two surviving Feoffees shall appoint others in their room, within two months next after the death of the last of the four deceased, who shall be possessed of the same powers. That within six months after the date of the Inquisition (September 3rd, 1656) the Feoffees shall take into their hands and custody all moneys belonging to the school, and shall invest it in lands of inheritance.*

---

* On February 2nd, 1690, the school land was leased to Henry Sale, of Hindley, tailor, for the term of 21 years, at a rental of 50 shillings. The lease was signed by Philip Langton and not by the Trustees, although they had then been appointed many years. Appended to the lease is the following memorandum : " That before

A Release given by Philip Langton, Esq., dated January 15th, 1682, to Mary Collier, widow, acknowledges the receipt of £10 left by her late husband, Randle Collier.

155 years ago the endowment was £10 6s. 6d. yearly, as appears from a memorandum among the school papers, of which the following is a copy :—

"An account given of the yearly profits arising to the Lowe Schoole, in Hindley, from lands and moneys at interest, &c.

"As foll., this 5th April, 1718 :—

	£	s.	d.
"In Mr. Langton's hands, £135	£6	15	00
"From the Schoole lands	2	00	00
"Mrs. Duckenfield's gift........................	1	00	00
"Mr. Crook's gift	0	11	6
In all...............£10	6	6"	

A small augmentation to the school funds was made in 1783 by Mr. James Eckersley. The codicil to the will securing it is in these words :—

" I, James Eckersley, of Hindley, Chapman, do make this codicil to my last will and testament. As I bear a very good will to the School of Hindley, of which I am a Trustee, in order to augment its income, I bequeath out of my personal estate to Holt Leigh, Esq., the principal Trustee thereof, the sum of ten pounds, to be by him invested or applied in such manner as he shall think most proper for the benefit of the Schoolmaster of the said School for the time being, for ever, in hopes that my said co-Trustee, Holt Leigh, Esq., will be pleased to make an augmentation to this my bequest, and promote a subscription for the further benefit of

the sealing and delivering of these presents it was agreed by the parties above-said that the town of Hindley shall maintain or keep up a little gate for the scholars to pass through, and shall repair the great gate at present, but for the future Henry Sale shall repair it, and Henry Sale shall have all the ashes burnt on the premises to be spent thereon."

the said School, which stands in need thereof.—Witness my hand, 3rd August, 1783.

"JAMES ECKERSLEY.

"Witnesses present,
"RA. PETERS,
"THOS. MATHER."

The Trustees next in order, of which we have any record, after those named in the Decree of the Commissioners for Pious Uses, dated 26th August, 1656, and in the Decrees of the Court of Chancery of the County Palatine of Lancaster, dated respectively June 5th, 1657, and October 22nd, 1657, were appointed on December 14th, 1747. Their names were :—

William Pugh, of Lowe (nephew and devisee of Edward Langton, Esq., of Lowe).

John Southworth, and } both of Hindley, Yeomen.
James Eckersley,

Holt Leigh, Gentleman (son of Alexander Leigh), of Wigan.

John Chadock, and } both of Abram, Yeomen.
John Leyland,

John Leyland survived all his colleagues, and on the 17th November, 1785, a new Trust Deed was executed, and the following persons were joined with him in the trust :—

Robert Holt Leigh, of Wigan, Esquire.

John Green, of Lowton, Gentleman.

Peter Ditchfield, of Hindley, Fustian Manufacturer.

Charles Worsley, of Abram, Fustian Manufacturer, and Ralph Peters, of Platt Bridge, Esquire.

Of this body Sir Robert Holt Leigh was the last survivor, and he died on the 21st January, 1843, without appointing successors.

The earliest master whose name has been preserved was Thomas Mort, who presided over the school in 1746. From a letter of his extant, dated Sept. 18th, 1746, addressed to Mr. John Southworth, he complains of injury resulting to the property of the school, in consequence of trustees not being appointed. This want was remedied, as I have stated, in the following year 1747. From existing memoranda, Thomas Mort appears to have been active in promoting subscriptions for the building of a "bay," as it was called, to the school, which was probably that part formerly used as the master's house.

In 1774 Mr. Richard Guest, of Standish, was appointed master, who was followed in 1782 by Mr. Enoch Clarke. The next master was a Mr. Forshaw, and the next after him Mr. John Clough, who resigned in 1829, and was the last master who taught at the old school.

The vacancy caused by his resignation was filled by Mr. Matthews, who was allowed to hold the school in the Sunday School of All Saints' Church, Chapel Green. He died in May, 1834. Sir Robert Holt Leigh, the only surviving trustee, then permitted the school to remain until May, 1842, eight years, without a master, when he appointed a young man named John Pollard, who held it little more than four years. Pollard resigned in November, 1846, and the school again fell into abeyance, there being then no trustees living, and no person having any authority or control over the estate. Things continued in this deplorable state until 1851, when the attention of the late Lord Kingsdown, then Mr. Pemberton Leigh, Sir Robert Holt Leigh's representative, was called to it, and in the following year he was the means of having new trustees appointed. The gentlemen he selected for the office were :—

The Right Honourable Francis Earl of Ellesmere.
The Rev. Edward Hill, Hindley, Clerk.
The Rev. John Dixon, Abram, Clerk.
Richard Pennington, Hindley, Cotton Spinner.
John Leyland, Hindley, Gentleman.
Thomas Gaskell, Hindley, Gentleman.
James Eckersley, Wigan, Cotton Spinner.
Richard Tickle, Abram, Yeoman.

The efforts of the new Trustees were first directed to secure the property of the school, which was in a fair way of being dissipated. Upon that being effected after the expenditure of much time and labour, they took steps to erect a new school, the old one being considered unfit for the purpose ; and the present site was selected as being in a more central position, and more accessible to the inhabitants of Hindley and Abram generally than that of the old school. The building of the new school was commenced in 1855, and completed in the spring of the following year. The cost of the school and master's house (including the site) was £1,301 17s. 2½d., of which £602 1s. 0½d. was raised by subscription, the remainder being liquidated ultimately from the proceeds of the mines under the old school lands.

The appointment of the new Trustees forms an important epoch in the history of the school, which from that time has assumed the character of a new foundation. A scheme was issued by the Court of Chancery for its government in June, 1854.

The first master appointed under the new system was the Rev. J. C. Airey, who opened the school in temporary premises, provided by the Trustees, opposite the end of Platt Lane, on the 2nd of October, 1854. The new school was opened on Monday the 31st of March, 1856, and, Mr. Airey having resigned, Mr. Joseph Hallas, the present master, was appointed in his place, and commenced his duties after the midsummer vacation in the same year.

The Earl of Ellesmere, the Rev. Edward Hill, and Mr. James Eckersley having died, and Mr. Tickle having become disqualified, the four following gentlemen were appointed in their place, on the 21st day of January, 1860 : —

> The Rev. Peter Jones,
> Alfred Pennington, Esq ,
> Nathaniel Eckersley, Esq., and
> Henry Jackson Whitley, Esq.

Mr. Alfred Pennington has since died, and Mr. Whitley has resigned.

The school seems to have been called originally the Free Grammar School of Hindley ; afterwards the Lowe

School, from its situation at Lowe Green, and in 1861 the Trustees gave it the name of the Hindley and Abram Grammar School.

The property of the Trustees consists now (December 31st, 1873) of :—

Yearly Income.

The new school and master's house (the latter occupied rent free by the master) ... £0 0 0

Small croft or field in front of the school ... 2 10 0

An acre and a-half of land (situate at Lowe Green, Hindley) of the large Cheshire measure, on which stands the old school and master's house 16 0 0

A wayleave, for a term of years, for a coal tramway over this land 5 0 0

The mines underneath are leased to the Duke of Bridgewater's Trustees, and produce at the present time £100 per annum. They are applied in accordance with a scheme issued by the Court of Chancery in June, 1854, and are now nearly exhausted.

A rent charge on lands in Mobberley, Cheshire, devised by Mrs. Frances Duckinfield 1 0 0

A rent charge on lands in Alston and Whittingham, Lancashire, devised by Thomas Crook 1 0 0

A sum of £400 lent on the security of their bond to the Mersey Docks and Harbour Board 17 0 0

A like sum of £400 lent on the security of their bond to the Mersey Docks and Harbour Board 17 0 0

A sum of £267 7s. 7d. consolidated £3 per cent annuities, and a sum of £278 3s. 3d. also consolidated £3 per cent annuities, which produced in 1873 net dividends 16 2 5

Cash balance of general account,
Dec. 31st, 1873, in the hands
of the Wigan District Bank...£138 2 4

Do. in the hands of the
Acting Trustee £18 3 5

Total balance general account 156 5 9
Cash balance Repair Fund
account, deposited with the
Wigan District Bank ... 0 6 6
Do., Thomas Gaskell's legacy
account, do. 54 12 9
Do., Mine account, do. ... 464 14 8

MRS. FRANCES DUCKINFIELD'S CHARITY.

Mrs. Frances Duckinfield, otherwise Croston, of
Bickershaw, widow, late wife of Robert Duckinfield, of
Duckinfield, in the county of Chester, Esq., by deed
dated the 29th of September, 1662, conveyed four
closes of land situate in Mobberley, in Cheshire, called
the Smithy Field, the Kiln Croft, and the two Cow
Heys, containing 14 acres to—
   Richard Hilton, of Westleigh,
   Robert Hampson, of Hindley, Yeoman,
   John Battersby, of Westleigh, Schoolmaster,
   Adam Richardson, of Abram, Yeoman,
   Mathew Astley, of Hindley, Yeoman,
   James Kay, of Hindley, Cooper,
   Henry Hilton, of Hindley, Husbandman, and
   Robert Sweetlove, of Hindley, Husbandman,
in trust for the following purposes :—That 50s. be given
yearly to the minister of Hindley Chapel, £4 to the
poor of Hindley and Abram, and 20s. to the master of
the Hindley Free School, and the rest to the heirs
of Ann Atkinson, daughter of Thomas Atkinson, of
Cockefoster, of Middlesex, by Elizabeth, one of the
daughters of the said Mrs. Frances Duckinfield. The
gift of 50s. to the minister of Hindley Chapel was contingent on a pew or other accommodation being provided
for Mrs. Duckinfield's family, her heirs and assigns, in

Hindley Chapel; and in the event of this not being had, the sum was to be bestowed on the worthy and orderly poor of Hindley and Abram.

A Lease and Release, dated December 18th and 19th, 1781, conveys the estate by the surviving Trustees, Robert Thomasson and James Green, to eleven additional Trustees, viz. :—

Henry Thomasson.	James Green.
Jonathan Thomasson. (1)	Hugh Stirrup.
James Eckersley.	James Leyland.
Jonathan Thomasson. (2)	John Leyland.
William Blundell.	Charles Worsley.
John Green.	

In 1804 the only survivors of this body were Henry Thomasson, Jonathan Thomasson (2), and Charles Worsley, who on the 24th of March in that year enlarged their number to ten by appointing—

James Lever, of Hindley, Gentleman.

James Mackie, of Lowton, Cotton Merchant.

Nicholas Marsh, of Westhoughton, Cotton Manufacturer.

James Bevan, of Lowton, Esquire.

Edward Ackers, of Newton-in-Makerfield, Surgeon.

Robert Bolton, of Wigan, Brassfounder.

Peter Arrowsmith, of Astley, Cotton Manufacturer.

The next Trust Deed is dated April 2nd, 1830. The existing Trustees were then—

James Mackie,	Hindley,	Yeoman.
and		
Nicholas Marsh,	do.,	do.

The new Trustees were :—

Henry Battersby,	Hindley,	Cotton Spinner.
Charles Battersby,	do.,	do.
Richard Pennington,	do.,	do.
John Aspinall, jun.,	do.,	Surgeon.
Thomas Gaskell,	do.,	Yeoman.
Peter Marsh,	do.,	Tea Dealer
John Marsh,	do.,	Linen Draper.

Samuel Banks,	Abram,	Farmer.
Adam Chadwick,	London,	Esquire.
John Whitley, jun.,	{ Ashton-in-Makerfield, }	do.
John Jolley,	Abram,	Schoolmaster.

An order of the Charity Commissioners, dated February 18th, 1870, recites that—

Thomas Gaskell, of Hindley, Esquire ;

Peter Marsh, of Southport, Tea Dealer ; and

Richard Pennington, of Westfield House, Rugby, Esq.,

wish to retire from the trust ; that the sole surviving and continuing Trustee is Samuel Banks, of Abram, Farmer, and appoints the following persons as new Trustees :—

John Leyland, of	Hindley,	Gentleman.
Richard Pennington, jun.,	do.,	Cotton Spinner.
Edward Grime,	do.,	Shopkeeper.
William Livsey,	do.,	do.
William Marsh,	do.,	Flag Merchant.
William Lyon,	do.,	Land Agent.
James Banks,	Abram,	Shopkeeper.
Charles Peter Ackers,	do.,	Gentleman.

MR. THOMAS CROOK'S CHARITY.

Thomas Crook, by his will, dated July 9th, 1688, devised a rent-charge of £20 per annum on land in Alston and Whittingham, in the County of Lancaster, for the poor of Preston ; St. Olave Jewry, London ; Abram, in the Parish of Wigan ; Mawdesley, in the Parish of Croston ; Walton-le-Dale, in the Parish of Blackburn ; for the Schoolmasters of Mawdesley, Walton-le-Dale, and Hindley ; and for the Ministers of Walton-le-Dale, Hindley, and Westhoughton. Of the £20, the Incumbent of All Saints' Church, Hindley, receives £1 per annum, and the Trustees of the Hindley and Abram Grammar School also £1.

Linen Cloth Charity.

Randle Collier founded this charity by a bequest in his will, dated September 8th, 1682, of £50, the interest of which was to be given in linen cloth every New-year's day to the poor of the township. His wife, Mary Collier, in her will, dated September 12th, 1684, also left £20 for the same purpose. The charity was afterwards enlarged by a gift of £20 from Robert Cooper, and of £10 from Edward Green. These various benefactions amount to £100, which accumulations from time to time have further increased to £137 2s. 9d. With this sum the Trustees of the Chapel purchased £151 6s. in three per cent consols, and receive dividends thereon amounting to £4 10s. 9¼d., which sum is distributed in the. manner described to the poor on every New-year's day.

The interest on £10 of the £50 bequeathed by Randle Collier was given to the Trustees, for their trouble in dispensing the charity; but they never claim it, and the entire proceeds go to the poor.

The proportion received by Hindley of the £4 given to the poor of Hindley and Abram by Mrs. Frances Duckinfield is £2 8s., and this sum has for a long period been given in linen cloth with the above charity.

Mr. Richard Mather's Charity

Dates from the 29th of April, 1852. On that day Mr. Mather conveyed to
John Leyland, gentleman,
Thomas Winward, warper,
William Mather, shopkeeper,
James Eatock, bookkeeper,
Richard Mather, the younger, shoemaker, all of
    Hindley;
John Pollard, printer, and
William Pollard, collier, of Wigan; and
Richard Tickle, of Abram, yeoman,

in trust for purposes specified hereafter, certain freehold property, situate in Hindley, comprising a room erected over a gateway in Chapel Lane, with the adjoining cottage on the north side, four cottages in the Wigan road, and a chief or ground rent near thereto, the gross yearly income of which amounted to £22 11s. 11½d. The deed of gift directs that the room over the gateway, in Chapel Lane, shall be used for a school for the teaching of infant children, and the adjoining cottage for the residence of the teachers. The balance of the income of the residue of the property, after deducting the expenses of repairs and collection, is divided into three portions, one of which is appropriated to the providing of the necessaries of the school, such as fire, cleaning, and books; another to the payment of teachers' salaries; and the third is expended in bread, and distributed among the poor of the neighbourhood.*

Mr. Thomas Winward, Mr. William Mather, and Mr. William Pollard, having died, and Mr. John Pollard having become disqualified, Mr. Richard Pennington, junior, Mr. Edward Grime, Mr. Thomas Atherton, and Mr. William Marsh were, by an order of the Charity Commissioners, dated October 18th, 1867, appointed in their place.

MR. THOMAS WINWARD'S CHARITY.

Mr. Thomas Winward, of Hindley, in his will, dated the eleventh day of June, 1860, bequeathed the sum of £40 to the Wardens of St. Peter's Church, when elected, the interest of which is to be distributed in bread to poor persons attending the church.

The sum of £42 2s. 9d., £3 per cent consolidated annuities, was purchased on the 29th of July, 1868, by the executors of Mr. Winward, with the legacy be-

---

* The bread is now given on the last Saturday in every month in the Infant Schoolroom.

queathed by him, and was vested in "The Official Trustees of Charitable Funds," pursuant to the provisions of the Charitable Trusts Amendment Act, 1855.

LAPSED CHARITIES.

The Commissioners appointed by the Crown to inquire into the state of the various charities in the kingdom, visited Wigan in the year 1828, and made a report on the charities of the parish, which was subsequently published, and to which I am indebted for the following particulars.

All the charities of Hindley of any value have been fortunately preserved. None have been lost except in the unimportant instances I am about to refer to.

MR. JOHN GUEST'S CHARITY.

In the report to which I have alluded, it is stated that "John Guest, by his will, bearing date 28th September, 1653, gave to the Ministers of the Parish Church of Wigan, and six other places, the yearly sum of £3 15s. each, charged upon his lands in Abram, to be bestowed in linen cloth on 45 of the poorest people within each parish, such as the said respective ministers should conceive to stand in the greatest need of the same.

"£3 10s. was received at the time of the commission as a rent-charge from a farm, called Bolton House, in Abram, which, from 1824 to that time, had been divided as follows :—

			s.	d.
" To the poor of Wigan		....	7	0
do.	do.	Billinge	14	0
do.	do.	Haigh	7	0
do.	do.	Abram	14	0
do.	do.	Winstanley	14	0
do.	do.	Pemberton....................	14	0
			£3 10	0"

"The other townships in the Parish [Hindley forming one of the number] formerly received a small portion of the charity, but this practice was eventually discontinued, probably on account of the smallness of the sum to be divided."

MR. EDWARD HOLT'S CHARITY.

"Edward Holt, by his will, bearing date 7th October, 1704, bequeathed £150 to James Holt and nine others of the town or parish of Wigan, upon trust, to put forth the same at interest, or to lay it in purchasing lands or a rent-charge, and to lay out the yearly produce thereof in oat bread, or any other sort of bread, as they should think most meet; and he directed that they should cause such bread to be distributed to such poor people as for the time being should inhabit and dwell within Wigan, and also within the townships of Haigh, Aspull, Ince, Pemberton, Hindley, Abram, and Winstanley, as the said Trustees or the major part of them should direct and appoint; the same bread to be distributed in the Parish Church of Wigan, in the manner following: (that is to say) 22 penny loaves every Sunday, viz.: one Sunday to the poor of Wigan, and the other Sunday to the poor of Haigh, Aspull, Ince, Pemberton, Hindley, Abram, and Winstanley, and so on alternately."

"In 1774 the principal sum of £150 was laid out on the Wigan Workhouse, and the interest has since been paid out of the Poors Rate." A few pounds were received by the Incumbent of Hindley from this charity for the poor of the township twelve or fourteen years ago, since which no claim has been made* by the township, and I am told that, as the bread ought to be distributed in the parish church of Wigan, any such claim would not now be allowed.

---

* Excepting in this instance no benefit has been derived to Hindley from the "Lapsed Charities" for a long period.

Mr. Edmund Molyneux's Charity.

" Edmund Molyneux, citizen of London, by his will, bearing date 8th October, 1613, devised all his lands, consisting of 53a. 2r. 33p., at Canewden, in Essex, which were £20 by the year rent, to be bestowed in penny bread, and given to the ancientest and poorest people at Wigan and at Holland, every Sunday throughout the year for ever, viz., at Wigan to 60, and at Holland to 30, of such poor people every Sunday, to each one penny loaf; and the remaining 10s. he gave to the Churchwardens for their pains at both the churches, equally to be divided; and if the Churchwardens should not perform this his gift according to his will, he directed that the land and the rent thereof should go to the use of a free school to be kept at Holland."

The share appropriated by Wigan "is made up in fourpenny loaves, and given away by the Churchwardens to the poor of such parts of the parish as attend Wigan Church, according to a list made out by the Churchwardens, upon the recommendation of any of the more respectable inhabitants. Whenever any extraordinary expenses are incurred the quantity of bread is accordingly reduced."

Mr. Edward Richardson's Charity.

" Under the name of Richardson's Charity, a distribution takes place annually, on the feast of the Ascension, of five loads of oatmeal, each load weighing 240lbs. Three loads are given to the poor of the township of Ince, one to the poor of Abram, and the other to the poor of Hindley. The meal is provided by Mr. Cowley, of Widnes, the owner of an estate in Ince, formerly the property of Edward Richardson, who, we are informed, directed by his will that this distribution should be made for 50 years from the time of his death.

"In the parliamentary returns of 1786 the year 1784 is given as the date of this benefaction."

The 50 years appointed for the distribution of the charity expired in 1836.

RECOLLECTIONS.

I am proposing to occupy the remaining pages with some notice of the principal people of the village in my younger days, and of the customs then prevalent, or which existed as I have been told in the preceding generation.

Before the introduction of manufactures and the opening of collieries, the village has been described as being what we may easily conceive it to have been — secluded and pleasant. The inhabitants were all known to each other; they were sociable, and an interchange of visits fostered a friendly feeling between the different classes.

The first factory was erected, as I have already stated, by Mr. Richard Battersby, at the Lowe Mill, which up to that time had been a corn mill, moved by water power. Mr. Battersby was an enterprising and prosperous man, and when he died, in 1806, bequeathed a handsome property to his children, who did not, however, with their patrimony inherit their father's prosperity. For some time afterwards they lived where their family had lived for several generations, at the Lowe Mill; but their property wasted away, and first one, and then another, removed or died, so that there is not one of them now left in the neighbourhood.

The example set by Mr. Battersby in factory building was speedily followed by the late Mr. John Pennington. This gentleman removed from an adjoining township to live on an estate his family owned about the year 1796. His was one of those master-spirits who leave their impress on after-generations. To him, and others like him, the cotton trade is indebted for its present colossal proportions. Though very much older, he honoured me with his friendship; and, perhaps, no one out of his own family circle had better opportunities, from long and frequent intercourse, of appreciating his talents. He was endowed with a mind of extraordinary power. I never conversed with him without being struck with the quickness of his perceptions and the sagacity of his observations. Whatever station of life he had been born in he would have distinguished himself, and would have risen to the foremost rank. As it was, from a moderate independence, he became the possessor of considerable wealth. At the outset of his career he employed only a few handloom weavers. As time went on these gradually increased in number. Subsequently he erected a spinning factory, afterwards one for power-looms of still larger size, and up to the time when he left the neighbourhood his works were continually increasing. In the spring of 1836 he removed to Liverpool, and the remainder of his life was spent there as a merchant, the works at Hindley falling under the management of his sons. Tall and powerfully made, and endowed with a vigorous constitution, he was enabled to get through an immense amount of work. The expression of his countenance was generally stern, but in social intercourse it softened and almost entirely disappeared. Like many other clever men, he played and much enjoyed whist, but he always loved to win. If the game went against him he became moody, and roused all his energies to turn the luck. It was no pleasant thing to be his partner on such occasions. Every move was watched with lynx-eyed attention, and a false step was commented on with unsparing severity. He died in August, 1850, at the advanced age of 82.

Another of the worthies of Hindley in those days was Mr. Edward Kearsley, a gentleman who resided on a property he owned in the village. Ivy Cottage—the name by which his residence was known—was the perfection of order, not a blade of grass being allowed to

G

grow out of its proper place. The efforts he made to maintain his house, grounds, and property generally in this condition were ably seconded by George Mort, a faithful servant, who had a taste as fastidious as his master's. But Mr. Kearsley had higher claims to respect than a mere love of order. As a husband, a father, and a neighbour, he set an example which it would be well for society if it were oftener imitated. Regular himself in his attendance at church, he saw that his children and servants attended likewise, and his religion was not put on one day in the week—it was every day the same.

Trouble fell upon him in his latter years, and after selling his property in Hindley, he went to live for a little while in Jersey; he then removed to Lytham, where, somewhat suddenly, when scarcely past the noon of life, he was taken away. In his death his friends mourned the loss of a true and loyal gentleman.

Mr. Peter Ditchfield was another of our leading men. All his family, which consisted of three sons and four daughters, are now dead. The two younger sons died first; the old gentleman himself followed next; then, with an interval of a year or two only between each, his four daughters. The remaining son resided elsewhere, and survived many years the other members of his family.

Among all the inhabitants of the village there was none better known than Richard Mather. Born in Crow Lane, Newton, in 1777, on an estate held in lease by his father from the Legh family, he became a resident in 1786 when nine years of age, at which time his father removed to Hindley in order to keep the Cross Keys public-house. This inn had then the most commodious stabling in the village, and was much frequented in consequence by travellers. Richard acted for some time as ostler boy, and received in that capacity many gratuities from travellers, every penny of which he carefully hoarded. In this way he amassed as much as £20. One Jonathan Thomason, a well-known man in the neighbourhood in his day, and a constant frequenter of his father's house, took care of his money, and encouraged him in his economy. A love of saving became thus a second nature, and clung to him to the very end of his life.

An older brother followed the trade of plumber and glazier, and in process of time Richard became his apprentice. Four years from the commencement of his apprenticeship his brother gave up the business, when Richard continued it on his own account. After following it for 22 or 23 years his health became impaired, and his doctor attributing the cause to his occupation, advised him to retire. The advice he acted upon, as the savings he had accumulated were more than sufficient for his maintenance. The severe economy he practised in his early years was continued after it became unnecessary, and a good bargain gave him intense pleasure even to the last. I have heard him tell a story of a speculation he made in glass, years before, with a good deal of unction. The probability of the Government of the day laying a tax on this commodity had been canvassed in the papers, and Richard had, therefore, thought it prudent to increase his stock much beyond his ordinary requirements. Early one morning he took up a newspaper, and saw that the tax had at last been resolved upon by Government, whereupon he set off at once without breakfast to the glass works at St. Helens, although he had made other arrangements for the day, gave an order for a considerable quantity, got the invoice, and saw a portion of it despatched home. Newspapers were not then read with the regularity they are at the present day, or the glass manufacturer would have been aware of the increased value the proposed tax had given to his wares. A builder named Fairclough got into his debt in the way of trade, to the extent of £130, and Richard having difficulty in getting the money, he determined to build a number of cottages, and by employing Fairclough in the building to recover the debt. This first led him to invest his money in cottage property, of which ultimately he became a considerable owner. When about five-and-twenty years of age he was persuaded to engage himself as a Sunday school teacher, although he had heretofore been a thoughtless liver, and a few years afterwards he became impressed with the truths of religion. From this period he took great interest in Sunday schools, and for a quarter of a century was a persevering and unwearied teacher in the schools connected with what was then called the Parochial Chapel. In conjunction with his fellow-teachers, he used to have a meeting of the scholars on the evening of Christmas Day, when the children recited short dialogues, hymns, or chapters of the Bible. Members of the congregation were invited to attend, and no one could have pleased him better than by forming one of the audience. At an early period in the history of infant schools he was the means of establishing one in the village, and ever afterwards took the warmest interest in its success. Surrounded by a number of young children, teaching them a verse of some sweet Christian hymn, he was at the summit of his ambition, and I verily believe would not have changed places with an emperor. Much credit is due to him for the invention of a machine for teaching children letters, numerals, spelling, and reading, and even sums in arithmetic. Although a similar instrument was used in ancient times in practical reckoning, and is said to be so still in China and elsewhere, the description he has given of its construction shows that he was but little indebted to extraneous aid. Playing one day with a child of his nephew's, there happened to be a tobacco pipe lying near, which he took up to amuse it with, and by a sort of accident formed a rude little block of wood, through which he bored a hole and ran it along the pipe. He next inscribed a letter on the block, and succeeded in teaching it to the child. Other letters were then tried, and with so much success that it induced him to try the principle on a larger scale. The first instrument he made was a frame of wood, not unlike the frame of a swing looking-glass, with square iron rods running horizontally, on which were threaded small square wooden blocks, having a letter of the alphabet inscribed on one of the sides. Accidentally making the hole of one of the blocks too large, it swung round when placed on the wire. Hence he saw the advantage of having the rods round instead of square, as he could have a different letter painted on each side of the block. Thus, little by little, with the suggestion of one friend or another, but principally by his own ingenuity, he constructed a very useful and complete machine. This was about the year 1837. It attracted considerable attention in the neighbourhood, and some of his friends recommended him to take out a patent for the invention, which however he declined to do. For a long number of years it was his custom to hold prayer-meetings every Sunday evening, when he would read a portion of the Church prayers, a chapter in the Bible, and a sermon, sometimes chosen from a published collection, and sometimes one of his own composition. These were held first at his house, but ultimately at one of his cottages, which he kept untenanted for the purpose; and as the attendance grew larger he was induced, in 1851, to build a room over a gateway for the express purpose, and large enough to contain a hundred people.

About this time—1851—he received an unexpected addition to his property from a distant family connection. His grandfather and a person named Rawlinson married two sisters, and from Rawlinson there descended a Mr. William Ainsworth, who acquired considerable property, which he bequeathed at his death among certain of his relations, to be divided when the youngest of them came of age. The testator excluded the four nearest of kin, of whom Richard was one; but he omitted to provide for the disposition of the accumulations of his estate, which, when the youngest interested in the property attained his majority, amounted to nearly £20,000; and the question was then raised, whether the legatees or the next of kin were entitled to the money. The Court of Chancery was appealed to, and decided in favour of the latter, and Richard received for his share upwards of £4,000. It was a curious result, that the very parties who were excluded by the will should receive so considerable a sum, and be put in actual possession of the money before those to whom the estate was devised could receive their portion. It affords a striking illustration of the truth of the proverb, "Man proposes but God disposes." This addition to his means led him to determine to devote some portion of his goods to charitable purposes, which eventually took the form of a deed of gift of freehold property of about £500 in value to certain trustees, the object of which, under the head of Mather's Charity, I have already stated.

Mr. Thomas Gaskell was the last survivor of the past generation who took any part in public affairs. He lived to reach his 87th year, and died as recently as 1870. Of the old yeomen, a class once common, and now almost extinct, he was an excellent representative. The house which witnessed his birth witnessed also his death, and he never lived in any other, through life—

> "Content to breathe his native air
> In his own ground."

The same fields his father cultivated he cultivated also; and if it be patriotism—as it has been said it is— to make two blades of grass grow where one grew before, Mr. Gaskell could have laid a claim to that virtue. The patrimony he inherited he brought into a high state of cultivation, and extended its bounds further and further, here a field and there a field. Throughout life he was a constant worshipper at the Presbyterian Chapel, of which he was the principal supporter. At one time or other he filled most of the public offices of the township, and served as trustee and executor to a great number of people, with un-impeached integrity.

In addition to those I have passed in review, there were others well worthy of a place in the annals of the village, discreet, keepers-at-home, who took no part in public affairs.   There were the families of the Eckersleys, the Southworths, the Thomassons, the Seddons, the Barlows, the Martlews, the Sumners.   There were Mrs. and Miss Clarke, Mrs. and Miss Heyes, and the Misses Green.

The Hargreaves family, long resident at Hart Common, were constant attendants at the Chapel, and took a warm interest in all that concerned the prosperity of the township.

The characters of many of our old friends who now rest from their labours, may be studied with advantage. Though being dead, they yet speak by their quiet, unostentatious, and virtuous lives.   Burns, in one of his letters to his friend, James Hamilton, says : "Among some distressful emergencies that I have experienced in life, I ever laid down this as my foundation of comfort, that he who has lived the life of an honest man has by no means lived in vain."

It remains for me now only to glance at some of the usages which were once common, and are so no longer.

The neighbourhood has been long known to be rich in coal deposits, and the upper seams were being worked long before the time I am speaking of. Factories existed, as I have more than once stated, seventy years ago, but they were fewer in number and smaller in size than the existing factories, and the number of people engaged in both occupations was comparatively small. The great bulk of the labouring class was employed either in hand-loom weaving or in agriculture. Cottages had all weaving-shops attached to them, some with space sufficient for two looms only, others for five or six. Taking all things into consideration, I question if the quality of modern cottages is better. Modern cottages are higher over head, and some possess lobbies and parlours—conveniences totally unknown in the days I am referring to ; but they are more huddled together, and have less breathing room outside. Most of the old cottages were either detached or semi-detached, and, excepting in rare instances, possessed their small garden plots.

Hand-loom weaving gave employment to entire families. The mother, with one of the younger children, wound bobbins, the father and the elder sons and daughters wove the coarser or finer calicoes, or fustians, according to their skill and ability. It is much to be regretted that the exigencies of trade, caused by the development of machinery, transferred this branch of industry to factories, as a father had the whole of his children working under his own roof, and under his own eye. Not only did the system lead to the parental authority being held in greater respect, but young people were exposed by it to fewer temptations.

A few years anterior to the time under consideration spinning was also carried on in cottages : cloth was thus spun, woven, and worn under the same roof. This cloth was of great durability, and continued in use in a family for one purpose or another for an entire generation.

Oatmeal formed the principal article of food of the operative class, and bread made of it, called "jannock," was commonly eaten. Families consumed only a single wheaten loaf in the week, bought by way of change or delicacy for the Sunday's meals. Few cottagers' houses possessed articles of mahogany furniture. An oak chest, a couch, an eight-days' clock inherited from a former generation, with rush-bottomed chairs and deal tables, were the ordinary articles of furniture.

A man still living told me an anecdote which curiously illustrates the sarcastic allusions of our old dramatists to shining shoes. He was a grown man (he said) before he ever had his shoes blacked, the universal custom among people of his class being to rub them with grease. One day he took a fancy to wear blacked shoes, and turned out from his home, proud at his unusual smartness. He lived in the Close Lanes, and he had not proceeded far towards the village before he began to have qualms of conscience as to whether he was really doing what was quite right. The misgivings grew upon him as he proceeded, and he became so heartily ashamed of his effeminacy that he daubed his shoes carefully over with mud, and was thus enabled to go on with head erect and a satisfied spirit.

The houses of the middle class were seldom or never entered by a lobby. The front door opened into the ordinary living room of the family, and this room led into the parlour, which was sometimes boarded and carpeted, but was oftener of bare stone. The latter apartment was only used on visits or family festivals. The ladies of these days did not possess the variety in dress their descendants think so essential. They were content with a single silk gown, which often lasted their entire lives. Chintz prints were generally worn, but even they were too valuable for everyday wear, as they cost from five to seven shillings the yard. The colours of these chintzes were so well fixed, and the cloth so durable, that after they had done service in the gown they were cut up and used in patchwork for quilts. I have seen several quilts made in this way, and have been surprised both at the strength of the cloth and the brightness of the colours.

The general mode of travelling was on horseback, and a lady would ride on a pillion behind her husband to church and market. The pillion had generally a covering of strong cotton velvet, quilted, and trimmed with fringe made for the special purpose, and presented a neat and tasteful appearance.

Christmas was then, as now, a festive season. Visits were interchanged, at which cards were the favourite amusement, intermixed, however, among the younger people, with blindman's buff, hunt the slipper, puss in the corner, and such like games. The holidays of Shrovetide, Easter, and Whitsuntide have diminished in importance, Shrovetide more, perhaps, than the others. Paste-egging was, and remains still, a popular amusement in Passion Week. Two kinds of paste-eggers were common—the white and the black. The white paid their visits in the day, as well as the night. They were decorated with ribbons, and acted a sort of drama, in which one Boldslasher was the hero, who fought and was slain; and there was a learned doctor, who, in travels to distant lands, had discovered a medicine that would bring back the dead to life. This he applied to the dead Boldslasher, who instantly rose up to life again. Our Lord's resurrection is evidently commemorated in this drama, which is probably a relic of the old mystery plays the Church of Rome was wont to represent at this season prior to the Reformation. The black paste-eggers made their calls in the evening after dark. They were simply mummers, masked, or with blackened faces, and dressed as hideously as they could devise. One in each band was surmounted with a stuffed horse's head, and was covered with a horse-cloth, the representative, doubtless, of the ancient hobby-horse. The custom of lifting on Easter Monday

and Tuesday, supposed to commemorate the lifting of
Christ from the cross, was common, but is now almost
abandoned. Rushbearing and morrice-dancing have
long since disappeared. A May-pole used to stand on
a green near the present Lord Nelson public-house. A
thatched house adjoining the present inn, pulled
down in 1846, was the old public-house, and bore
the sign of the Swan, of which seventy years ago
one Oliver Halton was the landlord. Before the
passing of the " Beer Act," or at least up to a short
period previous to its passing, there were only nine
public-houses in the township, viz., " The Bird i'th'
Hand," " The Red Lion," " The Lord Nelson," " The
Cross Keys," " The Bull," " The Hand and Banner,"
" The Swan," and " Brown Cow," Hindley Green, and
" The King William," Platt Bridge.

Mourning coaches were never used at funerals. If
the distance was short between the home of the departed and the place of burial, the body was carried on
a bier, the mourners following on foot. If the distance
was considerable, a hearse conveyed the body, which
was attended by relatives and friends on horseback.

A pretty custom, now confined to the lower classes,
and which even from them is now departing, formerly
prevailed at all funerals. Sprigs of evergreen, chiefly
consisting of rosemary, lavender, or box, were handed
round to the funeral guests. These were carried by
them to church, and thrown upon the coffin after it was
lowered in the grave, as emblems of immortality, and
tokens of their faith in the Resurrection.

One more story and I have done.

The authorities of the township used to walk the
bounds, as it was called—that is, they perambulated
every now and then the boundary line of the township,
in order to keep alive in the minds of the inhabitants
its exact and precise limits. It was easy enough to
inform the adult where the line was drawn, but they
had the rising generation to teach as well, maps, be it
remembered, being then scarce, and they hit upon a

notable expedient. They caught some lad they happened to meet, and carried him to any place where the boundary was not clearly defined, and gave him a good thrashing, thinking it would be a means of fixing the spot in his memory ever afterwards.

I have now brought my chronicle to a close. If it serves to preserve any fact relating to the township or any name worthy of being remembered, the object with which it was undertaken will be attained.

JOHN HEYWOOD, Excelsior Printing and Stationery Works, Hulme Hall Road, Manchester.

MEMORIALS OF HINDLEY.

BY JOHN LEYLAND,

OF

THE GRANGE.

PART SECOND.

"The past employments of passing hours."—BLAIR.
"Where are concealed the days which have elapsed."—KIRKE WHITE.

MANCHESTER:
JOHN HEYWOOD, 141 AND 143, DEANSGATE.

PREFACE.

———

THE writer of the letters contained in the following pages commenced at a very early period of his life to preserve copies of his correspondence. What motive induced him to do this is, at this distance of time, difficult to say; but assuredly it was not with the most remote intention of ever putting any of them in print. A release from official duties in the year 1870 gave him the opportunity he had long desired to examine and arrange his papers, and, while pursuing this task, he met with a large number of copies of his letters more or less perfect. Some of them were found to have been addressed to old residents of Hindley, and some to have contained references to what may be designated the history of the village. These he determined to print, and others were added in order to make up a volume of moderate size.

All have been revised, and some materially curtailed.

THE GRANGE,
November 17th, 1873.

MEMORIALS OF HINDLEY.

To Mr. John Marsh.

Hindley, March 14th, 1830.

My dear John,

I have been surprised at not receiving a letter from you before now; but I suppose you are pursuing your studies with such avidity that you have no time to think of absent friends. You will, perhaps, wonder at this letter being dated from Hindley. The reason is, that I am at home for the Easter holidays. I came on Thursday last, and found things much as I had left them.

The past winter has been severe in Southport. I could not have believed that the short distance between Hindley and Southport could have made so great a difference in the temperature. Southport is at this time of the year so dull that I have nothing new to tell. It is true there has been a wedding lately (and a wedding is a great event) between a Mr. Jolly, a former resident of Hindley, and one of the daughters of Mr. Greatbach, the Calvinist minister. A few families have been there during the whole of the winter; among them a clergyman of the name of Garrett, who has officiated frequently at church.

The owners and occupiers of cottages are now busily employed in beautifying their houses, and making other preparations for the ensuing season.

I am, truly yours,

JOHN LEYLAND.

To Miss Louisa Ditchfield.

Hindley, June, 1830.

Dear Madam,

Having an opportunity afforded by Mr. Pennington's visit to France, I use it to write to you.

I was happy to hear that you had arrived safe at your destination. I envy you the pleasures of your journey. The visit to a new country and people of which we have heard and read much cannot fail to be entertaining.

Of all things appertaining to your journey you will inform us on your return; and no doubt you will wish to hear something from home. On the whole, things are going on much as usual. I returned from school on the 16th inst., and your sisters left Southport a few days before. I have spent many pleasant afternoons with them during their visit, which I shall long remember. I daresay you know that they occupied Mrs. Peters's cottage. Up to a week previous to their return they had . the house entirely to themselves; then a Mrs. Jowsey, a lady from Norton, near Stockton-upon-Tees, a widow, and a very agreeable and chatty woman, took apartments, and established an acquaintance with them.

A large building, intended for news and billiards, is in course of erection. It is to be finished by September, and to be opened with a ball. The weather has been so unsettled lately that it has kept back visitors, and it has even caused many to return home who were already there. In summer it is a pleasant place, and a delightful occupation on a fine evening to watch the sun sink into the waters, to see the visitors inhaling the cool breeze, children climbing and running down the sandhills, and the various equipages driving along. One evening in particular your sisters and I enjoyed a walk we took on the banks of the Nile. The atmosphere was so clear that a chain of the Westmorland hills could be distinctly seen, and with the rippling sea in the distance, and such other sights as I have mentioned, the scene looked almost like Fairyland.

A Miss Manners, as you will doubtless have heard, is on a visit at your house. Yesterday I introduced her to the Sunday school, and as neither Miss Pennington nor you were there, her services were very acceptable.

Haymaking is not yet begun, owing to the bad weather. The crops are in general fair.

I am, dear Madam,
Truly yours,
JOHN LEYLAND.

To Mr. Charles Seymour.

Hindley, Sept., 1830.

My dear Charles,

I got home safely the day I left school. One of our men met me at Wigan, and you may naturally suppose my first question was after my father. The answer I got was that he had been easier since twelve o'clock. I then asked if his illness was dangerous, and he replied that he was very ill, but might possibly be better in a day or two. When I got near home I met Mr. Henry Battersby, a cousin to my mother, whom I have been in the habit of calling uncle. He said my father was very ill. I asked him, too, if his illness was dangerous, and he said, "I fear so." Imagine, Charles, how much I was shocked. How desolate the house looked on my arrival! All the windows and doors were open, and no one seemed stirring. I crept upstairs into my father's room, and there I found him lying insensible. I spoke the word "father," but he gave no sign of hearing me. He was breathing strong and heavy. My mother, who was in the room, said, "I am afraid he cannot last long." Until then I had no thoughts of him dying. It then occurred to me that his strong breathing, which I had just been supposing was a symptom of strength, might be the precursor of dissolution. What a long night that night seemed; the very minutes seemed hours. I laid down in an adjoining room about one o'clock, desiring to be called if any change took place.   Half-an-hour afterwards my aunt came to say he was passing away.

JOHN LEYLAND.

To Mr. Charles Seymour.

Hindley, Oct., 1830.

My dear Charles,

I avail myself of the visit of my friends, the Misses Ditchfield, to Southport, to write a few lines. I received your kind letter on Saturday, the 2nd inst. The books Mr. Brown has sent for to London, and I expect to get them in the course of a month. To me nothing is more welcome than a letter from an absent friend, hence—presuming you think the same—the reason of my writing to you. I may, perhaps, come to Southport in the course of a week or fortnight. Thank Charles Hargreaves for his letter, which I received along with yours, and tell him I am glad to have him for a correspondent. To-morrow I go to Manchester, where I am called on business about once a month.

What a loss I feel for my poor father; every day I seem to feel it more.

JOHN LEYLAND.

To Mr. and Mrs. Walker.

Hindley, Oct., 1830.

Dear Mr. and Mrs. Walker,

I am afraid you will think me forgetful in not writing before this, but I have been much engaged and a good deal from home. For the present Mr. Walker has sent me I am truly grateful, and for all the kindness I have received from you whilst under your care. There is little or no news stirring here. Mr. Evans, our curate, I am sorry to say, is leaving Hindley. The incumbent of the living, Mr. Hendrick, died lately, and Mr. Evans's services will not be needed by Mr. Hill, the new incumbent, who is at present senior curate of the Parish Church of Wigan. Mr. Evans goes to

Plimston, near Chester, but I am afraid the salary will be less than even the little he has had here.

I shall be happy to hear from you at any time.

Present my kindest respects to Mr. Dolling and all my schoolfellows. Believe me to remain,

Dear Mr. and Mrs. Walker,

Your affectionate friend,

JOHN LEYLAND.

To Mr. Roger Seymour.

Hindley, Sept. 16th, 1832.

My dear Roger,

Many thanks for your kind letter, which I should have answered sooner but that I have been so very busy, and time does pass so fast. I have nothing new; everything is going on here in the usual quiet way.

You inquire after our farm. In reply I have to tell you that we finished mowing on the Saturday after you left, and housing on the following Wednesday. Of course, we had a merrymaking, at the close of which there was both singing and dancing. I gave your "blessing," as you called it, to the mowers. They were much obliged, and returned you thanks and blessings of another kind innumerable. Johnson, the farmer at Strangeways, I saw the same day. He told me he had just killed two corncrakes. He calls them game, and he had had them dressed for cooking. I asked him to get me one in its feathers, and the next day he caught another and sent it to me. I have since had it stuffed, and intend bringing it, along with the dragon's tongue, when I next come to Manchester.

You remember our visit to the site of Atherton Hall. The reason of it being pulled down, I have since been told, was that a member of the family once sheltered rebels under the roof, and a yearly fine was in consequence imposed on the family by Government, to be paid as long as the building remained standing.

Alfred and Frederick Pennington returned home about a fortnight ago. Alfred is to remain at home permanently, and Frederick until Christmas only.

Mrs. and Miss Halton have been staying a day or two with us. I hope to be in Manchester on either the 2nd or 3rd of October. The havoc the cholera is making in Manchester is frightful to hear of. If it comes near you, come to Hindley; we shall be happy to see you.   JOHN LEYLAND.

To Mr. Charles Seymour.

Hindley, Oct. 20th, 1832.

My dear Charles,

After I parted with you at the door of the railway station I learned that the train did not leave for half-an-hour afterwards, and I immediately ran out to tell you, but you were already out of sight. I therefore had to wait alone in the office, and it was a good deal past six o'clock when it started. It became dark long before we arrived at Kenyon Junction. We had to wait there out of doors more than a quarter of an hour of the Bolton train, and I did not arrive at home until half-past eight. Fred Pennington called the day before my return for the "Romance of the Forest." I have seen Alfred since, and he says Fred is so much interested with it, and had entered into the spirit of it so earnestly, that he has time for nothing else. I am reading "Mansfield Park," by Jane Austin. An article in the *Liverpool Courier*, entitled "My Wife," amused me last night. Excuse this short letter. I shall, perhaps, be able to make up leeway the next time I write.

My mother and aunt join me in kindest respects to all your family, and believe me to remain,

Sincerely yours,

JOHN LEYLAND.

To Mr. Roger Seymour.

Hindley, Jan. 27th, 1833.

My dear Roger,

Do you remember your mother wishing us to write long letters to each other? I have determined to act up to her advice, and if I have delayed writing so long it has been in the hopes that I might have some news for you. Yet, notwithstanding the delay, I have nothing to fill my paper with. I had the packet entirely to myself on my journey home nearly to Worsley, when I had an addition of one as far as Astley. I was again alone until I got nearly to Leigh. It was twenty minutes past seven on my arrival at the latter place, and when I reached home it was half-past eight.

My mother approves of our arrangements; she thinks we all shall have a great deal more pleasure by the postponement of your visit. The weather will then be warmer, and the days longer. You will leave school on the 25th, and must come to Hindley about the 26th or 27th, or as soon afterwards as may be convenient to you. Yours sincerely,

JOHN LEYLAND.

P.S.—Give my best respects to all your family, in which my mother and aunt join. My aunt's arm has been worse since the frost set in. My uncle, too, has been confined to the house a fortnight through a severe cold.—J. L.

To Mr. Roger Seymour.

Hindley, March 3rd, 1833.

My dear Roger,

I write with the greatest pleasure, yet I must ask you to be content with a short letter. I had an opportunity of sending the accompanying songs which I promised to your sister, and I write in haste. Tell her she may keep them any length of time. There is one short of the number I promised, which I shall perhaps get by the time you come over. I had a letter from Charles Hargreaves this day week. He says Southport is full of visitors, and that Mr. Walker has eighteen boarders.

This embraces all my news. When you next write, say what day we may have the pleasure of seeing you. With kindest respects to your family, believe me to remain, Your affectionate friend,

JOHN LEYLAND.

To Master Charles Hargreaves.

Hindley, April 13th, 1833.

My dear Charles,

I am much obliged for your kind letter of February 19th, which I duly received. Only a few days ago I laid my hands on a letter you wrote to me in May last, which I never answered. For not answering the first, and for the long delay in answering the last, I ask your forgiveness. You inquire if I have seen or heard from the Seymours lately. In reply I have to say that I have had them staying a fortnight with me, and that they returned home only last Thursday. They have now left school entirely, and are to commence business to-day in their father's office.

The new church in Aspull I have not yet seen. I think it is about two miles from here. Mr. Evans, our old curate, I have just heard, is to be the first incumbent. It is very uncertain whether I shall be able to come to Southport this spring; if I do, I cannot stay more than a day or two. At any time I shall have pleasure in hearing from you.

I hope to see more of you at Midsummer than I did at Christmas.

Give my kindest respects to Mr. and Mrs. Walker and family, and to William, and believe me to remain,

Yours sincerely,

JOHN LEYLAND.

To Mr. Roger Seymour.

Hindley, May 16th, 1833.

My dear Roger,

Your kind letter ought to have been answered sooner. I am sorry to hear that you and all your family are unwell. The influenza has been afflicting the neighbourhood of Hindley to a certain extent. My mother, aunt, and myself have escaped, but many of our neighbours have been ill.

Two days, I am afraid, are all I can give you at the race week. I propose to come on Thursday morning, and to leave on Friday evening.

Our old curate, Mr. Evans, is appointed incumbent of the new church in Haigh, the church which you may perhaps recollect we passed on our way to Haigh Hall. The opening ceremony is fixed for Whit Sunday. My uncle, with some friends, visited Haigh Hall last week. Much work, he says, remains still to be done, and his opinion is that it will occupy ten years yet to complete, and may cost a further sum of £50,000. Alfred Pennington and his sister are both ill, and both went to Southport yesterday to recruit. Their aunt, Miss Pennington, has been there a week, and Mr. Richard and his lady go to-day. When I come I shall be the bearer of a great many compliments on your poetical talents. Mrs. Ditchfield, of Tyldesley, died suddenly last Tuesday. She was walking out, was seized with a fit, and died before medical assistance could be procured. The suppressed dedication to "Don Juan" you asked for I send herewith. I am almost at the end of my paper, so I must stop. Give my love to Charles, and remember me to all your family.

Believe me to remain, yours sincerely,

JOHN LEYLAND.

My mother and aunt desire to be remembered.

To Mr. Roger Seymour.

Hindley, June 6th, 1833.

My dear Roger,

I am sorry to tell you that Miss Ditchfield is so unwell that she will be unable to attend the concert. Her sister and Mr. Battersby do not like to come without her, and they commission me to thank you for your kindness, which they would certainly have availed themselves of but for this unfortunate event. I should have written sooner, but I waited to see if a day or two would give hope for a change in Miss Ditchfield's health. After you left me on the day I returned home I sauntered about for ten minutes, and then took my seat in a carriage, when who should enter but my friend, John Marsh. He was on his way from Cambridge, and expected to have got home the night before, but the coach he travelled by met with an accident, which had detained him all night in Manchester. Mr. Hill, our incumbent, is from home, and on Sunday we shall have either the rector of Wigan or one of his curates to perform service. Marsh spends that day with me, and I intend getting him, if I can, to read the lessons.

Believe me to remain, yours sincerely,

JOHN LEYLAND.

To Mr. Charles Seymour.

Hindley, July 12th, 1833.

My dear Charles,

We are in the midst of our hay harvest, and exceedingly busy. The weather last week was very favourable, but the present prospect is bad.

Miss Ditchfield is worse; her recovery is now scarcely expected. When you write, say when you can come to Hindley. If not too much trouble, get me Buonaparte's "Midnight Review." Frederick Pennington and Charles and Will Hargreaves are over for the holidays. Excuse this short letter.

Yours sincerely,

JOHN LEYLAND.

To Mr. Roger Seymour.

Hindley, Sept. 2nd, 1833.

My dear Roger,

I have been long in answering yours and your brother's kind letters, but, as usual, I must plead business and the want of news worth communicating. I was sorry you could not spare time to come to Hindley, for we should all have been happy to see you. Miss Ditchfield still continues very ill. She improved a little in strength last week, and the doctors recommended her to Buxton. Her friends made the necessary preparations, but when the time came she was found unequal to the fatigue.

Our annual charity sermons took place last Sunday.

Mr. O'Neil, curate of Wigan, preached. The attendance was numerous, but the collection was small. In former years we have generally had upwards of £20, this year we only got £18. Alfred has got a new boat; it came last Tuesday, and was launched the same night on the mill lodge. The name is "Alfred of Hindley." We are now busy in our corn harvest, but as this is a wet morning I have taken the opportunity of writing.

My mother and aunt join me in regards to all your family; and believe me to remain, yours sincerely,

JOHN LEYLAND.

To Master Charles D. Hargreaves.

Hindley, Oct. 29th, 1833.

My dear Charles,

I have been expecting to hear from you ever so long, and you have not sent me a single line. I was glad to hear from George that you like your new school. Poor Will! I have wondered many a time how he goes on by himself. A person told me last week that Mr. Walker had a pretty good school, for he had counted twenty boys in the playground. The late high tides in Southport have done considerable damage. Mr. Whiteley's wall and an observatory on the beach have been washed down. At the Banks, two miles beyond Crossons, the sea broke through an embankment which had been standing sixty or eighty years, and submerged three hundred acres of land. A great number of new houses are now in building at Southport. Here there is nothing new stirring, except that Alfred has got a boat on the lodge, called the "Alfred of Hindley." It holds about a dozen people.

Believe me to remain, yours sincerely,

JOHN LEYLAND.

To Mr. Roger Seymour.

Hindley, Nov. 2nd, 1833.

My dear Roger,

Scold me if you will for not writing sooner, but forgive me this *once*, and I really will be more punctual

in future. I got home well, and had a pleasant journey.
There were two or three Hindley gentlemen on the
coach, and a gentleman who was a little "over the
line," who sung and talked, and amused us much.

I arrived at home about half-past seven.

Frederick Pennington leaves school at Christmas.
Dr. Pulford is retiring from his profession, or he would
have stayed longer. Charles is well, and likes his new
school. My mother and aunt join me in regards to all.

Ever yours,

JOHN LEYLAND.

To Mr. Roger Seymour.

Hindley, 1833.

My dear Roger,

Yours and Charles's kind letters deserved a
more punctual acknowledgment. I am writing on the
24th of December (Christmas Eve). It is a merry
time, but you Manchester people don't wait for the
arrival of Christmas to make merry, as you carry its
festivities with you the year round. I look forward
with great pleasure to our meeting both in Manchester,
and here at the time of the Wigan ball.

I am obliged to the two fair friends of yours who have
honoured me with their good opinion. Though you
don't say, I guess who they are. I am innocent of the
soft impeachment. A quiet, rational, bachelor sort of
life is what I am aiming at. Do you know the story of
the bottle of vinegar? If you don't, I will repeat it for
your benefit. Twelve young men, carousing one night,
pledged themselves, one and all, that whoever was the
"*last*" bachelor of the party would drink a bottle of
vinegar. The vinegar was brought, solemnly sealed,
and delivered, with an agreement signed by each, into
the custody of the host. Ten years after, the very
individual who made the proposition sat in the same
room, and the shudder he gave every now and then as
he eyed a dingy-looking bottle standing before him was
utterly incomprehensible to the waiter in attendance.
At last he opened a packet, which contained the agree-

ment and eleven letters which his old friends had written. The last of the eleven had been married that morning, and had written wishing him joy of his vinegar. Each advised him to marry; each said he was happy; yet each warned him of some foible or other. The wife of one was too pretty; of another, too ugly. One said never marry a woman of wit; another, avoid one remarkable for simplicity. All of them gave him a warning; so that the poor fellow began to think that after all there was the least acid in the vinegar.

A Mrs. Barlow, of our neighbourhood, has just died suddenly. Her son, a friend of mine, who lives in Warrington, was over the Sunday before, and invited me to tea with him. I went, saw his mother, who was in good health and spirits, in which she continued until the following Wednesday. On that evening she retired to rest at ten, was then taken ill, and died before twelve.

Fred Pennington, and Charles Hargreaves are home from school. My mother and aunt join me in regards to all.　　　　　　　Yours sincerely,

John Leyland.

To Mr. Charles Seymour.

Hindley, 1834.

My dear Charles,

I have received Roger's kind letter, and am much obliged by your invitation. I will be with you, all keeping well, on the 9th inst. The mode of conveyance will depend on the weather. It was odd Roger and I should both write on the same day. Christmas has begun, I find, with you, for in both of Roger's last letters he told me of having attended balls. Neither my mother nor my aunt are well, the damp weather having affected them. I write on New Year's Day, and wish you, Roger, and all your family, a happy New Year.　　　　Yours sincerely,

John Leyland.

B

To Mr. Roger Seymour.

Hindley, January 21st, 1834.

My dear Roger,

Forgive my negligence in writing, and don't follow my example. I got home comfortably.

The bachelors' ball came off last night. 150 guests were expected. There are only 30 subscribers, who will be mulcted, they say, in £15 each. I don't know who they are. I have not yet heard for what day the dispensary ball is fixed. Ever yours,

JOHN LEYLAND.

To Mr. Roger Seymour.

Hindley, March 17th, 1834.

My dear Roger,

It is now too late to remove the dragon's tongue. I have been waiting for an opportunity of sending it, or I should have written sooner. I am expecting to be in Manchester shortly.

The dispensary ball never took place.

The governors had received an apprentice fee, and had therefore no occasion for one. I only heard this a week since.

Marsh visited me the other day. He has left Cambridge, and got his B.A. degree.

Our man is going to Wigan, and is waiting to post my letter, so excuse haste. My mother and aunt are still complaining. Yours sincerely,

JOHN LEYLAND.

To Mr. Roger Seymour.

Hindley, April 11th, 1834.

My dear Roger,

On the very day I posted my last letter to you I received yours, a few hours afterwards. I have been expecting to be called to Manchester on business for some time past, which has caused me to delay writing; but the business is now arranged, and my journey dispensed with.

What say you to the Cheshire jaunt? The time is arrived when birds of passage migrate.

The Misses Ditchfield have taken wing for Southport. Alfred and his sister are gone there likewise. Our incumbent, Mr. Hill, and his family, are in Worcestershire, called thither by the death of his father, at more than eighty years of age. A few more flights, and I may wander forth spouting "Sweet Auburn." My mother and aunt are better in health, and I too am better. The doctor advises my aunt to go to Buxton or Southport, and so do I; for if she goes I shall probably be her companion. By the way, your visit is now due here. Write and tell me you are coming: days are now long enough, and the weather fine enough. Say you will come. My mother and aunt join me in kindest regards to all your family, and believe me to remain,   Yours very faithfully,

JOHN LEYLAND.

To Mr. Roger Seymour.

Hindley, May 19th, 1834.

My dear Roger,

I have got yours and Charles's kind letters of April 10th and May 14th. Letters from Manchester are a long time in reaching their destination, yours of the 14th being only delivered here on Friday night. I should have written on Saturday, but I had no means of sending my letter to post.

I cannot join in your gaieties, I am sorry to say. The disappointment is not small, as I have been anticipating the pleasure some time, but I am over head and ears in farming work. The heavy rains of the winter and early spring have caused much work to want doing all at once. We are busy draining, and have a good deal of manual labour and team work to get through.

I am obliged for the hints you gave me in your letter of April 10th respecting letter-writing. I certainly wish you could drive me into writing long letters. There is nothing I myself like better than to receive a good long letter, and nothing I hate worse than to receive one of an opposite character.

You inquire about a reference I made in a former letter to "Sweet Auburn." Auburn is the name of Goldsmith's "Deserted Village," and the first line of the poem is—

"Sweet Auburn, loveliest village of the plain."

John Marsh spent yesterday afternoon with me. He is on the look out for a curacy. I was glad to hear of Mr. Thomson's ordination. I never told you that I read an interesting letter of his a few weeks since in the *Manchester Courier*, on the subject of botany.

When I call to mind the events of last year's races, I can scarcely believe that a year has since elapsed. My memorable day of disappointments, I am sure, will be fresh in your recollection. In the first instance, being too late for the railway; late again on arriving at Brook-street; and then missing you on the race-stand.

Alfred and his sister are returned from Southport. The Misses Ditchfield are staying there another month. Alfred invited me to spend a few days with him when he was there, but I was obliged to forego the pleasure. Another year I may perhaps be able to participate in your racing festivities.

My mother and aunt join me in kindest regards to your family, and believe me to remain,

Faithfully yours,

JOHN LEYLAND.

To Mr. Charles Seymour.

Hindley, July 4th, 1834.

My dear Charles,

Do you know that I have had an attack of cholera? The Sunday after I had been at Manchester I went to bed quite well, and when I awoke the following morning I was seized with this very unpleasant complaint. For two days I was exceedingly ill, but quick medical assistance doubtless prevented it from becoming serious. Yet, short as was the attack, it has reduced me much.

I was sorry to see from the papers the death of your aunt Cartwright. We are busily engaged in our hay harvest, and with a prospect of favourable weather.

Give my respects to all your family, and believe me to remain, Yours very faithfully,

JOHN LEYLAND.

To Mr. Roger Seymour.

Hindley, Sept. 24, 1834.

My dear Roger,

My own silence has been longer than yours, and I have not illness to plead as you have for an excuse. I was very sorry to hear of your indisposition.

In reference to my own negligence, may I quote the words attributed recently to a certain noble lord, and say: " I am so sensible of my grievous faults, that I can offer nothing in my justification." Forgetfulness, assuredly, is not the cause. When you were at Hindley Miss Ditchfield was ill. Since then Miss Louisa has been also ill, and got well again. Miss Betsey has been attacked, and now she is better, though not well. Their sister, Mrs. Croudson, last week gave birth to a boy, and mother and child are both doing well. Marsh, with a fellow-collegian, visited me on Monday. Dreadful to tell, he is on the point of carrying away one of our Hindley ladies! It is an actual fact, I assure you.

My mother and aunt join me in regards to your family, and believe me to remain,

Faithfully yours,

JOHN LEYLAND.

To Mr. Roger Seymour.

Hindley, Nov. 13th, 1834.

My dear Roger,

As usual, I am behindhand in writing. I enjoyed my journey home, where I arrived in comfortable time for dinner. I have no news, excepting that one or two of the weddings I told you of are to take place speedily. I am going to Chester in a few days. The object of my journey is at present a profound

secret, but if in a week or two you care to con a particular column of a newspaper, you may possibly receive
some light on its object. I am going to Wigan this
morning, so excuse a long epistle.

My mother and aunt join me in respects to your
family, and I remain,

Yours very faithfully,
JOHN LEYLAND.

To Mr. Roger Seymour.

Hindley, Jan. 28th, 1835.

My dear Roger,

I received your and your brother's letters of
Nov. 27th, and also yours of the 17th inst., in due
course. I hardly know what plea to urge in extenuation
of my long silence. I suppose I am generally dilatory,
and I have had occupation with the county election.
This is all I can prefer as an excuse. A lecture like the
one you gave me in your last will do good service.

I was truly sorry to hear of the severe indisposition
of so many members of your family. Your mother, I
was hoping, would by this time have recovered from
the effects of her accident.

I had a great treat in my journey to Chester. The
papers have long forestalled me in announcing its
object—the marriage of Mr. Henry Battersby with
Miss Elizabeth Ditchfield. The ceremony took place
in St. Oswald's Church, which forms the south transept of the Cathedral. Miss Louisa officiated as bridesmaid, I as groomsman. The Rev. Richard Battersby,
brother of the bridegroom, performed the ceremony.

Anyone fond of seeing the relics of past ages must be
delighted, as I was, with Chester. The venerable
Cathedral is deservedly a glory and a pride to the
county. The city is difficult to describe, the "Rows" give
it such a curious and antique appearance. These are
covered walks on each side the street on the first storey.
Salford Cloth Hall may give you some idea of them.

The different churches I admired much, particularly that of St. John's, which is of pure Norman architecture, and stands outside the walls. Originally it was a collegiate church of immense size, one part of which only is now standing, the other and larger part being in ruins. The old city walls are in existence, and afford a curious and interesting promenade. On one side are still fields, called the jousting crofts, where the ancient tournaments were held. Here brave knights displayed their prowess, their valour stimulated by

> "Stores of ladies, whose bright eyes
> Rained influence, and adjudged the prize."

Several towers still remain on the walls, the most extensive being the "Water" and "Phœnix" towers, from the latter of which Charles I. saw one of his armies defeated. In St. Mary's Church are the effigies of "Gammel" and his wife, who gave succour to that unfortunate monarch.

The Roodee, the Castle, the Shire Hall, the new bridge (a single arch of two hundred feet span), the different gates into the city, are each and all objects of great interest. I remain, faithfully yours,

JOHN LEYLAND.

The dragon's tongue I send per packet on Saturday, the 31st inst.

To Mr. Roger Seymour.

Hindley, May 30th, 1835.

My dear Roger,

A month or two at Lytham will be highly beneficial to the members of your family after their long indisposition. For several years past I have promised myself an outing to Southport. If I can get down during their stay I will cross over to see them. Not a word can I offer in vindication of my neglect in writing. That thief, Procrastination, the cause of so many errors, will, I hope, get hung some day along with all other thieves. I am obliged by your kind invitation to spend the race week with you. Pray excuse me, as I prefer visiting you at a quieter time.

My mother and aunt desire me to say for them, and I also say for myself, that a visit either from Charles or you will give all of us much pleasure, either now, or in a month, or whenever it may be convenient to you.

We have had our chapel broken into four different times during the last fortnight. Last Tuesday night the constables were on the watch, and about two o'clock two men entered, who were both secured. They had put a quantity of powder inside the lock of the iron safe, intending to blow it up. If they had succeeded they would have got nothing by it, as the communion plate had been removed. On their three former visits they had stolen Prayer-books and Bibles. One proves to be an Irishman from Manchester, the other a person from the neighbourhood. Forty-five pawntickets were found on them.

A few friends and myself have been establishing a Conservative Association, to which the name of the " Hindley True Blue Club " has been given. I fill the office of secretary. Our next meeting is to be on Monday, the 1st of June.

Sincerely yours,
JOHN LEYLAND.

To Mr. Roger Seymour.

Hindley, July 2nd, 1835.

My dear Roger,

I am venturing to hope that my punctuality on the present occasion will atone for some past omissions. I thought I had better write before hay harvest, as I might otherwise get again into disgrace. We commence to-morrow.

I was at Warrington the other day, and saw a friend of yours, who, you will rejoice to hear, still remains in single blessedness. Mrs. Mellor (a sister of Alfred Pennington) arrived in Liverpool last week, with her husband and family, after an absence of seven years in South America. Adverse winds detained them five weeks longer than the usual period of the voyage, and caused their friends much anxiety. Since their arrival

in Liverpool Mrs. Mellor has been confined of two fine
girls.   Excuse a short letter; after the hay harvest I
will write again, and I hope we may then have the
pleasure of seeing you and your brother at Hindley.
My mother and aunt join me in regards, and believe me
to remain,　　　　　　　Yours faithfully,

JOHN LEYLAND.

To Mr. Roger Seymour.

Hindley, Sept. 21st, 1835.

My dear Roger,

Ever since I was in Manchester I have been in
daily expectation of receiving a letter from you, and I
write now concluding you may perhaps be waiting for
me to write first.   I was disappointed to miss you
when I was over.

The last few weeks we have been occupied with the
harvest.   Our corn is not yet housed, and the weather
is at present unfavourable.

Your family are before now, I presume, returned
from Lytham.   I wished much to have got down to
Southport during their visit, and have crossed over to
see them, but I could not manage it.

I met our old schoolfellow, Maddocks, last week.
Since you and I saw him in Wigan I have never fallen
in with him, although he now resides altogether in the
neighbourhood.

My mother and aunt desire me to ask you to name
an early day for your visit.   It will give them and me
much pleasure to see you.

Yours faithfully,

JOHN LEYLAND.

To Mr. Charles Seymour.

Hindley, Nov. 26th, 1835.

My dear Charles,

The last two or three weeks I have been unwell
with a bad cold, which, happily, has now almost left me.
I hope the invalids at your house are also better.   You

have not yet said when you are coming to Hindley. You will find the place becoming more and more populous.

Mr. Pennington is extending his works, and a new mill is being built by a Mr. Walker. When these get completed a large increase of inhabitants must follow. In a short time it will doubtless rank as a small town. Send me, if you can, the songs I asked for. A neighbour of mine, who visits Manchester every Tuesday, will convey them if you will leave them, addressed to me, at 8, Duke-street. Yours very faithfully,

JOHN LEYLAND.

To Mr. Roger Seymour.

Hindley, March 29th, 1836.

My dear Roger,

A long time has passed since I had either the pleasure of hearing from you or of writing to you. My dear aunt has been seriously indisposed since November, which has afflicted us much, and has been the chief cause of my silence. The last week or two has brought some little amendment of her condition. I have thought much of you, and wish to hear from you.

The visit you promised has been long since due. Cannot you at once pay it? I have no news that you will feel an interest in. No fewer than four new mills, it is said, may be built here in the ensuing summer. Hands are become so scarce that whole families have been brought from the agricultural districts to supply the want. I am obliged to Charles for sending my songs.

Present my regards to all your family, and believe me to remain, Sincerely yours,

JOHN LEYLAND.

To Mr. Roger Seymour.

Hindley, May 19th, 1836.

My dear Roger,

I have only now received your letter of the 14th inst. I am happy to hear that your sister is better, and that all the rest of your family are well. My aunt, I am rejoiced to say, too, is better. Since the warm weather came she has improved rapidly. The rest of us are hearty as bucks.

Thanks for your kind invitation to the races and to other amusements, but it is quite out of my power at present to accept it.

I remain, yours faithfully,
JOHN LEYLAND.

To Mrs. Hannah Halton.

Liverpool, Jan. 31st, 1837.

My dear Mrs. Halton,

I grieve that I have to acquaint you of the death of my dear aunt. Her usual health, which you know has for some time past been delicate, continued up to Thursday, the 19th inst., when she was taken worse. Dr. Chadwick was called in, did all he could, but gave little hope from the first; and at ten minutes before three o'clock in the afternoon of Sunday, the 22nd inst., she left us for a better world. A holier and purer spirit never left its earthly tenement, and the gain to her must be great: to us the loss is irreparable.

I am, my dear Mrs. Halton,

Yours very truly,
JOHN LEYLAND.

To Mr. Roger Seymour.

Liverpool, January 31st, 1837.

My dear Roger,

It is a long time since any intercourse passed between us, and I little thought when I last wrote that my next letter would contain the sad news I have this day to communicate. My dear aunt is dead. On Sunday, the 22nd inst., at ten minutes before three o'clock in the afternoon, she left this world for a better, after only four days of severe illness. I was in Liverpool when the event happened. The Sunday previous I had been at Hindley, and I left her on Monday morning in her usual health.   My mother and I are much distressed, for she was very dear to us.

I am, yours very faithfully,

JOHN LEYLAND.

To Mr. Henry Battersby.

Liverpool, July 5th, 1837.

My dear Sir,

We have been much disappointed at not seeing you.   We begun to fear either that Mrs. Battersby or you were unwell.   Rigby never called until Wednesday, the day after you had fixed for your visit.   We were sorry to hear of Mrs. Croudson's illness.   Mrs. Rogerson called yesterday to tell us she was going to Wigan, so I take the opportunity of writing by her.   May I trouble you to give George Martlew my claim to vote?   Electioneering here is in all its glory.   The Conservatives think Lord Sandon's success certain, and they are sanguine also of Mr. Cresswell's.   Most likely I shall be over at the county election.   My mother is well, and joins me in regards.

I am, in haste, faithfully yours,

JOHN LEYLAND.

To Mr. Roger Seymour.

Liverpool, August 1st, 1837.

My dear Roger,

A friend has kindly undertaken to deliver a letter for me in Manchester, and I am taking advantage of his offer to send you these lines.   You are aware, I think, of my mother's residence in Liverpool.   As I am likely to be stationed here a few years, she thought it advisable after my aunt's death to come to me.

Our domicile is at No. 36, Ashton-street.   Mr. and Mrs. Battersby were staying a few days with us last week.   They told us they had met you in Manchester the week previous.

Miss Francis is in Liverpool, officiating as bridesmaid at the wedding of a Miss Rowbotham.   Probably you would hear of the death of poor John Marsh. To Miss Francis it must have been a great disappointment. My mother joins me in kindest regards to all your family.

In haste, I am, yours very faithfully,

JOHN LEYLAND.

———

To Mr. Henry Battersby.

Liverpool, October 11th, 1837.

Dear Sir,

We were expecting you anxiously during the whole of September. The *Wigan Gazette* of the 29th ult. was duly received. Thank God, both of us continue well.

I dare say you would see from the papers the death of Mr. Burrell. He went to London for the benefit of surgical advice, and died there. His remains were interred at Kendal, of which place he was a native. If you have opportunity to write, we shall be glad to hear how you are. It seems long since we had news from Hindley. Cannot this fine autumn weather tempt you to come here for a day or two?

I saw in the paper the announcement of the wedding of a Mr. John Sharples, of Hindley. I suppose John is a mistake for Thomas. The young lady's age was given, but not her name.

Either my mother or myself will be over in November. Accept our united regards. I remain, truly yours,

JOHN LEYLAND.

———

To Mr. Henry Battersby.

Liverpool, May 25th, 1838.

My dear Sir,

My mother desires me to write to tell you that she got safe and comfortably home.

As she says we are not to expect you here until your new house is covered in, I wish you favourable weather, and everything that may speed the building onwards. I was glad to hear you were both well. My own health is good. I join my mother in kind regards,

And remain, faithfully yours,

JOHN LEYLAND.

To Mr. Henry Battersby.

Liverpool, Jan., 1839.

My dear Sir,

From Mr. Scott we have just learned that you are not yet gone into your new house. Whenever you remove I hope you will manage to spend a few days here.

I was glad to hear that you escaped without injury in the late awful storm. So lucky were we that we had not a single pane of glass broken, although in the immediate neighbourhood of our house, as well as in the town generally, the devastation was terrible. The streets the following morning bore abundant evidence of the fury of the gale. Bricks, slates, and chimney mugs were strewed on the pavement, and on every side chimneys might be seen blown down and windows out. The fear of falling slates and bricks prevented me from going to the river. A gentleman more venturesome told me he was there at an early hour, and he described it as being one grand sheet of foam, and the spray falling with the force of a hailstorm. Both of us are well, and desire to be remembered to Mrs. Battersby.

I am, faithfully yours,

JOHN LEYLAND.

To Mr. B. J. Barlow.

Liverpool, March 30th, 1839.

My dear Sir,

Your letter of the 27th inst. only reached me this morning.

The arrangement enabling us to proceed together on the morning of your marriage I heartily concur in. I will therefore be with you in Warrington by the six o'clock train on Wednesday evening.

Nothing has occurred to me to improve your plan. Since your visit to Liverpool we have had Mr. Gaskell over, and since that again I have been at Hindley.

I would recommend you to acquaint Mr. Gaskell with your marriage. I sincerely join you in your prayer

that the step you are taking may in very truth prove
to you a happy one.

I remain, very faithfully yours,

John Leyland.

____

To Mr. Henry Battersby.
Liverpool, Sept. 14th, 1839.

My dear Sir,

According to your request, I enclose a few
designs for gates. They are rough, and struck off
without much care. If you are not wanting your gate
immediately, say, and I will try and think of something
else. An infinite variety of designs, from the simplest
to the most complex, may be had by varying the
position of geometrical figures. The architects in the
palmy days of Gothic architecture seem to have acted
upon this principle to a considerable extent, as is
evidenced by the tracery of the windows and other
decorations in the works they have left us. A gate
should correspond with the style of the house it leads
to. Many people have their gates and lodges of a
totally different character, which to me seems an
incongruity.

My mother's health, I am glad to say, is improved.

I meet your nephew occasionally. He tells me his
father has taken a house in Finch-street.

We hope to see you for a few days before winter. If
you can spare time, write and say when. I will take
care not to be absent this journey.

My mother joins me in kindest regards.

I remain, truly yours,

John Leyland.

____

To Frederick Pennington, Esq.
Liverpool, January 13th, 1840.

My dear Sir,

I regretted after I left you on Saturday evening
that I did not recommend you to attend the very
interesting course of lectures now delivering at the
Mechanics Institute on the early English opera. The

first of a course of six was delivered last Wednesday. None but subscribers are admitted ; but if the lecture of Wednesday be a fair earnest of those which are to follow, I should say the course will be well worth the year's subscription. I think they would highly gratify you.·   Yours faithfully,

JOHN LEYLAND.

———————

To Mr. Henry Battersby.

Liverpool, January 16th, 1840.

My dear Sir,

The . reduction of postage has induced me· to trouble you with a few lines, though I have nothing to communicate. I desire, though somewhat late, to pay the compliments of the season, and wish, with great sincerity, Mrs. Battersby and yourself a happy New Year. My mother and I are both in good health. Your brother's family are also well.

I remain, yours faithfully,

JOHN LEYLAND.

———————

To Mr. Henry Battersby.

Liverpool, Feb. 5th, 1840.

My dear Sir,

When you see another letter from me I am afraid you will wish the charge for postage had remained at its former rate.

My present object in writing is to request your company, and that of Mrs. Battersby, on the day of Her Majesty's marriage, which I am in the hope will be kept in Liverpool as a general holiday. You spent the day of her coronation with us, and it will be something to say we spent all the great festivals of her reign in the society of our friends. Monday next is the day fixed for the ceremony. Let us hope to see you.

I was shocked to hear of Mr. Pigott's death. ` How often it happens that good men are taken away, and sometimes in the very midst of their usefulness, whilst others, whose hearts are steeled against every generous

feeling, live on selfishly and uselessly, and survive the
blasts of winter after winter. The last time I heard
Mr. Pigott preach was the funeral sermon of the late
rector of Wigan. He chose for his text words which I
think may be emphatically applied to himself—" He was
a good man." My mother joins me in kind regards to
Mrs. Battersby. Hoping to see you on Saturday,
I remain, ever truly yours,
JOHN LEYLAND.

To James Bent, Esq.
Liverpool, Jan. 1st, 1842.
My dear Sir,
I forgot to mention to our friends at school last
Sunday that I purpose absenting myself from them
to-morrow. It may, perhaps, prevent my class waiting
if you will be good enough to tell Mr. Webster that I
shall be away. I never feel the full value of God's day
so much as at these seasons when my time is so fully
occupied with business. If I may use a metaphor, it
seems like a peaceful oasis in a stormy desert, a spot
where the traveller may obtain rest, composure, and
refreshment for his ensuing journey.
I am, faithfully yours,
JOHN LEYLAND.

To Mr. Henry Battersby.
Liverpool, July 18th, 1842.
My dear Sir,
Since your visit to Liverpool we have been
anxious to hear from you. Your letter of the 15th
inst., informing us of the improvement which had taken
place in your health, and of your call to the assizes,
gave us much pleasure.
We trust your restoration may be complete before
your services are required in the law courts. Don't by
any means seek to evade the requisition.
The wrangling of the lawyers, and the excitement
incident thereupon—enough, by-the-bye, in some cases,
c

to fever any man's blood—will, under your circumstances, be just the specific you require. We shall be glad to see you, and at the time you mention will be on the look out for you, and have a bed well aired.

My mother joins me in kindest regards.

I remain, truly yours,

JOHN LEYLAND.

To Mr. Henry Battersby.

Liverpool, Jan. 2nd, 1843.

Many thanks, my dear Sir, for your kind letter and friendly wishes. My mother unites her prayers with mine, that every social happiness which this season so especially calls forth, and which lends to Christmas some of its most cherished associations, may be yours and Mrs. Battersby's, and that every blessing may await you in this and in many a year to come.

In haste, truly yours,

JOHN LEYLAND.

To Mr. Henry Battersby.

Liverpool, July 27th, 1843.

My dear Sir,

I was sorry to receive from your nephew an unfavourable report of your health. The previous accounts which had reached me since I saw you had been such that I was in expectation of hearing of something very different. I hope that you may have drawn for him a more gloomy picture than your condition warrants.

Health is the gift of the Almighty, and if He thinks fit to withhold it a perfect submission to His will is doubtless required. But it is a support in trial when we can see God as its immediate author—God, who never willingly afflicts, and who has graciously promised that "as our day our strength shall be." The dispensations of His providence, which now seem afflicting, may be as full of mercy as those we think joyous. When the veil which conceals the motive of His dealings is removed, we shall see Him in all things as a tender father watching anxiously over the welfare of His children. Let any man look back on his past life, and he cannot but see a special providence to have been about him delivering from evil and bringing help, and when help seemed far off.

I am sure you will rejoice at the account I have to give of my mother's health. Since the warm weather came her amendment has been progressive. She is free from pain, and her limbs are almost daily gaining strength. She joins me in kindest regards.

I remain, very faithfully yours,

JOHN LEYLAND.

To Mr. B. J. Barlow.

Liverpool, Sept. 4th, 1843.

My dear Sir,

I have received your newspaper, for which accept my thanks. Although I have nothing to communicate, I am hoping my letter may afford you the same pleasure your newspaper did to me.

Old friends are like old clothes—pleasanter for every-day life, and we enjoy them with similar freedom from restraint. May not you and I be a little proud that your family and mine are friends now in the third generation?

I was over at Hindley not long since, and found our mutual friends, Mr. and Mrs. Gaskell, enjoying their wonted good health. Everything besides in the village was also going on as usual. I dined lately with Will Hodgkinson. His brother, nephew, and I formed the party. All the Hodgkinson family are well, Will especially; his spirits seem never to flag.

If I ever put in execution a plan I sometimes amuse myself in dwelling upon, of making a pedestrian journey to London, I shall certainly include Bishop's Stortford in my route. Very likely you will laugh at the idea of walking all the way to London in these days of steamboats and railways.

However, what I say is a fact. I shall be glad to

hear from you at any time, and trust you will take an early opportunity to let me know how you are.

With kindest regards to Mrs. Barlow,

I am, faithfully yours,

JOHN LEYLAND.

To Mrs. Hannah Halton.

Liverpool, Oct. 18th, 1843.

My dear Mrs. Halton,

I should have written, according to my mother's promise, last week ; but she continued so unwell for some days after her return home, that I thought it better to delay writing until I could inform you of her recovery. She is now nearly as well as she was before her late attack, and perhaps almost as well as she can ever hope to be. When the frame has stood for seventy winters, it cannot be expected to be free from the symptoms of decay. It is well it should be so. If the strength, and the energy, and the comeliness of youth, with its ardour of mind and elasticity of spirit, were to continue unimpaired through the term of human life, we should think this our tenement of clay a lasting habitation. A merciful Providence warns us, by the infirmities weight of years bring with them, that we are hastening to the end of our pilgrimage ; and if we give heed to the admonition, it quickens our preparation for the life of eternity opening before us.

My mother joins me in kind regards to the various members of your household.

I am, very truly yours,

JOHN LEYLAND.

To Mr. Henry Battersby.

Liverpool, Dec. 18th, 1843.

My dear Sir,

I was much shocked when I heard of the death of Mrs. Battersby, so short a time after seeing her in almost her usual state of health. Death, awful at any time, becomes doubly so when its stroke is sudden and unexpected. "In the midst of life we are in death" is a portion of Scripture the truth of which, in our course through life, we are forced to confess painfully and repeatedly. Surely we need these afflicting visitations, or we should not be called upon to undergo them—need them to keep us in constant mind of the uncertainty of life; to weaken our affections for surrounding things; to stir up thought and care for the world to come. Painful as they are, and often as they are forgotten, like all God's works, they insensibly teach and lead men to look to the future for rest. The contemplation of death should not inspire fear to any but the impenitent and hardened.

A Christian can claim His help who hath triumphed over the grave, and deprived death of its sting. To him, careworn and weary, it offers rest and a release from sickness and sorrow. May you, dear Sir, and I, and all that we hold dear, be enabled, in humble confidence, to say—"Though I walk through the valley of the shadow of death, I will fear no evil; for Thou, O God, art with me; Thy rod and Thy staff comfort me."

We are very anxious to hear how you are, but don't write unless you feel quite able.

My mother continues tolerably well; she desires her best love. I am, my dear Sir, very truly yours,

JOHN LEYLAND.

To Mrs. Hannah Halton.

Liverpool, February 16th, 1844.

My dear Mrs. Halton,

You mention Henry Battersby's death in your letter to us of the 6th inst., but you seem not to be aware that his wife's death preceded his by just six weeks.

Our old friends and acquaintances are indeed fast passing away. Dr. Johnson justly inculcates the necessity of making new friends in the place of those we lose; otherwise, if a man live but to middle age he may find himself alone in the world, a last survivor of

the associates of his youth.   Henry Battersby's decay was
so gradual that he must necessarily have been sensible of
his approaching end.   A lengthened sickness, grievous
as it may be to bear, affords a season for repentance and
preparation for the coming life.   He had his full share
of misfortune and trouble here, and I hope and believe
that he is now at peace.

My mother has been a little unwell the last fortnight,
her old complaint having slightly returned upon her.
She joins me in kindest regards.

I remain, very truly yours,

JOHN LEYLAND.

To T. D. Hibbert, Esq.

Liverpool, Feb. 19th, 1844.

Dear Dorning,

I beg to return my best thanks for the first
volume of " Mosheim," which I have just finished, and
shall feel obliged at your convenience for the following
volume.   It is an interesting work, but requires to be
read with close attention.   I hardly ever feel satisfied
with my reading of books of this nature : they demand
the renovated energies of the morning instead of the
worn-out powers of the evening, which is all I can at
present bestow upon them.

I am, truly yours,

JOHN LEYLAND.

To Thomas Harcourt, Esq.

Liverpool, March 12th, 1844.

Sir,

I have taken the liberty of addressing you for
the purpose of bringing before your notice a poor widow
of the name of Mary Blackburn.   Her maiden name, I
believe, was Smith, and previous to her marriage she
lived in the service of the Harcourt family.   Her father

served the same family in the capacity of gardener for a quarter of a century. She now lives in a cellar in Gerrard-street, in this town, and endeavours to gain a livelihood by selling bread from door to door, through which my own acquaintance with her originated.

This she follows during all kinds of weather, although age is creeping fast upon her; but latterly her trade has proved so insufficient for her subsistence that she has been compelled to seek relief from the parish, and even with this addition to her means she is barely able to obtain common necessaries. The comforts which smooth the pathway of life, and which declining years require, she cannot procure. It is the happy privilege of the wealthy to cheer the lot of the poor, and every true Christian rejoices at an opportunity of aiding a needy and worthy object. I think, therefore, I need not apologise for bringing the case of this poor woman before you. I may add that I understand the late Mr. Harcourt continued to extend his bounty to her to the close of his life; and perhaps I ought also to state that I have taken this step without any solicitation or knowledge on her part.

I remain respectfully,
Your most obedient servant,
JOHN LEYLAND.

To T. Dorning Hibbert, Esq.

Liverpool, March 12th, 1844.

Dear Dorning,

I have at length finished the second and third volumes of "Mosheim," which I now return with many thanks. The third volume brings the events of the Church down to the time of the Reformation, when the human mind broke the fetters with which ignorance and superstition had so long enchained it—a period of history to me of all others the most interesting.

I am, truly yours,
JOHN LEYLAND.

To T. Dorning Hibbert, Esq.

Liverpool, May 31st, 1844.

My dear Dorning,

Your adventures in the great city I shall be all anxiety to hear. I did not expect Roger Lowe's diary would have afforded Mr. Hunter the pleasure you say it has done. What interest it possessed I supposed to be entirely of a local character. The writer, I imagine, would have been rather astonished if he had known it would be carried a journey of two hundred miles for the purpose of being read. If he had fallen asleep some day after making his customary entry, and dreamed that what he had just written would, after the lapse of a couple of centuries, be conveyed in a carriage drawn by a sort of fiery dragon, and at a speed of such extreme velocity that houses, trees, bridges, and every other feature of the landscape seemed to rush by as if borne on the wings of the wind; that the carriage stopped in the centre of a city numbering near two millions of inhabitants; that his manuscript was read by a light kindled from vapour by the touch, as it were, of the wand of an enchanter; that from the windows of the apartment where his document rested an immense tide of population might be seen ebbing and flowing, numerous equipages driving along, and stately buildings stretching on every side far as the eye could reach; he would have supposed it to be the capricious wanderings of a wild imagination, instead of being prophetic of what has literally come to pass.

Possibly you may recollect me telling you that I had two friends of the name of Seymour living in London. Since I saw you it has occurred to me they may be descendants of the Bishop Cartwright whose diary Mr. Hunter has edited. I know that a Dr. Cartwright, a bishop, was an ancestor of theirs; but I do not know over what see he presided, nor at what period he lived. One of my friends, in consequence of his descent from the dignitary I have named, bears the name of Cartwright, and I recollect a portrait of the prelate in

his episcopal robes used to hang in his father's
library in Manchester.

I am, faithfully yours,
JOHN LEYLAND.

To Mr. Hugh Kendrick.

Liverpool, July 25th, 1844.

My dear Sir,

The low spirits you laboured under when you
called to say good-bye, and the aversion with which
you seemed to look upon your voyage, pained me much.
The love of home and country is in some natures, I
know, very deep. A separation from either would to
me be hard to bear. Pope said he could not part with
the stump of a tree he had known from childhood without emotion. The sentiment is not confined to one
class, nor to one nation ; it is widely diffused. The
mountaineer loves his hills, and the lowlander his plains.
Our affections centre in the place we call home. In no
race has the love of country been exhibited in greater
intensity than among the Jews. The pages of Scripture record in the most touching language their love
for Jerusalem. When their Chaldean conquerors
demanded from them one of the songs of Zion, what
can exhibit their grief at their exile more beautifully
than their exclamation—" How shall we sing the Lord's
song in a strange land ? If I forget thee, O Jerusalem,
let my right hand forget her cunning." Daniel, eminent
for piety and faith in God, and for a large endowment
of the prophetic spirit, even he prayed with his face
towards Jerusalem, showing the love he had for the
city of his fathers. And when God restored them in
the fullness of time to the land they loved, we read no
more of them lapsing into idolatry. God's providences
are mysterious—seemingly inevitable evil turns to the
greatest good, and apparent good is often fruitful in
misery. What we should try to say is—" God's will be
done." Our finite capacity cannot fathom the reason of
His dealings. The history of Joseph is a further

illustration of this truth. Torn by his unfeeling brothers from the care of a tender father and from the comforts of his father's house, and sold as a bondsman in a foreign land, he could then doubtless see in it nothing but an overwhelming affliction. As another of his race in the time of trouble in a later age expressed, "he was come into deep waters, where the floods overflowed him." Afterwards he could acknowledge to the same brethren, "it was not you who sent me here, but God." But men, instead of making a salutary use of affliction, generally fret, and grieve, and spend their time in unavailing murmurs; thus adding bitterness to their sorrow, until it becomes what they themselves have made it—a certain and unmitigated evil.

I was glad to learn from your brother of your safe arrival, after a speedy and prosperous voyage, and I shall be gratified to hear direct from you, if you can at any time make it convenient to write.

I am, sincerely yours,

JOHN LEYLAND.

To Mr. B. J. Barlow.

Liverpool, Aug. 12th, 1844.

My dear Sir,

Penny postage and steam-engines are doing wonderful things.

John o' Groat's House and the Land's End are brought next door to us at whatever part of the kingdom we may locate ourselves. America is but half the distance it was a few years ago.

Despatches arrive in due course from Kamtschatka and New Zealand, and even from the Celestial Empire.

Success often leads to presumption. So much has been achieved that I had even hoped postal communication might have been established before now between here and Bishop's Stortford. Certainly I have been disappointed, but surely another century will accomplish so desirable an event.

I have heard nothing direct from you since you removed to that distant spot save and except a newspaper, which I suppose you sent, and which I acknowledged in a letter about a year since.

Indirectly I have heard nothing either for a considerable period. I conclude you are well and prosperous. I am sure I wish it, although you do not think it worth while to tell me.

For this indifference you deserve punishment, and I have therefore determined to say nothing more in this letter.

No! not one word will I add whether I am well or ill—whether I have news or I have not. Advice only will I give.

As in the most sequestered regions there are occasional opportunities for communicating with the rest of the world, so if a post should leave Bishop's Stortford any time in the course of the next twelve months, pray take advantage of it, and write to your old friend,

JOHN LEYLAND.

To Mrs. Hannah Halton.

Liverpool, Sept. 5th, 1844.

My dear Mrs. Halton,

Before I received your letter I was afraid you might be expecting me at Sutton, and when it came I was just on the point of writing to explain how I am at present placed.

You know how difficult it is for me at any time to leave home, and since my Hindley journey in May last my mother has been too unwell to allow me to quit her even for a single night. If her health will improve, so that I can leave her with any comfort, you may rely upon seeing me. The recent change in the weather will be most beneficial both to the farmers and the country generally. Seed time and harvest never fail. Why should the long-continued rain fill us with alarm, even though the corn be fully ripe? The Great Ruler of the earth—He whose power causes the seed to germinate, who strengthens the tender blade, and who sends His sun to ripen the ear—tells us He is all-sufficient to supply our wants.   We but want, dear Madam, a perfect trust and confidence in His wisdom and goodness, and the concerns of this world will yield us no disquiet.

Mrs. and Miss Gaskell left us last Saturday after a week's visit.   We had been in daily expectation of seeing them for a month previously, but the wet weather delayed their journey.   My mother desires to be remembered.   I am, truly yours,

JOHN LEYLAND.

To Edward Nugent, Esq.

Liverpool, Oct. 2nd, 1844.

It was the end of August, my dear Sir, before I heard of your removal from Hindley, which, I understand, took place two months before; and I only learned your present address a few days ago, or I should sooner have written to express my concern at losing you from the neighbourhood.   Although I have now lived in Liverpool eight years, I still look upon Hindley as my home; and if I return there, as it is probable I may in a few years, there is no person whose removal I shall more regret than yours.   The native spot maintains a tenacious hold upon the affections.   Years may pass over; we may settle in other places, from necessity or even from choice; yet the heart clings, with a constancy nothing can wear away, to the home of early youth.

I was much rejoiced on hearing from your nephew (to whom I am indebted for your address) that the change of residence has proved of benefit to your health; and I was also glad to learn there was a possibility you might eventually again settle in your old county.   I have no immediate prospect of being able to see Jersey; but my engagements must be pressing to prevent me sometime or other from visiting it if it should become your permanent residence.   Wherever you are, you have my best wishes, and my best prayers, for your health and prosperity.   The comfort flowing from a sure confidence that our Heavenly Father orders all things for our good—that wherever His unerring wisdom leads, He is with us, as with the Israelites of old, a guiding cloud by day, a protecting fire by night—I know you experience.

My mother's health has caused me, lately, much anxiety. Happily, she suffers little pain, but her weakness is so great that she is almost entirely confined to her room, and her advanced age, I am afraid, precludes the hope of any considerable improvement.

I am, truly yours,

JOHN LEYLAND.

To Mrs. Hannah Halton.

Liverpool, Dec. 6th, 1844.

My dear Mrs. Halton,

You will be glad, I know, to hear that my mother's health has improved somewhat since your visit : she has continued free from pain, slept better, and, on the whole, I think her a degree stronger. I hope the next account you receive may be still more favourable. Any of your family will be welcome guests whenever they can come over ; and I know them well enough to be sure that a visit will not be withheld because sickness is in the house.

I remain, my dear Madam, sincerely yours,

JOHN LEYLAND.

To Mr. Hugh Kendrick.

Liverpool, 21st Dec., 1844.

My dear Sir,

The little time I have at my own disposal has been lately much broken in upon from various causes, and these things, together with the continued illness of my mother, have prevented me from writing to you sooner. The long distance you are from home will, I know, make you value a letter, even though it may contain no news. Your many relatives will, I have no doubt, keep you posted up with everything that goes on here of any importance, and nothing, therefore, remains for me but to say that your friends still think of you. There is something melancholy in reflecting how very soon the absent are forgotten. Ties which but yesterday were as the sun to our being lose to-day their potency. Time quickly heals the wounds he makes. Fresh objects excite our sympathies, and engage our affections. Do we need further evidence to show that this is not life, but only the prelude of it ? I was shocked at the account you gave of the desecration of the Sabbath at Maranham. I considered that, like as in other Catholic countries, it might be a day partly for religious observances and partly for amusement, but I did not suppose it would be so recklessly profaned. Amidst much that is encouraging at the present day there is enough to fill the thoughtful with alarm. The light of the Gospel has penetrated to the most distant regions, and the healing influences of Christianity are at work where but recently they were unknown. In England, whence these blessings, under God, have mainly sprung, the Church is rent by divisions, and attempts are being made to substitute forms and ceremonies for the pure and simple faith Christ and His apostles preached. Maybe we have not, as a people, sufficiently valued the privileges we have enjoyed ; maybe we have been lukewarm and " neither cold nor hot ; " maybe we have looked to the increase of our goods, and dreamed that we needed nothing ; and the insulted majesty of Jehovah may determine to remove our candlestick to another place.

I am, truly yours,

JOHN LEYLAND.

To Mr. B. J. Barlow.

Liverpool, March 13th, 1845.

My dear Sir,

Your kind letter, which followed with so much expedition the last I addressed to you, deserved an earlier acknowledgment. It has been a source of much.

regret that I could not accept your kind invitation, more especially as it bore the promise of so pleasant a companion homewards, and I can only console myself by remembering that I have the visit yet to anticipate.

My mother has been very ill for a long time. Her complaint is a troublesome one on the nerves, and has caused her intense suffering. For three years she has been ailing more or less, and many a time I have trembled for the result. I was glad to hear that you had in a great measure overcome the difficulties of your new duties.

The situation of your residence in an agricultural district, near to a small town and within a few hours' journey of London, must be agreeable.

Unlike us in Lancashire, you are free from the smoke of manufactories. But trade, or perhaps I should say the inordinate pursuit of it, generates worse evils than smoke. It is causing the good old-fashioned characteristics of the nation to disappear.

Simplicity of manners, straightforward honesty in dealing, and the contentment which enriches and gives so great a charm to life, are giving place to an eager thirst after money. Gold has begun to be reckoned the chief good, and a man is valued, not for the worth of his character, but just in proportion to the ability he has for getting money.

Your friend, Dorning Hibbert, has chosen the law for a profession, and become a student of the Middle Temple, where he has already kept two or three terms.

I am, truly yours,

JOHN LEYLAND.

To Mr. Hugh Kendrick.

Liverpool, June 5th, 1845.

My dear Sir,

I have received to-day your letter of the 19th of April, and one written some time before, which I never acknowledged. The time I can at present devote to correspondence is so very little that I am afraid of my friends charging me with remissness. From the tone of your two last letters I was happy to infer that you are being reconciled to your present residence, and that you are under no fears of the climate impairing your health.

The Maynooth Endowment Bill has been with us, as the papers will have informed you, a great cause of excitement and interest for some months past. Your old pastor, Mr. M'Neill, has resisted the measure strenuously, and it is to be deplored that the determined opposition it has called forth in the country should have been so utterly disregarded by the Prime Minister, who seems to have forgotten that no government can long exist which rules in defiance of public opinion.

I am, my dear Sir, sincerely yours,

JOHN LEYLAND.

To Mrs. Hannah Halton.

Liverpool, June 26th, 1845.

My dear Mrs. Halton,

You residents in the country are favoured people. The abundant showers and the warm sunshine we have recently had must have clothed everything around you in beauty. I quite long to live among the green fields again. Whatever advantages a town life may bestow, they are but indifferent compensation for the loss of the flowers and the fields. Town life has doubtless its advantages: facilities for acquiring knowledge exist; there is mind to sharpen mind, and congenial companionship. On the other hand, the country holds fewer temptations to vice; its employments, habits, and amusements are more rational; and moral and religious influences are stronger. The great book of nature is ever open, and offers a fertile and delightful source of enjoyment. There is—

> " A present godlike power,
> Imprinted on each herb and flower."

At present I am unable to speak with any certainty when I can visit you.

My mother's health is in no way different from what it was when Mrs. Garnett saw her. She joins me in kind wishes to all your family.

I am, truly yours,
JOHN LEYLAND.

To Alfred Pennington, Esq.
Liverpool, 14th July, 1845.

My dear Sir,

Yesterday morning I left you so abruptly as to make it necessary for me to apologise. On leaving you I hoped I should have been able either to have rejoined you immediately or to have seen you further on in the day. In both expectations I was disappointed, and having to return to Liverpool in the afternoon, I could not even call upon you.

I remain, truly yours,
JOHN LEYLAND.

To Edward Nugent, Esq.
Liverpool, Aug. 11th, 1845.

My dear Sir,

I cannot refrain from offering the little consolation I possess, unavailing as it may be, and expressing the sympathy I feel for the loss you have sustained. It is a heavy trial, and I pray God that He will support you under it. God's knowledge embraces all things, and His providence directs all things; and this knowledge should stay some of the bitterness of grief, more especially when His Word declares Him to be merciful, tender, compassionate, and kind. Some gracious purpose, we presume and believe, is to be accomplished by these dispensations. The character of God may be summed up in the word Love. Love is, as it were, the sun in the system of the Great Divine, round which all His other glories and attributes revolve. Love is written in golden letters on the works of His hands; love created us, love redeemed us, love will glorify us.

D

It is love which checks the growth of earthly affections, if they are striking too deep a root.

"This present affliction is but for a moment, and worketh out for us a far more exceeding and eternal weight of glory."

I have to thank you for the kind letter you wrote to me in April last. Your better health, I trust, continues. There has been no amendment in my mother's condition since I last wrote. The greater part of the time she has suffered severe pain, and she has now almost lost the use of her limbs. She does not leave her bed day or night. Yet, what is a great mercy, she is generally composed and cheerful.

I am, truly yours,
John Leyland.

To Mr. Hugh Kendrick.

Liverpool, Sept. 12th, 1845.

My dear Sir,

Although I am well assured you are always glad to hear from your friends, I do not yet well know what to write about. You have such a host of relations that one or other of them will be continually writing to you; and, very probably, you may know better than I do what is going on at home. I mix little with the world, and from channels other than newspapers I scarcely hear anything. In proof, I may tell you that not long since a fire occurred in the West Derby Workhouse, which, you may remember, is situate directly across the fields in front of our windows. An alarm was made—fire-engines came to the spot—a scene of considerable noise and bustle ensued—but the first intimation I had of it was from a London newspaper.

Puseyism, thank God, seems to be losing some of its influence. A year since the cloud was darker than it is now. Even in the dioceses of London and Exeter, where the clergy, with episcopal sanction, have sought to introduce innovations in the old way of conducting public worship, less is said of it. Happily, the laity

met the movement with a bold front. I hardly ventured
to hope for so strong a display of Protestant zeal as the
mistaken views of these autocratic priests have called
forth.

The religious movement going on in Germany is full
of interest, and has become so widely extended that it
has began to be called the second Reformation.

My mother just now is somewhat freer from pain
than she has been recently, but the perfect uselessness
of her limbs renders her situation, at the best, very
trying.   I am, faithfully yours,
                                JOHN LEYLAND.

To Thomas Dorning Hibbert, Esq.
                Liverpool, Dec. 20th, 1845.

Dear Dorning,

I cannot reply to your letter of the 8th inst.
as fully as I should like, for want of the necessary
time ; but its friendly spirit struck a kindred chord in
my heart, which would not let me rest until I had made
some sort of acknowledgment, although it be a brief one.

Well, Sir, I mean to accompany you in your Christmas excursion. Now, don't start and fancy your old
friend will, in a few days, be treading with you the dull
and gloomy precincts of the Temple, or—pleasanter
scene—roaming with you among the comfortable homesteads and fertile fields of Essex, or meet you where

> " Christmas blocks are burning ; "

where

> " The wassail round in good brown bowls,
> Garnished with ribbons, blithely trowls."

Not in person, but in spirit I will be there. Christmas
Day will present to my mental, if not to my bodily eye,
all your happy faces ; and I shall wish each of you,
though you won't hear me, many happy returns of the
season.   I am, faithfully yours,
                                JOHN LEYLAND.

Remember me cordially to Benjamin and his lady.

To Mrs. Hannah Halton.

Liverpool, 12th March, 1846.

My dear Mrs. Halton,

Like a many other people I fancy I have a great deal more work than time ; and whether it be really so or only an illusion of the fancy, it serves equally as an excuse when an excuse is wanted. I have delayed writing to you so long that I am really ashamed of myself, and yet I know you will forgive me, your good-nature is so wide.

I spent last Sunday at Hindley, but neither there nor here is there any news. My mother's health has continued without much change through the winter. My own has been uninterruptedly good. We are both anxious to hear how you are, and shall be glad to see you whenever you can make it convenient to come over.

With our united regards,

I remain, sincerely yours,

JOHN LEYLAND.

To Mr. John Wilton.

Liverpool, May 16th, 1846.

My dear John,

Thank you for the letter you sent me from Douglas. Dilatory in writing as I am, I can yet honour and admire punctuality in another.

Our friend Williams told me of the chivalrous feeling you displayed on your voyage, when, ill yourself, you rendered help to a sick lady ; and in your letter to me you recount the valorous deeds you wrought on landing from the steamer. This gallantry and valour are worthy of the olden time. Often are we told that chivalry is dead ; but no ! the spirit which animated Bayard and Sidney still lives.

I have no news worth sending. I could, it is true, discourse on the bank's stock of gold and silver, or risk speculations on current bills of exchange, but one glance at the scene around you, on the green fields, the stately mountains, or the restless ocean, is worth a hundred

times more than anything my lucubrations could produce.   So I may as well break off; and, with best wishes
for your health and enjoyment,

I remain, truly yours,

JOHN LEYLAND.

To Mr. Hugh Kendrick.

Liverpool, July 22nd, 1846.

My dear Sir,

So long a time has passed since I last wrote,
that I feel not a little perplexed to find what may seem
to you a reasonable excuse for my silence.   Let me say
that I have never once forgotten you; but what with
my office engagements, my mother's illness, and my
private business, I assure you I have very little leisure.
So great have been the demands on my time, that I
have been obliged latterly almost to discontinue reading.

My mother's health is, I grieve to say, worse than
when I last wrote.   She becomes more and more feeble.
She, and indeed I too, feel the need of help from above
to enable us to bear an affliction so long continued.

You will doubtless have learned from the papers what a
grand festival we are to have in Liverpool next week, on
the occasion of the foundation stone of the new " Sailors'
Home" being laid by His Royal Highness Prince Albert.
A general holiday is in contemplation, and if my
mother's health be so that I can leave her, I shall run
away from the bustle and spend the day in the country.

With all good wishes for your health and happiness,

I remain, sincerely yours,

JOHN LEYLAND.

To Mr. Hugh Kendrick.

Liverpool, March 16th, 1847.

My dear Sir,

I have to thank you for your letter, the only one
you have favoured me with for a long period.   If I was
more punctual myself, I should grumble at your silence;
as it is, it will not do for me to cast the first stone.

It is fortunate that the climate continues to agree with your health. Much as I should like to travel, I have no wish to follow you to South America. If I ever travel it will be in the Old World, not the New. Half my enjoyment would consist in the associations the places I visited called forth. If Egypt, Greece, and Rome possessed fewer memorials of the past than they do, they would be worth seeing. It is not the Nile, or the Ilissus, or the Tiber, as rivers, which are the objects of interest, but the men and the actions of men with which they are associated.

It is an awful reflection that every individual, as well as every nation, has an influence not only on his own day, but in after ages as well.

Spite of my predilections for the Old World, I must admit that the traveller will find abundant room for contemplation, and that of no ordinary kind, in the New. There is something sublime in its vastness. Nature there has been more prodigal of her gifts. The rivers are mightier, the mountain ranges loftier, the plains wider. What its ultimate destiny may be is a curious problem for inquiry.

My mother continues in much the same state— weaker, if at all changed. She knows I am writing, and desires to be remembered.

I remain, yours truly,
JOHN LEYLAND.

To James Bent, Esq.

Liverpool, June 21st, 1847.

My dear Sir,

Although you are not a distant neighbour, I have no prospect of being able to ask you how you are for some weeks to come save through the medium I am at present employing, owing to the duties which devolve upon me at this period of the year. The extraordinary state the money market has been in for some time past has thrown bankers' business out of the ordinary channels, and considerably increased their labours ; and this, with the noways lessened tie at home, has prevented me from seeing you lately. I have nevertheless twice knocked at your door, but in both instances I was unfortunate. Once you were from home; the other time you were engaged.

I trust you are well and enjoying the fine weather, which, though not so genial as the "leafy month of June" should be, is yet delightful, after the long and severe winter we have undergone. This long winter will be a season much to be remembered. The destroying angel has passed over us, famine has done its work, and now pestilence is at the door. I cannot conclude my few observations better than in the words of Luther to Melancthon, used on some occasion when danger threatened : "Avert the wrath of God from us by your faithful prayers."

I am, truly yours,
JOHN LEYLAND.

To James Bent, Esq.

Liverpool, July 13th, 1847.

My dear Mr. Bent,

God has taken my poor mother to Himself. Severe and long her sufferings have been, but they are at an end for ever. Now I feel assured she is a saint in glory. Her departure was sudden at the last. I left her not much worse than usual on Saturday morning, and when I came home in the afternoon I found her exceedingly ill, and she died before eight o'clock. The fears of death, which had so much harassed her, were taken away. She said she was not afraid to die, and I do not think she experienced either terror to the soul or pain to the body, but sunk asleep as calmly and as gently as a child in its mother's arms. There could not be a more peaceful end. She has been to me the best of mothers : her life she would willingly have laid down for me ; and although I am persuaded the change is for her unspeakable gain, yet the pain of parting is very bitter.

Pray for me that God of His goodness may help me through it. I am, very truly yours,

JOHN LEYLAND.

To Mrs. Hannah Halton.

Liverpool, July 26th, 1847.

My dear Mrs. Halton,

I have to thank you for your kind letter and inquiries. I am better than I could have expected to be after the trying event which has occurred. No one can live in daily and confidential intercourse with any one from childhood to mature years, without feeling keenly a separation when it comes. We have lived together as happily as mother and son ever did live, and the grief at her loss will not soon be got over.

The thought that her state of existence now is happier than what it could have been with me, had I possessed every power which this world can bestow of ministering to it, affords me consolation.

It is unnecessary to add that I shall be glad to see you whenever you can come over.

Remember me to all your family, and believe me that I remain, truly yours,

JOHN LEYLAND.

To the Rev. Richd. Battersby.

Liverpool, Aug. 21st, 1847.

My dear Sir,

I have to thank you for the kind lines you wrote to me on the festival of St. Swithin, and to apologise for not sooner acknowledging them. The great loss I have had, you will readily believe, has unfitted me for many duties. Helpless and infirm as my poor mother was, I feel her removal severely. Not only was she the guide and support of my childhood, but the friend and almost sole companion of my maturer years.

To its last pulsation her heart overflowed with love and affection towards me. Her death is like the taking away of some vital part of my own being.

I am sensible there is much to console me. She was spared longer than I could have expected, considering the state of her health during the past few years. As you remind me, she lived to the age of man, and her mental powers continued clear to the last. She enjoyed many earthly comforts, and, what is more than everything, I have good ground for hoping she is now happy. I can look back on her long illness, and rejoice that she was counted worthy to suffer; and the reflection is pleasant that, instead of lying on a bed of pain, she may at this moment form one of that happy throng who are ever before God's throne, and whose work it is day and night to praise Him.

I am afraid there is little prospect of my being able for some time to accept your kind invitation. The earliest opportunity I have I will however take to visit Lathom. I am, yours truly,

JOHN LEYLAND.

To Mrs. H. F. Ingham.

Liverpool, Nov. 29th, 1847.

My dear Mrs. Ingham,

We are, I find, companions in sorrow. I only knew when I was in your neighbourhood a week since that your bereavement had followed so quickly that of my own. I wished much to have called upon you, but I was so straitened for time that I could not. In a great sorrow the soul recoils from human consolation, and refuses all comfort save what comes from above. It is to the great Master Ruler, the beneficent source of all good, that we turn in affliction, and we turn to find that He ever remembers we are but flesh, and tempers His supporting love so equally with His chastening rod, that we are never wholly cast down.

"Death," it has been pleasantly said, "is the gate of heaven." Death, much as we dread it, releases us from the sorrows of time, and opens an entrance into the everlasting habitations Redeeming Love has prepared. Again, and for ever, it unites the loved companions of earth freed from the power of sin, with affections spiritualised, and the perceptions of the soul quickened and refined. The contemplation of these sublime truths might well inspire the Apostle to exclaim—"O death, where is thy sting? O grave, where is thy victory?"

I am, very truly yours,

JOHN LEYLAND.

To Mr. Hugh Kendrick.

Liverpool, December 4th, 1847.

My dear Sir,

I received your letter of the 8th of July in due course. Two days after you wrote that letter my poor mother breathed her last. The pain of a long illness, and the cares and sorrows of this life, she then exchanged for a new state of being, which I doubt not will yield her unalloyed happiness. Death, come how it may, is an awful thing. I was not unprepared for the event: for a long time it has been like a load hanging over me by a slender thread, ready at any moment to fall. It has made on me a deep impression. I have shared so much of my time and my thoughts with her, that now she is gone I feel a loss that, speaking as I at present feel, nothing ever can replace. To fill up the void it has occasioned in my heart appears simply impossible. Her high-minded nature, her scrupulous honesty, her love of truth, her reverence for goodness, now they are buried with her in the grave, make me feel as if left alone amidst a crooked and perverse generation.

I am, your sincere friend,

JOHN LEYLAND.

To Mrs. Edward Nugent.

Liverpool, January 21st, 1848.

Allow me, dear Madam, to express my sympathy in your sorrow. Very sincerely can I say that I regret the loss of your dear husband, deeply; he had so many qualities to command respect. How great must be YOUR grief my own recent bereavement enables me to estimate. In all God's afflictive dispensations something is found to afford consolation : He tempers the wind to the shorn lamb ; He promises that as our day our strength shall be. The reflection of your husband's well-spent life, and the hope that at the great day of assize he will be found to have been faithful in the discharge of his various duties, must comfort you. The Christian has many sources of consolation on the loss of godly friends, not the least of which is the assured hope of a reunion when a few more years have passed away.

With kind regards to your son,

I remain, dear Madam, faithfully yours,

JOHN LEYLAND.

To Master S. Wilton.

Liverpool, 26th April, 1848.

My dear Simeon,

I well remember the pleasant evening I spent with you and your brothers, a day or two before you returned to school, at the house of our friend, Mr. Williams. That evening, I dare say, is fresh in your recollection as well as in mine, and likewise a certain promise I then made to write to you, which I have been, I am afraid you will think, a long time in fulfilling. It was a cold, snowy night, the night I refer to, and days were then nearly at the shortest. Now, the days have increased considerably in length ; there are more than twelve hours of sunshine ; the snow is all gone, the cold winds are leaving us, the buds of the trees, swelled to bursting, promise ere long to clothe in leafy verdure the twigs and boughs which have been bare and naked through the winter.

Several months have passed since we met ; they have gone by quickly and quietly, but nature, you see, has not been idle ; neither, I dare say, have you. Many days and weeks you have had for your books and studies, and the result of these days and weeks will be seen, I doubt not, in the progress you have made in whatever your attention has been directed to.

The holidays will soon be here again, and the sap which has risen from the roots of the trees, and shown itself in the bursting buds I spoke of, will, before you come home, aided by the warm sun and the refreshing rain, make further progress, and the trees, which are yet bare, or have but a scanty covering, will then be fully decked in their own peerless beauty. Don't forget these trees : the time you have been enabled to give to your books, and the instructions you have received from your masters, will warrant your friends in expecting you to make a somewhat similar progress.

I am, your sincere friend,

JOHN LEYLAND.

To Mrs. Hannah Halton.

Liverpool, May 1st, 1848.

My dear Mrs. Halton,

My conscience has been restless for some time at the omission I have been guilty of in not writing to you for so long a time. I still find it very difficult to leave home, and it is only when I am absolutely compelled that I get away. I trust you and all your family are well. I am hoping that now the days are got a pleasant length, and the cold weather passed away, you will be able to spend a day or two here. Do if you can, and let us have a chat about old times.

With regards to all your circle,

I remain, truly yours,

JOHN LEYLAND.

To Master S. Wilton.

Liverpool, Oct. 10th, 1848.

My dear Simeon,

If I must speak the truth, I believe that but for my promise I should have allowed the half-year to pass without writing to you. While I am honest enough to say this, you must not suppose that it would have been through any want of regard. My engagements are numerous, and occupy every day from morning until night; but the promise I made has every now and then kept recurring to my mind, and at last I am penning a few short lines. Schoolboys have more time for correspondence than their elders, who have to fight the battle of the world. I am, therefore, only proposing what is fair when I say that for every letter you receive you should return three at least. Consequently, I shall expect to receive three letters before another becomes due from me. If I were a schoolboy again, as sometimes I half wish I was, I would make a better use of my time than I did when I was a lad. Unfortunately, I had then a great deal too much of my own way. Now I can see that it was not for my good. At the present time you are in a position many grown men would rejoice to exchange. I advise you to improve it, and never to waste time: very soon you will become sensible of its inestimable value.

I am, your sincere friend,

JOHN LEYLAND.

To Mr. John Wilton.

Wigan, Nov. 18th, 1848.

My dear Friend,

I am not, you see, an imitator of a certain gentleman, who, during something more than a fortnight's sojourn in a country where nature has spread her pleasantest scenes in lake, valley, and mountain, where there was everything to inspire eloquence, and from whence a letter would have been peculiarly acceptable to a poor stay-at-home fellow, never once took pen in hand during his absence. Such conduct I look upon as the perfection of naughtiness, and I never mean following it; hence this missive.

I wish I had you here in this ancient and loyal borough, not for the purpose of exhibiting to you its lions (they are so very commonplace), but for the pleasure of having a friend at my elbow.

I am, affectionately yours,

JOHN LEYLAND.

To Mr. T. W. Gore.

Liverpool, Nov. 28th, 1848.

Dear Gore,

My friend, John Wilton, favoured me with a sight of the letter you have just written to him. The event you relate, I can easily suppose, must have made a great impression on the boys of the school. It comes home when one circumstanced in every respect like ourselves is suddenly taken away. I recollect a similar event occurring to a boy named Brierley, when I attended the Wigan Grammar School, and how deeply it affected me. Youth readily receives impressions, but then they are as quickly effaced. With you, as a senior boy, this occurrence may have a more abiding influence. If we are apt to lose sight of one truth more than another, it is this, that " in the midst of life we are in death."

I thank you for your kind remembrances of me. Give my affectionate regards to the Wiltons. Tell them I shall be exceedingly glad to see them home again at the coming holidays. Truly yours,

JOHN LEYLAND.

To Mr. John Hall.

Liverpool, 27th Jan., 1849.

My dear Sir,

There is something to me so attractive in a place which has been, age after age, the abode of learning, and been hallowed by intellect and genius, that I cannot help envying you your residence at Cambridge. I wish the pursuits of the inhabitants of this good old town of Liverpool were of a kindred nature, but we are content to tread on lower ground, and to aspire to objects of a different character. Like you, we certainly study, and what is more, seek our purpose with a perseverance and an avidity unknown, I suspect, in your tranquil and sober haunts. Gold is the god of our idolatry. " Get money, honestly if you can, but get money," is the prevailing creed ; and the man who dared to doubt its truth would be considered guilty of weakness and folly— a man behind his age, and given up to effete and exploded opinions. The prophets of the present day tell us that the increase of riches is the increase of a nation's greatness. Utter a contrary opinion, and the Ahabs will say, " I hate Micaiah : he is a prophet of evil."

I should much like to see Cambridge, and I hope before any great length of time elapses to be able to pay it a visit ; meanwhile I shall be glad to hear anything about it you choose to relate. I have reason to believe that its river, the celebrated Cam, partakes of the qualities of the ancient Lethe ; and the exhalations from its waters to produce on those who ramble on its banks oblivion of absent friends, and of any promises they may have made to write to them.

Our good friend, Wilton, is well. I acquainted him with my intention of writing, and he desired me to say all sorts of civil things on his account.

Not long after you left, I had to congratulate him on a no less important event than the attainment of his majority. How much he has increased in dignity, and how well his new honours sit upon him, I will leave to your imagination to conceive, rather than attempt a cold and unimpassioned relation.

I have read Blanco White's "Poor Man's Preservative Against Popery," which you were good enough to lend to me.

Until now I never knew so much of the author's personal history. The book is of peculiar value, coming, as it does, from one trained up as a priest in an intensely Roman Catholic country. The simplicity and force of his arguments, and the practical object he aims at, contribute to its usefulness.

Englishmen have reason to rejoice in their free country, and Churchmen on being members of a Church jealous of the soundness of her faith, as is evidenced in the provision made in her Liturgy for bringing the whole of the Scriptures periodically before her people.

I return my thanks for the loan of the book, which I have already returned through your brother.

I am, yours truly,
JOHN LEYLAND.

To Mrs. Hannah Halton.

Liverpool, Feb. 2nd, 1849.

My dear Mrs. Halton,

I wish I was nearer, that I could come to you and speak a word of consolation. As it is, I must be content with expressing in this way the sympathy I feel for your loss. I will not ask you to dry your tears and shut out the thoughts of what has happened : I would rather say, weep on. Sorrow brings humility ; and with the humble and contrite spirit God loves to dwell. When the road along which we travel is dark, and dangerous, and perplexing, when things around are found to have no reality, and to prove only a delusion and a snare, then we turn to the unerring oracles of God, and try to spell syllable by syllable the divine will.

Our nature is dead to spiritual things—even regenerate men need line upon line, and precept upon precept.

Trials, like bitter but wholesome medicine, work out, under the grace of God, a healthy condition of the soul. "Blessed are they that mourn, for they shall be comforted." I am, my dear Madam,

Very faithfully yours,

JOHN LEYLAND.

To Mr. John Wilton.

Liverpool, Feb. 17th, 1849.

My dear John,

I was glad to be assured of the condition of your health, and of your safe arrival at the end of your journey.

We have managed well at the office since you left : so far your absence has occasioned no inconvenience. It is fortunate that you are comfortably fixed in lodgings. Doubtless you will like them better than a constant residence in Dr. Gully's establishment.

When you write again let me know something more of Mr. Lee. I remain, affectionately yours,

JOHN LEYLAND.

To Mr. John Wilton.

Liverpool, March 4th, 1849.

My dear John,

Tuesday morning brought me a letter from you, and on the evening of the same day I wrote in reply. I addressed my letter according to your instructions, but I have since learned that I ought to have added the words "Chapel House," and this omission may have prevented it from reaching you. Do not neglect to write if you do not receive from me letter for letter, as you know how much I am occupied.

To-day is the good Sunday, a day on which I have always avoided writing letters. Indeed, I do not think that in the whole course of my life I have written more than half-a-dozen letters on the day. I shall, however, have no scruple in writing to you.

If I could give you health, you should not be long ailing. The only thing I can do is to bid you look to the source whence sickness and health flow. If I were to tell you that your illness is a blessing, you might think it unfeeling; still it is the decree of One who loves and cares for you. I have often thought that, circumstanced as you have been, your deafness has been morally beneficial. It has kept your mind from being tainted by many a coarse jest and impure observation, and the sickness now laid upon you may, and doubtless will, in some way or other bring good. Use every means you can to compass your recovery, but bear it patiently, and pray to Him who aids our necessities, not so much in accordance to our wants, as to the fervency of our petitions.

I am, affectionately yours,

JOHN LEYLAND.

To Mr. John Wilton.

Liverpool, March 8th, 1849.

My dear John,

It gave me pleasure to receive so good an account of your health. The experiment you are trying—for such I regard it—bids fair to be suc-

E

cessful; and that it may be so to the uttermost I ardently wish.

I felt much interested in the account you gave of Mr. Lee's family. You have been fortunate in meeting with so comfortable a home. From your description I don't know which to admire most—the kind lady, her worthy husband, or their engaging children. If I am to have a helpmate after the model of Mrs. Lee, as you say you wish, I ought at once to come over and make acquaintance with her. Yet, if the sight of the lady should affect me as I have read the sight of a painting affected a Romish priest when celebrating mass, it would be safer to keep away. The eyes of the good father, it is said, chanced, in an unlucky moment, to fall on the painting of a female saint of exquisite beauty, which ruffled him so much, and occasioned such a perturbation in his breast, that he declared he would rather encounter the hurricanes of a stormy sea he had once navigated than undergo again a season of such disquietude. Perhaps I am more impenetrable than the priest. I can boast this now, however I may feel after seeing Mrs. Lee.

I am, affectionately yours,

JOHN LEYLAND.

To Mr. John Wilton.

Liverpool, March 14th, 1849.

My dear John,

There was one paragraph in the letter I received from you last Sunday which gave me great satisfaction. You say, "I firmly believe that I came here by the direction of an all-wise and all-merciful Providence." Assuredly a good Providence guides us always. He has led you where you are, and not there only, but from the moment you first drew breath to the present hour. "In God's hands our breath is, and He orders all our goings." This truth carefully cherish. If men and women would take the pains to note the various events which happen to them, they would see the guiding and protecting power of God as clearly as if it was made palpable to the eye of sense.

How much they lose, how many anxieties they store up for themselves, by not fully receiving the truth of the particular providence of God! It stills every fear and murmur to remember that all that is good God's mercy will provide—all that is hurtful His power will keep away. Herein is a marvellous thing, that the Being who called into existence the grand and immeasurable universe, and whose own greatness far exceeds the boasted powers of man even dimly to conceive, should condescend to supply man's special wants, and to guard him from special evil. The Hebrew poet might well exclaim, "Lord, what is man that Thou art mindful of him ?"

Let us pray frequently and earnestly; let us lay every want before Him, and every trouble. Nothing is too small, nor anything too great, for His power to accomplish. I am, your affectionate friend,

JOHN LEYLAND.

To Mr. John Wilton.

Liverpool, March 25th, 1849.

My dear John,

I have been wishing to hear something more about your health, and you do not once mention it in your last letter. Let me know how you are soon.

You ask for particulars of the death of poor Alexander Brown. All I know I will tell you. Although his illness was long, and the result not unlooked for, yet his death was not expected so soon. I was delivering the message you sent to his brother George respecting the treatment of dropsical complaints by hydropathy, the day after I got your letter, and when I had said my say I perceived he was moved by some unusual emotion. He then told me he had received two letters that morning, one written by the person with whom his brother was lodging, informing him that there were no hopes of his recovery ; the other, dictated by his brother, who was unable to write, requesting him to come to him at once. He set off the same night to Paignton, and arrived at one o'clock the following day. Alexander, on his arrival, was insensible, but he soon after rallied for a few minutes—the last flickering of the life within him—and was able to speak. An hour afterwards he peacefully expired. The quotation you made from Young beautifully sets forth the lesson events like these carry with them. The present existence, with its trials and its bereavements, would indeed be sad if man had no concern beyond its boundaries. The future—the mysterious, impenetrable future—inspires us with courage, and nerves us with strength in our daily conflicts; and the light it even now yields guides and cheers us in our struggles.

I am, sincerely yours,

JOHN LEYLAND.

To Mr. John Wilton.

Liverpool, April 1st, 1849.

My dear John,

Your mother, as you are probably aware, is contemplating a journey to Malvern, and by the time you receive this she may be with you. I am in hopes she will bring back a good account of your health. Great reason have you to be thankful for the large number of mercies you enjoy. You have a most affectionate mother, and there cannot be on earth a greater blessing.

> " A mother is a mother still,
> The holiest thing alive."

I have had as kind a mother—indeed I have had two, for my aunt was a second mother to me. I do not think it possible for there to exist individuals possessing tenderer natures, or more devoid of selfishness. Their memory I very dearly cherish.

I am, sincerely yours,

JOHN LEYLAND.

To Alfred Pennington, Esq.

Liverpool, April 2nd, 1849.

My dear Sir,

Allow me to congratulate you on becoming the proprietor of "Birchall's Farm." It is an excellent situation, and before long I hope to see you comfortably domiciled there. The hand of taste may transform it into as snug a home as any that can be found amongst all the pleasant homes for which good old England is famous. I have only just heard of your purchase.

I am, truly yours,

JOHN LEYLAND.

To Mr. John Wilton.

Liverpool, April 4th, 1849.

My dear John,

I am glad to hear you speak so confidently about the crisis which you say necessarily results from the medical system you are pursuing. I am also rejoiced to hear that your physicians consider your internal condition better, and that they are sanguine of gaining, at no distant time, the mastery over your complaints. If you come home cured, I shall be ready to canonise Dr. Gully, the Rev. Mr. Lee, and everybody else who has been instrumental in bringing about such a happy result.

Since you went to Malvern we have had a number of workmen making alterations in the cellars of the bank. Our friend McLaughlin had unluckily stowed there a small stock of Burgundy. One day the porter, happening to be near the spot where the wine was deposited, looked at the case, which he thought bore the appearance of having been disturbed. On further examination it was found that nearly half the bottles had been emptied of their contents, and replaced by water. The workmen on the premises were charged with the misdemeanour, but they one and all declared their innocence ; so I suppose it must be that malignant elf called " Nobody," who goes up and down the world doing so much mischief.

Believe me to be, sincerely yours,
JOHN LEYLAND.

To Mr. John Wilton.

Liverpool, Easter Day, 1849.

My dear John,

A great and solemn festival we celebrate to-day— a festival which ought to call forth our warmest thanksgivings for the great event it commemorates. The Church, it has been well remarked, celebrates the resurrection of her great Head at a season of peculiar fitness, when a new life is bursting on the material world. Nature, like humanity, has its youth, its prime, and its old age : a springtime of promise, a summer replete with matured beauty, a hoary winter, when strength decays, and beauty withers leaf by leaf, when life gradually disappears in the tomb, and a snowy pall is spread around. Springtime follows the clouds and darkness of winter, and nature begins to show symptoms of life. At this juncture the Church stands forth and preaches the doctrine of the resurrection—" Christ is risen from the dead, and become the first-fruits of them that slept." Our bodies, " sown in dishonour, will be raised in glory." The atoms of which they are composed may each have an individuality, and, widely as they may be scattered, again be collected, and arise anew spiritualised, and yet the same body. The gardens and fields on every side emphatically repeat the Gospel lesson. From every expanding leaf, and from every opening flower, the doctrine of immortality is enforced. The two volumes God has given to instruct us are Nature and Revelation. The former is an illustration of the latter, and in it may be found the confirmation of many a Christian doctrine and many a Christian grace. The book of Nature, like the book of Revelation, we do not study half enough.

I wish Dr. Gully would pronounce the word " better"
finally, and send you home again.

I am, affectionately yours,

JOHN LEYLAND.

To Mr. John Hall.

Liverpool, April 20th, 1849.

My dear Sir,

I have just re-read your letter of the 21st of
February, and the impressions it conveyed on the first
reading are confirmed by a second perusal. You seem
determined to lessen my veneration for Cambridge, and
to disabuse me from the belief of its being a place of
immaculate purity or of unquestioned usefulness. I feel
loth to change my opinions, and must beg you to
remember—

> " He that's convinced against his will,
> Is of the same opinion still."

I am unwilling to believe the city noisy, the Cam
muddy, the undergraduates disorderly. If these things
are, they ought not to be. After all, the conviction
will sometimes force itself on the mind that our two
universities might be rendered more efficient. Time
passes quickly; and institutions which in time past
have been well suited to the wants of the age may not
be the best adapted for the present. Whenever any
change is made, however, it should be done in a
reverent spirit. Men who clamour loudest for reform
use it commonly as a means, not an end—as an instrument to enable them to work out their own secret and
mischievous designs. Many good men oppose reform,
not from a wish to defend even the shadow of an abuse,
but from the fear lest a change may bring about a worse
state of things than before, especially when the change
is advocated by those whose known desire is to uproot,
and not to strengthen or renew.

Our friend, Wilton, is at Malvern, as probably you
are aware, trying the hydropathic system under the
care of Dr. Gully. Already he has been there nearly

two months, and is likely to remain some time longer. He seems sanguine of obtaining a perfect cure in the end.   I remain, faithfully yours,

JOHN LEYLAND.

To Mr. John Wilton.

Liverpool, April 22nd, 1849.

My dear John,

In reply to your inquiry concerning the bank I have to state that everything has gone on satisfactorily during your absence. Although now and then we have been hard pushed, on the whole there has not been much business doing. ——— has managed the out-tellings well. It is true that, according to the French proverb, "*Il a un pied de nez,*" yet I believe he has done his best. He has come early, occasionally stayed late, and, after all, been grumbled at more pitilessly even than his predecessor. When he has lived a little longer he will find it to be the way of the world. ——— told me one day that a fatality seemed to preside over his balancing. His cash was often perversely wrong—sometimes over, sometimes short. One day I was passing him soon after he returned from his rounds, when he pointed with great triumph to a paper before him, which showed the same figures on the debtor and creditor side. He had balanced at once, and it appeared an exceedingly welcome event.

I do not think your absence was expected to be as long as it is likely to prove. The opinion now seems to be that it may be prolonged to an indefinite extent. Not being authorised by you, I have not, of course, intimated its probable duration ; indeed, I scarcely ever mention your name, except in reply to inquiries. The present opinion is, as I state, that you will not return for a long time to come, and arrangements have just been made for the duties of your department to be carried on by another.

I am, sincerely yours,

JOHN LEYLAND.

To Mr. John Wilton.

Liverpool, April 29th, 1849.

My dear John,

Many thanks for your two kind letters. I shall look forward with pleasure to the end of May, if it is to be the time of your return. Yet, when you speak of the cold and biting winds which have predominated so long giving place to gentle and balmy airs, and when I think that you can now wander, at your own sweet will, along the healthy mountain range of a district abounding in varied and delightful scenery, I feel it is a sin to wish you back. I confess I should like to have a ramble with you to the many pleasant spots round Malvern, and to none better than the secluded ruins of the old church you describe. You say I must not expect you to send news. I want none. When I write I generally write what I happen to be thinking of at the time, unless you make a special inquiry, as you did about the bank, and I shall go on in the old way. Nevertheless, if any great event was to occur, I should deem it right and proper to acquaint you. If, for instance, our worthy stipendiary magistrate, Mr. Rushton, were caught in the act of shoplifting; or if the good Corporation of this town were to form themselves into a community of monks; or if the Parochial Chapel of St. Nicholas, wearied with the site it has so long occupied from the time when its shadow fell on the green sward where now it rests on piles of buildings, thickly clustered near it—if, I say, it was to grow wearied with its old site, and be found some morning quietly located in Barlow-street, to the great astonishment of the inhabitants of that place; or if the Mersey was to take a sudden fancy to resume its ancient course to the sea—if any or all of these things were to occur, doubtless I should edify you with the minutest particulars; but, if nothing happens of the marvellous, expect me to fill my letters as I have been in the habit of doing.

I remain, affectionately yours,

JOHN LEYLAND.

To Mr. John Wilton.

Liverpool, May 6th, 1849.

My dear John,

You commence your last letter by telling me you have nothing to say, and you go on by imparting as much news as can well be comprised within the limits of a letter. First, you give an interesting account of a severe thunder-storm your neighbourhood has been visited with; then you describe a walk you have had with Sheridan Knowles, one of the greatest of living dramatists; and you wind up with the agreeable information that your recovery is satisfactorily progressing. What more could any one desire in a letter? Evidently you are fishing for compliments, and, to spite you, I won't pay them.

I have been pleased to observe in many of your letters expressions of thankfulness for the mercies you receive from the Giver of all good. I have purposed saying a word or two on the subject sometime, and so I may as well take the present opportunity. My aim is simply to fulfil that part of a Christian friend's duty which requires us to build each other up in the faith. Nothing can be plainer in Scripture than that a return of praise is imperatively required for the good things bestowed upon us with a lavish hand by a beneficent Providence.

In the long array of eminent men whose history Scripture has preserved this grace shone forth in their character with surpassing lustre. If we wish to tread in their footsteps, to prove ourselves heirs to the same inheritance, gratitude must become a living principle in the heart. As everything that concerns us, be it little or great, should form a subject for prayer, so every blessing we receive should call forth our thanksgivings. If we value anything we possess, there can be no more effectual means to ensure its continuance. A thankful heart and an earnest purpose to use God's gifts rightly will bring down on us other blessings.

I am, affectionately yours,

JOHN LEYLAND.

To Mr. John Wilton.

Liverpool, May 12th, 1849.

My dear John,

Your letter came this morning with a punctuality much to be commended. I was not equally pleased with what you had to say of your health, which improves slower than I wish.

To-day is old May-day. If I were living in the olden time I should now be wandering in the green meads, instead of being sat quietly at home writing letters. Both occupations have their respective charms. We are growing such a working and trading people, that we can afford little or no time now for holidays. For my part I confess to a liking for them, and for old customs also. Putting aside the religious interest connected with Christmas, Easter, and Whitsuntide, they are otherwise pleasant seasons for the mind to think upon. To the great mass of the people they are like water-springs, investing the dreary waste of memory with refreshing verdure; like milestones to the way-farer, telling of the journey he has travelled, and in the cheeriest way. Former days are again enjoyed in the recollection; and if sometimes they remind us of past troubles, the keen smart is healed by time, and the recollection tends to soften and humanise the heart. Many a bright colour and curious device these holidays furnish for the web memory weaves in every breast. Reverence for the past needs not make us forgetful of the blessings of the present—advances in physical comforts, liberty better understood and more per-manently secured, a wider dissemination of knowledge, modern times have brought. Nevertheless, I would not even for these exchange the manly simplicity and the sterling honesty which have been for ages the pre-dominant features in our national character.

I am,

Sincerely yours,
JOHN LEYLAND.

To Mr. John Wilton.

Liverpool, May 17th, 1849.

My dear John,

In your last letter you say you suppose the officers of the bank are rather hard worked, and that you should be glad to render them assistance. You have made the observation before. You, who have been living so long in the pleasant county of Worcester, who can wander the livelong day with fancy for your guide, or, if you list, take

> "Moonlight walks, when all the fowls
> Are warmly hous'd, save bats and owls—"

you desire to be mewed up between four brick walls, like a rat in a hole! Umph! I would as soon see you home again as believe it.   Sincerely yours,

JOHN LEYLAND.

To Mr. John Wilton.

Hindley, May 20th, 1849.

My dear John,

I have much pleasure in dating a letter from this place. I came yesterday, and remain until to-morrow. If I were to tell you that the sun shines nowhere so bright, that the sky is nowhere so clear, the fields nowhere so gay, the flowers nowhere so sweet as here, I daresay doubts would insinuate themselves in your mind. But "there is a good time coming," and I hope it will see you familiarly acquainted with the neighbourhood. You can then judge for yourself whether I am giving an honest description, or whether I am misled by a partial judgment.

I have just risen from the hospitable breakfast board of an old friend, and have called to write my letter at a house, to me, full of valued associations. Many members of my family have stood beneath its oaken rooftree, and I feel here more at home even than in Barlow-street. I do not know how old the house may be, but it is, at the least, two or three centuries. When first reared it might look with scorn on its lowlier neighbours, yet the pretensions it once may have possessed are now almost altogether gone, and in its old age it is devoted to the purposes of an inn. What a fertile subject for meditation is an old house! One cannot help pondering on its history, and the changes it has witnessed, and picturing to the mind its former inhabitants. Their forms, clad in homespun garments of quaintest fashion, once more fill the old rooms; their furniture comes back again—capacious wardrobes of polished oak, chests of profound extent, chairs with towering backs, and tables whose solidity seems to fit them for the service of generations. What a different scene has been looked on from the windows of the apartment I am in! Not as now—a number of cottages closely huddled together, brick built and slated, with groups of children playing in the door-ways, in the rear of which are huge chimneys vomiting clouds of smoke which darken the fair face of heaven; but green fields, gently undulating, a brook whose crystal stream murmured at the pebbles obstructing its course meandering in the midst. At no great distance in front rose the thatched roof of the " Low Mill," with a sheet of water before it, reflecting in its placid bosom the rural scene around; while nearer, a little to the right, stood the village inn, and, on a patch of greensward adjoining, the maypole—a spot where youthful parties blithely revelled. Perhaps from these same windows a troop of cavaliers may have been seen riding past, burning with zeal to avenge the death of a venerated king; or a company, who, by their closely-shaven locks, and the strains of some old Hebrew melody they join in as they pass onwards, distinguish them as belonging to the opposite party in the state, which for a period was successful in subverting the ancient constitution of the land. Trains of pack-horses doubtless have been seen journeying along, the song of the drivers making pleasant music with the jingle of their horses' bells; and wondering eyes may have gazed on the first wagon as it was drawn lumberingly on its way. What hopes and what fears, what gladness and what mourning, these apartments must have witnessed: infancy growing up to manhood and sinking into old age; the cradle and the tomb in the retrospect seen side by side of each other; and life as a tale that is told. I am, sincerely yours,

JOHN LEYLAND.

To Mr. John Wilton.

Liverpool, May 27th, 1849.

My dear John,

It is Sunday morning; I have little time, and am writing in great haste, as the quarterly collections in support of the place of worship I attend take place to-day, and I purpose being present at both the fore-noon and afternoon services. I have also my usual class to look after, and in the evening I am expecting the visit of a friend; so that you see my time for the day is pretty well laid out. I wrote to you last from Hindley, and I have since received yours of the 21st inst. The notable walk you took to Worcester I shall long retain in my recollection. If I do not henceforth hold you up as a model of intrepidity, I shall do you grievous wrong. The account of your journey, however, has occasioned me some remorse. I am afraid lest the insinuation I made in a former letter, of your being unwilling to return to your duties at the bank, you have taken in sober earnest. Allow me to say that I am quite sure you would not absent yourself a single day without urgent need. I was sorry to learn that your return is likely to be further delayed.

I am, affectionately yours,

JOHN LEYLAND.

To Mr. John Wilton.

Liverpool, June 3rd, 1849.

Dear John,

I am circumstanced much as I was when I last wrote; and if I was to detail all the duties I have to discharge to-day, I should leave room for nothing else; so I will at once pass on to other things. I hope you are not indulging in irony when you say I never say anything about myself. What can I have to tell of so lone an individual that can possibly interest you ? When I was last at Hindley my friends thought me looking better; but, to set against that, an old friend, who lately paid me a visit here, said I had a very careworn appearance. Like everybody else, I have my daily fears and fightings ; work I have in abundance, even more than I care for, and I am longing for the rest which I expect soon to have.

God bless you, my dear friend, and believe me to be,
Sincerely yours, JOHN LEYLAND.

To Mr. John Wilton.

Liverpool, June 10th, 1849.

My dear John,

In the short visit I paid to Hindley three weeks since, I could not help noticing the sear and dingy appearance of the evergreens, which through the long dull winter have so faithfully asserted the undying powers of nature, and given so cheerful an aspect to the landscape, when standing side by side with the fresh-opened spring leaves. Even then there were trees in full foliage, while the buds on others were only opening. The oak was late, not more than a faint tinge of green marking its branches. This backwardness seemed, to my fancy, indicative of its nature. As it defies sturdily the storms of hundreds of winters, so, too, it would resist the gentler influence of the sun. A drive to Hale last night with a friend gave me another peep into the country, which I never saw looking better. Oak, as well as all other trees, were in full leaf.

This afternoon I have been visiting at 99, Islington. Not a word yet has been heard of Dr. Gully's letter. If it has been received, it has certainly not been made known. John Hall is returned from the University. He gave me a call on Friday, when I was unfortunately out. Sincerely yours,
JOHN LEYLAND.

To Mr. John Wilton.

Liverpool, June 17th, 1849.

My dear John,

I was agreeably surprised this morning by the post bringing me a second letter from you since I last wrote. Both letters are written in so lively a strain as to serve as a tonic on my languid system.

If ever my spirits are as buoyant, it will certainly not be when business claims as many hours out of the twenty-four as it does just now. If these periodical visitations serve no other purpose, they are at least an excuse for grumbling, and grumbling is the grand privilege of an Englishman, who, it is said, cheerfully submits to any amount of inconvenience, provided he is left free indulgence in the national amusement.

Two subjects of your letter of the 11th inst. need a passing notice.

First, as regards Hindley. Don't let your fancy lead you astray. There cannot well be a greater contrast than between Hindley and Malvern. The former place is flat, and is interspersed with manufactories and collieries. In some corners people may be found who may possibly stand as low in the moral scale as in the worst regulated town in the kingdom. Still, on the whole, it has a tolerably pure atmosphere, and contains here and there pleasant rural spots. To those, like myself, whose infancy and youth were spent in the neighbourhood, it is dear from its old associations. I can take up the parable of one of our poets and say—

> "Like as the hare when hounds and horns pursue
> Pants to the place from whence at first she flew,
> So do I wish these long vexations past,
> There to return and die at home at last."

The second thing I wish to mention is my concurrence in the views you express on retirement. Active life should not be followed by idleness. When a man has fewer occupations, and especially if he has larger means, the responsibility lies clearly upon him to use his advantages in promoting the welfare, temporal and spiritual, of his neighbours.

I am, sincerely yours, JOHN LEYLAND.

To Mr. John Wilton.

Liverpool, June 24th, 1849.

My dear John,

I have been attending the funeral to-day of a neighbour of mine—John Cave—who was, if I mistake not, an old schoolfellow of yours. You cannot be more shocked to hear of this event than I was. A few days since, and he was in perfect health : youth and health, however, are no securities against death. A short but severe attack of cholera has cut him off before he has reached his prime, and gives one more lesson to us who are left behind of the uncertainty of life. "He was the only son of his mother, and she is a widow." Her grief must indeed be great. May He who alone can sound its depths extend to her His mighty help.

I am, ever yours, JOHN LEYLAND.

To Mr. John Wilton.

Liverpool, July 1st, 1849.

My dear John,

On my return home, a little before one o'clock this morning, I found your letter waiting.

I shall abstain from offering an opinion on the course you should pursue in the emergency you are placed in, and content myself with reminding you that a good Providence counsels wisely all who go to Him.

After the harassing week I have had I am so worn out that I cannot write more than these few lines.

I am, yours affectionately, JOHN LEYLAND.

To Mr. John Wilton.

Liverpool, July 8th, 1849.

My dear John,

As you seem to expect my advice from your letter of yesterday on the step you are considering,

F

I will say a few words, although I should have preferred remaining silent.

In the first place I wish you to know that my faith in the hydropathic system is diminishing fast, notwithstanding the details you give of your improved condition. Still, if you are determined to persevere, a longer stay at Malvern follows as a matter of course.

In the next place I beg to suggest whether it would not be the most proper course to break your connection with the bank at once. You have already been four months absent, and, according to present appearances, you may be four or six months longer. Are you, then, justified in retaining your office under these circumstances? Certainly, the duties of the bank are being discharged; but if the directors think a certain number of officers necessary to carry on their business, are you justified, I repeat, with your present prospects, in maintaining the connection? Personally, I should much regret any step which would have the effect of rendering our intercourse less frequent; but there are other reasons besides those I have named to incline me to think you might do worse than resign your office. The bank holds out no prospect of any great advancement in life : you may spend the best of your days, and get nothing at the end better than a few hundreds a year.

The confinement it entails is another strong reason for your consideration. In my opinion a farming life offers the most suitable occupation for you, taking into account the state of your health. Think over it.

I am, affectionately yours,
JOHN LEYLAND.

To Mr. John Wilton.

Liverpool, July 15th, 1849.

My dear John,

The suggestion I threw out of a farming life suiting your health better than any other occupation, I again repeat, in spite of the disinclination manifest towards it in your last letter.

From what I know of your constitution I feel sure no calling will agree with you better, nor even as well; and if you have any opportunities of acquiring a knowledge of agricultural pursuits where you are, let me advise you to embrace them.

I thank you for your sympathy respecting my health. I need change, and the next few Sundays I purpose spending somewhere in the country. How eagerly my imagination roves to the green knolls, warm and bright with sunshine! I seem even to hear the voice of murmuring branches, whispering—

> "Under the greenwood tree,
> Who loves to lie with me?"

I am, affectionately yours,

JOHN LEYLAND.

To Mr. John Wilton.

Liverpool, July 21st, 1849.

My dear John,

I told you in my last letter that I purposed spending a few Sundays in the country. To-morrow, therefore, I go, God willing, to the neighbourhood of Woolton, and I am taking the opportunity of writing a few lines to-night. You have been vegetating so long in so healthy and agreeable a spot, that I don't know whether you will be able to believe in the advantages a slight change of air may afford. Wherever I go—that is, if in this immediate neighbourhood—I cannot hope to enjoy a prospect equal in beauty and extent to that of Malvern, unless I call in the aid of imagination, and through its transforming power gaze on an illimitable expanse, yielding nourishment, not to plants of such common growth as the oak, the elm, or the ash, but to the graceful palm and the stately cedar, watered, not by streams narrow as the Severn or the Avon, but by majestic rivers, like unto the Ganges or the Mississippi. The vine displays there its purple clusters; the pomegranate its crimson fruit; the air is

laden with perfume from the blossoms of the orange ;
and the sun which illumines the scene is—

> " Not as in northern climes obscurely bright,
> But one unclouded blaze of living light."

What is Malvern in comparison ?

Sincerely yours,

JOHN LEYLAND.

To Mr. John Wilton.

Liverpool, July 28th, 1849.

My dear John,

You have placed a great temptation before me,
but the bank stands in the way of my accepting it.
For the present I must be content to picture to my
mind's eye the Chapel House, and the diversified prospect it commands. I see it even now before me—the
old Abbey Church, with the scattered houses on the hillside, and the windings of the Severn through a vale of
surpassing beauty. Yonder rise the grey towers of
Worcester, suggesting thoughts and awakening associations of overwhelming interest. A king, who disgraced
his high station by shameful vices, found there a nobler
spot than he deserved to sleep his quiet sleep. Another
king must have watched with terrible anxiety from the
great tower of the great Minster the issue of the battle
which made him a fugitive for a time from his own
kingdom.

When contemplating grand and majestic temples like
Worcester and Gloucester, one cannot help comparing
the earnestness of the faith of the men who reared them
with the apathy of this generation.

———— is contemplating a trip on the Continent, but,
entre nous, I don't think he will be able to carry it out
just yet. ———— is threatened with an attack of gout,
and opposes the project.

I am, affectionately yours,

JOHN LEYLAND.

To Mr. John Wilton.

Liverpool, August 4th, 1849.

My dear John,

I have just had a venerable old clock repaired, if that has any interest for you. Faithful it has been for many a long year to old Father Time in recording his movements, yet he had not permitted it to escape his ravages. It is true he had touched it with a gentle hand. The fingers, which had travelled so often round the dial-plate, were perfect, but they had become rust-eaten, and the figures which marked the hours well-nigh effaced. Fingers and dial are now renovated, and, by the aid of silvering and lacquering, the old clock stands proudly in the chimney corner in almost its pristine freshness. I look up in its face and moralise: The hand which fashioned thy curious wheels has been long since cold. More than one generation has gazed, as I gaze now, upon thee, and where are they? Gone to render an account of the employment of the time the rapid and stealthy flight of which thou didst so faithfully record. Thy fingers, in their circuit, brought them hours of enjoyment and of health; hours for the fulfilment of the duties of their station, for repentance of sin; and they carried in their train a summons which has taken them hence.

What a shadow is man! Even the clock he constructs for his daily convenience outlives him. I wonder how men managed before clocks were invented. But I am forgetting. The lights in the firmament count the hours, and a careful observer can as accurately note the passage of time as by these mechanical contrivances.

It was a royal gift the illustrious and refined Caliph of the East sent to the energetic and powerful Emperor of the West. The intricacy of the wheels, and the regular performance of their office, must, one can imagine, have caused wonder to contend with admiration in the breasts of the household of the great Charles.

Having nothing else to say, pray accept these cogitations. Sincerely yours,

JOHN LEYLAND.

To Mr. John Wilton.

Liverpool, Aug. 23rd, 1849.

My dear John,

The newspapers will have given you so full a report of our Fancy Fair that it is needless for me to attempt any description of it. The commercial gentlemen who live in complacent dignity on the banks of the Mersey were more than merry for the three days it lasted. It was delightful to see them throw aside their ledgers, and cease fingering their money-bags, to hurry after pleasure like boys in their teens. And wouldn't they breathe the freer, and wouldn't they sleep the sounder for it? Everybody went, and if the houses could have stirred I verily believe they would have gone too, and the deserted site might have presented the appearance it bore six or eight centuries ago. It was well they couldn't, or they might have had a fancy to stay, and then what a heap of labour it would have been to get them back! Only think, if the Town Hall had taken a position on a choice spot in the park, and persisted in remaining, spite of coaxing or entreaty; or if a sunny knoll on the confines of Aigburth had wooed the Exchange buildings and won their affections, and they could not have been persuaded to forsake their love— what a predicament for the Mayor and the merchants! It is well stone and mortar haven't legs of their own and wills of their own, or it would add immensely to our troubles. I think all the better of the Liverpool folks for indulging in a holiday, and wish they would take one oftener. The joyous heart and the smiling countenance in the moral world are like the sunshine and the flowers in the physical mercies, which the great beneficent Ruler sends to gladden us in our pilgrimage here. And you, who are no cynic, condemn all festival observances!

About the harvest I have little or nothing to say from personal observation. In going to and returning from Wigan last Saturday I noticed several fields of oats cut, but none of wheat. Lancashire, you must bear in mind, is always a week or two later than Worcestershire. The various grain crops here are all, I believe, promising, but everything depends on the weather of the next few weeks, and just now it seems particularly unsettled.

Williams started on his tour a week since to-day.

Affectionately yours,
JOHN. LEYLAND.

To Mr. John Wilton.

Liverpool, August 30th, 1849.

My dear John,

The cholera, I hope, is subsiding here. I have heard less said of it this week, and the deaths, happily, have become fewer. I cannot say I have been free from alarm on the subject. I was so much shocked by the death of poor John Cave that my fears were perhaps needlessly excited. In truth it is an awful thing to be called with little or no warning into eternity. Like Dr. Dodd, I am no stoic as regards death. A prospect of immediately entering "that undiscovered country from whose bourne no traveller returns," may well fill poor weak man with fear and awe.

Some little time ago you asked me whether I thought a person justified in dealing in spirituous liquors, as they so often prove the cause of vice and misery. It appears to me that spirits, like wine and the rest of the gifts of Providence, are good in their use, evil only in their abuse. In my opinion they may be traded in without any breach of religion or morality. Doubtless, it is a nice question, and deserves careful handling. If any person were to be deeply convinced that the evils resulting from their use outbalanced the good they bestowed, he would hardly be justified in dealing in them ; nor would the consideration lessen his culpability, that if he were to withdraw from the trade it might not in the least degree affect their consumption. If he did not do it, others would, is a weak argument. To be just, he must wash his hands clean of the trade altogether.

I am, yours affectionately,
JOHN LEYLAND.

To Mr. John Wilton.

Liverpool, Sept. 10th, 1849.

My dear John,

Your letter is perplexing. You name so distant a period as the probable time of your return that I begin to think you never mean to come back at all. I was supposing that the air of Malvern was pure, its waters medicinal, and even that its doctors had some skill to boast of. These advantages combined, I thought, would surely effect your cure in a marvellously short time; but I am grossly deceived. Of the merits or demerits of the doctors, out of respect for the profession, I will not speak; but, judging from results, I should like to know how the air and the waters of these vaunted hills are better than those of smoky Lancashire. Seriously speaking, my faith in the efficacy of the system you are trying is growing weaker and weaker. Don't, however, suppose that I shall be sorry to find myself mistaken.

Williams returned from his tour a week since. He travelled over a large tract of country—far more than I should have ventured on with only the time at my disposal that he had. Very likely he will give you a full account of his journey, so I will not forestall it by a secondhand version.

It is always pleasant to have one's opinions in unison with one's friends, but as regards festivals you and I must be content to differ. A moderate enjoyment of holidays could not do harm, and might be productive of good. One fact goes against you—as festivals have declined, intemperance has increased. Men need relaxation, and where it is denied they fly to the excitement of the public-house.

Periodical holidays, I believe, would contribute largely to the happiness of the middle and lower classes, both mentally and physically.

I am, truly yours,

JOHN LEYLAND.

To Mr. John Wilton.

Liverpool, Sept., 23rd, 1849.

My dear John,

I should have wondered at your silence if I had not been told that the crisis you have been so long expecting had at last arrived. A crisis, accompanied with pain in a greater or less degree, is an inevitable result, I understand, of the hydropathic treatment, and therefore, however disagreeable, there is nothing in it to excite alarm. On the contrary, it is pleasant to know that you have reached a point at which recovery may be expected to be rapid. I will not weary you in your present condition with sending a long letter for you to read, and will only add that you have my best wishes for a speedy and favourable issue through this and every other stage of your malady. When you are able, let me know how you are.

I am, affectionately yours,

JOHN LEYLAND.

To Mr. John Wilton.

Liverpool, Oct. 3rd, 1849.

My dear John,

I was glad to hear by your letter that your health is better than I was fearing it might be. It is well you have no pain, and although the sickness you are troubled with must be unpleasant, comfort yourself with the prospect of a speedy recovery. This phase of your illness will, I dare say, only be of short duration, and when you have got through it I trust you will mend apace. Affectionately yours,

JOHN LEYLAND.

To Mr. John Wilton.

Liverpool, Oct. 15th, 1849.

My dear John,

Some people fall into the mistake of supposing the period of education to be confined to the time spent at school : on the contrary, education is the work of the entire life. It commences in the schoolroom, or rather on the knee of the mother ; but the daily avocations, the mixing with those who have knowledge, and indeed with those who have not, call into action the faculties of the mind.

Observation and reflection on the everyday incidents of life, even sickness and trouble, are all so many avenues by which man is continually influenced and instructed. A man's faculties are perpetually expanding. With his years he gathers, or ought to gather, knowledge to the very end of life :

> "The soul's dark cottage battered and decayed,
> Lets in new light through chinks which time hath made."

I have got a little too serious for my present purpose, which is merely to tell you I have just discovered that the vernacular of Worcestershire differs widely from what is common here. There is a game children sometimes play at, called the "rule of contraries," the sport of which is, when they say hold fast, they mean let go ; and when they say let go, hold fast. This rule seems to hold good in Worcestershire, and when people say they will write *often*, mean *rarely*.

I am, sincerely yours,

JOHN LEYLAND.

To Mr. John Wilton

Liverpool, Oct. 23rd, 1849, half-past 12 a.m.

My dear John,

I was glad that the letter acquainting me of the attack of your brother's illness acquainted me also of his partial recovery. The next report you make I trust will be that he is still better. The kind and assiduous nursing he is fortunate in having will do much to facilitate his recovery ; but although I can understand his illness must have encroached to a certain extent on your time, I am nevertheless at a loss to discover what makes you so desperately busy. Your letters now are like angels' visits—few and far between. A mutual friend to whom I took the liberty of showing your two last letters remarked that you might have the care of a nation on your shoulders from the way you speak of your occupations. Of course, I do not presume to speculate. Many of them may be of a nature of which I am wholly ignorant. For instance, the widow lady and her family of daughters you once mentioned to me, and towards whom you have so carefully refrained for a long period from referring, may, for aught I know, occupy a large share of your time. From your silence I could indeed imagine that no introduction had ever admitted you into their society. Mind, I do not blame you if this be the case. The society of good and sensible women is of great value to young men : it softens their manners, and refines their naturally rougher natures. Nothing coarse can be spoken in their presence, and the discipline of the tongue must have its influence on the heart.   I am, affectionately yours,

JOHN LEYLAND.

To Mr. John Wilton.

Liverpool, October 28th, 1849.

My dear John,

I am going to make one thing or another an excuse for writing a short letter ; but I was desirous that the day should not pass without offering to you my congratulations, and expressing the hope that you may live to see its return again and again, even until those sandy locks of yours are bleached by a long succession of winters.

The other evening I went to see Banvard's Panorama of the Mississippi, now exhibiting here, and which is well worthy of a visit. In the course of the evening, when dilating on the fertility of the prairies in the neighbourhood of that mighty stream, Mr. Banvard said that, to use an American metaphor, a tenpenny nail had only to be planted there at night to be found a crowbar next morning. I trust I shall not transgress the rules of decorum if I say it reminded me of a transformation that partook of the marvellous some of us were witnesses to a year ago, when the sun set on the 27th of October on a youth the law, doubtless with much propriety, declared to be irresponsible for his actions, and rose next morning on the same individual and found him matured, and capable of self-government.

I am, truly yours,

JOHN LEYLAND.

To Mr. John Wilton.

Liverpool, Nov. 8th, 1849.

My dear John,

The unusual duty devolves upon me of acknowledging the receipt of a letter from you. If it had not come I should either have imitated your silence, so powerful is example, or else have written an ill-tempered letter. I was not aware that your brother had been as ill as you say he has. The last mention you made of him he was better, and I have been supposing ever since that he was quite well. Partly from indisposition, and partly from want of opportunity, I have lately been rarely in Islington. Since midsummer I have either been unwell or fancied myself so, and office business has been exceedingly heavy. These causes have obliged me almost wholly to discontinue visiting.

I am, sincerely yours,

JOHN LEYLAND.

To Mr. John Wilton.

Liverpool, Jan. 14th, 1850.

My dear John,

I am half inclined to emulate the good wife of "Tam o'Shanter," and "nurse my wrath to keep it warm," in order that I may pour it on you in cumulative force for your long silence. Surely in these many weeks you might have found an opportunity to pen a few lines. As an Englishman loving fairplay, I would have you to plead at once any excuse you may have, lest I perform the functions of judge and jury in my own person, and condemn you unheard. For myself, I have been working all the time more like a galley-slave than a freeborn Briton. I have reason to be thankful that I have at last got through my periodical visitation. Weeks ago, when I saw such a load of work before me, my spirit quailed, and I nearly succeeded in persuading myself that I was very ill. Now it is past and gone, I turn joyously to the sunshine, and feel I am breathing again the free air of heaven.

May the good God bless and prosper you.

Affectionately yours,

JOHN LEYLAND.

To Mr. John Wilton.

Liverpool, Jan. 29th, 1850.

My dear John,

I must, I suppose, give up all hopes of receiving another letter from you. I have done all I could to induce you to write, and in vain. Nothing, therefore, remains for me but to submit, which I do the more readily as I hear that your residence at Malvern is now drawing to a close, and that we shall shortly have you home again. With many of your other friends I shall give you a hearty welcome, and I trust that your lengthened absence may have accomplished the purpose for which it was designed.

I am, sincerely yours,

JOHN LEYLAND.

To Mr. Worsley Battersby.

Liverpool, March 23rd, 1850.

My dear Worsley,

At last I have determined to run away from the good old town of Liverpool. The noise, the elbowing, the overreaching, the ignorance, and the vice form a catalogue of ills, enough to weary, in a period of nearly fourteen years, a man of brass. Turning to the sort of life I may lead in the future, how can it but be bright by the contrast, when it promises opportunities for encasing my nether man in drab inexpressibles, of uttering sage judgments anent the weather, and of entering with due gravity on the study of the properties of manures? If, when you contemplate the prospect, an evil genius should insinuate aught concerning hobnailed shoes, or remind you of the foolish saying of a foolish statesman that country heads are as heavy as the clay of their acres, heed it not; nor even let it permit you to think I may be subject to troubles from the blight in wheat, the rot in sheep, or the fly in turnips. I shift my tent somewhere about the end of June, if I live so long; between and which time I hope to have the pleasure of seeing you.

I shall be glad to hear that your father's health has improved. I am, truly yours,

JOHN LEYLAND.

To Mr. T. Dorning Hibbert.

Liverpool, March 25th, 1850.

My dear Dorning,

I may not possibly occasion you much surprise when I tell you that I am leaving Liverpool, and returning to the neighbourhood where your eyes and mine first opened to the light. I am sick of town life, and long to renew my acquaintance with that early friend I never knew how much I loved until we had shaken hands and parted. A rich and right bountiful friend Nature is. The verdant carpet she spreads under our feet is studded with a thousand gems. She paints the tulip and the poppy, the rose and the honeysuckle receive from her their fragrance, and the melody streaming forth from wood and hedgerow on a summer's morn is her inspiration. The subtlest inquirer cannot penetrate her secret workings. She has " sermons in stones, and good in everything." What an old divine said of the book of Revelation may likewise be said of her :

"There are shallows in which a child may wade, depths in which leviathan may swim." Before I leave, which I expect will be about the end of June, I hope you will favour me with a visit.

I am, sincerely yours,
JOHN LEYLAND.

To Mr. John Wilton.
Hindley, July 19th, 1850.

My dear John,

Many thanks for your kindness in forwarding the letter which had been left at the office for me, and for your own letter which accompanied it. I was wishing for some communication with you before the arrival of your packet, and I should not have waited for you to have written, but that since I came here I have been not a whit the less busy than I was towards the close of my connection with the bank. I have made little progress yet with my house. In a neighbourhood like Hindley there are difficulties in procuring workmen of the precise kind you want at a short notice. The next time I write I hope to be able to report better progress.

Your account of the calamities which befell our friends at the bank after the festivity of Wednesday se'nnight (must I own it?) considerably amused me. I trust they have all long since recovered from them, and that they are at the present time well and hearty. Give to each of them my cordial regards.

I must scold you for the much too complimentary strain of your letter. If you go on in this way, my good fellow, I shall become vain, and not know what to do with myself. Like Gulliver, after his residence among the Brobdingageans, I may fancy that men and women of six feet high are less mortals than myself, and if I meet them in the highway, call to them to stand back lest I should trample on and crush them. "No more of this, Jack, if thou lovest me."

Ever affectionately yours,
JOHN LEYLAND.

To the Rev. Richard Battersby.

Hindley, July 22nd, 1850.

My dear Sir,

Your letter, informing me of your visit to Hindley, was forwarded to me from Liverpool here. I thank you both for your letter and for your visit, and regret much that I was not upon the spot to give you welcome. I am obliged for your suggestions respecting my house. I scarcely yet know what to do with it. Already I have pulled a portion of it down, and for the present I shall content myself with putting in order only so much as is absolutely indispensable for a bachelor to live in. The place has been called Cheetham House some two or three centuries. Cheetham— cheat'em—I don't like it, and feel half disposed to change it. What say you to " The Grange"?

I am in better health than I have been, and as soon as I can discharge my workmen I think of making an excursion somewhere. Before I go I will, if I can, run over for a day to Lathom.

I am, my dear Sir, faithfully yours,

JOHN LEYLAND.

To Mr. John Wilton.

Hindley, Aug. 1st, 1850.

My dear John,

I am so completely immersed in bricks and mortar that it engrosses both all my time and my thoughts, so that I cannot do more than scribble a few hasty lines. Excuse, therefore, long, prosy letters at present. In a little while it shall not be my fault if you are without soporifics. I intend coming to Liverpool on Saturday, as Mr. Finney probably may have informed you.

I am, sincerely yours,

JOHN LEYLAND.

To Mr. John Wilton.

Hindley, Aug. 30th, 1850.

My dear John,

I received your letter yesterday at noon, and am sorry I could not acknowledge your kindness in forwarding its enclosure with such promptness before to-night. I ought to think myself a favoured man—as I do—in possessing so excellent a friend.

A pious bishop of our church made a rule never to praise a man before his face, nor to call him behind his back, so out of reverence for this rule I forbear to say more. It would be a blessing to society if the admonition was invariably acted upon, the latter portion of it especially, as a step would be thereby gained towards carrying out that new commandment, which contains the very essence of the Christian faith, " Little children, love one another." Affectionately yours,

JOHN LEYLAND.

To Mrs. Mary Cave.

Hindley, Sept. 30th, 1850.

My dear Mrs. Cave,

I received Miss Cave's note on Friday evening. I beg to thank you for the promise to housekeep for me during my absence, but I am afraid the house is in such dire confusion that you will reap little comfort from your visit. At the earliest, I find I shall not be able to leave before the 15th of October. If that be too soon for you to make the necessary arrangements, inform me, and I will wait until you are ready. In the course of next week I will write again.

With kind regards to Miss Cave,

I remain, dear Madam, truly yours,

JOHN LEYLAND.

To Mrs. Mary Cave.

Hindley, October 7th, 1850.

My dear Mrs. Cave.

These plaguey workmen lead me a dog's life.

G

Their stupid delays have obliged me to defer my journey until the 22nd inst., but, God willing, I shall start early on the morning of that day. Whatever may be incomplete then shall be left undone for the present. Therefore, pray do not come later than Monday, the 21st inst., and as much sooner as you please.

When you have completed your arrangements let me know when I may expect you. Remember me kindly to my good friend, Miss Cave, and believe me to remain,

Faithfully yours,

JOHN LEYLAND.

To Mr. John Wilton.

Cheetham House, Hindley, Oct. 17th, 1850.

Dear John,

In addressing a letter to you from this house I have one subject for congratulation, which is, that I do not write from an unknown country. You have been and surveyed the land, even though you had no luxuriant fruit, like the Israelitish spies, to carry back in token of its fertility. I have been disposed to change the name of the place, but I have been persuaded otherwise. Cheetham House has been its name for many a long year, and must continue so, I suppose, for the future.

I purpose starting early next Tuesday morning for London, whence I trust there will be an interchange of letters between us. I am, sincerely yours,

JOHN LEYLAND.

To Mr. A. McLaughlin.

London, October 23rd, 1850.

Here I am, my dear McLaughlin, in this wilderness of brick and mortar, without knowing that in the greater wilderness of human beings there is a single person with whom I have an acquaintance. It has been often remarked there is no situation so depressing as the being unknown in a great city, but the saying does not hold good in my case, for my spirits are exceedingly buoyant. I should not have written at this early period of my visit, saving that I wished to acknowledge the receipt of your letter, which arrived about noon last Saturday, just as I was setting out on a journey of some twelve miles from home, from which I did not return until Monday afternoon, and the following day I came up to town. I was more particularly anxious to write as you seemed to think I had been guilty of neglect in not calling upon you when I was last in Liverpool. I was only there two whole days, besides Sunday, and as I had much business to transact in the time, I trust you will clear me of blame. I have not hitherto been able to read the paper which accompanied your letter, but I have got it with me here, and the first opportunity I have I will read and return it as requested.

As yet I am not in regular quarters. I am writing at a place of entertainment in Fleet-street, the name and the number of which I am ignorant, where I called for the express purpose of writing this letter; nor have I seen any of the wonders that are round me. Everything seems to wear an ordinary sort of aspect; even the very paving-stones, about which so much has been fabled, appear as the rain plashes on them (for the day is wet) to be destitute of a single particle of gold. However, although I have hitherto seen nothing, I am on the tiptoe of expectation, and I don't know how soon I may have to communicate to my friends in the north the becoming possessed of a lamp like Aladdin's, or the discovery of the coveted elixir which transmutes the basest metals into gold. In the meantime believe me, with sincere wishes for your welfare and that of my old colleagues, to remain,   Faithfully yours,

JOHN LEYLAND.

To Mrs. Mary Cave.

London, October 25th, 1850.

My dear Mrs. Cave,

You will be glad I daresay to hear that I am safe in this land of multitudes; at all events, believe me I am glad I can assure you of the fact. I got through my journey pretty well, though towards the end of it I began to feel much wearied. The two days which have passed since my arrival have been really dismal—one almost constant dripple of rain, without even a gust of wind or a gleam of sunshine to enliven them. Still, notwithstanding the unpropitious weather, I have managed to settle down in comfortable lodgings, to see Westminster Abbey, St. Paul's Cathedral, the Exchange, and the Post-office. The fires are execrable; the very sight of them starves one. Convey to Miss Cave my regards, and accept my best wishes for yourself.

I am, dear Madam, your sincere friend,

JOHN LEYLAND.

To Mr. John Wilton.

Rheidol Terrace, Islington, London,
October 26th, 1850.

Good Friend John,

I am presuming that you and others of my friends are wondering what I am doing in big and busy London. Well, I am installed in comfortable lodgings, in an airy and agreeable neighbourhood. Two out of the three days I have been here have been miserably wet, yet, notwithstanding, I have seen a good many of the sights. If I stay as long as I purpose, and see as much in proportion as I have already seen, I shall have much to tell when I come back. My father used to relate a story of an acquaintance of his who was in the habit of visiting London occasionally when he was a young man. The journey in those days was a difficult undertaking, and whoever made it enjoyed the reputation of being a great traveller. The gentleman I have named used to be puffed up so much with the dignity, that for some time after his return home he spoke such an unintelligible jargon that nobody could understand him. I will endeavour to avoid his example, and save my friends from that species of martyrdom.

The country I passed through in my journey hither differs widely from Lancashire. There are gentle valleys, flowing rivers, bonny green knolls, deep and wide-spreading woods, and fields cultivated like gardens. The greater part of yesterday I was in the British Museum. I have also seen Westminster Abbey and St. Paul's. To the former I have only as yet paid a cursory visit; the latter I examined more carefully, and attended service. Whatever may be said by prejudiced people respecting the service of our cathedrals, as it was conducted at St. Paul's nothing could be more devotional. The chanting was grand. The anthem sung on the occasion was taken from the Psalm commencing, "In Jewry is God known; His name is great in Israel." The words struck me as being singularly appropriate to a spot where tradition says an apostle planted the first Christian church in the land, and the magnificent temple which echoed the words proclaims that His name is indeed accounted great.

I am, sincerely yours,
JOHN LEYLAND.

To Mr. J. P. Williams.

London, October 30th, 1850.

My dear Williams,

I am becoming experienced. I have crossed London Bridge, stood beneath the dome of St. Paul's, and passed under Temple Bar. I have been in streets bearing the familiar names of the Strand, Holborn, Ludgate-hill, Cheapside, Lombard-street, Cornhill, and Leadenhall-street. Nay, I have actually crossed underneath the bed of that famous river which in past times bore on its bosom the fleets of the Roman, the Saxon, and the Dane, and which now floats ships from every portion of the globe. I did think when I was under, about middle way, that if great Father Thames was to come through he would quickly put an end to me and my adventures; but it would have been unbecoming his dignity to extinguish so humble an individual, and to destroy a magnificent work of art. I have stood in Fleet-street, too, and watched the great tide of humanity as it ebbed and flowed like one for whose memory I entertain a deep reverence. Bolt Court I have found out, and my fancy pictured the good doctor issuing forth, attended by his faithful and admiring biographer. At Marlborough House, which I visited on Monday, I saw an interesting picture of Dr. Johnson in the ante-chamber of Lord Chesterfield. He is represented sat down in company with others, waiting for an audience with the fine gentleman of literature, and his indignation at the delay is admirably expressed. His presence appears to impose a restraint on the party, and a beau, bedizened with lace, returning from the presence chamber, with a young lady as gaily dressed as himself, is apparently telling her who the visitor is. She eyes him at the end of her fan, but their self-complacency is too evident to permit them to extend to him any courtesy. The first time I was in St. Paul's I walked by accident up to the doctor's monument, and felt as if I had met with an old friend. The artist has clothed his statue in Roman costume, perhaps not inappropriately, as he was so great a lover of classic literature; but the majority of the statues I was glad to see sculptured in the dresses the individuals they represented were in the habit of wearing. A stranger to the history of our country, viewing the monuments in St. Paul's, would evidently conclude, either that we have had more men eminent in war, so greatly do the monuments to naval and military officers preponderate, or that we honour less the men whose virtues and talents have distinguished other walks of life. I remain, faithfully yours,

JOHN LEYLAND.

To Mr. John D. Finney.

London, Nov. 2nd, 1850.

My dear John,

My journey has afforded me much gratification. As the saying is, "I have let no grass grow under my feet" since I came, for I have worked hard, and the weather has, on the whole, considering the season, favoured me.

Notwithstanding, as I tell you, I have been gratified, several things have fallen short of my expectations. The streets and the shops generally have not that elegance I was prepared to expect. The public buildings, too, although many of them possessing great merit, are so hemmed in by houses, that their effect is in a great measure lost. With no place was I more disappointed than Trafalgar Square. If it be true that the National Gallery occupies the finest site in Europe, it is equally true it spoils it. The space is noble, and the Nelson column a fine ornament. These are the two grand features of the Square. Many things gave me an odd sensation at first. When I saw the omnibuses inscribed with such names as Battersea, Putney, Chelsea, it required an effort of the mind to believe they came from the real places. I was puzzled, too, with meeting with the *Times* early in the day, and had to reflect that it was a morning and not, as with us in Lancashire, an evening paper. The first time I visited the British Museum I had the good fortune to meet with an artist friend who was engaged in sketching from the Elgin marbles, and I had afterwards the privilege of visiting in his company the National and the Vernon Galleries of Paintings. The Vernon pictures, as you are probably aware, are exhibited at Marlborough House, but the collection embraces many more works than were contained in Mr. Vernon's gift, munificent as it was. Most of the modern paintings have been removed there from the National Gallery, so that one now may be said to form a collection of ancient, the other of modern masters.

I leave town in a day or two on a short visit into Hertfordshire, but purpose returning. There appears to be indeed so ample a field for observation here, that as my agricultural operations do not for some months require my attention, I am hesitating whether or not to stay the whole of the winter. The veriest trifle would determine me.

Persuade your father to join me for a week, and tell him if he will follow me for that length of time in my long daily rambles, it will drive away the gout for ever so long a time to come.

I am, yours truly,
JOHN LEYLAND.

To Mr. John Wilton.

London, Nov. 7th, 1850.

My dear John,

Your two letters arrived in due course. I have sympathised with you in the excessive labour you have had to undergo, for I know well from experience what it is, and I now congratulate you on the prospect of its being mitigated. I am here still, you see, having deferred my journey into Hertfordshire in order to see the Lord Mayor's show on Saturday. In one of your two letters you say you hope to find me the same person on my return that I was when I left Liverpool a few months ago. My good friend, how can you expect such a thing? Do you think that the refinements of the capital, even though they be only enjoyed for a short period, are to be lost upon me? Small thanks, if these be your reasons! Besides, physiologists tell us our frames are perpetually undergoing change : one set of vessels are continually at work carrying away decayed bits of bone, and muscle, and flesh, while others are as constantly employed in replacing the decay, and at certain intervals we stand forth altogether and completely a new person. How can I gather up the decayed bits of muscle and of bone, when I don't even know how they go nor when they go ; and would you have me cut out the newly-formed healthy parts? Why, Shylock's pound of flesh is nothing in comparison!

Last Saturday was the commencement of Michaelmas term, and the judges on that day make a state entry into Westminster Hall. Eleven o'clock, I had previously been informed, was the hour fixed for the ceremony; and as I did not wish to miss it, I was punctual, and almost the first person in the hall. Much to my annoyance, they did not arrive until nearly two o'clock, by which time a large crowd had assembled. The Lord Chancellor, according to custom, entertains them previously to breakfast, and I presume, as it was the first given by his lordship, it was so bountiful an affair that even the moderation of a judge might have been put upon trial. At last the cry went round "they come"; and come they did, the Lord Chancellor first, wearing his state robes, profusely ornamented with gold, preceded by a Marshal and followed by an officer bearing his train, dressed in black, with ruffles at his breast, a cocked hat under his arm, and girt about with a sword. A similar formality was observed with others of the judges, who were, I presume, highest in rank; and nearly all were preceded and followed by officers whose correct titles I did not hear. The names of the distinguished men I learned from the bystanders. A more venerable set of countenances I never beheld, every one of them displaying great intellectual ability. I liked Talfourd's and Lord Campbell's best, perhaps because of my prejudice in favour of men of letters. At any rate, the lines of genial temperament seemed conspicuous in their countenances.

I am disposed to remain here the winter. My farm does not yet need attention, and my house is well cared for, so that I neglect nothing if I stay.

Affectionately yours,

JOHN LEYLAND.

To Mr. John Wilton.

Cambridge, Nov. 14th, 1850.

My dear John,

Few people will deny that Fortune is a fickle goddess, and that her frowns are dispensed with greater prodigality than her smiles. For once she has looked on me with a pleasant countenance, for the Cam is flowing near me, and temples dedicated to religion, and halls devoted to learning, raise their venerable fronts around. Yesterday I made an excursion to Dunmow, in Essex, a place well known amongst the honourable fraternity of antiquaries, to which I belong, from a certain farm being held by the tenure of supplying a flitch of bacon to any couple who, at the expiration of a year and a day from their marriage, can say they have never repented entering the matrimonial state. I saw the farm, and sat in an old chair kept in Little Dunmow Church, in which such happy couples have been accustomed to receive the reward of their extraordinary fortune. Bachelors can afford to laugh when they find that next year will make a full century since the flitch was claimed. What! not one happy marriage in a hundred years!

I am just going to call on our friend John Hall. Write, if you can, and address me at my old lodgings in Rheidol Terrace. I am, sincerely yours,

JOHN LEYLAND.

To Mr. John Wilton.

Cheetham House, Hindley, Nov. 29th, 1850.

My dear John,

I am home once again, you see, after a longer ramble than I ever had before. I have enjoyed it much, and the health and spirits I am in are pretty sure tokens it has done me good. Business requiring my personal attention obliged me to return; but I am not sure I shall remain, as I feel rather disposed to spend the winter elsewhere. I wrote to you last from Cambridge, immediately on my arrival, and when I had seen nothing of that celebrated city. I was there only a day and a night, yet I saw much, thanks to the good offices of our friend Hall (who is well, and who made many kind inquiries after you), and to the bright, cheerful weather. I had the good fortune to witness the confirmation of degrees in the Senate House, a ceremony usually confined to two periods in the year, the time of my visit not being one of them. The Vice-Chancellor

and other magnates of the University were present,
and amongst them Adams, the discoverer of the new
planet, "Neptune." The proceedings were short. The
candidates for degrees were presented to the Vice-
Chancellor by the Masters and Doctors, after which the
usual oaths were made. There was much solemnity in
the last stage of the ceremony, when each candidate
knelt down, and placed his hands within those of the
Vice-Chancellor, a fine old grey-headed man, and repeated, I presume, the words of the oaths, for what was
said was inaudible where I was stationed in the gallery.
I visited the University Library and the Fitzwilliam
Museum : the former a magnificent collection, and in a
building every way worthy of it; the latter is also a
splendid edifice. Internally, it is far from being com
plete. It contains a few good pictures, a small number
of antique sculptures, and a many casts. I saw the
outside of most, if not all, the colleges, and the interior
of the halls of one or two. I attended service in the
famous King's College Chapel, and in the chapel of St.
John's College; yet the greatest treat I had was in the
college walks or gardens. The various University buildings are fine, but the trees in the gardens are much
finer. An avenue of limes at Trinity College has a
deserved reputation for especial beauty. In London
there are a many grand sights—works of art, executed
by men of the rarest genius the world in ancient and
modern times has produced; but the graceful forms of
the trees, their gnarled and twisted branches, in the
different parks, possess a beauty no work of art can
equal. I am, sincerely yours,

JOHN LEYLAND.

To Mr. J. P. Williams.
  Cheetham House, Hindley, Dec. 5th, 1850.
 My dear Williams,
  I take shame to myself for not sooner acknow-
ledging the kind letter you wrote to me some weeks

ago.   A friend's letter received at a distance from home is sure to be, as yours was, very welcome.

After your raillery on my Johnsonian style, I should have been afraid to write to you again, if I had not been confident of your good nature, and that any slips my luckless pen may make will meet with generous indulgence.

My London journey will form my stock-in-trade for talk for many a month to come.   By-the-bye, I must not omit to tell you that I saw the Lord Mayor's show. The 9th of November saw me, as you may readily suppose, sally forth in high glee, with spectacles on nose, to gaze on this time-honoured pageant.   I stationed myself for the purpose in Cheapside, within sound of Bow bells, and, as they pealed forth their music, tried to fancy they said, " Turn again Whittington, Lord Mayor of London," and half persuaded myself I succeeded. I am not going to give you a detailed account of the procession, as you might possibly read of it at the time in the newspapers.   All I shall say is that it was really a fine sight.   If I had been ignorant before of the vast population of London, the crowd on this occasion would have removed it. The streets through which the procession passed were closed to carriages, and such a mass of human beings filled them as I never saw.   Turn where you would there were heads, heads, and nothing but heads.   Yet, in spite of the vast population, living, I suspect, is tolerably cheap.   I noticed the price of provisions in the shop windows, and they struck me as being so reasonable that I have little doubt a family may house-keep comfortably there on a moderate income.

With best wishes for your health and prosperity,
I remain, faithfully yours,
JOHN LEYLAND.

____

To Mr. James Finney.

Wigan, Dec. 9th, 1850.

My dear Mr. Finney,
I was glad to hear yesterday week that you are

alive and well. I have had my apprehensions, for I could not tell what effect the late extraordinary display of Protestant zeal would have upon you. It is well you bear up so manfully. I ought, though, to have remembered that if it had fallen on you Papists with even greater fierceness, you could console yourselves with the thought that your names in a future age would shine forth as martyrs. I think—nay, I am sure—it would be wiser, whilst you are whole in skin, to forsake your dangerous practices, and embrace a more popular, and, at the same time, a better and a safer path. Come, now, cut your cloth after the fashion of the Church of England, which neither encumbers her children with too great superfluity of dress as do you of Rome, nor yet, like Dissent, invests them with such a straitened garb that, if it does not wholly hinder, it at the least impedes their progress.   I am, truly yours,

JOHN LEYLAND.

To Mr. B. J. Barlow.

Cheetham House, Hindley, Dec. 13th, 1850.

My dear Sir,

I staid in London until the Thursday next following my return from Bishop's Stortford.

The day I left (Monday) was extremely wet, and with having to return into Lancashire early on Thursday morning, I had but two whole days; and as days were short, and I had one or two places to see, I gave up the excursion I mentioned to you.

On taking a retrospective view of my journey, I think I have seen as much as I could reasonably have expected; yet, instead of being satisfied, I feel rather stimulated to attempt something more. In this admission there is food to moralise on. The infirmity of human nature peeps forth, ever restless and troubled, and craving for something not yet won. The prospect to the mountain traveller expands the higher he rises, and height upon height opens before him. " I am but as a child," said the greatest of our philosophers, "with the undiscovered ocean of truth stretching before me, and playing with a pebble its waves have cast up at my feet."

I shall have much pleasure in hearing from you at any time, and, with regards to Mrs. Barlow,

I remain, faithfully yours,   JOHN LEYLAND.

To James Bent, Esq.

Cheetham House, Hindley, Dec. 20th, 1850.

My dear Sir,

I called in Bedford-street about the end of September, but it was only to learn you were out of town. During the month which has since passed I have kept wishing to do what I am only doing now, that is, to write to you. The repairs needed at my house proved more extensive than I expected; and although they are now completed, I am at the present time confined to a small portion of the house, it being all that is thoroughly aired; so that you may picture me vegetating in a sort of mousetrap, which will continue, in all probability, until the March winds set me at liberty.

For the first time in my life I have been spending several weeks in London. By virtue of my visit I can, by way of relief to this quiet retirement, indulge in reveries on what is doing in the city, or at the court. I can meditate among the tombs in the abbey, loiter about the clubs, or even, like the " boy Jones," creep into the palace of royalty itself.

I trust you and Mrs. Bent are enjoying the blessing of health, and that you may long continue to possess it, with every other good, is the sincere wish of

Your faithful friend,   JOHN LEYLAND.

To Mr. John D. Finney.

Cheetham House, Hindley, Dec. 24th, 1850.

My dear John,

As you anticipated, I was surprised at the event the enclosure in your note acquainted me with.

I could almost have thought of anyone marrying sooner than Haylock. His facts and his figures, his inferences and deductions—civil, social, and political—seemed to hedge him round with so complete and impregnable a fortification, that one would have supposed there was not a single weak point for Cupid to attack. His genial nature, however, must have been spied at some little loophole, and the shaft shot through which has carried him into the ranks of "family men." I hope he has got a right-down good woman for a wife, for he is every way worthy of one.

The "Papal aggression" subject caused as small a stir here as in any part of Her Majesty's dominions. There was a petition got up against it, which I never saw, and only heard of too late to sign, even if I had been so disposed. When I was at Cambridge the excitement seemed to have reached its climax. The walls, and even the pavements, were covered with such phrases as "Down with the Pope," "Hang Dr. Wiseman," and there were sketches of gallows with a body suspended to represent one or other of those distinguished offenders. Lord John Russell's letter I consider highly indiscreet.

If kindly dispositions lurk in the breast, time has brought us once again to a season sure to call them forth. I have many for your associates at the bank, and I pray you to express them for me as warmly as you can. I am, truly yours,

JOHN LEYLAND.

To Mr. John Wilton.

Cheetham House, Hindley, Jan. 3rd, 1851.

My dear John,

Blessings have often been invoked on old Father Christmas for the good things he brings—the respite from toil, the beef and the pudding, the merry quips and laughter-stirring tales.

Blessings, too, for bringing distant friends together, and sending loving thoughts to those whom the iron hand of necessity shuts out from family gatherings.

It is fifteen years since I last spent Christmas here, and, notwithstanding the joyous spirit of the season, I experience a feeling of sadness difficult to shake off, when I look round and compare then with now.

> "There's many a lad I loved is gone,
>   And many a lass grown old;
> And when at times I think thereon,
>   My weary heart grows cold."

With the good old phrase, "A merry Christmas and a happy New Year," I will draw bit and bridle, and subscribe myself,   Affectionately yours,
                                        JOHN LEYLAND.

To Mrs. Hannah Halton.
  Cheetham House, Hindley, Jan. 14th, 1851.
 My dear Mrs. Halton,
  The promise I made to write to you from London I did not fulfil. Instead, however, of filling my letter with apologies for a fault which I know your goodness will at once pardon, I will spend what time I have in giving some account of my journey. In the first place, I may tell you that I expected to find the streets, shops, and public buildings, as a whole, to be finer than they are. You know Liverpool pretty well, and I shall therefore make myself more intelligible to you if I institute a comparison between that town and London.

The principal streets in Liverpool have a better appearance than any in London, with the single exception of Regent-street, which certainly is grand and spacious.

In no part of London within the same area will so many handsome shops be met with as in Bold-street, Liverpool. The public buildings in Liverpool are, moreover, well situated, with space around which, if not ample, is still sufficient for them to be seen to advantage; while in London they are so huddled up with houses that a fair view of them can hardly be obtained. Then there is the Thames, which neither in volume nor purity can be compared with the Mersey. After having seen London, I think much better of Liverpool. London is yet a wonderful place. In extent and population, preconceived opinion falls infinitely short of the reality. One is inclined to wonder at the houses how they can all get filled, and at the people where they can all be housed. A walk in the leading thoroughfares of the city at four or five o'clock in the afternoon is enough to astonish any stranger. I don't know whether the carriageways or footways are then most crowded; both are gorged.

Vehicles of all kinds, private carriages, hackney coaches, and omnibuses, literally choke the carriageway, and are often at a total standstill from want of room to proceed. One of the pleasantest features is the public squares, which are numerous, and meet the visitor at every turn. They have all railed enclosures of ornamental garden ground; the trees in some of them astonished me by their size and luxuriance. The equestrian and other statues likewise contribute to their handsome appearance. I cannot here help echoing the sentiments of those who have charged the ruling powers with raising monuments to individuals distinguished merely by conventional rank, leaving unhonoured men of distinguished character and genius. Statues of kings are plentiful, "marquises, dukes, and a' that," but I saw none to men who have enriched the republic of letters by their talents or research, nor to any of our distinguished divines, nor (excepting a few statesmen) to the many other worthies who crowd our annals. Observe, I speak only of outdoor monuments. As regards St. Paul's and Westminster Abbey, this reproach cannot be urged.

The extensive parks, with convenient walks, and adorned with fine old trees and ornamental sheets of water, are among the chief attractions. In these agreeable resorts I experienced a difficulty of realising that I was in the midst of a city containing two millions of inhabitants. A curious custom exists with respect to street crossings. In most towns they are swept by the public authorities. In London private individuals

H

keep them clean—that is, men and women appropriate
to themselves a crossing, at which they stand with their
besom the whole of the day, and maintain themselves
on the pence given by passengers. Some are reckoned
of considerable value, and realise as much as 8s. per
day. Fights have been known to occur for the possession of these lucrative situations. If the touch of
the hat and a whining supplication for money are
disregarded by the pedestrian, the sweeper sometimes
revenges himself by a fling of the besom and bespatters
him with mud. One of the sweepers I observed to
be a female apparently advanced in life, dressed in
mourning, to all outward appearance a gentlewoman.
She wore fur round her wrists, and black gloves.
Whether misfortune had reduced her from a position
to which her dress would indicate she had belonged, or
it was assumed for the purpose of extorting sympathy,
I cannot tell.

I have now given you a few general impressions of
the city; its sights, properly so called, I have not
touched upon; and as I have spun out this letter to a
considerable length, I must reserve an account of these
until I have the pleasure of seeing you. Remember
me to the various members of your family, and believe
me to remain, Dear madam, faithfully yours,

JOHN LEYLAND.

To Mr. John Wilton.

Cheetham House, Hindley, Feb. 4th, 1851.

My dear John,

On reading the account of the bridal preparations
in your letter, I felt no wonder it had been so long
delayed, and that I ought to congratulate myself it
came at all. The blind god is wonderfully active just
now. Right and left are his arrows flying; one
despatch follows another with the record of his triumphs,
so that one can scarcely help a feeling of consternation
at the extent of his power. Who next may fall his
victim it is difficult to say. Well! what there is no

preventing is useless bewailing. In all seriousness, my good friend, I sincerely wish the event which has occasioned the preparations you describe may afford much happiness to the parties most interested, and to the root and branch as well of the families about to be connected.

It seems a little out of place to send you an account of delving and ditching in the midst of your rejoicing, but I have nothing but such like news to tell. I have already begun operations on my farm. I have been ploughing a field which has not been broken up within the memory of anyone living. A neighbouring farmer, who has known it for sixty years, tells me it has been in grass the whole of that time, so it may be considered virgin soil. Very soon I shall be over head and ears in gardening, and my friends need not have to search far for an application of the lines—

> "Oft would he cry delve, delve the hole,
>   And prune the tree and trim the root;
> And stick the wig upon the pole,
>   To scare the sparrows from the fruit."

I shall have much pleasure in seeing you here whenever you can make it convenient to come over.

I am, sincerely yours,
JOHN LEYLAND.

To Mr. J. P. Williams.

Cheetham House, Hindley, Feb. 10th, 1851.

My dear Williams,

  I am disposed to rate you soundly for not fulfilling the promise you made when you last wrote. Rightly or wrongly, I have concluded that the storm you were in has settled into a calm, and that all the anxieties it occasioned have passed away. I hope it is so, for I have no wish my old companions in arms should be called upon to undergo needless marchings and counter-marchings, but, on the contrary, to enjoy as much quiet during the rest of the campaign as the necessary duties of the service will permit. Notwithstanding, I am desirous of having a full account of all that has happened, and what is now going on in ever-memorable Water-street. Does ———— continue his physic, and ———— his wig? Is ————'s cravat as prim as it was, and the spirit for trading in ———— as active as ever? I can fancy my worthy friend ———— make his morning's entry in the office with quick and important step, laden with duodecimos and octavos; and while drawing off his spectacles with the dignity which could only be assumed by one in whose veins runs the ancient royal blood of Denmark, dilate on Mr. So-and-So's speech in the House last night, and the intelligence contained in the latest edition of the *Sun*. I can see ————, duster in hand, buried in the *Globe*, and hear the wail of Mrs. ———— describing her various ailments, and admire the courage which in the midst of weakness would slay a whole legion of Papists.

Thank God, all my recollections of the place are pleasant; and although I had my share of difficulties when I was there, I have not a grain of bitterness left towards so much even as a stool of the bank.

I shall be very glad if you and M'Laughlin, to whom give my affectionate remembrance, would come over here some Saturday afternoon—the next of all, if convenient. Let me know by return of post if I may expect you.

Perhaps as neither of you have seen Wigan, you may prefer stopping there, and walking on afterwards to Hindley. Do, however, as you feel disposed: at either place I will meet you, if you will let me know by what train you travel.

I remain, faithfully yours,

JOHN LEYLAND.

To Mr. John Wilton.

Cheetham House, Hindley, March 3rd, 1851.

My dear John,

I was much concerned to receive the account you have sent me of your health. The plan you are proposing, to sleep every night in Southport, is perhaps as good a thing as you could devise, and retain your connection with the bank. I sincerely hope it may have the effect you anticipate. I am very busy with my farm, and as forward with my work as any of my neighbours. My garden has been so chopped and changed, it hardly looks like the same place. The old hedges which enclose it I am pulling up and planting new, laying drains, planting and transplanting fruit trees. It has been disgracefully neglected. I question if the fruit trees have been pruned for ten or twenty years. I had purposed employing an experienced gardener; but by a sort of accident I tried my hand on it one day, and did it, in my own opinion, so well, that I mean now to complete the task. I won't say I do it right, for I cut away furiously. My aim is to make handsome, shapely trees, and the buds on the heaps of cut wood on the ground, big with blossoms, evince that I have a noble disregard for profit.

One result of my labours is the gaining an excellent appetite. Dinner is never ready soon enough, and in health generally I was never better. Would that I could persuade you to imitate my example. Don't wait until time has traced furrows in your brow, and smitten baldness on your head, before you venture on such peaceful and health-giving pursuits, or maybe, like Blinkhoolie, the abbot-gardener, you will murmur at not finding out their pleasures sooner.

> " Come hither, here shall you see
> No enemy, but winter and rough weather."

Can you obtain for me the price of guano, and ask if it can be had in small quantities ? To me it is a new fertiliser; I have not yet even seen it, and the organ of cautiousness is too largely developed in me to permit of much in the way of experiment.

I am, yours truly,

JOHN LEYLAND.

To the Right Honble. Thos. Pemberton Leigh.
  Cheetham House, Hindley, March 20th, 1851.
Sir,
      The inhabitants of the townships of Hindley and
Abram generally entertain considerable anxiety at the
position in which the Lowe School, in the first named
township, has for a long time been placed. The
importance of the subject will, I trust, form a sufficient
excuse for the liberty I take in drawing your attention
to it. Perhaps I may feel a greater interest in it than
many, as two years of my early boyhood were spent
there, endeavouring to unravel the difficulties of the
"rule of three," and similar perplexities.

I doubt not the full particulars of the existing state
of the trust have at one time or other been laid before
you, but as I have entered on the subject I may as well
briefly glance at them. The annual value of the school-
house, and land adjoining, together with sundry small
payments, amounts to about £25, and this sum has
been increased £5 or £10 in the last few years by
a railway from a colliery crossing the property, and will
eventually be further augmented by the coal underneath
the estate being brought into the market. Up to the
year 1829 the school was held at the old schoolhouse at
Lowe Green, but on the appointment of a new master
in that year it was transferred to the Sunday School
connected with Hindley Chapel. Mr. Matthews, the
master elected in 1829, died in May, 1834, and from that
time until May, 1842, the office was held in abeyance,
when a young man named Pollard received the appointment, who, after conducting it until November, 1846,
resigned. Since then the office has been again vacant.
Thus it appears that for thirteen years out of the last
twenty the neighbourhood has been deprived of the
benefits of an institution which, though certainly of no
great magnitude, must have yet produced an appreciable
amount of good, and impressed some portion of the
surrounding youth with the duty they owe to society.
This is more especially to be deplored when it is
remembered that the district around the school has a

fast-increasing population; that from 1831 to 1841 the numbers of the two townships rose from about 5,000 to more than 6,000; that the census of the present year may show a similar increase; and that if a recent report of the Lancashire School Society be correct, the neighbourhood stands at the very lowest point in the scale of education of any in the county. These considerations render the subject of paramount importance. The increasing value of the estate from its proximity to an extensive colliery, and the accumulation of the rental, which should amount to upwards of £300, form additional grounds for claiming the attention and assistance of all who have at heart the wellbeing of the neighbourhood.

In making these observations, I am far from imputing any blame to you; but though you, sir, are not the author of the evil, nor does the delay in appointing new trustees rest with you, still the exertion—the active exertion—of your influence (not too much to expect from us who are accustomed to your benevolence) would do all that is needed.

I have the honour to be, Sir,
Your most humble and obedient servant,
JOHN LEYLAND.

To Mr. J. P. Williams.

Cheetham House, Hindley, April 4th, 1851.

My dear Williams,

It is just a fortnight to-day from one of the two public holidays of the year, and I daresay you have already begun to meditate how to make the most of the occasion.

I know it to be a disagreeable predicament for one attraction to pull in this direction and another in that, so as to place one like Mahomet's coffin, which, it is said, is suspended in his tomb midway between the floor and the roof; or like the perplexed Mrs. Honour, who, when starting on a sudden journey requiring little baggage, could not prevail on herself to leave behind one gown because she had bought it recently, a second because she had had it long, a third on account of its being a gift, and a fourth for an equally cogent reason. My purpose in writing is to throw another ingredient in what may be an already brimming cauldron of difficulties.

When I was in Liverpool last week I entered into covenant with John Wilton either to spend Good Friday with him in Southport, or for him to give me his company at Hindley. I have been since thinking he might like to gratify a wish I know he has long had to visit the Rivington Hills; and as I have heard you also express a similar desire, I shall be glad if it should meet with his and your approval to accompany you there. If you decide to go, I would recommend you to start by the earliest convenient train for the Hindley Station, where I will be in waiting, from whence we can proceed direct to Horwich, a village at the foot of the hills, and arrive in plenty of time for church; after service visit the Pike, admire the extensive prospect, and return to Hindley by four o'clock in the afternoon. Bear in mind, it will be a walk of nearly twenty miles, and that the Rivington air is a powerful whet to the appetite.

The inhabitants of that neighbourhood are often, I suspect, in a dilemma similar to some of the people here, who find an appetite much sooner got than a dinner. When you have resolved this momentous question, advise me thereupon.

I am, truly yours,
JOHN LEYLAND.

To Mr. John Wilton.

Dog and Partridge Inn, Wigan, April 10th, 1851.

My dear John,

Yesterday's post brought me a letter from your friend John Slingsby, saying he had forwarded me by railway five bags of guano. To-day I have sent him cash in payment, and I have to thank you for your kindness in ordering them for me. The place whence I am writing must be my apology for a short letter. I am sure *you* would never expect it to be a fountain of inspiration. Besides, one thing is enough to do at a time, and at present I am imbibing home's-brewed. Take care you don't condemn me. Remember my creed is—we honour a kind Providence better in using His gifts temperately and thankfully, than in putting them from us and calling them evil. I tolerate excess in no form.

Should you fall in with the suggestion I made through Williams, I shall see you at Hindley next week. I will have a bed in readiness for you on Thursday evening; but write before, that I may be certain when to expect you.

I am, faithfully yours,
JOHN LEYLAND.

To Mr. Thomas Brereton.

Cheetham House, Hindley, April 23rd, 1851.

My dear Sir,

On the 18th day of March, in this memorable year of 1851, I addressed a letter to you at the lodgings you were in when I last saw you in London. For some weeks after I had written it I enjoyed the pleasing satisfaction of thinking I might be present to your mind, together with the agreeable anticipation of receiving a letter in return; when lo! the post one morning brought a packet from that place of evil omen, the "Dead Letter Office," which on opening I found to contain my letter to you, inscribed—"Gone away—not known where." I am not, you will perceive, giving up the pursuit of you, for it has since struck me that a letter might find you if addressed to the British Museum. I am therefore comforting myself with the hopes that the lines I am penning may be seen by you, may freshen me up in your memory, and bring back a reply. In return for my perseverance, I may justly claim a letter of considerable length. Tell me of your good father and mother, of yourself, and of anything you may have to relate about your profession.

I am busily engaged in farming operations—manuring, planting, sowing, and harrowing. Whatever may be the ultimate result of these proceedings, the effect hitherto is to cause my appetite to wax keener, my face to become browner, my hands to grow horny, and my purse lighter.   I am, truly yours,
                                JOHN LEYLAND.

———

To the Right Hon. Thos. Pemberton Leigh.
        Cheetham House, Hindley, April 24th, 1851.
    Sir,
        In the reply with which you honoured a letter I addressed to you on the 20th of March last, relating to the Lowe School, you invited suggestions for the best way of promoting its future interests. I therefore beg to lay before you the following observations.

The present school buildings are much dilapidated, and a considerable outlay will be necessary to place them in substantial repair. I should not, however, recommend these repairs to be done with any view of using the buildings for their former purpose, for the master's house is small and inconvenient, and the schoolroom, now used as a labourer's cottage, is neither large enough nor high enough overhead. The school-room and house well repaired and laid together might afford a comfortable residence for the master; but a new school I consider the first and most necessary want after the appointment of trustees. The land belonging to the school is about an acre and a-quarter of the large Cheshire measure in extent, and between it and the public road a field intervenes of perhaps an acre of the same measure, owned by the Bridgewater Trustees, through which there is a right of road to the school. This field would afford an excellent site for a new school, and extend the school property up to a good road, if it could be acquired. Considering the large property owned by the Bridgewater Trustees in Hindley and the surrounding neighbourhood, it is possible they might present the field to the trustees, if the request came to them from an influential quarter. The statutes of the school will probably require Latin to be taught free. The sort of education required at the present day for the lower classes—who will be chiefly benefited by the school—is very different, I need not remark, from what was formerly imparted. Those excellent institutions, the Diocesan Masters' Training Schools, are perhaps more likely than any other to furnish a master with the necessary qualifications, and the trustees would do well to fix the terms of instruction at as low a rate as possible. The Parochial Chapel of Hindley is situate a mile from the school on the north, and Abram Church a mile on the south ; other places of worship belonging to the Established Church being at a much greater distance.

Many houses, chiefly for the labouring classes, have been recently erected not far from the school, and more are contemplated; so that a population of some extent will be soon gathered in its immediate neighbourhood. Should the trustees think fit to select a master from the training schools to which I have referred, the bishop might admit him into orders, and license the school for public worship. Without interfering with the duties of the school, service could be performed every Sunday, and religion would thus be brought nearer the doors of many who, owing to insufficient church accommodation and little pastoral supervision, may otherwise be altogether neglected. The Pastoral Aid Society, or the society for providing additional curates in populous places, might be induced to make a grant to the master for his Sunday services, which, if effected, would produce two desirable ends—firstly, in increasing the stipend of the master; and, secondly, in stamping the school with greater respectability. The chief difficulty will be to raise funds for repairing the old school and building the new—a difficulty which is not, I trust, insurmountable. The accumulations would go some way

towards this end, and I know no other mode of providing the remainder than a public subscription.

I have the honour to be, Sir,

Your most humble and obedient servant,

JOHN LEYLAND.

To Mr. John Wilton.

Cheetham House, Hindley, April 28th, 1851.

My dear Friend,

Very likely you may have been wondering how I
got home from Southport the other day, and as I like
having my own curiosity gratified, I will, as well as I
can, satisfy yours on this point—that is, presuming you to
have any.   When I parted from you at the railway
station I inquired the nearest way to Scarisbrick, and
found, as I suspected, a shorter way than turning back
through the village, with the additional advantage of it
possessing the charm of novelty.   This road is a direct
continuation of the one in which the railway station
stands, and after crossing the moss joins the public
highway near the new church in Scarisbrick, some four
miles distant.   The morning, you will remember, was
fine, and, as a natural consequence, gave animation to
the spirits.   The road traverses a flat country.   A long
line of sandhills skirt the horizon behind and to the
right, the tower and spire of Ormskirk Church rise from
an eminence distant some miles in front, and nearly in
front too, though much less remote, the spire of the
pretty church of Halsall (which I well remember once
visiting when a lad in company with my schoolfellows
from Southport, and with which some red-letter day I
wish to renew my acquaintance), are all the objects,
besides a few cottages and farmhouses, in view.   I had
scarce started on my journey when I fell in with a party
in humble life, consisting of a young woman, a girl, a
man of about five-and-twenty, whose occupation I could
not rightly divine, and a farming lad just verging upon
manhood.   The youth proved a lively and agreeable
companion, and I acquired from him sundry scraps of

information concerning the district through which we were travelling. Mr. Scarisbrick, the proprietor of all the land thereabouts, has an excellent reputation, he said, as a landlord. At the coming rent day he has given notice that he will return 15 per cent to his tenants. A striving and orderly farmer obtains always any reasonable thing he requires.

On the moss we all of us heard the notes of the cuckoo for the first time this spring. The elder of my male companions said his father had told him that if he had money in his pocket when he heard the cuckoo the first time in the season he would never be without the year after, and he had found this to be true. Fortunately, my own purse was not quite empty, so rejoice with me on the pleasant prospect the information has opened. My companions left me a little before I arrived at Scarisbrick Bridge. The rest of my way I pursued alone and on foot. I could not help observing signs of prosperity during the whole of the route. Numerous houses are being built, and a better class of farm buildings; new hedges are in planting, field cultivation is skilfully attended to, and here and there new churches are rising up. I sat down to tea at home about the same hour as I thought you might be sitting down to yours in Southport, after the performance of your day's duties. The twenty years which have run their course since I was last in Southport have passed like a dream. Much of the time is as if it never had been. It seems as if but a few days ago I was a schoolboy poring over my tasks, or wandering among the hills or on the beach for recreation. Another twenty years, if I live to see them, may pass as swiftly; and then, through a short vista, will be seen the term when " our little life is rounded with a sleep." How true are the descriptions of life in the Bible: "It is as a dream when one awaketh;" "Man walketh in a vain shadow;" " He is like grass which groweth in the morning, and in the evening is dried up and withered."

I am, sincerely yours,

JOHN LEYLAND.

To Mr. John Wilton.

Cheetham House, Hindley, May 30th, 1851.

My dear John,

If I admit your apologies, I must beg you to understand that I shall strongly condemn such conduct in the future. I had begun to think that the great crystal loadstone which is drawing men towards it from the extremities of the earth had subjected you to its influence, and I have been wondering what affinities you might be forming under its magic roof.

At last I am become a real farmer. I have got three live cows, with horns and tails all complete. I have got a dairymaid, too; but lest your ideas should be of the ordinary sort respecting so necessary an appendage to a farmer's establishment, it will be necessary for me to describe her. Poets commonly picture a dairymaid as young, rosy, and light-hearted, singing over her milk-pail, and coquetting with admiring rustics. Reality often dispels the most generally received opinions. Mine has weathered sixty odd winters; and although it would be untrue if I were to say there is anything especially ungainly in her person, yet these many years have taken the lightness from her foot and the jauntiness from her carriage. By the way, how differently we speak of age at different periods of life. Of one we say he is a youth of twenty summers; of another he has seen seventy winters. Youth, it seems, is reckoned akin to the sun and flowers, and age to clouds and storms. And winter will come to all of us if life continues! Well, never mind; a sure-founded hope will give light and warmth within, and the remembrance of a well-spent life will be as the evergreens without, and winter we shall find a cheery time after all.

I continue the Sunday evening labours you refer to. Last Sunday week we opened our new room, and I read a sermon before nearly a hundred people.

It was a grand display. We had a fiddle big enough, if the lid had been taken off, to cradle two or three babies. We had also a surprising machine of brass, with I can't tell how many curious twistings, and another brazen instrument which the skilled artist contracted and expanded in a marvellous manner. The Vicar of Wakefield remarked on the occasion of a merry party, "that he did not know whether there was as much wit as usual, but he was certain there was more laughter, which answered the end quite as well;" so I daresay our musicians satisfied the assembly with their noise, if not with their harmony.

I shall be glad to see you on either of the days you mention, along with our young friend, to whom kindly remember me.   I am, sincerely yours,

JOHN LEYLAND.

To Mr. James Finney.

Hindley, June 18th, 1851.

My dear Mr. Finney,

I was disappointed you could not come here when I wrote a few weeks ago, and it is now so near your half-yearly balancing that I know it would be nothing more than a compliment to ask you until you have taken that bull by the horns, pitched him behind you, and are fairly out of the hearing of his bellowing.

I was honoured by the visit of two pillars of the bank on Saturday, who supplied me with an account of your wellbeing.

Tell John I consider myself a letter in his debt, and will pay off my score at an early opportunity.

I am, my dear Sir, truly yours,

JOHN LEYLAND.

To Mr. Thomas Brereton.

Cheetham House, Hindley, June 17th, 1851.

My dear Sir,

I had begun to fear the second letter I sent you was doomed to meet the fate of the first, when, happily, your welcome reply dissipated the misgivings I had for its safety.   I was rejoiced to hear that you and your parents were well, and I hope all of you will long continue so. I was also happy to learn that your professor thinks well of your future prospects. If an earnest love of art for the sake of its spiritualising influence, combined with patient and assiduous industry in aiming at the highest excellence, be the way to success, that success, I feel sure, will one day be yours.

A residence in London at the present time, when so many choice works of art are thrown open, will prove not only interesting, as they are sure to be to all educated persons, but to you inestimably useful. I wish I had the seven league boots of Jack the Giant Killer, which could transport me thither every now and then for a brief space.

I heartily concur with you in believing there can be no earthly pursuit more gratifying than the study of nature and the watching her continual changes, every one of which exhibits a fresh aspect of beauty, and manifests skill and wisdom man can only by little and little scan and appreciate. The telescope and microscope are grand auxiliaries. The discovery of the one was quickly followed by that of the other ; and it has been well said that, whilst the first seemed to remove the Great Creator farther from us, the latter brought Him nearer.

Unassisted by these aids, man could never have dreamed of the vast infinity of the heavens, that near and far systems of worlds revolved, many immensely larger than the earth, or that in the earth the very air he breathed was full of creatures rejoicing in life.

Towards September I think of making a tour somewhere, and very likely I may find my way again to London. I am, faithfully yours,   JOHN LEYLAND.

To Mr. John Wilton.

  Cheetham House, Hindley, July 15th, 1851.

 My dear John,

  After a longer delay than I have wished, I am taking up my pen to reply to your last letter.

Like yourself, I have been continually occupied. In addition to the superintendence of my new buildings, I have had to gather in my hay, the greater part of which I had the good fortune to house in capital condition. Before I had quite finished the weather unfortunately changed. The clouds like an invading army assembled, discharged their artillery, and spread devastation around. When watching the descent of the huge perpendicular drops of rain, and the gusts of wind sweeping fitfully across the fields, I thought the expression Horace Walpole used to employ of "fishing for hay" not much of an exaggeration. At last the clouds rolled away, the sun condescended once more to shine, the wind blew until the moisture had evaporated, and my barn doors closed with the whole crop safely stowed, much to my satisfaction.

I have no hesitation in giving the advice you solicit. I say, stay where you are for the present. Reconsider the subject in the middle of the half-year. As far as hours go you are better off than I was, and I stood it many a long year. When I did leave, friends in whose judgment I placed great reliance expressed doubts as to the policy of the step I was taking.

I was at Warrington last Monday morning, and at Newton Junction I thought I caught a glimpse of you on the platform. Tell me when you write if you were there. Truly yours,

JOHN LEYLAND.

To Mr. J. P. Williams.

Cheetham House, Hindley, July 25th, 1851.

My dear Williams,

The last time we met you complained of my being a letter in your debt ; and as debt suggests duns, bailiffs, and state and circumstances more than disagreeable, I am sending this letter in order to ward off a train of miseries, and to settle my account in your books. Yet, although I have nothing better to speak of than the growth of cabbages, or the dismal feelings

I

engendered by watching a field of hay in the rain, you will accept such lucubrations, I hope, in discharge of my debt :

> "Let not ambition mock their useful toil,
> Their homely joys, and destiny obscure,
> Nor grandeur hear with a disdainful smile
> The short and simple annals of the poor."

Through my residence here I have come to appreciate the change the neighbourhood underwent during the time I lived in Liverpool. The thirteen or fourteen years has sufficed almost to revolutionise both the place and the people.

Formerly I used to know nearly every person in the place; now the faces I meet are for the most part strange. When a lad I remember spending—I had almost said wasting—five good years in trudging backwards and forwards to the Wigan Grammar School, the district between which place and my home was then the pure country. Amberswood Common lay in the way, dreadful in those days to cross in the dark, and the very spot for robbery and murder.

Buildings on this line of road now almost connect the two places. The old common is there still, and unenclosed. Hungry cattle crop its scanty herbage, and flocks of geese wander among the gorse bushes as formerly, but what a different scene it presents! A railway has cut it in two parts, and red brick cottages and tall chimneys, instead of wide open fields, are on its borders. If the lark should rise from its sod, it would as likely be lost in clouds of soot and smoke, as once it was in the brightness of the azure of heaven.

The neighbourhood is wholly destitute of literary resources; and I have often to regret the distance I am from my reading friends in Liverpool, and the agreeable evenings I used to spend at the meetings of our literary society.

Remember me with all kindness to our learned friend the Secretary of the Philomathic Society, and believe that I remain, Sincerely yours,

JOHN LEYLAND.

To Mr. J. P. Williams.

Cheetham House, Hindley, Sept. 3rd, 1851.

My dear Williams,

I do not think you really misunderstood the observations I made in the last letter I wrote to you, and therefore I need not explain them. Along with you, I hope that for a long time to come there may be an interchange of letters between us. I ought to have said what I did not, that I don't like arrears on any side with correspondents. Finney told me you were going to London ; the account of your journey, therefore, did not take me by surprise, nor your report of the delight you experienced, as I know how heartily you enjoy an excursion. I was yet much gratified to have so early a confirmation of my anticipations under your own sign manual.

And so the Exhibition surpassed your expectations. It must, in truth, be a beautiful sight, for all the reports I have heard from those who have seen it concur in your opinion. I don't, though, intend taking any of your reports for granted, but to judge for myself. Afterwards I should like, either at Hindley or Liverpool, whichever will suit you best, to compare notes. I have been looking forward to a four or five weeks' holiday, but my new buildings have given me such a world of trouble, and get on so slowly, that I am afraid I shall have to compress it within shorter limits. I have said I was not surprised to hear of your journey, nor of the pleasure it imparted; and if now I say another communication in your letter did not surprise me either, you will begin to think the organ of wonder to be but faintly developed in my brain. So, however, it is, for the marriage of our friend I looked for as a matter of course. With all my heart I wish him many a long year of happiness. For *you*, procrastinating man, I am in a sea of fears. Don't you see that all your friends are getting noosed, and becoming docile, tractable creatures, while you remain in untamed wildness? The truth must be spoken. You are a stranded vessel, sir, from which the tide is continually receding. Be alive to this fatal position, and make one vigorous effort before the waters are gone quite out of your reach.

I am, truly yours,   JOHN LEYLAND.

To Mr. John Wilton.

London, Sept. 30th, 1851.

My dear John,

When I tell you I only came here last Saturday, and that I am living under the same roof with a friend with whom I have to share what time I can spare from sightseeing, you will understand why I have not written sooner.

Another reason may prevent me from writing again during my stay, and one no less important than the charge of four ladies who are come to town, like myself and thousands of others, to look at the great show, and who rightly think, as old neighbours, that they have some claim to attention. As I have only yet paid a single visit to the Exhibition, I will reserve any mention of it until another opportunity.

I came here, as I said before, on Saturday, and considering the day was none of the finest, I had a pleasant journey enough. Railway travelling is certainly convenient, but it is a poor way of seeing the country. If curiosity be excited in any passing scene, it is only to suffer disappointment—a bridge, the belt of a plantation, the rising embankment, shut out all further prospect. The sight of some of the mansions on the line of route, with their outstretched woods, suggestive of long rent-rolls, luxuriant apartments, choice libraries, and polished society, stirred up for a brief moment the leaven of the old man in the shape of covetousness.

I am, faithfully yours,   JOHN LEYLAND.

To Mr. J. P. Williams.

London, Oct. 6th, 1851.

My dear Williams,

My travels are so circumscribed in comparison with yours, that if it were not for the friendship you extend to the writer, anything I have to say about them would fail to be interesting, more especially on the present occasion, as I am writing from a place you have so lately visited. The first sight of the Exhibition, prepared as I was for its grandeur, exceeded my anticipations. Further examination scarcely kept up the impression. I experienced a feeling of weariness in looking upon heap after heap of shawls, and case after case of cutlery. The greatest wonder far is the building itself, which cannot receive too extravagant praise. I derived much amusement from watching the heterogeneous multitude of spectators. The Koh-i-Noor, the sculpture courts, and the machinery in motion, were the principal centres of attraction, but above all stood the refreshment rooms. The enthusiasm here it was impossible to mistake. So crowded were they that the waiters had difficulty in moving to and fro. One of them, carrying a cup full of coffee in either hand, diverted me with his shrewdness when endeavouring to open a passage through a crowd of ladies. As he advanced step by step he called out, "Scalding, ladies; greasy, ladies," and the ruse succeeded. It reminded me of the man who stole the bones of St. Mark from Alexandria, who cried "Pork, pork," as he passed through the Mahometan inhabitants. I have also been busy with other sights. One day I drank a pot of beer at "The Tabard," Chaucer's hostelrie, in Southwark; on another I inspected the antiquities of the churches of St. Mary Overy and St. Bartholomew, and to a paper in the "Sketch Book" I owe a pleasant ramble in Little Britain. I admired the propriety of the inscription on the hospital of St. Bartholomew: "The Lord comfort him when he lieth sick upon his bed;" "Make thou all his bed in his sickness;" "Blessed is he that considereth the poor and needy, the Lord shall deliver him in the time of trouble."

And when I read over the portals of the chief edifice of commerce, the Exchange, "The earth is the Lord's, and the fulness thereof," I was even more gratified.

I am, truly yours,   JOHN LEYLAND.

To Mr. A. McLaughlin.

Cheetham House, Hindley, Oct. 18th, 1851.

My dear McLaughlin,

After a fortnight's absence, I returned home about a week since.

The comparatively solitary lanes and fields in my neighbourhood present a wide contrast to the tumult of a city containing two millions and a-half of people. It is not my purpose, however, to moralise on the weal or the woe of so vast a multitude, but to say a word or two about my journey. I did not follow your advice in taking a guide to the Exhibition, for two reasons. In the first place, I had previously made myself tolerably familiar with the plan of the building; and in the second, I had to act as cicerone to a party of ladies. The first view of the building outwent all my anticipations. It seemed more like entering some enchanted edifice in fairyland than a building in real life. Whether its many splendours, or an examination into its varied stores, taxed the observant powers too keenly, I cannot say, but I soon felt it pall upon the mind. The sights of the City, and the excursions I made into the suburbs, I enjoyed far better.

I took your counsel, and went to Hampstead and Highgate, which, apart from any literary reminiscences, are worth seeing. I made, also, other literary rambles. One day I dined in Bolt Court, out of veneration to Johnson. I visited Leicester Square, where Reynolds lived; saw Newton's house, and the site of the house where Hogarth lived and executed many of his works; and Brick Court, where poor Goldsmith died.

When next you write tell me if you have had any recent accounts from our transatlantic friends, Russell and Suliot. I am, faithfully yours,

JOHN LEYLAND.

To Mr. John Wilton.

Cheetham House, Hindley, Oct. 23rd, 1851.

My dear John,

Our postman, who is a curious character, brimful

of news as postman should be, and by no means chary of
imparting it, accompanied by his dog, about which he tells
extraordinary stories, surprised me the other morning
with a large packet forwarded from London, containing
no less than three letters and two newspapers, all from
you. If I was ungrateful for so bountiful a contri-
bution, I should deserve to go to those disagreeable
places where wandering ghosts in old times used to be
banished by candle, book, and bell.

You ask for an impossible thing when you ask me to
criticise the letter you refer to. I am utterly incompetent
for any such task ; yet I may say, so far, that no person
could take offence at the goodnatured raillery it contains. The power of expressing ones ideas fluently and
correctly with the pen is a most desirable art. Nothing
is more useful to this end than practice. To read some
of the best authors, and write immediately afterwards
either an abstract of what you have read, or your
thoughts on other subjects, has been often recommended.
Dr. Johnson says : " He who would write with elegance
and ease must give his days and his nights to Addison."

I abandoned my intention of visiting the eastern
counties, having in my recent excursion gone to, and
returned direct, from London. I may possibly write
again soon, if opportunity serves, with some recollections
of my journey.   I am, sincerely yours,

John Leyland.

To Mr. Thomas Brereton.

Cheetham House, Hindley, Oct. 28th, 1851.

My dear Sir,

I had a speedy journey from London the other
day, for I stood in the Wigan market place before four
o'clock in the afternoon. Either I, or the companions
Fate threw me with, must have been remarkably unsocial,
for we scarcely exchanged a word during the whole of
the journey. I was fortunate in the weather, though
with having recently passed through precisely the same
line of route on my way to town, I was not tempted to

look much abroad, but yielded to the seductive pages of Washington Irving, which lent wings even to a locomotive.

The approach of winter is much more marked here than in London. We have trees with not a leaf left on their branches—spendthrifts, I call them, who have parted with their last shilling. Some are like voluptuaries, arrayed for a brief moment only in gorgeous colours, and a few are yet thick with foliage—misers clinging to their wealth to the very last.

You will laugh when I tell you why no letters reached me in town. To avoid errors being made in the address, I arranged for my letters to be sent to a neighbour, who undertook to re-address and forward them. This person is one of the old school, not much versed in the usages of society, and carried out his task in a most original manner. Every letter he opened and read; and as there were none in his opinion worth sending, he kept them all until I came back. It was lucky I was engaged in neither love-plot nor treason, else, sure enough, I should have been discovered.

I remain, truly yours,
JOHN LEYLAND.

To Mr. A. McLaughlin.

Cheetham House, Hindley, Jan. 2nd, 1852.

My dear McLaughlin,

There are times when it would be inexcusable not to communicate with ones friends; and as you are one of the most devoted admirers of the late Foreign Secretary, his recent retirement from office demands from me a few words of condolence.

The event has caused a great sensation in the country. It is true there is a dearth in politics just now, and talkers, like drowning men, catch at straws; but the resignation of a minister whose indomitable spirit has stirred, time after time, the very heart of Europe, is no light affair after all. Some people say his retirement will break up the ministry, while others pertinaciously urge that his embroiling this country continually with foreign powers is a convincing proof of the necessity of the step which has been taken.

These conflicting opinions trouble one sadly when aiming at that too often distorted and disfigured thing called truth. I can only hope that you and I may both live long enough to see what judgment the calm and deliberate historian may pronounce on his labours when existing prejudices are forgotten. Meanwhile rest assured of my sympathy.

In conjunction with a few friends I am labouring to establish an operative reading-room here, which is to open for the first time on Monday; but I am not over sanguine of its success, as the numbers who have hitherto come forward to give it support are very few. The committee guarantee to make good any deficiency for the first three months; and, if it lives no longer, it will, at least, show if there be a taste for reading in the neighbourhood.

Wishing you and all my old friends and associates a happy new year,   I remain, sincerely yours,

JOHN LEYLAND.

To Mr. John Wilton.

Cheetham House, Hindley, Jan. 7th, 1852.

My dear John,

Instead of this season being with you what it ought, a season of sober festivity and rational social enjoyment, I know it is one of extraordinary labour and peculiar hardship. Occupied as you are, if you cannot find time to write, I trust you may at least find time to read what I am writing.

I remember promising you some account of my excursion to the south, but I never got asked for it, so I presume it was not wanted. The principal, and indeed the only present news I have, is, that I am aiding a few friends in establishing an operative reading-room. We have engaged a comfortable apartment in a central position, and have undertaken to supply it with the

London *Times*, some of the local papers, and a variety of magazines. I feel anxious for its success, as there is no place in the neighbourhood besides for recreation or amusement for young men but the public-house. Intellect here is like one of the buried mines of the district—few dream even of its existence, still fewer of its wealth.

Whether our scheme will succeed or not I cannot say, but I earnestly hope it may.

I remain, sincerely yours,
JOHN LEYLAND.

To Mr. John Wilton.

Cheetham House, Hindley, Jan. 28th, 1852.

My dear John,

Do not mistake me; I am not presuming to undertake the reformation of the neighbourhood. I will not affect what I do not feel, and pretend I have no influence. All men, whatever their rank or station, have that—some much, everyone a little. I wish the truth was oftener realised that what appear trifles, such as opinions expressed in conversation or ideas carelessly thrown out, may influence the destiny of those around us through time and eternity. Our responsibility would then stand out too clearly defined to be shunned.

Concerning our reading-room, about which you express so lively an interest, I am glad I can report that it is going on favourably. On the whole, it has met with more friends than I anticipated. The subscription being fixed at a low rate, in order to suit the means of the humblest, will be insufficient to meet the expenses. To be a lasting institution, it should be independent of casual donations.

Our Sunday evening meetings are likewise prospering. The numbers who attend have gradually increased, and the new room is generally as full as it will hold.

I am, truly yours,
JOHN LEYLAND.

To Mr. John D. Finney.

Cheetham House, Hindley, Feb. 11th, 1852.

My dear John,

We country folk live (intellectually, and as regards news) upon simple fare, on dishes compounded for the most part from the homely productions of the neighbourhood. A condiment occasionally from London or foreign parts gives a zest to our ordinary diet, and a bit of scandal is sometimes added by way of garnish. You townspeople vegetate upon dainties, sit down to breakfast with papers supplying the rarities collected by hundreds of caterers north, south, east, and west, and the metropolis is ransacked every morning to add variety to your feasts at night. You will not, therefore, expect news from me after this exordium.

I shall not probably much surprise you when I say I am going on badly with my farm. After the usual preliminaries I bought cows and engaged a dairymaid. The latter was an unlucky venture, for she upset completely the quiet routine of my establishment. Then people came to the house haggling with her about pennies, so I gave up the thing in disgust, sold my cows, and turned my dairymaid adrift. Send me a full account of the " Athenic Society," both collectively and individually. The last time I was in Liverpool I was surprised to find, in a dark-whiskered visage which greeted me, the once smooth face of Arthur Hunt, and was glad to see him hearty as of old. And from the announcement in a recent paper that Haylock's wife had presented him with a daughter, I infer that he, too, is well and happy. Of the other pillars of the State, which are all of good vein and quarry, I have for a long time heard nothing.

When you have no better engagement for a vacant afternoon come over here. I shall be rejoiced to see you.

I am, faithfully yours,

JOHN LEYLAND.

To Mr. John Wilton.

Cheetham House, Hindley, April 10th, 1852.

My dear John,

I have so long an array of debts in the form of letters and newspapers to acknowledge, that I must beg of you not to imitate the merciless creditor in the Scriptures, and say, " Pay me that thou owest."

The melancholy account you give of your brother Abraham I am sorry to receive. Your greatest consolation must be in his peaceful and happy condition; and if things are well with the soul, it matters little comparatively what happens to the body. Earth is so full of cares and griefs, the soul is dragged so low in the mire of corruption, that, truly speaking, it should rather be a cause of rejoicing than of mourning when our friends near safely the end of their painful and perilous journey.

A modern writer has a phrase, " Immortality, the spiritual desire, is the intellectual necessity." Its justness cannot be questioned, for dulness and distraction oppress the soul in our present condition, even in religious investigations.

I am, sincerely yours,

JOHN LEYLAND.

To Frederick Pennington, Esq.

Cheetham House, Hindley, April 17th, 1852.

My dear Sir,

I received your kind note of yesterday, with the accompanying volumes, this morning, for both of which accept my sincere thanks. A memento of any friend could not to me be in a more valued form than in books, nor in books more welcome than those you have selected. I do not pretend to the possession of any great wit; but I must be duller than I am willing to acknowledge if I could not appreciate the beauties of perhaps the first of living poets, or the sentiments of a writer who, happily for the credit of the taste of this generation, is attaining a place in our literature scarcely surpassed by another. There is always something sad in saying the word "farewell;" and I will not cloud your mind—full as it must be with preparations for your voyage, and touched as I am sure it is on parting with your friends—with suggesting ills which never may come. I hope we shall meet again at no distant day, well, and in the possession of mutual friends, if changed at all from now, in a not lessened but widened circle. I am, faithfully yours,

JOHN LEYLAND.

To Mr. John Wilton.

Cheetham House, Hindley, April 22nd, 1852.

My dear John,

"Sorrow not as those without hope." The words are consoling to the bereaved. They form a message of love, speaking of peace now and happiness hereafter. Many privileges the Christian inherits, and he only can comprehend the fulness of the comfort the words convey. When I heard of the fatal certainty of your fears, I was troubled for you. Need I say that I sympathised with you individually, and with every member of your family. The peace which marked the latter end of your brother—certain token of the "good hope through grace" you possess—must tend to assuage the bitterness of your loss. Mysterious are the circumstances time brings forth, and what there may be stored up for us in the hidden future none can tell. Yet this we know, that, if trouble comes, the merciful Dispenser of events has peace and comfort ready to dispense in abounding measure. I am, affectionately yours,

JOHN LEYLAND.

To Mr. J. P. Williams.

Cheetham House, Hindley, June 5th, 1852.

My dear Williams,

Your letter was a reviving cordial, yet the matter

it contained gave me grief as well as joy—joy in the assurance of your good health, grief for your troubles, and, most of all, for the illness of your old housekeeper, and the loss you sustain from her invaluable services. We are worse than fools if we neglect to profit by experience. At some parts of my life I have thought that if I could get rid of something which troubled me, or gain the possession of something which held out the promise of good, I could wend my way in comfort, but if I succeeded in being free from the one or obtaining the other, I found I was just like the man who fought the monster in the ancient fable, who no sooner cut off one head than another sprung up in its place. I have at last come to the conclusion to take everything by the smooth handle, and seek content in whatever happens.

I derive much gratification from watching the bursting of the buds, and the putting forth of the tender shoots in the young trees and hedges I have been planting. The cold dry spring has been unfavourable to the newly-removed plants, yet, spite of the drought, they look healthy and promising, and amply repay me in pleasure for the trouble and expense I have been put to. I don't remember if I told you that about last Christmas I assisted a few friends in establishing an operative reading-room in this neighbourhood. Notwithstanding it was a novel experiment, it will, I think, ultimately take root and thrive. We have just been forming the germs of a library. By dint of some exertion, the committee has obtained sufficient funds to purchase a collection of about a couple of hundred volumes. Can you tell me who is the author of a series of articles which have appeared in the *Liverpool Albion*, entitled, "Liverpool a few years since, by an Old Stager?" They evidence such an acquaintance with, and love for, letters, that coming, as I presume they do, from some of the merchants of your good old town, they have greatly surprised me.

You and McLaughlin were once to have made a journey hither together, and I don't see what there is to hinder you from putting the scheme now into execution. If you can I shall be most happy to see you.

I am, yours truly,
JOHN LEYLAND.

To Mr. Isaac Ellison.

Cheetham House, Hindley, June 16th, 1852.

Dear Mr. Ellison,

A few gentlemen established here, in the middle of last winter, an operative reading-room.

The committee appointed to conduct it have rented a room in a central position, and supplied it with one London and several local papers and various magazines. A small entrance fee and weekly subscription are charged. It is, perhaps, too soon to say the scheme has succeeded; but it has met with as much support, under the circumstances of its being a new and untried thing in the neighbourhood, as its promoters had any reason to expect. Including the committee, the members number about fifty. The aim of the committee is to conduct it without any sectarian bias, either in religion or politics.

So far it has been attended with a money loss, which the committee have defrayed. A small library, the result of a subscription, has been recently added, comprising some of the cheap and useful publications of Chambers and Charles Knight; and if this were extended it might make the institution still more attractive. My object in bringing it before you is to ask if you think Mr. Pemberton Leigh would give it any assistance. No doubt he has many calls on his purse, and I should be unwilling to press the institution unduly on his notice; but if you think he would have pleasure in aiding it, perhaps you will be good enough to mention it to him.

The trustees have not made much progress yet in re-establishing the Lowe School. It has been found necessary to apply to the Court of Chancery for powers to deal with the mines—a process which, unfortunately, may absorb a great part, if not the whole, of the accumulations. Until this is settled the trustees think it would be unadvisable to take further proceedings.

I am, truly yours,
JOHN LEYLAND.

To Mr. J. P. Williams.

Hindley, July 20th, 1852.

My dear Williams,

I feel sure I shall surprise you when I say that in the course of about ten days I am expecting to reside again in your ancient town. I have accepted an appointment offered by two of your directors in a new public company they are establishing, but I cannot at present say whether the engagement will extend for any length of time.

The event has burst suddenly upon me, for at ten o'clock on Saturday forenoon I knew nothing of it, and soon after one the matter was settled.

Acquaint McLaughlin and Finney with the news, and tell the former that, although I shall be occupied with preparations for leaving home, I will endeavour to execute his friend's commission if he will send me immediate directions. If he and his friend can come over, I shall be glad to see them.

I am, faithfully yours,
JOHN LEYLAND.

To Mr. J. P. Williams.

July 26th, 1852.

My dear Williams,

I am giving myself credit for self-denial in the step I am taking, for, spite of the many drawbacks of this neighbourhood, it would be a keen trial if I thought I was to leave it for good and all.

When I am shut up between brick walls, the windows of which open to a prospect of sloping roofs of different degrees of altitude, and long chimneys and short chimneys, now hidden or revealed, as the curling smoke gathers or disperses, with a glimpse perhaps of a busy thoroughfare, where men and women are hurrying to and fro as if their existence depended on their haste, and a din rising up as from the strife of a battlefield, my mind will be apt to recur to scenes where—

> "At morn the skylark singeth,
> At noon the wild bee hummeth,"

and invest them with hues of more than their legitimate brightness.

I have heard nothing yet from McLaughlin. I thought Saturday might have brought him over, and now I have so little time left that I am afraid I shall be unable to render any service to his friend.

I am, faithfully yours,
JOHN LEYLAND.

To Mr. John D. Finney.

19, Hope Place, August 2nd, 1852.

My dear John,

The shifting of the scenes of the great drama in which we are all actors brings about so many strange situations, that unlooked-for or unexpected events need scarcely excite our wonder; yet I do feel surprised on finding myself once again, however short may be the time, a resident in Liverpool. Of course you will have heard of it, as I sent word to your father some days ago.

I am, truly yours,
JOHN LEYLAND.

To Mr. A. McLaughlin.

August 21st, 1852.

My dear McLaughlin,

I return your Paris letter and the "Bubbles," with many thanks. Your warm eulogies of the capital of our Gallic neighbours have strengthened a wish I have long entertained to give it a personal visit, which fortune, I hope at no distant day, may permit. The "Bubbles" are entertaining. The style is somewhat

K

rough and slipshod, but the writer is evidently a close observer, and not without his share of quiet humour.

I am, truly yours,

JOHN LEYLAND.

To Mr. Richard Mather.

19, Hope Place, Liverpool, Sept. 4th, 1852.

My dear Richard,

I was at home a week since for a day, as you would probably hear; but, being jaded and not over-well, I kept close house, otherwise I should have contrived to have seen you before returning. I have fears lest my absence (the duration of which I really cannot at present assign the limits) may interrupt to some extent your Sunday evening meetings. It is superfluous, I know, to remind you of their usefulness, or that, if help fails you in one quarter, it will be supplied in another. Assuredly it is a duty to disseminate God's word, the promise attending upon which will in due time receive its accomplishment. A double blessing, indeed, follows: "He that watereth shall himself be watered;" "Cast thy bread upon the waters, and it shall be found after many days."

Believe me to remain your sincere friend,

JOHN LEYLAND.

To Mr. James Eatock.

Sept. 29th, 1852.

My dear James,

I will trouble you to lay the enclosed letter before the Committee of the Hindley Operative Reading Room at their approaching quarterly meeting.

I am, truly yours,

JOHN LEYLAND.

To the Committee of the Hindley Operative
Reading Room.

Liverpool, Sept. 29th, 1852.

Gentlemen,

I regret much that business has called me where

I am unable to render personal service to our Reading Room. The end of the third quarter of its existence is now approaching, a period which I hope to learn may have proved as prosperous as either of the preceding quarters. If the same principle that has maintained it hitherto be continued, I shall be glad to subscribe to the coming quarter, and will remit my subscription to the Secretary, along with my share of the deficiency of the past, on being informed of the amount.

You will pardon me, I am sure, if I urge you, collectively and individually, to use every exertion to establish its success. Nothing, in my opinion, can exceed its importance. The Institution may, under the blessing of Providence, be a great means in a neighbourhood like Hindley to stir up moral and intellectual life.

Its few supporters and narrow operations should not be permitted either to damp our zeal or paralyse our exertions. We are as if watching the seed germinate, or rather only casting it into the furrow; by-and-by if our endeavours relax not, I have faith to think we shall see the fresh green blade maturing into the vigorous stem, and ripening to a plentiful harvest. Of this I am sure that, however long may be the term of our several lives, there will be no one thing we shall ever look back upon with greater pleasure than this effort to impart to our less fortunate neighbours some of the pleasures derived from reading.

I am, Gentlemen, your sincere friend,
JOHN LEYLAND.

To Richard Pennington, Esq.

Liverpool, October 1st, 1852.

My dear Sir,

I am afraid it may seem that I have been deficient in courtesy in running away from the neighbourhood for these many weeks without even the formality of saying "good-bye." I may, however, allege in excuse, that at the time of my leaving home the duration of my absence was uncertain, as, indeed, it remains to the present moment, only that now, in any case, I can say it is unlikely I shall very soon return.

I have not, meanwhile, been unmindful of the interests of the Grammar School. You are, of course, aware that it was the trustees' wish to obtain powers, in the pending application to the Court of Chancery, to invest the proceeds of the mines at their discretion, but so many difficulties were raised by the Chancery barristers whom we were forced to consult, and so decided was their opinion of the unlikelihood of the court granting such powers, that with much regret I have advised Mr. Taylor to abandon the attempt. The money will, therefore, have to be invested in Government securities, which bring in a low rate of interest.

I am, faithfully yours,
JOHN LEYLAND.

To Mr. Richard Mather.

Liverpool, Oct. 8th, 1852.

My dear Richard,

When men arrive at threescore years and ten they are justified in expecting to ground their arms and enjoy their "*otium cum dignitate*" in peace. It yet not unfrequently occurs that a man's labour, however advanced may be his age, ends only with his life. Believe me, my good friend, I do not willingly disturb the repose of your venerated seventy-six years, but I have a little commission which no one can perform as well as yourself, and which I think will afford you some pleasure. With this letter you will receive a bundle of tracts, which I wish to be distributed, weekly or fortnightly, until they are exhausted, in the close lanes, beginning at the Dog Pool, and going as far as James Mort's house in one direction and Alice Prescott's in another. The district here intimated embraces a little community within itself, apart from the rest of the neighbourhood, and in which I am specially interested.

I am, faithfully yours,
JOHN LEYLAND.

To Mrs. Hannah Halton.

Liverpool, October 22nd, 1852.

My dear Mrs. Halton,

My hands have been fully occupied since I last saw you. For three months I have been engaged in business here, and before that time I was up to the elbows in bricks and mortar—a tribulation than which surely nothing in a Papist's purgatory can be more acutely tormenting. The fact of my being here again will, no doubt, excite your surprise. Although the time of my stay is uncertain, it promises to be long enough to have warranted me in renting a cottage, which I am to enter upon in the course of a few days. Cheetham House is to be tenanted during my absence by an old friend. It is odd how readily we fall into old habits. I turn out to the office every morning to attend business as mechanically as if such duties had never received a moment's interruption. Still I miss what I have left. Instead of enjoying, through the organs of sense, the changes the seasons effect on the landscape, I have to draw upon my imagination to picture its present aspect. The bright green upland changed to a dingy brown, streaks of light breaking through trees that all the summer have been impenetrable masses of verdure, and the wind sporting with the fallen leaves, now, like fickle Fortune, bearing them towards the sky, and now whirling them in the mire to be trodden under foot. Do not imitate my delay in writing, but let me hear soon from you ; and may the blessing of a good Providence rest upon all of us.

I am, your sincere friend,

JOHN LEYLAND.

To Mr. John Wilton.

Oct. 22nd, 1852.

My dear John,

The enclosed piece of silver will repay you the sum laid down for me at the ferry the other evening. I deserve I can't tell what for not sending it sooner.

Faithfully yours,   JOHN LEYLAND.

To Mr. John Wilton.

Oct. 25th, 1852.

Most worthy Sir,

I beg to make a formal apology for the indiscretion of which I have been unwittingly guilty. I am sure I little anticipated that the small piece of coin I sent you would have raised a hurricane so dire; if I had, I would have taken good care it should have kept brightening in my pocket.

I am, your humble servant,

JOHN LEYLAND.

To Mr. John Wilton.

Oct. 27th, 1852.

Thanks for the relief you have afforded me. Money, I begin to perceive, is like a sharp-edged tool, dangerous to meddle with. I'll be careful henceforth, and permit it, if I can, to lie as undisturbed at the bottom of my pocket as Truth in her well. I thought of nothing more in this terrible affair than paying what I considered a just debt. I know wits sneer at such things, but then I don't aim at being a wit. After all, I cannot help thinking an imp of mischief must have lurked in that unlucky coin, else it would never have evoked so terrible a commotion.

I remain, as in duty bound,

Your humble servant,

JOHN LEYLAND.

To Mr. Richard Mather.

Liverpool, Oct. 29th, 1852.

My dear Richard,

It is never a welcome task to convey unpleasant tidings, and I am sorry a duty of this sort now devolves upon me. I have been flattering myself that I have been of some use at your weekly meetings, and for this reason I feel loth to say that I have decided on remaining here some time. Nevertheless, I am looking forward to a not-very-distant future, when my services may be again at your disposal.

The providences of God are inscrutable : we tarry a little here and a little there, led, as the unthinking would say, by mere accident, when all the time we are instruments in the hand of Omnipotence, working out ends we neither seek nor foresee.

I remain, your sincere friend,

JOHN LEYLAND.

To Mr. Thomas Brereton.

Liverpool, Dec. 20th, 1852.

My dear Sir,

The address of this letter will inform you whence I am writing. If it occasions you surprise, the surprise may possibly be heightened when I tell you that I have connected myself with an Electric Telegraph Company. "What!" I can fancy you exclaiming, "an antiquary in taste, and a Tory in politics, working at the Electric Telegraph! It is satire surely!" So, however, in sober truth it is. I have accepted an. offer from the promoters of the company to fulfil certain duties which are not very dissimilar from those I formerly discharged at the bank.

Whenever I see a notice of modern paintings in the papers I always look amongst the artists' names in the hope of finding yours. If I have failed in finding it hitherto, I feel assured I shall see it some day, and with honourable mention. Hard labour is necessary to attain skill in any study, and when it is obtained still more labour is needed to produce any important work, and the term of life is almost exhausted by the time men are fitted to commence its duties. Of all plain things nothing is plainer than the truth of the text, "By the sweat of thy brow thou shall eat bread."

I am, faithfully yours,

JOHN LEYLAND.

To Alfred Pennington, Esq.

Liverpool, December 20th, 1852.

My dear Sir,

I shall have much pleasure in dining with your

mother on Christmas day. So many of these days have been spent in your and your relatives' society, that when the custom is broken, as broken, I suppose, like every other earthly thing besides, it must be some time or other, I shall feel, if I am a survivor, very considerable regret.

The extraordinary rains that for so long a time have kept falling must have done a serious amount of damage in the country. I have not heard how your neighbourhood has fared. The north generally has escaped better than the south and midland districts, although the rains have been pretty equally distributed. The reason may possibly be that the distance between the two seas in the north is narrower and the rivers deeper and wider, which have drawn off the waters sooner. A friend of mine, whose family lives near Salisbury, a district that has suffered considerably from the floods, informed me the other day that one of his neighbours had his orchard buried in the waters, and another had not seen his farm for six weeks. Next year's wheat crop must suffer heavily in consequence.

I was at an excellent performance of the Messiah last week, at the Philharmonic Hall. The orchestra was large, and every part ably supported. It would have been a high treat to you, loving, as you do, sacred music so much. The choruses were gone through grandly, and often as I had heard them before, I could not help admiring anew the sublime genius that could conceive them.   I am, truly yours,

JOHN LEYLAND.

To Charles Seymour, Esq.

Liverpool, Dec. 22nd, 1852.

My dear Sir,

About ten days ago I was in Manchester for a short time, and four or five years since I was also there. These are the only visits I have paid to Manchester for the last twelve or thirteen years. On both occasions I went on business, and was compelled to make an immediate return. On my first visit I stayed only two or three hours; on the last, although I was there a night, I arrived late in the day, and returned by an early train the following morning.

It seems necessary to enter into these explanations when addressing one with whom Manchester in former years was in my mind identified. I do not know why the intercourse between us ceased. I have always regretted it on my part, and I have kept hoping that some lucky accident would throw us together again. I have made inquiries at different times about your family, but I have learned little. I have been told that you have lost a brother, which, from the description given to me, I guess to be William.

An advertisement in a newspaper of your old house in Upper Brook Street being to let, and stating it to have been the residence of the *late* R. Seymour, acquainted me with the death of your father.

This is all I know of the events which have occurred in your family since we met.

The last time I was in Manchester I searched the directory for your name and found it, whence I obtained your present address.

I looked in vain for Roger's.

My own history is soon told. Like other people, I have had my troubles; but, on the whole, the twelve or thirteen years—a large proportion of any man's life—has been with me as little diversified as it well could be. You will, no doubt, remember my becoming connected with a bank in this town, which connection continued until the summer of 1850—nearly fourteen years—when I gave it up in order to spend, as I thought, the remainder of my days where I first drew breath—at Hindley. In the middle of last summer I was induced to come hither again—not to the bank, but to a new telegraph company that two of the bank directors are promoting. Soon after I first came to Liverpool to reside I lost my aunt, and ten years after that my mother, so that for some years I have been alone in the world. It is needless to say that the hope of hearing from you gives me pleasure—a pleasure certainly not unmixed with apprehensions, for all at once I have to hear of the changes of so many years.

Believe me, my dear Sir, I am, sincerely yours,

JOHN LEYLAND.

To Mr. John Wilton.

Dec. 27th, 1852.

My dear Friend,

I have returned "Southey's Life," along with two other books, for which I return you many thanks. They have afforded me much pleasure.

Anyone must rise from the perusal of Southey's correspondence, of which chiefly the "Life" consists, with a higher opinion of his character as a man than he would obtain from a study of what may be properly called his works. At first I thought he was scarcely what one could call a loveable man. Between his disposition and that of Walter Scott there seemed to be a wide difference ; but as he advanced in life, and as domestic sorrows gathered round him, his better qualities developed. It is the manifestation of the old truth—affliction is the crucible in which the metal is refined. One cannot help regretting that a mind like his should have been disturbed by anxieties for providing the ways and means for his family. How much more might he have done if his position had been one of thorough and perfect independence. Give me an evening soon, and we will talk these things over.

I wish you all the good wishes of the season, if you are quick in poking me up. If not, why, even then I wouldn't wish the Christmas to be a sad one, nor the New Year to bring you anything but happiness.

Affectionately yours,   JOHN LEYLAND.

To Mr. James Eatock.

Liverpool, Dec. 29th, 1852.

My dear James,

I have not heard a single word for some time about the reading-room. I do not know whether its old supporters continue their help, or so much as if the little fire we tried with so much difficulty to ignite be still alive or has died out. If its prospects are not what its friends could wish, they should not be discouraged. Assuming that it is bad, perseverance will eventually do something. If it be carried on as before, I will thank you to place my name again on the committee; and when you have made up your last quarter's accounts to let me know what my share of the deficiency is, and I will find some way of sending it to you.

I have not heard anything either of your Sunday evening meetings, but I have less anxiety for them than for the reading-room, as those whom they interest may be better counted on than the supporters of the reading-room. Our venerable friend Richard I trust keeps well. I wrote to him after the last visit I paid to Hindley, and thought perhaps it might have provoked a reply, but I have been disappointed. Pray give to him my kind regards, and believe me to remain,
Sincerely yours,
JOHN LEYLAND.

———————

To Mr. John Wilton.

Jan. 3rd, 1853.

My dear Friend,
I beg to thank you for your kind note of yesterday, and for the book which accompanied it. As you know, I am a very miser in books. Judge, then, how I shall value your gift, which, apart from its literary value, is so beautiful in type and binding.

You refer to our long friendship. Certainly there has never been a shadow of coldness between us, and I have no fear for it in the future. Friendship in this troubled state is precious. To me, having no household ties, life without it would be terribly dreary.

I was concerned to hear of the illness of your brother; but do not needlessly alarm yourself—a few days may bring about a favourable change in his complaint.
I am, affectionately yours,
JOHN LEYLAND.

To the Trustees of the Lowe School.

Liverpool, January 4th, 1853.

Gentlemen,

I am sorry I shall be unable to meet you at the approaching annual meeting, so as to give an account personally of my stewardship for the past year, but I will, instead, make as full a statement as I can by letter.

The proceedings connected with the application to the Court of Chancery, ordered at the last annual meeting, have not yet, I regret to say, been brought to a conclusion. Several legal difficulties have arisen to prevent the trustees from obtaining the powers they desire, the nature of which Mr. Taylor (who intends being present at the meeting) will be better able to explain than me, as well as the position in which the application at the present moment stands. The first business of the meeting is to examine, and, if found correct, to pass the accounts for the past year.

You will next have to determine on the advisability of investing £150 out of the £178 8s. 7d. now standing to the trustees' credit at the bank.

The treasurer of the Liverpool Corporation asks for an indemnity to be given to the corporation for the missing bond of £150. You will remember that £250 is lent altogether to the corporation, and if £150 more be added, the treasurer proposes to give one new bond for £400.

The present abundance of money may perhaps determine the corporation to offer a lower rate of interest on the new bond. If so, it will be requisite to fix what terms the trustees will accept.

As I probably may remain here for some time, it would be well if you were to appoint some other person in my place to fill the office of acting trustee, as just now the school is at a critical period of its history.

The collector of the Crook and Dukinfield charities refuses to pay the sums he has received until the school be re-established, and it will be for you to decide whether you will wait his time, or compel him to make immediate payment.

The only other business requiring the trustees' attention is to take into consideration the following proposal: I am willing to give 400 square yards of the land I own near the Strangeways Hall, for a site for the new school, on condition that the mines be reserved for my use, and a fence-wall be raised of at least five feet high round the boundary. If the trustees accept this offer, I shall have much pleasure in contributing the land as my subscription to the new school. Money for the erection of buildings would then only have to be raised. An architect here has furnished me with a design for the new school, which he estimates to cost £500. The design accompanies this letter. If the subscriptions prove successful, any overplus may be expended in repairing the old buildings. I also send a plan of the plot of land I offer, and a statement furnished by the bank of the transactions with them for the past year.

I am, Gentlemen, truly yours,
JOHN LEYLAND.

To Mrs. H. F. Ingham.

Everton, January 5th, 1853.

My dear Mrs. Ingham,

When I called upon you a few days before I came here I was uncertain of the length of my stay, and now, nearly six months afterwards, I cannot yet say anything definite : it may be a year, or even years. But whatever uncertainty may exist on this point, I am satisfied it is time to inquire if you and your family are well.

Your daughters are, I daresay, making progress with their music and drawing. When I think of them, recollections occur of what I suppose I must now call a past generation. It seems only yesterday that I was looking at their mother's drawings, and one of a gipsy woman I remember as vividly as if it were before my eyes at the present moment, and their mother's mother pointing out a patch stitched crosswise on her check apron, which I thought a very marvel of excellence.

One of your daughters, on some convenient opportunity, may perhaps favour me with a few lines informing me of your welfare.   I remain, sincerely yours,

JOHN LEYLAND.

To Alfred Pennington, Esq.

Liverpool, Feb. 5th, 1853.

My dear Sir,

There is to be a meeting of the trustees of the Grammar School on Wednesday, the 16th of this month, at which I have promised to be present.   Since I made the arrangement to come over, a thought has struck me, which I will give you the benefit of.

I remember a conversation occurring one evening in the committee of the Reading Room on the desirability of having a merry-making at Christmas in the shape of a tea-party, as it might tend to make the institution more popular.   Now, if you have already had nothing of the kind, if it meets your approval, if you think it may succeed, if the 16th inst. be convenient for the purpose (a good many *ifs* by the way), why then it would afford me considerable gratification to be present. The Reading Room is calculated to do a great deal of good, and I therefore feel anxious for it to prosper.

I am, faithfully yours,

JOHN LEYLAND.

To Mr. John Wilton.

Feb. 10th, 1853.

My dear John,

Herewith I return, with many thanks, the " Successful Merchant."   It is something out of the common run of books, both as regards the subject and the manner in which it is treated.

Mr. Budgett was a wonderful man, wonderful for the quickness of his perception, for his energy, for his perseverance, for his success, for his bounties.   But there was one grand defect in his character—the keenness of his bargaining.   His biographer, I was glad to see, condemns it freely.   If he had been less hard in his buying and selling, his character would have been a model worthy of imitation. I like the book, though not as a biography. According to the modern system of biography, the subject of the book is made to relate, in diaries, letters, and records of conversation, his own history. Mr. Budgett's biographer, on the contrary, uses the events of his life just as so many opportunities for uttering maxims of religion and morality.

I am, sincerely yours,

JOHN LEYLAND.

To Mr. John Wilton.

Dog and Partridge Inn, Wigan, Feb. 16th, 1853.

My dear Fellow,

I am in a state of exuberant felicity. The animating spring within gushes forth with unwonted vigour, while a tender sympathy urges me to channel its overflowing stream to refresh any waste there may be in dingy Water Street. The scenes of this neighbourhood are dear to me, notwithstanding their sootiness.

At the present moment I am seated in the snug apartment of an old-fashioned inn, with a glowing fire in the grate, recent papers lying on the table, and a vessel of crystal filled with a beverage clear, sparkling, and, in the estimation of men of an oddish turn of thinking, delicious as the nectar of the ancient gods.

Two hours hence will be a meeting of our Grammar School trustees, which I expect to result in measures for the speedy re-establishment of a school, interesting to me if from no other reason for two years' associations of happy boyhood. After the meeting comes the first annual celebration of our Operative Reading Room. Was ever day before so lucky! Mark it, John, with red in the calendar; and, d'ye hear—let the 16th of February be observed henceforward as a perpetual holiday. No more toiling on it, mind that. Hurrah! If I was out of doors now, wouldn't I fling up my hat. Ay! high as the clouds, if there be any. Hurrah!

JOHN LEYLAND.

To Mr. John Wilton.

11 P.M., Feb. 17th, 1853.

My dear Friend,

In the flush of my joy yesterday I stretched out my hand to bestow on you its over-abundant issue; to-day I have humbly to crave you to return it to me again. An unnatural tension is invariably followed by as unnatural a collapse. The thermometer, from standing at the temperature of the tropics, has gone down to zero, and what constitution can bear so rapid a transition? Would that I could evoke the spirit of last night, and unrol the exciting picture: the faces of youths and maidens radiant with glee; the fountains of tea and coffee; the piles of bread and butter, the oranges and lemonade; the interminable dance—up, down, back again, round, round, and round! A great phenomenon occurred. The lights in the room where we had our gathering became infected with the motion of the dancers, and whirled slowly round at the echo of the fiddle-strings.

On going home, the very houses reeled in a courtly sort of step, and, what is still more extraordinary, the stately buildings in this grave old town of Liverpool, have had all day a disposition to start off in a waltz. What can have caused such remarkable occurrences?

> " Sleep dwell upon thine eyes,
> Peace in thy breast."

Good night,

JOHN LEYLAND.

To Richard Pennington, Esq.

Liverpool, Feb. 23rd, 1853.

My dear Sir,

The school meeting was badly attended, Mr. Gaskell, Mr. Tickle, and myself, being the only trustees present. The business transacted was briefly as follows:—The accounts for the past year were examined and passed. Mr. Taylor was instructed to hasten the proceedings in Chancery, and to proceed against the collector of the Crook and Dukinfield moneys. I was authorised to invest an additional £150 with the Liverpool Corporation, and requested to continue to be the acting trustee, to which I consented, Mr. Gaskell having promised me his assistance.

The offer I made of a site for the new school was considered. Mr. Tickle raised objections to it; and although Mr. Gaskell and myself were in its favour, we thought it prudent to defer a decision· until a fuller meeting.

It was, however, agreed unanimously that a new school should be built by subscription.

I submitted a design for the new building, prepared by an architect of this town, which was approved by the meeting. The design is to be lithographed, five hundred copies taken, and I am to draw up a circular to accompany it. I acquainted your brother with our proceedings, and he suggested that a site should be fixed upon before subscriptions are solicited, as many may refuse giving if there were any uncertainty where the school is to stand. I agree with him, and think that a meeting had better be called for the special purpose of deciding the question.

If my offer of a site should be declined, I would recommend the trustees to lease from the Bridgewater Trustees a plot of land up to the public road, directly in front of the old school, so that the question may be put fairly to rest, and subscriptions at once set on foot.

I am, very truly yours,
JOHN LEYLAND.

To Miss M. J. Ingham.

Liverpool, March 23rd, 1853.

My dear Friend,

Thank you for your kind letter. The pleasure it gave me was increased by the promise you make to write frequently. I will reply as often as I can, but I am afraid I must not be depended upon regularly. Gentlemen, you know, are occupied with business the chief part of every day, and what little time remains has to be apportioned among a variety of occupations. With young ladies it is different. Letter-writing ought to be one of their principal duties, inasmuch as it is an important way of adding to their proficiency in English composition—an art which, if pursued with the earnestness it deserves, is a means of contributing largely to their happiness and usefulness in after-life. The two most accomplished letter-writers of any age or country have been ladies. The racy wit and sterling sense of one—Lady Mary Wortley Montague—have charmed the book-loving world for more than a century; and the vivacity and playful sallies of the other—Madame de Sevigne—have captivated her readers for nearly two. A host of ladies have distinguished themselves in modern times in the lighter branches of literature; and even in the department of the sciences, a path usually considered unsafe for females to tread, the name of Mrs. Somerville fills a distinguished place.

In referring to these examples I have no wish to stimulate your ambition. Ambition is a vice; therefore it must not be cherished. Nevertheless, it is an important duty to cultivate the faculties God has given us. By so doing new sources of enjoyment are opened of the highest and purest character.

The learning of French, about which you inquire, is likewise of importance, almost as much, indeed, as English composition. Twenty or thirty years ago it was looked upon merely as an accomplishment, now it has become a necessity. You will perhaps find more difficulty with the ear than the tongue. When the language is spoken quickly the words run into one another, and seem different from what they really are. A good master will make the study perfectly easy. The elementary works I should recommend are—De Fiva's Grammar, De Porquet's Le Tresor, Chambaud's Fables, and L'Echo-de-Paris, with which, for a time, you may get on very well.

Your master, however, will no doubt wish you to

study from the books he is in the habit of using. After you have advanced a certain stage, and made good your footing, you may then pursue it without a master, but by no means begin without one.

I am, faithfully yours,

JOHN LEYLAND.

To Mr. Thomas Brereton.

Liverpool, April 1st, 1853.

My dear Sir,

This year's Liverpool exhibition of paintings was, as I daresay you would learn from the papers, unusually good. Unluckily, I put off going until the last week, and when I presented myself at the door, found, to my great disappointment, that I was just a day too late. The pre-Raphaelites were in great force, and carried away the chief prize.

Did you ever notice, during your residence in Liverpool, a painting on glass in Brownlow Hill, over an inn door, representing a female shielding a light with one hand, which she was carrying in the other? Behind the hand a jet of gas was placed, and when lit up at night had a very striking effect. The design is old, but the application was to me entirely new.

In the same street I remember another work of art, perfectly unique, I should say, in its way. This was the signboard of a tailor, bearing the portentous announcement, "Gentlemen's own materials made up." No further explanation was given, and how the barbarous occupation was conducted remained, so far as the signboard was concerned, an impenetrable mystery.

Both these curiosities may be still in existence, though I have not seen them for some time. They were brought to my recollection recently from observing the names of "Dodge," "Daggers," and "Payne," on the signplates of certain gentlemen of the legal profession. The law may well have terrors when accredited officers bear such ominous names. In rivalship with these are the titles of certain mercantile firms. A few years ago there were in this town, and may be yet for anything I know to the contrary, two remarkable for the odd contrast of names they present : one was " Moore and Christian," the other " Brown and Green." In London there is " Flint and Steel," who, by the rule of right, should follow the gunmaking or hardware business ; and I have heard elsewhere of " Bury and Graves," who, by the same rule, ought to be undertakers or gravediggers.

Having said my say, I will add nothing more than that,

I remain, sincerely yours,

JOHN LEYLAND.

To Mr. John Wilton.

Liverpool, April 25th, 1853.

My dear Friend,

But for the consideration of your colleagues, who, I suppose, are affected more or less by your absence, I should advise you to stay where you are longer than you propose. You derived so much benefit from your former sojourn, that I have no doubt you will in time receive equal advantage now. How can a week or two's change remedy the wear and tear caused by many times the number of months of close application ?

Although I have never been near Malvern, yet, from the letters which passed between us during your former visit, and the talk we have had about it since, I seem to be familiar with its noble hills, the extended valleys stretching below them, and the rich green pastures, making the cattle feeding on them fat and lazy, the teeming orchards, and the proud historic memorials they contain. The motley crowd of migratory visitors will afford you amusing material for observation. Many, doubtless, come vainly hoping that a purgatory of water may purify the body from the sins of a life of dissipation, just as others trust to a purgatory of fire to cleanse the sin of the soul.   I am, faithfully yours,

JOHN LEYLAND.

To the Right Hon. Thomas Pemberton Leigh.

Liverpool, April 26th, 1853.

Sir,

I am sure it will afford you pleasure to hear of the progress which is being made in the affairs of the Hindley Grammar School.

The new trustees, on their appointment (for which they are indebted to your kind exertions), found the estate in the following condition :—

The schoolhouse was in the occupation of a man who refused to pay rent. Two rent charges of a pound each had for years been received by the administrator of other charities in a neighbouring township, and distributed in that township. The sum of £250 invested with the Liverpool Corporation was safe, certainly, interest as well as principal; but the mines underneath the freehold were claimed by the trustees of the Duke of Bridgewater, and leased by them for their own profit. Very nearly the whole property was being appropriated by others.

Now, although the estate has suffered several years' loss of income, so much has been realised that, with the accumulations of the interest on the Liverpool Corporation bonds and a balance of moneys lying in the hands of Mr. Ellison, the trustees have been enabled to increase their investment with the Liverpool Corporation from £250 to £400.

The trustees directed their attention early to ascertain the grounds on which the trustees of the late Duke of Bridgewater claimed the mines under the school estate, and in this inquiry they were met in the most courteous spirit by the law agents of those trustees, who no sooner found their claim to be unjust than they at once relinquished it. It then became requisite to obtain powers from the Court of Chancery to deal with the mines. The application is now pending, and the trustees confidently hope this will in a short time also be settled.

The trustees now deem it desirable to commence raising funds for the erection of a new school, as the accompanying circular will inform you. The object of my letter rests in this last paragraph, which is to solicit your aid towards this desirable object.

    I have the honour to be, Sir,

        Your very humble and obedient servant,

JOHN LEYLAND.

To Mr. Richard Mather.

Liverpool, April 27th, 1853.

Dear Richard,

    The enclosed circular will inform you that the trustees of the Grammar School purpose erecting a new school. I am sure you will aid them in effecting so desirable an object, and if you will permit your contribution to pass through my hands I shall esteem it a favour.

    The Reading Room is another pet institution of mine, and wants help also, but I must content myself with recommending one of these institutions at a time. The school cannot fail of doing good in a manufacturing and rapidly-increasing population like Hindley. To those blessed with abundance no better way can be found to evidence their gratitude to the Great Giver than by promoting establishments for the training of the young in order and virtue, and for providing for those of older years wholesome provision for the mind. I am greatly deceived if the influence of these institutions does not, in time, become apparent : a little leaven leavens the whole lump. The foundation you made last year will add strength to the movement.

    James Eatock tells me you wish me to be present at a meeting of your trustees, which you are desirous of having. I do not know when I shall next be over, but I daresay it will be in course of the next five or six weeks. As soon as I can name the day I will acquaint you.   I am, your sincere friend,

JOHN LEYLAND.

To Mr. John Wilton.

Liverpool, April 29th, 1853.

My dear John,

If it be your intention to adhere to your original plan of returning home to-morrow, this letter may possibly reach you just before setting out; but if it should not, or if it miss you altogether, you will suffer no loss, as I have nothing to say. Opportunity served me to write, and I would not forego it. I can think of nothing. My mental faculties might be subject to a frost so severe as not to let a stray thought escape from its icy grasp. I have looked up at the ceiling and down at the floor, and peered into the fire, without finding aught to stimulate my ideas.

My pen is in order, and my inkstand is filled with ink, but what of that? In some hands even so desperately fixed they would prove as effective as a well-tempered broadsword and valiant heart would to a warrior in the heat of battle, but even this conviction does not wake my apathy. I am like an angler in fishless waters; and as anglers are proverbial for their patience, so in that point also the resemblance holds good, for, believe me, I am full of that exemplary virtue, and I can close my letter in the best temper with myself. I remain, your sincere friend,

JOHN LEYLAND.

To John Pennington, Esq.

Liverpool, May 6th, 1853.

My dear John,

I have pleasure in enclosing a year's subscription to the proposed "Hindley Cricket Club," and trust it may meet with adequate support.

I agree with you in thinking it will be beneficial to the neighbourhood, and it may prove so in more ways than one. There is no need to refer to the healthy exercise it affords—that is patent to everybody; but what I value quite as much as that, or, indeed, rather more, is the opportunity it will afford of different classes meeting on a common ground, and having an interest in the same pursuits. A deep gulf unfortunately separates the rich from the poor in this country.

Your Cricket Club and our Reading Room may tend possibly to bridge over the gulf, at the least, at Hindley.

If you should ever have an anniversary dinner or anything of the sort, I will attend if you will give me timely notice.   I am, yours sincerely,

JOHN LEYLAND.

To Col. the Hon. C. B. Phipps.

Liverpool, May 9th, 1853.

Sir,

The trustees of an old grammar school, called the Lowe School, one of whom I have the honour to be, are endeavouring to raise funds for the building of a new master's house and school, an account of which will be found in the accompanying circular. The neighbourhood it is situated in contains few families able to assist in accomplishing a work necessary anywhere, as is evident from the public and private efforts now being made throughout the kingdom for the extension of education, but especially so in a place where the population has rapidly outgrown all provision both for education and religion like Hindley.

The motive I have in sending the circular is to ask of you the favour to lay it before Her Majesty the Queen, in the hope that she may graciously permit the trustees to place her name at the head of the subscription list. Her Majesty's name would be a tower of strength to the trustees in asking aid, as they must do, from those who have no tie or connection with the neighbourhood.

I have the honour to be, sir,
Your most humble and obedient servant,
JOHN LEYLAND.

To Richard Pennington, Esq.

Liverpool, May 11th, 1853.

My dear Sir,

Absence from home yesterday prevented me from receiving your letter of the 9th instant until several hours after post time.

The letter you mention having addressed to Hope Place I never got, but I will have it inquired for.

The circulars were equally divided among the six trustees and your brother. The latter, not being a trustee, seems at present unwilling to take any active part in the task. If he continues in the same mind, the circulars he has can be transferred to you. I sent Mr. Eckersley an equal number with the rest, enclosing them in Mr. Gaskell's parcel. When I heard they had not reached him I made inquiries, and found Mr. Gaskell had never delivered them. I wrote on Monday to Mr. Eckersley telling him this.

The original plan of the school, you will remember, was to give accommodation for fifty boys, and the estimated cost £500. Afterwards we decided to increase the schoolroom to double the size. Taking into account the repairs required at the old buildings and the increased cost of the new, it would have been better if we had started by saying we wanted £1,000 or £1,200.

I have gone on badly here. Everybody I ask tells me the school is too far off for them to give it any help.

It seems you have been in communication with Mr. Pemberton Leigh as well as me. I had a letter from him before I knew you had written, in which he says he will contribute £25.

I have also written to the Earl of Ellesmere, but I have not yet had a reply. I expect to be over at Hindley at the end of next week, and if the circulars your brother has should be insufficient for your requirements, let me know before then, and I will bring some of mine with me, though I have not many to spare.

The Liverpool Corporation have behaved handsomely. Not only have they agreed to allow the old rate of interest on the new bond, but they have remitted certain fees they are in the habit of charging.

I am, truly yours,

JOHN LEYLAND.

To Richard Pennington, Esq.

Liverpool, May 16th, 1853.

My dear Sir,

You are working bravely. Keep on; don't let your zeal slacken, and the rest of the trustees will have nothing to do but to send a cheer now and then of congratulation.

I have put my own name down for £25; Mr. Pemberton Leigh's £25, and a guinea each from two other persons, are all I have got. As I told you before, I doubt I shall not be able to do much here, still I hope to do more than I have done yet.

I enclose the plan as requested. The schoolroom, you will see, can be drawn out to any length without interfering with the rest of the building. Has Mr. Eckersley got his circulars? If you are likely to want more than you have, let me know before Friday.

I am, in haste, truly yours,

JOHN LEYLAND.

To Charles T. Bright, Esq.

Liverpool, May 18th, 1853.

My dear Sir,

I have called twice at 38, Kensington, since you left. The first time I was unable to gain admission; the second I went over the whole house from the attics to the coal cellar, and I have to report that everything is in perfect safety. The good lady in charge appeared overjoyed to see me. It is her miserable fate to have no one to talk to, and as dammed-up waters often find some mode of escape, so my visit was a vent for her long-smothered loquacity.

Many years of happiness, I hope, lie in store for you and Mrs. Bright, in the relations you have so recently assumed. I am, faithfully yours,

JOHN LEYLAND.

To Colonel The Honourable C. B. Phipps.

Liverpool, May 24th, 1853.

Sir,

I beg to thank you for the reply you made to the letter I addressed to you on the subject of the " Lowe Grammar School." The tenor of it, I need not say, was different from what I could have wished it to have been. I do not know whether my good or evil genius has influenced me to renew the subject, but, at any rate, I trust that the step may not be construed into any wish to press my suit beyond the bounds of courtesy and respect.

The rule Her Majesty has laid down to limit her charities to objects which are of general application is, no doubt, reasonable and just, and I am free to admit that the school whose interests I advocate does not fall within the limit. At the same time there are one or two reasons to justify an exception in its favour.

It is an old foundation ; for at least two centuries it has had an influence in moulding the youth of the neighbourhood into loyal subjects and useful citizens ; moreover, Her Majesty is duchess of the county in which it is situate.

To me the school is endeared by early associations. It was the first boys' school I attended, and the rudiments of what little I know were learned there ; so that I feel desirous of doing what I can to promote its welfare. The idea forced itself upon my mind that I might gain for it the patronage and support of royalty, and it became to me what the fresh weeds and the thorn branch with berries on it were to Columbus in his voyage of discovery—an encouragement of success. Excuse me for still clinging to this hope. I cannot, however, say or do more. The facts are before you, and, if not presuming too much, I would request you to reconsider whether the school may not be commended to Her Majesty for her support.

·I have the honour to be, Sir,

Your most humble and obedient servant,

JOHN LEYLAND.

To Mr. George Orton Owen.

June 11th, 1853.

My dear Owen,

If it has ever been your lot to watch a grocer's apprentice attempt to fold some commodity possessing little or no cohesive power—coffee-berries, for instance—in a small piece of paper, how, if he has the luck to make good one end, out they burst at the other, or if in a propitious moment he secures both, how they escape from the middle, you may form an idea of my present difficulty in seeking to compress in this small note the many apologies I have to make for keeping the "Faggot of French Sticks" so long, and the many thanks that are due for the great pleasure the reading of it has afforded me. The day I brought home your book I deposited it carefully on a bookshelf, and I am ashamed to say never once thought more of it until, by a sort of accident the other day, to my great surprise, I found a strange-looking volume, which proved to be no other than it. The book contains much information, and ought to be given to every Englishman to ruminate upon who has an overweening admiration for his own country. I am, faithfully yours,

JOHN LEYLAND.

To James Bent, Esq.

Liverpool, June 11th, 1853.

My dear Sir,

I was vexed to find you had left town without saying good-bye. I called in Bedford-street before the time you had fixed for leaving to learn that you were then staying with Mr. Guest, and I presume you must have gone away direct from his house.

Happily, your new home is not at too great a distance to shut out the hope of an occasional meeting. I know well what the trouble of removing is, and can understand that, although two months have since passed, you are not yet perfectly settled. The most disagreeable part of the business, however, must be over, and your anxieties sufficiently laid at rest to permit you to enjoy the pleasures of this month of June in your country neighbourhood. Lilacs and laburnums and the superb flower of the chestnut are now with us, as no doubt with you, in the fulness of their glory.

Old green lanes—though here they are not—I can picture, gay with the golden gorse flower, and the pleasant rambles they invite, made pleasanter by the skirting hedges perfuming them with the scent of hawthorn blossoms.

The month of June, like a queenly dame, wears precious gems in her diadem. The great Being who has scattered the flowers, evidences of His goodness, in the pathway of even the humblest, may, I hope, grant you and Mrs. Bent health and long life to admire and enjoy them, and the unction of His spirit, that you may be fitted for that future state which the setting of every sun is fast hastening.

I remain, my dear Sir, sincerely yours,

JOHN LEYLAND.

———

To John Pennington, Esq.

Liverpool, June 29th, 1853.

My dear Friend,

I take the first opportunity which has occurred since receiving your letter to express the satisfaction I experienced on reading so flourishing a report of the Cricket Club; a result due, I am sure, to your own indefatigable exertions. Especially I congratulate you on securing the powerful support of Mr. Pemberton Leigh, whose example in promoting good objects we should all do well to imitate. If possible, I will join your festivities in August. I am, faithfully yours,

JOHN LEYLAND.

———

To Mr. Richard Mather.

Liverpool, July 18th, 1853.

Dear Richard,

I have wished much to write to you ever since

the last hasty interview I had with you at Hindley, but before the present moment I have not had a fitting opportunity to express the sorrow I feel at your refusal to help the Grammar School trustees in their task of building a new school. The reason you gave pained me even more than the refusal itself. It is a principle you have not yourself hitherto acted on ; for if it be right to withhold assistance from a good work until those of larger means give the precise sum they ought, every scheme of benevolence would be nipped in the bud. The better way is to set an example to such as part with their money grudgingly, and shame them into a noble emulation. If we let their example stop our own efforts, we are guilty of the very conduct we condemn. The charity in question is of vital importance. Morally speaking, education is clothing the naked, and giving bread to the hungry ; it is opening the blind eyes, and healing the feet of the lame. And if there be one place where it is more imperatively required than any other, it is Hindley. Only give the lads who run idle in the highway picking up all sorts of vice, an education befitting their station, and the contrast of their after-life to their present condition will be as great as was that of the man possessed with the legion of unclean spirits, when he lived in the mountains and in the tombs in a state of ferocity which no man could tame, to the time when he sat clothed, and in his right mind, at the feet of Jesus. You will not hold back, I am sure, on further consideration, in so necessary and excellent a work. Help us with your purse generously, help us with your counsel, help us with your prayers, and you will enjoy the sweet reflection that generations yet unborn may be made better by the wise use of the gifts Providence has entrusted to your keeping.

I am, very faithfully yours,

JOHN LEYLAND.

To Mr. B. J. Barlow.

Liverpool, July 22nd, 1853.

My dear Sir,

You and I are both dilatory correspondents. I believe no communication has passed between us since we met at the house of our friend Thomas Gaskell, in the spring of 1851. I was in London the same year at the Great Exhibition, and I remember purposing to write to you before leaving town, but somehow or other the resolution never got carried out.

Mr. Gaskell will, I daresay, have told you that I have engaged myself again with business in Liverpool. Although I have been here nearly a year, I did not come with any purpose of remaining permanently, nor can I now say I have any such intention. My future motions will possibly be determined by circumstances.

I hope your health and condition, and that of your family, are such as your friends would desire to see. Your eldest son must by this time be getting into a big lad. What do you purpose doing with him ? By all means let him choose a profession early. A profession gives a man a certain fixed and definite aim in life, and calls forth energies which might otherwise lie dormant. I feel in my own case the evil of having been brought up without one. If I am not mistaken, you went to the Hindley Grammar School when you were a lad, and will, therefore, read with interest the enclosed circular.

The trustees will be glad if you can assist them in carrying out their object. To you, who are well acquainted with the neighbourhood, I need not state how very useful an efficient school would prove.

With regards to Mrs. Barlow,

I remain, faithfully yours,

JOHN LEYLAND.

To Mr. John Wilton.

Dublin, September 2nd, 1853.

My dear John,

Thanks to the omnipotent power of steam on

land and water, I arrived here safe last night, and, with certain allowances, comfortably. I started early in the morning from Birkenhead, with a bad prospect of weather, which luckily was not verified. After leaving Chester the whole route was new to me. From Chester to Bangor I had the Irish sea almost continually in sight on the right, while on the left a series of mountain views opened to the eye in rapid succession. The scenery in Anglesea was less interesting. The land there is barren and badly cultivated, large tracts lie waste, and there is little wood. The cattle are of the small black breed of little esteem in English markets, and the houses have all a poverty-stricken look. Altogether the island seemed to me a century in the wake of England. I had three hours to spare at Holyhead, which I spent in sauntering about the town. It possesses remarkably few attractions. There is a small church, of sufficiently ancient date to render it inviting to the antiquary, although its architectural merits have never been great. At the present time it is the only church in the place; another, however, is now being built. But if the good people want churches they don't want taverns, which exist in liberal profusion. The town, as I have stated, is not prepossessing. The buildings are poor, and the streets narrow and dirty. The beach stretches in front of the whole town, and is at ebb tide nothing but a mass of slime and mud. The new harbour, when completed, may yet cause it to become a place of importance. The works are of great magnitude, and will cause the port to be one of the first in the kingdom. The steamer sailed for Dublin at six o'clock, and as soon as I put foot on board my enjoyment ended. I was wretchedly sick, and landed at Kingstown as much dead as alive. A night's rest has restored me, and I have been occupied to-day in looking at this city, which I find much finer than I anticipated. More at another time.

I am, sincerely yours,

JOHN LEYLAND.

To Edward B. Bright, Esq.

Dublin, Sept. 3rd, 1853.

My dear Sir,

I made my journey here pleasantly on Thursday, so long as I continued on land, but I no sooner changed that element for water than it became the very reverse. The rocky extremity of Anglesea had scarcely disappeared from view when the vessel appeared as if it was seized by a spirit of mischief. It commenced heaving and falling in a most disagreeable manner, and wherever I trod, the boards spitefully shifted themselves from under my feet. Levity of conduct, even in a steamboat, is reprehensible, so I retired into the cabin, and tried to close my eyes to its folly. Soon after a fellow-passenger came down in serious distress, but looking so comical withal, that, ill as I was, I could scarcely repress laughter. Suddenly I was seized with the same malady, and kept in misery by it until we arrived in the harbour of Kingstown. The sight of Dublin has, however, been a sufficient compensation for the unpleasantness of the voyage. It is certainly a handsome city. The two powerful attractions of Her Majesty's visit and the Exhibition have crammed it with visitors. Yesterday morning I saw Her Majesty and suite pass through the streets, without any ostentation, on their way to the Exhibition. Later in the day I was at a grand review in the Phœnix Park, which drew a large concourse of spectators. Prince Albert was present with a brilliant staff. The sight would, no doubt, be considered attractive; but I have so little relish for military display, that I am afraid it was in some measure lost upon me.

The Viceregal Lodge, though a tasteless edifice, stands well, and commands a fine prospect of the Dublin and Wicklow mountains.

The surrounding park is short of timber, and would be greatly improved by planting. There are yet a number of large thorns, which, when in blossom in springtime, they say, present a beautiful sight.

I am, faithfully yours, JOHN LEYLAND.

To James Bent, Esq.

Sept. 5th, 1853.

My dear Sir,

I was glad to have the wishes I entertained for your and Mrs. Bent's health and happiness satisfied by your welcome letter.

As you become more settled in your new home, you will be able to fall into those quiet and regular habits which I know are so dear to you. I am writing from Dublin, where I have been drawn by the Exhibition, and before I return I purpose visiting Cork and the Lakes of Killarney.

I shall have much pleasure in accepting your kind invitation, though I am afraid my present journey will oblige me to defer it for some time.

Dublin is overflowing with visitors. The Queen is here, as, of course, you will be aware. The city has good claims on the admiration of strangers. The chief streets are spacious; the public buildings numerous, of elegant design, and advantageously placed. The Liffey flows through its very heart, and, as the tide rises to a considerable height, must be a valuable sanitary agent. In the best quarters of the city many poor people are seen, and if you diverge from the principal streets filth and wretchedness are abundantly conspicuous. It is well St. Patrick banished vermin, or the state of things would be intolerable.

I paid a visit to the Clares lately; and you will be glad to hear they were then well.

With kind regards to Mrs. Bent,

I remain, very truly yours,

JOHN LEYLAND.

To Mr. J. P. Williams.

Dublin, Sept. 5th, 1853.

My dear Williams,

Thanks for your kind note of Saturday. The time I have spent here has, of course, been devoted to the city and its sights.   My first impressions were favourable, and these have been strengthened by further examination.   Dublin does not owe its beauty to any advantages of position—for it stands on level ground—but to the good taste with which it is laid out and adorned.

Paramount among the public buildings is St. Patrick's Cathedral.   In my mind this edifice is almost wholly identified with Swift, and I paid that homage at his tomb which his inimitable genius demands.   Yet he was a man I never greatly admired. His works abound so much in satires of his contemporaries which the present generation cannot, like the men of his own day, appreciate, that, excepting to a lover of books, they are now comparatively little read. "Gulliver's Travels" will, however, be popular both with old and young in all time to come.   "The Battle of the Books," short as it is, is my favourite.   He had here a legitimate subject for satire, which, in a vein of the richest humour, he wields with the hand of a master.   The episode of the "Bee and the Spider" is apt and witty, and contributes in rendering the paper exquisitely charming.   Poor Swift!   Notwithstanding his genius and his fame, his career is not to be envied. If he had lent his ear more to the still small voice of the Gospel he had been a happier man.

I was sorry to find the Cathedral in a state of complete dilapidation.   Christ Church Cathedral, which contains the tomb of the renowned Strongbow, is likewise in the same decayed condition.

Surely the *amor patriæ* of Irishmen ought to prompt them to restore these ancient fanes to a state befitting the taste and opulence of the age.

To-morrow I go to Cork.   Galway and the wild district around tempt me, but time and the distance forbid.   The weather is delightful.

Yours very truly,

JOHN LEYLAND.

To Mr. John Wilton.

Cork, Sept. 6th, 1853.

My dear John,

Until my journey hither I had seen nothing to call essentially Irish. Dublin being the capital of the country, and the resort and residence of numbers of Englishmen, has little to distinguish it from an English city. The tract of country lying between the two cities is, however, unmistakably Irish. Immense tracts of bog, mud hovels, with their turf heaps and dung-hills, scattered at distant intervals, and men, women, and children, clothed in rags, are the characteristic features.

The Exhibition is good. I speak generally of the the contents; its external appearance is certainly not attractive. From the engravings I had been supposing the domes to be wholly of glass; they look as if they were covered with tar sheet, and give it a heavy and tomb-like appearance. The interior, on the contrary, is light, airy, and elegant.

At the London Exhibition I remember observing the superior artistic skill with which the French arranged their wares. I fancied I could trace an improvement in the general disposition of the various products in the Dublin Exhibition by our countrymen, which may possibly be owing to the lesson our Gallic neighbours then taught us; but even yet our inferiority is apparent. The chromatic decorations are executed with judgment, and, as a whole, it is a show well worth crossing the Channel to see.

The library of Trinity College deserves examination. It is a noble apartment, and contains nearly a hundred thousand volumes.

God bless you, my dear friend; and believe me to be,

Sincerely yours,

JOHN LEYLAND.

181

To Alfred Pennington, Esq.

Muckross Hotel, Sept. 9th, 1853.

My dear Sir,

Instead of taking mine ease in mine inn, I thought I should act a less selfish part if I were to acquaint you that I am having a ramble in Ireland, which has brought me much enjoyment, and to endeavour to persuade you to follow my example.

I came by way of Dublin, where I was during part of the time of Her Majesty's visit. I saw her twice: *first*, as she was going one morning, with little ceremony, to the Exhibition; and, secondly, on the evening of another day, on her return. On the latter occasion there was much crowding. I happened to be walking accidentally in the direction of Carlisle Bridge, when—

> "I heard as if an army muttered,
> And the muttering grew to a grumbling,
> And the grumbling grew to a mighty rumbling,
> And out of the houses the folks came tumbling."

Curiosity seemed to draw them, though, rather than loyalty, as there was little or no display of feeling.

I have also been to Cork and Queenstown. The scenery of the Lee merits well its great reputation.

I have, moreover, been at Blarney Castle, which you may perhaps remember is famous for a stone possessing extraordinary virtues. The legend is that whoever kisses it three times becomes the possessor of a power of eloquence no lady can resist. The stone is now broken in two pieces, both of which are embedded in the masonry of a lofty tower. For fear of mistaking the wrong piece, I kissed both. Believe me, I shall be as eager to test the virtue of the charm as was Ali Baba the efficacy of the mysterious password of the enchanted cave. The scenery of the Lakes of Killarney cannot surely be excelled the world over. Take a friend's advice, my good sir, and come and spend a month in the country. The Exhibition is worth a visit. If it be inferior to its London parent, it is so only in size. Dublin is worth a visit, Killarney is worth a visit, the

Blarney stone is worth a visit. Let your spindles twirl
as they may, put on a travelling dress, a change of linen
in your portmanteau, a fifty-pound note in your pocket,
and if you don't enjoy yourself you deserve the basti-
nado.   I am, very truly yours,

JOHN LEYLAND.

To Mr. Wm. R. Fitzpatrick.

Limerick, Sept. 11th, 1853.

My dear Sir,

The disagreeable weather on the morning we
parted in Liverpool was not, luckily, an index of what
I was to have during my journey, for the very same day
it cleared up, and it has since been as fine as I could
desire. I am much pleased with Ireland. On all hands
it is admitted to be a remarkably fertile country, and a
short visit will satisfy any person possessing ordinary
powers of observation that it is so. Unfortunately, it is
evident also that the land is not half tilled, and that the
people are in a state of great poverty. The natural
inference to be drawn from these premises is that the
blame rests with the people. I met a gentleman at the
hotel I staid at in Cork, a native of the place, who was
on a visit after a twenty years' absence, and he said
there had been no progress made in the country in the
interim, and that he believed it would never improve so
long as it was peopled by its present inhabitants.

If he spoke the truth, the emigration now going on,
together with the transfer of large tracts of land from
encumbered proprietors, by the law at present in operation, to English capitalists, and the introduction of
railways, may make the Ireland of another generation a
different land from the present. It is lamentable to see
lads of all ages up to manhood, barefoot, and barelegged,
with rags scarcely covering their nakedness, and men
of mature age too, idling away their time from morning
to night. Seemingly they prefer to earn a precarious
living by carrying a portmanteau from a railway station,

or guiding a party of tourists up a mountain, to regular employment.   And, in the midst of all their poverty, they are as lighthearted as if surrounded by affluence.

Their shrewdness and humour are most amusing, and, if time permitted, I could give you some amusing illustrations.   I am, sincerely yours,

JOHN LEYLAND.

To Edwd. B. Bright, Esq.

Limerick, Sept. 11th, 1853.

My dear Sir,

When I left Dublin I arranged for my letters to be kept waiting in College Green until my return, as I was uncertain what route I might take, so that I do not know whether you, or any of my other friends, have since done me the favour to write.   God willing, I shall be there again to-morrow or next day, when I hope to find a full budget of news.   I came to Limerick by way of Cork, Killarney, and Tarbert—from the latter place by steamer on the Shannon.

This river is broad and spacious, but the banks are low, and possess no features of particular interest. Higher in its course, I understand, the scenery becomes more varied.   In making the tour of the lakes I started from Muckross in a car, which set me down at the entrance of the Gap of Dunloe.   The gap, as its name implies, is a rent or chasm in the mountains, extending a distance of four or five miles, and of as wild mountain scenery as can be imagined.   At the head of the upper lake I had a boat in waiting, and was rowed through the three lakes, and landed again near to Muckross, whence I started.   On the lower lake are the picturesque ruins on a small island of Ross Castle.   The island is laid out in pleasure grounds, and is kept in excellent order by Lord Kenmare, to whom it belongs.   It forms one of the show places of the district.   Ireland is in truth a fine country, and it is a thousand pities that a large portion of the people are in such a deplorable state of wretchedness.   The influence of the priests is evidently unbounded, and as pernicious to the people as the idle habits of the people are to the country.

I am, faithfully yours,

JOHN LEYLAND.

To Mr. John Wilton.

Bray, Sept. 13th, 1853.

My dear John,

On my return to Dublin yesterday I found your two letters waiting for me, and very welcome they were.

Much to my regret, business obliges me to return to-morrow, and I may possibly be in Liverpool even before you receive this letter. I shall be a good deal occupied on my return in clearing off the arrears of office work, which, no doubt, have been accumulating during my absence, and I may be unable to call upon you in town for some little time. Therefore, make your way up to my place with what dispatch you conveniently can. I say I return with regret, for I am greatly interested in the Irish people, and the time I have spent among them is much too short to permit of accurate observation.

Peculiarities on the surface are abundant. Among them may be seen men of all ages basking idly in the sun, as if, like Diogenes, they had no other wish than to enjoy its beams. Women's time seems likewise to be of no value : they wander up and down mountains in the tracks of tourists, wasting whole days for the chance of selling a shilling's-worth of goat's milk and whisky. Both sexes are the most pertinacious of beggars. If you take a drive in the country, and your car for any purpose draws up, the inhabitants in the vicinity surround it instantly with outstretched arms imploring charity, and if you even pass their houses without stopping, they turn out and run three or four miles after the carriage whining for coppers. Their persons are singularly handsome, their motions graceful, and every muscle in their countenance betrays the possession and appreciation of the lively humour with which nature has so liberally endowed them.

I stayed a night at Mallow, and on emerging from the railway station on my way to the town, from which it lies a short distance, I had some difficulty in freeing myself from the tribe of idlers congregated at the station. At last I managed to get clear of all, excepting one lad, a fine fellow of fifteen or thereabouts, who followed me spite of my repeatedly expressed determination to have nothing to say to him. "Show your honour the Spa and the Castle, what all the gentlemen look at," he kept repeating, as he walked side by side of me, to which I gave not the slightest attention. Seeing me turn to look at a house we were passing, which stood in a park-like sort of meadow, he at once began to give me the history of the occupant, and he did it in a most amusing manner, casting towards me at the same time every now and then an arch glance to see what effect his eloquence was producing. I laughed outright, and was fain to enlist him as a guide to all the sights he chose to carry me to. A fellow-traveller related that the other day he asked a ragged urchin he met "who his tailor was," when the lad replied, "Bedad, sir, and whoever he is, I don't owe him as much as your honour does yours." Another gentleman told me he was passing two women on one of the hot days we have recently had, both of whom were wearing the long blue heavy cloaks which are in common use, and he asked them however they managed to wear them in such weather. One of the women pertly told him to mind his own business, but the other checked her, saying, "Hush wid ye now, isn't the gintleman, sure, going to give us shawls apiece." These have the ring of the true Irish metal, and possess the merit, moreover, of being struck off fresh from the mint. I am, sincerely yours,

JOHN LEYLAND.

____

To John Pennington, Esq.

Liverpool, Oct. 10th, 1853.

My dear Friend,

All keeping well, I will be with you without fail on Thursday. My opinions, as you know, on such meetings are that they foster a healthy feeling between the different classes of society, and do as much good in their way as sermons. What a commotion there will be to be sure among the cooks the next few days, and what consternation in the hen roosts! The hostess of the "Bird" will, even now, be deep in preparation; and, gracious me! if the savour of the roast is not diffusing itself around me already!

Sincerely yours,
JOHN LEYLAND.

To James Bent, Esq.

Liverpool, Nov. 5th, 1853.

My dear Mr. Bent,

Never was there such an unlucky fellow as I am. Have I not been to Blarney Castle, mounted a ruinous tower at a height enough to make a sober man dizzy, and have I not kissed the prescribed number of times the charmed stone it possesses, and departed pluming myself on possessing the virtues with which it is said to impart to its votaries, to discover afterwards, when too late to remedy, that I should have performed the rite kneeling, instead of, as I did, standing, and that consequently I remain just the same leaden-tongued individual that I was ever? And now, when I had begun to forget the disappointment, my peace of mind is again invaded by the offer of an opportunity for the meeting of an old friend, which the iron arm of Fate will not permit me to embrace! Seriously, my dear sir, I am much troubled that I cannot accept your invitation, not only as it will deprive me of the pleasure of seeing you and Mrs. Bent, but also of the gratification of accompanying your relative in the journey.

The main lines of the telegraph company I am connected with are expected to be ready for opening about the time you name, and my presence at the office, I am sure, will then be considered indispensable. Since I received your letter I have looked at the question in every point of view, in the hopes of finding a solution

of the difficulty, and, I am sorry to say, without
arriving at any other result. I have not the faculty of
making new friends, and I shall never willingly throw
away an opportunity of cementing afresh the bonds
which lighten so much the toils we have all to go
through in this life.

With kindest regards to Mrs. Bent,

I remain, my dear Sir, sincerely yours,

JOHN LEYLAND.

To Miss M. J. Ingham.

Liverpool, November 11th, 1853.

My dear Miss Ingham,

My visits to your neighbourhood are generally
on business, and generally short, so that I am never
able to get as far as Peel House; but if I cannot find an
opportunity to call the next time I am over, I will
promise to make a special journey for the purpose.

Your recent excursion into Derbyshire would, no
doubt, afford you pleasure, especially if it was your first
visit. Those who live in a flat district like Hindley or
Ince enjoy with double satisfaction varied and romantic
scenery. If you can spare the time, I shall be glad to
receive some account of your journey.

I trust you will heed the good advice my old master,
Mr. Spry, has been giving to you. One thing is, indeed,
needful, and it must be sought earnestly. No half
measures will avail. But, then, whatever struggle or
sacrifice the salvation of the soul may cost, even in this
life it is recompensed. Religion sweetens every lot. In
the trials of everyday life it is an unspeakable consolation, and to all earthly blessings it adds a further and a
higher pleasure.

I have no news. My time is divided for the most
part between my office duties and my books, the latter
of which have for me a continually-increasing charm.
Books are friends I never weary of. They are never
unsociable, never churlish. What they have they give,
what they know they tell; and, I was going to say,

they are never dull ; but, then, if by any chance you take up a stupid volume, you have only to lay it down and exchange it for another.

Give my kindest regards to all your circle, and believe me to remain,　　　　　Your sincere friend,

JOHN LEYLAND.

To Alfred Pennington, Esq.

Liverpool, Dec. 2nd, 1853.

My dear Sir,

I was very sorry to hear of your loss. You had, indeed, in some degree led me to expect it ; but we are so unwilling to think of these bereavements, that no preparation is ever sufficient to enable us to bear them with composure when they come. I cannot but share deeply with you in your regrets, knowing your mother, as I have done, so intimately. How curiously the good and evil of the present life, the hallowing influences of home and friends, and the beauties of external nature, are blended with disappointments in mind, body, and estate—the first to content us during our stay, the latter to remind us of the uncertainty of its tenure. And as the instinct of animals leads them to seek shelter on the approach of storm, or night, or winter, so do the higher principles in man gather strength in trouble, and guide his perhaps unwilling steps to that Rock which yields a safe refuge in every tempest.

Believe me, my dear Sir, to be sincerely yours,

JOHN LEYLAND.

To Mr. John Wilton.

Liverpool, Jan. 6th, 1854.

My dear Friend,

As to-day is your last day at the bank, and occupied, as you must be, with many arrangements, you can, I am sure, very well dispense with unnecessary interruptions; but as I was present the day you entered the bank's service, and as the intervening years have many recollections interesting to both of us, so I would have a share, too, in your parting thoughts. You will have your regrets on leaving, as we all have when we come to part with anything we have been long accustomed to, even if it may have been accompanied with disagreeable surroundings. In casting past events through her crucible, memory rejects the dross, and preserves only the sterling metal. Differences are forgotten; even painful events become, by the lapse of time, pleasanter and pleasanter subjects for reflection, just as the stars of evening first glimmer in the heavens, and, as the night advances, burn with a brighter and steadier lustre. The same laws are observed even in inanimate things. If a fair landscape be invaded by the spoiling hand of man for any unsightly work, nature begins by a hundred channels to repair the wrong. Seeds are wafted near and far to the fresh upturned soil, and soon clothe it with a verdant covering. Ivy mantles the falling tower; moss grows on the decaying tree; and many a flower unfolds its beauties on the ruins of ancient dwellings. Providence decrees that neither the eye of the body nor the eye of the mind shall long rest on anything calculated to impart pain.

I am, faithfully yours,
JOHN LEYLAND.

To John Pennington, Esq.

Liverpool, January 9th, 1854.

My dear Friend,

With to-day I believe will expire the time allotted for the performance of your great walking feat. As the weather has proved so unfavourable for its execution, I have been racked with all sorts of apprehensions on your account. Sometimes I have fancied you beset by robbers in a lonely place in the dead of night; and although you may not want courage, yet the stoutest arm must yield to overwhelming numbers. Sometimes my fears have foundered you in a snowdrift, rescued perhaps by an old village crone skilled in the virtues of herbs, who, with the best intentions for your recovery, may have compelled you to swallow deep potations of sage tea, or fomented your frozen body with embrocations of rue. Then I have thought of your limbs aching as they never ached before, and pictured to myself your dismayed face at your exulting uncle pocketing his money. For the sake of your friends never, I beseech you, enter into so foolish a compact again, and if you have strength left to take up a pen, relieve my anxieties. Remember they are as disagreeable to bear as stiff joints and sore feet.

Sincerely yours,

JOHN LEYLAND.

To Mr. Michael Stevens.

Liverpool, January 26th, 1854.

My dear Sir,

Since our last meeting at the Reading Room I have given the subject we discussed—the propriety of excluding the journal in question—a careful consideration. Knowing, as I said, nothing whatever of the merits or demerits of the publication, I have yet come to the conclusion that its admission ought not to be continued, partly from the prejudicial effect it might have on the institution, if it became known that a publication was admitted which had been openly censured by a clergyman of respectable character and moderate views, and more especially with that portion of the public who are either inclined to look upon the institution with suspicion, or disposed to lend it a helping hand without being quite sure whether they are doing right or wrong; partly, also, by the conviction that, if what our reverend friend says be true, we ought not to hesitate a moment in refusing it admission, however popular it may be with the readers; and if he should even be prepossessed against it without sufficient cause, we only err on the right side by so doing. Few works of fiction, I admit, will be found destitute of faults if rigidly examined, even among those written by men of genius, and which find their way into unexceptionable circles.

Nevertheless, we have not only to abstain from evil, but from the appearance of it. Our efforts in a good cause may be rendered unavailing by indiscretion or want of judgment. It is better for a time to submit to what we may think unreasonable, rather than run the risk of injuring a scheme which ultimately may effect considerable good. I am, truly yours,

JOHN LEYLAND.

To Alfred Pennington, Esq.

Liverpool, March 24th, 1854.

My dear Sir,

Although I am unable to speak decisively on the subject of your letter of the 1st of February, I thought, as so many weeks had elapsed since it was written, I ought at least to say that the advice it contained was receiving the attention it merits. It has certainly set me a-thinking, which with some people, you know, is an unusual and difficult operation. It serves, indeed, as a dam to the ordinary current of their motions, their crude ideas and half-formed purposes bubbling and swelling and inundating everything within the compass of their vision, so that they can never tell whereabouts they are until the perplexing process is discontinued, and the elements, stirred up, again become stagnant. Observe, I speak with no reference to the subject or persons on the carpet. I confess, however, to being puzzled, and as much as if placed in one of those dear old mazes which are occasionally to be met with in the gardens of mansions of the olden time, where the pathways turn in the most unexpected manner, and involve the unwary adventurer in an inextricable labyrinth.

Believe me, dear sir, that, whatever I may do in the affair, I am truly obliged for your counsel, and remain, as ever, your attached friend, JOHN LEYLAND.

To Richard Pennington, Esq.

Liverpool, April 17th, 1854.

My dear Sir,

The situation you have selected for the new school is, on the whole, suitable, and all that now remains to be done is to secure it on the most advantageous terms. It would be better to wait until the 3rd of May, the day fixed for the adjourned meeting, it being so near, rather than summon a special meeting to decide upon it.

Mr. Mosely, the manager of the Magnetic Co. in Manchester, has received instructions to show you everything there is to be seen in the working of the telegraph instruments. He is prepared to expect a party, as I thought Mrs. Pennington, or some of the other members of your family, might perhaps wish to accompany you. An hour may profitably be spent in watching the mode of operation.

I am, faithfully yours,

JOHN LEYLAND.

To Alfred Pennington, Esq.

Liverpool, April 24th, 1854.

My dear Sir,

I beg to acknowledge the receipt of your letter of the 22nd inst. in reference to the Grammar School, and to thank you for your handsome and liberal offer. I will lay your letter before the trustees at their next meeting, which is fixed for Wednesday, the 3rd of May, and acquaint you afterwards with their decision.

I am, faithfully yours,

JOHN LEYLAND.

To Alfred Pennington, Esq.

Liverpool, April 27th, 1854.

My dear Sir,

At the last meeting of the Grammar School Trustees a committee was appointed to select a suitable site for the new school, and your brother, a member of

the committee, has since written to me to say they have fixed on the field between the workhouse and James Martlew's house (the projecting corner, if I understand him rightly), but your generous offer, with the stipulation annexed, alters the case completely. Would a site at the top end of the field, opposite the Dog Pool House, fall in with your views? It was suggested to me by the remark in your letter that, if the school was built anywhere between Cheetham House and Hindley House, it could be approached easily by the Abram people. This position is healthy, near to Abram, easy of access to Hindley Green, Chapel Lane, Castle Hill, on one side, and Mill Lane and Wigan Road on the other. Let me have a line from you before Wednesday morning.　　　　　I am, faithfully yours,
JOHN LEYLAND.

To Richard Pennington, Esq.
Liverpool, May 1st, 1854.

My dear Sir,
　　　　I have received a letter from your brother, within the last few days, in which he offers to double his subscription to the new school provided the trustees place it somewhere between Cheetham House and Hindley House. His offer will therefore oblige us to take the question of site again into consideration at the coming meeting. I have since suggested to him the top end of the field opposite to the Dog Pool Farmhouse, as being near Abram, and easy of access to the different parts of Hindley. His reply is in effect that this situation may do, but that perhaps a better may be found. If you have the two plans of the school which were drawn up a year ago, bring them with you to the meeting.　　　　　I am, faithfully yours,
JOHN LEYLAND.

To John Wilton, Esq.
Liverpool, May 11th, 1854.

My dear Friend,
　　　　Well, I was at the wedding on Monday. Yes,

N

sir, and I pray you to bear it long in your remembrance that I was considered a necessary auxiliary in that august ceremonial. It has added vastly to my consequence. I begin to feel myself a man of mark, useful to the world, knowing, distinguished. I am mounted on a pair of stilts, and can see nothing nearer the earth than the tops of trees and the weather vanes on church steeples. These elevated regions I find to be eminently refreshing. The breezes, like a conquering army, come laden with spoil. Perhaps I may rest here, and hold perpetual feast; but if I should descend into your prosaic, every-day sphere, I don't know whether I shall companion again with anybody beneath the dignity of a duke or an earl of a dozen descents. I may make exceptions. I shall see.

Accept, sir, the assurance of my high consideration.

JOHN LEYLAND.

To James Bent, Esq.

Liverpool, May 25th, 1854.

My dear Sir,

Our mutual and worthy friend, Mr. Clare, told me the other day that he had received a letter from you, in which you had asked after my welfare. At first I thought the inquiry might have been addressed with greater propriety to myself; but, on second thoughts, I concluded you had acted wisely, as no person can ever obtain true ideas of an object from viewing it in too close a proximity. It is always necessary to stand at a little distance, to look at it this way and that, and compare it with neighbouring phenomena, in order to become acquainted with its just proportions. Then, we all love self so much, that any account we may give of ourselves is sure to be one-sided. If every man's opinion of himself was to pass current, society would be composed of very amiable people. It may, therefore, be prudent to inquire from another; but to gratify me, always, I beseech you, apply direct to myself.

I was hoping Easter might have brought me a

sufficient holiday to have allowed of a journey into Yorkshire, but my office duties now absorb so much of my time, that I have scarcely the opportunity even to write a letter. But wait a little, say I to myself, wait a little, good cash books, ledgers, pens, ink, paper, and the rest of ye, wait a little, and won't I send ye a packing. Covetous mercenaries ye are, grudging even stray thoughts to purling brooks and daisy-jewelled meads, and intercourse with books and friends. Away varlets, and find some sombre den for your resting-place, I will have none of ye. I am yet wrong. Pens, ink, and paper I must retain. They are among my penates, charms against the evil one. Luther hurled his inkstand at the devil, and got rid of him, as the stains on Wartzburg Prison walls to this day do plainly testify. They are pioneers of civilisation,

> "Steeds of light,
> Adorned with manes of gold, and heavenly bright"—

angels of comfort to separated friends—heralds publishing in earth's utmost bounds "good tidings of great joy to all mankind."

If I tell you that I have been at a wedding lately, you must not suppose that I refer to an ideal ceremony of romance, the actors in which I have followed with hopes and fears through two or three volumes of print. Nor must you suppose it was one of those pictures the mind is apt to form when the body is steeped in sleep, where like as not the gentlemen may figure in silk hose and coats of embroidered velvet, and the ladies in starched ruffs, hoops, quilted satin petticoats, and trains borne up by pages. I am speaking literally. It was a true, real, genuine, veritable wedding, performed legally by an authorised clergyman, inside a church, in the broad daylight, and before credible witnesses. In these days news travels fast, and the event may possibly have become known in Yorkshire, and you may have already anticipated that I speak of that of Miss Clare with my old bank colleague, Mr. Kershaw.

Never, I sincerely think and seriously say, has man

made a wiser choice or secured a surer prospect of his home being made permanently happy.

With kind remembrances to Mrs. Bent,

I remain, your sincere friend,

JOHN LEYLAND.

To the Misses Ingham.

Liverpool, May 23rd, 1854.

My dear Friends,

Want of sufficient leisure has compelled me to let the letters you were each good enough to write to me remain so long unanswered, and for the same reason I am addressing both of you at one and the same time.

I was glad to find that you had enjoyed your excursion into Derbyshire. The visit you mention having paid to the printing works of your relative would no doubt prove both instructive and entertaining.

All kind of information is useful at one time or other of our lives. Just as every part of the body has its purpose in contributing to the supply of our necessities, or everything in the economy of nature its appointed office, so will every new fact we gain be found of service in its season.

You are both now young, and may be looking forward to a future of many years' duration; yet remember the Scriptures say "all flesh is as grass"—green in the morning, cut down and withered before night.

Observe, the longest life is characterised thus. One lesson then is obvious—that we have no time to be idle. Kind friends and competent teachers may do much by their direction and assistance in making clear any branch of study at an age like yours; but, after all, everything depends on a person's self. I see much more clearly than I used to do that work, constant, unceasing work, is the inevitable lot of every one in this life. Plans of leisure and retirement are often formed, and may in a certain degree be realised, but this law of our nature cannot be evaded; so that we may as well look it fairly in the face at the outset.

If we are spared the necessity of working for our daily bread, there is plenty of other work in discharging our social obligations, in acquiring information, and in preparing our souls for our future state.

On reading over what I have written, I find I have been very serious. Nevertheless, I am sure you will receive what I have said in a friendly spirit.

With kind regards to your father and mother,

I remain, sincerely yours,

JOHN LEYLAND.

To Mr. Thomas Gaskell.

Liverpool, June 9th, 1854.

My dear Sir,

I enclose Mr. Nightingale's letter to Mr. Pennington, on the subject of the site for the new school, which, I am sure, you will rejoice to find favourable. We may, therefore, I hope, consider the question as at last set at rest.

Mr. Pennington is gone from home for three weeks; on his return, be good enough to return to him Mr. Nightingale's letter.

I trust Mr. Dixon will approve of the site. Tell him it is more favourable for Abram than Hindley; that it contains more of its unsophisticated breezes, for the nourishment of the young urchin blood, than the vapours of mixed and doubtful odour which prevail in some portions of the sister township. And as Mr. Dixon is the representative of that township, he should do something for his good fortune. He is lying idle and basking in the sunshine; draw him if you can within the shadow line of duty, and ask him to swell, with a good heavy lump, the building fund.

I am, faithfully yours,

JOHN LEYLAND.

To Frederick Pennington, Esq.

Liverpool, June 30th, 1854.

My dear Sir,

Lifelong friends, as you and I have been, must of necessity feel a lively interest in everything that touches the welfare of the other; and though I know you would at all times give me the credit of "rejoicing with you when you rejoice," yet the late event in your life is so notable, that I cannot withhold my special and very hearty congratulations thereupon.

There can be no question about the policy of such a step on your part, or the propriety of your choice. You are too prudent, and have seen too much of the world, to make a mistake in either. I remember you saying, when you first acquainted me with the event, that you had already begun to look on life with feelings of enhanced value, and I can understand that marriage unlocks heretofore unknown springs of sympathy and affection, and causes them to flow forth freely to delight and beautify existence. I can understand that the father of a family discharges a noble duty in educating his children so that they may fill their place in society virtuously, and use their influence for the general good; and there is little doubt in my mind that the man who does this carefully and conscientiously is a greater benefactor to his country than many of those soldiers and statesmen who have filled the world with their fame.

I would not be thought unduly to lessen the value of such services to the State, if I compare them to the thunder-shower falling on parched and hardened ground, of seeming greater utility than it really is. It falls grandly, but its waters rush into the brooks and rivers; while the home influences I have named are as the silent and gentle rain, which makes the earth, as the Psalmist expresses it, "soft with its drops," as "a fleece of wool," and "very plenteous."

Although I have not yet the pleasure of being known to Mrs. Pennington, I pray you to remember me to her kindly, and to believe that I am ever,

My dear Sir, sincerely yours,   JOHN LEYLAND.

To Mr. John Wilton.

Glasgow, August 5th, 1854.

My dear John,

Presuming you to take your usual interest in your friends, I have taken pen in hand with the intention of giving some account of my journey. I started from home early on Thursday morning, and first stopped for about an hour at Preston. Once, and once only, when a lad, I visited Preston before, in company with my father, on our way to Lancaster.

I remember so well that visit to Lancaster, long as it is since. The town, with its grand castle and its beautiful environs, made a deep impression on my youthful imagination. It was assize time, and the pomp and majesty attending the administration of the law had doubtless also their influence. May I give you a word of advice ? If you should ever become a father, accustom your children in their early years to scenes of innocence and beauty : the recollection will remain with them in after-life, and lead them ever to delight in such pleasures.

My next stopping-place on the present journey was Carlisle ; but the half-day I stayed there was insufficient to see it with the deliberation I like. You know I am slow in everything : I read slowly, write slowly, eat slowly, walk slowly, and even my very thoughts run slowly. What is of slow growth is generally of sterling value, but general rules are proved by exceptions, and these receive additional confirmation from my failings. I have said that I read slowly, and I might hence hope to retain all that I read. Unfortunately, the reverse is the case. At one time or other I have read much ; yet somehow or other I forget much. Oddly enough, some things stick by me. For instance—when I was at Cork last autumn, some rogue picked my pocket as I was crossing St. Patrick's bridge. Now I verily believe I shall never again cross that bridge without thinking of the theft, and wishing the culprit had got a good whipping for his pains.

You will be glad for this egotistical letter to be brought to a close. I will therefore only add that I have seen Lanark, the Falls of the Clyde, and am now busy with Glasgow.

If opportunity serves I will write again.

I am, faithfully yours,
JOHN LEYLAND.

To Edward B. Bright, Esq.

Perth, August 10th, 1854.

My dear Sir,

The bustle of an inn is not a favourable place—at any rate to me—for writing the details of a journey, so I will content myself on the present occasion with a few hasty and random observations.

The route I purposed taking at the outset, which I think I acquainted you with, I have not deviated from. Carlisle and Glasgow I saw, and both cities exceeded my anticipations.

From the latter I sailed down the Clyde, through the Kyles of Bute, Loch Fyne, and the Crinan Canal, up to Fort William.

The rich and varied scenery this route presents I saw under the most favourable circumstances, for the weather was fine, and the water had not even a ripple to disturb its surface. At Fort William I stayed a night, and walked early next morning to Banavie, the head of the locks on the Caledonian Canal, a distance of two or three miles. I enjoyed this walk exceedingly. It was in the grey of the morning, not absolutely dark enough to shroud any portion of the landscape, nor yet sufficiently light to divest it of the mystery and solemnity of the night.

The objects the eye could drink in through the walk were the little cluster of houses forming the town, Loch Linnhe stretching placidly before it; the picturesque little fort which gives the place a name; the ruins of Inverlochy Castle, the plain memorable from the defeat of the Campbells under Montrose, and the circling hills around; Ben Nevis, the monarch of Scottish mountains, outtopping all, his head far away among the clouds. I continued my route by the Caledonian Canal to Inverness, and by coach to the "Fair City" whence I am writing.

I am, faithfully yours,

JOHN LEYLAND.

To J. P. Williams, Esq.

Linlithgow, August 12th, 1854.

My dear Williams,

For the directions you were good enough to give me for my journey, the value of which I tested first at Carlisle, and afterwards frequently on this side the Border, I return my hearty thanks. By-the-bye, I never knew exactly when I crossed the Border, and was therefore spared the emotions the knowledge would have occasioned. The district affords such ample scope for the imagination. The old sequestered towers, and their history from the hot days of their youth and prime, down to the peace and honours of their old age, are full of interest. So are the feuds, and the fights, and the raids of the ancient inhabitants. I fancy I can see one of their bluff old warriors before me this moment, his wild, jovial eye bespeaking him ready either for frolic or foray.

A pleasanter life, I take it, was theirs than counting money, as you do, all the day, shut up within four square walls. Possibly you may have the advantage in honesty, though, for the matter of that, honesty goes for as little in these days as it did then. But I must proceed—I have much to tell; prepare to listen. I have been as far as —— I ought, though, to narrate circumstantially.

I will resume the thread of my narrative where I left it at the Border. Like a picture of one of the "grand old masters," the Border is a subject one loves to linger over. The very word is of large signification. Young ladies often talk of "borders"—rug borders, handkerchief borders, robe borders. There are borders of flowers of exceeding beauty, and there is the border of matrimony, which I have heard people say is very pleasant.

I have covered my paper, and must therefore reserve the remainder of my history until I return. Remind me that I left off at the Border.

I am, faithfully yours,

JOHN LEYLAND.

To Mr. John Wilton.

Edinburgh, August 14th, 1854.

My dear John,

It was late on Saturday evening and nearly dark when I arrived in Edinburgh, and I was gratified to find a letter from you waiting at the Post Office. I always like to arrive at a city of any historic eminence, on a first visit, in the dark. In passing from a railway terminus to one's hotel in daylight, one is sure to recognise some feature made familiar either by prints or reading, and a casual glance dissipates to some extent the ideas previously formed in the mind, which a more careful examination may possibly strengthen. Then, the complacent feelings on retiring to rest go for something; the fantastic dreams of the night, the gush of delicious emotions on awaking next morning, so soon as the wonder at the strange bed curtains and apartment has subsided; golden fruit, ready gathered, lying on the richly-hued chalice of imagination yet untasted! But I will not dilate on all that may pass then before the eye of the imagination. I will only say that I esteem as a rare luxury a first morning's reveries in a strange city. I have been as far north as Inverness, and stopped at many intermediate places, reminiscences of which will afford subjects for conversation when we meet; till which time I reserve further details.

At the Inversnaid Hotel, where I passed a night, I saw, from the visitors' book, that your mother and uncle had preceded me there only by a few days.

I am, sincerely yours,

JOHN LEYLAND.

To Alfred Pennington, Esq.

Edinburgh, August 14th, 1854.

My dear Sir,

I have been in Scotland the last ten days, in consequence of which your letter of the 7th inst. only reached me late on Saturday evening.

I am always glad to hear from you, and on the present occasion your letter, as it gives me an excuse for writing, is of essential service.

Travelling produces on me something of the same effect that fuel does on the boiler fires of your steam engines : one generates steam, the other ideas, or at least what pass for such, which is much the same thing. In either case there must be an outlet or a catastrophe. I am therefore making you my safety-valve.

A first visit to Scotland must be memorable to any person. To me the interest is considerably heightened by its numerous legendary and historical associations.

Edinburgh pleases me immensely. Its situation is so picturesque, and the embellishments it has received from art so judicious. It is a city of the past as much as of the present. I confess to cherishing an antipathy to modern towns. The red brick of their new buildings is like a tropical sun, painfully oppressive ; it is everywhere ; there is no escape from it ; no venerable shadow of walls

" From old heroic ages grey "

to fly to for shelter. I dislike the regularity of their streets, the uniformity of their buildings, their parallel lines, their right angles, their unmistakably exact squares. I never had a taste for mathematics. How Pythagoras could fall into such extravagant ecstasy on simply discovering that the square of the hypothenuse of a right-angled triangle is equal to the sum of the squares of the sides, is to me incomprehensible.

Old cities like Edinburgh have histories we are familiar with. They have had their worthies who have left posterity rich legacies of thought—men whom we have learned to honour, and perhaps taken into close companionship. I do not mean to assert that men formerly were better than now; far from it. Human nature has been ever the same.

I ought, however, to apologise for filling up my paper with speculations, instead of telling you something of my journey. I am afraid I can do nothing more now than simply mention the route I have taken. I went by railway to Carlisle and Glasgow; from the latter city by steamer through various beautiful lochs and the Caledonian Canal to Inverness, by coach to Perth, and by railway, coach, and steamer alternately through Stirling, the Trossachs, Loch Katrine, and Loch Lomond, to Edinburgh.

I purpose taking Durham and York on my return, in order to have a look at their respective cathedrals.

I am, truly yours,

JOHN LEYLAND.

To Alfred Pennington, Esq.

Liverpool, August 28th, 1854.

My dear Sir,

I am obliged to you for forwarding the notice of objection to my vote. From the trouble my political opponents take to prevent me from voting, I am beginning to think they consider me a formidable adversary. I have been served with so many objections, at one time or another, that they have totally lost the power of annoyance. A fellow, you see, gets accustomed to kicks, and acquires, in process of time, a skin as tough and impenetrable as a rhinoceros, or perhaps loses the sense of feeling altogether.

I have been at home about a week, but I have since had such a multiplicity of things to look after, that I have been unable, before now, to take pen in hand to write to you.

My Scotch trip has given me much gratification, and I promise myself further pleasure in talking it over with you. I did not experience the same admiration for the people that I did for the country. Most of those who came under my observation were dry, caustic, wary, captious—men of the Shylock stamp, who exact the uttermost farthing in a bargain. Their stern and rigid features seemed as if they could never relax into amenity. I can fancy them living wholly by rule—rising every morning at the same hour, dining punctually every day to the minute, and eating to a scruple the same quantity. If in these things they are exact, they compensate themselves by unlimited indulgence in others. Like a quicksand, they swallow any quantity of liquid, and, like it, too, retain all the while a calm and unruffled surface.

I am, faithfully yours,
JOHN LEYLAND.

To John Pennington, Esq.

Liverpool, August 29th, 1854.

My dear John,

Two days ago I promised a friend to hold myself in readiness all week to meet a few friends at his house. He could not then name a day, and it is possible Thursday may be fixed upon. If it be, I shall be unable to accept your invitation; if not, I will be with you, as I should be sorry not to join in the congratulations on so auspicious an occasion.

My desk is unhappily full of papers, which seem filled with scores of eyes gleaming angrily as I write. I dare not, therefore, longer withhold from them the suit and service they so imperiously require.

I am, truly yours,
JOHN LEYLAND.

To Mr. John McLaughlin.

Liverpool, August 29th, 1854.

My dear Sir,

Yesterday I received your circular announcing the opening of the coming session of the Philomathic Society. I have so ill discharged the duties I owe it as a member, that I am convinced I ought, in justice to the society, to ask you to strike my name from the list. Other reasons, which I am unwilling to trouble you with, strengthen the propriety of a request, which I assure you is anything but agreeable to me to prefer. If it be consistent with your duty to receive my resignation, without publicly intimating it to the society, pray do ; if not, you are

"Too fond of the right to pursue the expedient,"

as I hope I am, also, to desire it.

Unless the members are reminded of me, I shall never be missed. Should a ray of recollection of my face or person ever shoot athwart the memory of any of the members of more retentive power than the others, it would even there be as indistinct as the fading figures on the tapestry hangings of an antiquated apartment. The difficulty of deciphering what personages or events some of these productions of the ancient loom pourtray would be about as great as the Philomaths who sought to give shape and individuality to their vague conceptions of   Your very humble servant,

JOHN LEYLAND.

To Mr John McLaughlin.
Liverpool, Sept. 7th, 1854.

Believe me, dear Sir, that I am grateful for, and highly value, the many friendly expressions contained in your letter. Out of deference to your request I have reconsidered my resignation, but, I regret to say, without being able to think the step the less necessary.
I am, yours very truly,
JOHN LEYLAND.

To Richard Pennington, Esq.
Liverpool, Sept. 7th, 1854.
My dear Sir,
I send you herewith the draught of a circular I have drawn up. I have done it to the best of my

ability, but there is plenty of room for the correction it will receive in passing through your hands. If you approve of the time I have named for opening the school, it will be well to place it in the hands of the printer without loss of time. A number of bills for posting on the walls, containing the same matter, would also be useful. It appears to me unnecessary to particularise in greater detail the course of instruction to be pursued, until we see the sort of lads we have to work upon. The books we put into Mr. Airey's hands will be his best guide, and about these I should like to have a talk with you. The five first Reading Books of the Irish Board are, I am told, useful; Chambers's Educational Course is highly so, I know; and Cornwell's School Geography is spoken of as an excellent work.

I can get these, or any others, easier and cheaper in Liverpool probably than you can do in Wigan, and, if you wish, I can also have the circulars printed here. We must not forget to give orders for the school to be opened and closed daily with prayer.

I am, truly yours,

JOHN LEYLAND.

To John Wilton, Esq.

Liverpool, September 18th, 1854.

My dear Friend,

Aversion to letter-writing is an affliction so common, at one time or another, to everybody, that I ought not to expect an exemption from it. Yet perhaps I never experienced it more than since I received your last letter, now a week old.

The reasons are many, and may equal in number the ingredients employed in compounding our national dish of plum pudding. First in the list come my office duties, which are increasing continually, and shortening, in consequence, the time I have been in the habit of devoting to reading and writing. I have, next, several private business matters requiring attention, and, to pass over others, I am struggling with a severe depression of spirits. Under these circumstances, I beg you will give me credit for magnanimity in rejoicing, as I sincerely do, at your emancipation from business.

Of Ilkley I know nothing, save what you tell me. I am glad you are in so pleasant a neighbourhood. The name your house goes by—"The Cow Pastures"—suggests pleasant thoughts of ruminating kine, rich cream, and the many luxuries of rural life, just as the name of your landlady, Mrs. Teal, does of autumn, though, at the same time, sporting, its ugliest feature, follows in the train of thought. The indifference generated by long-established custom prevents us from seeing the barbarities of which the horn of the hunter and the gun of the fowler are the signal. William Howitt somewhere says he believes that it is more a love of nature which animates sportsmen than the pursuit itself. I hope it may be so, but the sooner this love is divested of its inhuman accompaniments the better. Nature fills her votaries with peace, purity, gentleness, love. Let sportsmen study her more, and they will leave unoffending birds and animals in the enjoyment of the existence they delight in. I may go even further, and say that a wanton destruction of the lives of these creatures—and for mere amusement—is contrary to the spirit both of the moral and divine law. Believe me, I am ever, sincerely yours,

JOHN LEYLAND.

To Richard Pennington, Esq.
Liverpool, September 25th, 1854.

My dear Sir,

I send you herewith the circulars and advertisements, which I hope will meet with your approval. Of the former I have had 150 impressions taken, of the latter only 50. You will see that I have struck out the names of the trustees from the advertisement, and on the circular, in place of my own name, I have substituted Mr. Gaskell's and Mr. Tickell's; these two gentlemen, with yourself, forming the committee appointed by the trustees for making arrangements for the opening of the school.

I am glad you have agreed for the house in the New Road, as it is by far the most eligible in the neighbourhood for the purpose. There are two desks, and, possibly, some forms also belonging to the school, lying in the reading-room. They were sent from Lowe Green to Chapel Green, when the school was transferred thither many years ago, and were removed again along with the school to where they now are. Whatever else may be required, get as cheaply as possible, as nothing will, in all probability, come in for the new building.

I will do nothing about the books until I either see or hear from you.   I am, faithfully yours,

JOHN LEYLAND.

To John Wilton, Esq.

Liverpool, October 2nd, 1854.

A very pretty life you are leading, John Wilton! So, Venus, and Apollo, and Diana, are at your merry-makings! Do you know these are rank, heathenish names? The old Puritan blood of my ancestors fires in my veins at the bare recital.

"I grow full of anger, Sir Lucius."

I am, nevertheless, rejoiced that the place suits your health, and, as for your spirits, they seem incapable of improvement.

It is like exchanging the exciting pages of romance for a dry chapter of metaphysics to turn from you to myself. What I said to you recently about my health was strictly true. Yet, don't think me worse than I am. Ill I am not, in the proper sense of the term, nor, on the other hand, am I well. Sickness, even in a modified form, has its use. "We begin to feel the worth of water when the well offers to go dry."

To-day will be memorable in the annals of our

Grammar School at Hindley, as the day on which it was reopened, after being closed, and lost to the neighbourhood, for the greater part of twenty years.

I enclose a circular, which will put you in possession of further particulars. The trustees have found it no easy task to effect. Discouragements of all sorts they have had to encounter, but the result illustrates the text, " Ye shall reap in due time if ye faint not."

Sincerely yours,
JOHN LEYLAND.

To John Pennington, Esq.

Liverpool, Oct. 9th, 1854.

My dear John,

I can manage to eat a dinner if I cannot wield a bat; and, as I can promote the noble art of cricket in no other way, I am content to do it by feasting upon sirloin, venison, or other dishes of equivalent reputation. I should therefore have certainly joined you on Thursday if it had not been for a severe cold I caught a few days ago, which, though much better, remains sufficiently bad to render it imprudent for me to venture at present from home. I can scarcely fancy that 365 times 24 hours have passed since our last anniversary. Poor Westhead, the waiter, or rather factotum of mine host of the " Bird"! I see him still, spellbound in the dining-room by the manifold calls on his services, in much the same way as we read of certain animals being transfixed by the basilisk.

Now he bows to one, now to another; smiles on all; puzzled whose wants to supply first, remains yet irresolute, and attends upon none. At last he moves; he approaches your uncle and me, and asks " what we wud loike fur to soap."

Certainly it was a pleasant meeting, but there is a *leetle* fear mixed up with my reminiscences lest we conducted ourselves somewhat too noisily. Your influence can easily prevent its recurrence on the coming occasion. The Hindley Cricket Club has a character to maintain, and I shall make no apology for directing your attention to the subject, for, as a member of so distinguished a body, I hope to be pardoned even an excess of jealousy in watching over its dignity.

I am, ever truly yours,

JOHN LEYLAND.

To Mr. W. R. Fitzpatrick.

Liverpool, Oct. 14th, 1854.

My dear Sir,

The post delivered punctually your letters of the 24th of September and the 6th of October.

As you know how fully from morning to night I am every day engaged, you will excuse me, I am sure, for not sooner replying. Everything is going on here as usual. There has been little news stirring since your departure. The festivities incident to the opening of St. George's Hall were, I think, then about taking place. They passed over unsatisfactorily; the high prices to the performances, as well as their indifferent quality, were the subject of general animadversion. We had next the Congress of the British Association, which brought many distinguished men amongst us, and I feel mortified to say that my occupations would not allow me to hear them.

The all-absorbing subject of interest, at the present time, is the war in the Crimea, and the last fortnight has been fertile in supplying stimulants to the previous excitement. At one time we made sure of the possession of Sebastopol, and were congratulating ourselves on having secured comfortable quarters for our troops for the coming winter; more even than this, on advances having been made which might lead to a speedy termination of the war itself; when we were suddenly and unpleasantly awakened to the knowledge that all this has still to be accomplished.

I am, faithfully yours,

JOHN LEYLAND.

To Richard Pennington, Esq.

> Liverpool, Oct. 16th, 1854.

My dear Sir,

I should not myself be disposed to give up the field, because Mr. De Trafford will not make himself responsible for any damage which may be caused to the buildings by working the mines. We are told they are very deep, and not likely to be got for many years to come. If they ever should be, the trustees for the time being can then make arrangements with the lessees for such pillars of coal to be left as will leave the buildings secure.

Some neighbouring cottager had better be engaged to light fires in the school for the present quarter, and the bill can be discharged at Christmas along with Mr. Airey's salary.   I am, faithfully yours,

> JOHN LEYLAND.

To Richard Pennington, Esq.

> Liverpool, Oct. 21st, 1854.

My dear Sir,

You will, I am sure, be as glad to hear as I am to inform you that the Bridgewater trustees have paid £434 1s. 8d. on account of mine rent, and that Mr. Taylor has placed the money to the credit of the trustees with the District Bank.

We seem now to be gradually getting things to rights, and I am in hopes that Christmas will find us with nothing upon our hands to look after but the building of the new school.

> I am, faithfully yours,
>
> JOHN LEYLAND.

To John Wilton, Esq.

> Liverpool, October 21st, 1854.

My dear John,

I have to tell you that I have had a remedy prescribed for my various ailments, the efficacy of which is vouched for by the members of an extensive fraternity

who have long benefited by its extraordinary virtues. If
I was to leave you to guess what it is until next Christmas you would never find it out, so I may as well at
once tell you. It is, then, nothing more nor less than
tobacco smoking. If you should be sceptical of my intention to venture on the experiment, I must bespeak
your careful attention to what I have to say. In truth,
then, I am learning to smoke, and have already been
initiated into the art of puffing. Chibouks, meerschaums,
cherry-wood sticks, amber mouthpieces, are become the
objects of my study. Even now I experience its salutary influence. Although seated by my own fireside, I
seem to be in an eastern kiosk, reclining on a divan
covered with the richest cashmeres. The virtue of the
plant I inhale (the finest Shiraz) has soothed away all
irritation and despondency, and produced in its stead a
pleasant, calm, and benignant state of feeling. The
smoke curls from my pipe in graceful cork-screw windings, half hiding, half disclosing, the cypress trees, and
the minarets, and the olive groves, that are glowing in
the rich sunlight of the landscape stretched before me.
The air is still, yet the breeze comes in grateful freshness, and softens into a lulling melody as it plays
among the acacias overshadowing my summer house.
A cunning hand strikes the chords of a lute in a
neighbouring alcove, and a voice sings—

> " There blow a thousand gentle airs,
> And each a different perfume bears,
> As if the loveliest plants and trees
> Had vassal breezes of their own,
> To watch and wait on them alone."

I grow thirsty. What ho, there! bring coffee. The
aroma reaches me this moment, and lo! here comes, in
tiny cups of oriental porcelain, encased in silver filigree
work, the essence of the precious berry itself. It was
the one thing wanting to fill my cup of luxuries to the
brim.

And what are you doing, poor man? The thought of
your cold water and wet sheets makes me shiver.

Excuse me if I drop your acquaintance. Luxurious people cannot think of misery, even if it needs relief; it shocks too much their sensibilities. Adieu.

JOHN LEYLAND.

To Richard Pennington, Esq.

Liverpool, Oct. 25th, 1854.

My dear Sir,

I send you herewith a dozen gutta-percha ink-stands, of a medium size. Philip & Son's is the best house for educational works in this part of the kingdom. They are the only agents in Liverpool for the sale of Chambers's and the Irish Board's publications. The packet of books I sent you some weeks ago I had from them. I have ordered a course of maps, which will be ready in a week. They have any quantity in stock, but the mounting on rollers and varnishing cannot be done in less time. I will forward them as soon as they are ready. I am, faithfully yours,

JOHN LEYLAND.

To John Wilton, Esq.

Liverpool, Oct. 25th, 1854.

Pity me, my dear friend, my smoking has ended; not in smoke; alas no!—would that it had—but in absolute, horrible sickness. The first unpleasant feeling it caused me was giddiness; then my head felt as if it was seized with an irresistible desire to fly into the upper regions, like a balloon filled with gas, and as if it was kept in its place on my shoulders only by ropes of sinews, and other integuments, holding it fast down. Afterwards a languor overspread my whole frame, even to the tips of my finger nails. This presently changed into a total prostration of the system, and, worst of all, was followed by actual vomiting. It is true, I assure you. I have been upon my hands and knees vomiting violently. How sad that so bright a prospect should be thus suddenly overcast! A few days ago, I received a present of a beautiful pipe, and a pouch of rare tobacco. I have had them put out of sight, for I cannot bear to look upon them now. Heretofore, if the morning or evening breeze carried the odour of the weed from the pipe of a passing traveller, I thought it agreeably fragrant, especially in clear, crispy weather; but how shall I describe the commotions, the unutterable loathings, a faint whiff in the street yesterday occasioned in my very inmost being? I say, with Charles Lamb—

> "Filth of the mouth and fog of the mind,
>   Africa, that brags her foison,
>   Breeds no such prodigious poison."

I am, your unfortunate friend,
JOHN LEYLAND.

To Richard Pennington, Esq.
Liverpool, November 2nd, 1854.

My dear Sir,

I have just received the maps from Philip's, and shall send them to you by train this evening. As they are well packed, I think they will escape injury from the carriage. I hope no further difficulties have arisen about the purchase. Did you send the drawings of the new school to Mr. Eckersley? He asked for them, you will perhaps remember, at the trustees' last meeting.

We shall have to decide very soon now about building. I shall try to have everything made straight for the annual meeting.

I am, faithfully yours,
JOHN LEYLAND.

To John Pennington, Esq.
Liverpool, November 15th, 1854.

My dear John,

I was waiting for tidings of the anniversary proceedings of the Cricket Club with some impatience, when I fortunately met with your uncle, who informed me that they passed off satisfactorily. I was sorry I could not join you, and, was going to add, that I hope to be with you another year, but I must check myself, for a year is so long a period to look forward to that, if even life and health be spared, there is no telling what changes may occur, or what part of the compass the winds of fortune may carry one to.   I am going on only in a dull sort of way.   The daily life I lead is a life of complete routine, something, indeed, like travelling through a flat, sterile country, without a hill or a tree, or a house to look at.

The remains of my cold hang about me still, which I remind you of, as it may explain my disposition to be querulous.

It may, perhaps, interest you to know that I have lately been making efforts to acquire an accomplishment in a science in which you long since graduated. Some of my friends here hold in supreme veneration the virtues of the pipe as a sovereign remedy for many of the ills human flesh is heir to, and, at their instigation, I was induced to become one of its votaries.   I tried, then, to smoke, and for a day or two all went well. I had begun to fancy all sorts of grand things.   In fact, I had got completely among the clouds (of smoke) when my soaring ideas were dashed suddenly to the ground. The tale has a melancholy sequel, and is long to tell, but the gist of it is that I found out nature had denied me the powers necessary to obtain skill in the art.   The internal throes that I experienced before coming to this conclusion I will not stop to describe, nor dwell longer, indeed, on an unpleasant subject, than to say I am now satisfied, if I was not before, that the smell of tobacco is as odious, as the practice of smoking is abominable.

I am, faithfully yours,

JOHN LEYLAND.

To Alfred Pennington, Esq.

Liverpool, Dec. 2nd, 1854.

My dear Sir,

It is near midnight and Sunday morning.   I have been longing all day to take pen in hand, and have never before now had the opportunity, in order to thank you for your good offices for me at Wigan.

I am, faithfully yours,
JOHN LEYLAND.

To Alfred Pennington, Esq.

Liverpool, Dec. 5th, 1854.

My dear Sir,

I owe you an apology for replying to your letters at the fag end of the day, when I am half asleep and altogether weary, for it is nearly as late an hour to-night as it was the other evening when I wrote ; but, in truth, my various engagements keep me so busy that I scarcely know which way to turn. I am like Attorney Dowling in Tom Jones, who was wont to say that if he was cut up into four quarters he could find employment for every quarter. If you are inclined to make merry with my labours, you will say, perhaps, that Chaucer's description of his man of law offers a better parallel :

> " So besy a man as he thaer n'as,
> Yet seemed besier than he was."

Believe me, dear sir, to be,

Sincerely yours,
JOHN LEYLAND.

To the Misses Ingham.

Liverpool, Dec. 18th, 1854.

My dear Friends,

Time hurries along with such terrible rapidity that wide gaps are soon made in the periods of intercourse with friends living apart from each other. Summer had scarcely attained its maturity when I last saw you, and now Christmas fires are lighting the long evenings, and winter stories usurping the place of rambles among the green fields. The changes of the seasons, like all the other works of Providence, are eminently adapted to minister to our happiness. To me, and doubtless to most people, they are a source of continual pleasure. If we can think for a moment what a dreary thing it would be to live without the succession of day and night, and summer and winter— to live even in perpetual summer and sunshine—we can realise better the enjoyments the several seasons, in their appointed order, bestow. Who would have winter, bleak and cold as it is, blotted from the year? Who cannot but admire the trees in their naked grandeur, the rough and fantastically-twisted branches of some, the gracefully-curved and flowing lines of others, and the wonderful feathery tracery in which they terminate, which are hidden by their foliage in summer? Then the Great Author of All "giveth snow like wool, and scattereth hoar frost like ashes, and casteth forth His ice like morsels."

When I last saw you, I was contemplating, you will remember, an excursion to Scotland; and as my time has since passed monotonously, I will fill up the rest of my paper with telling you something of my journey. I first went to Glasgow, thence by steamer round the western coast and through the Caledonian Canal, to Inverness, the capital of the Highlands. One of the most enjoyable days' travelling I ever had was the journey I made outside the coach from Inverness to Perth. Every variety of scenery presented itself on the road by turns. Stirling, Loch Katrine, Loch Lomond, and Edinburgh, I afterwards saw, and returned home, by way of Melrose, Berwick, Newcastle, Durham, and York. The whole of Scotland abounds with beautiful scenery, and with localities renowned in history and tradition, to many of which the pen of Sir Walter Scott has added an additional interest. I spent a day in visiting Abbotsford, and the ruins of Melrose and Dryburgh Abbeys. These three celebrated places stand within the compass of a few miles from each other. They excited in me vivid emotions of the man from whom they derive their chief attraction.

I do not know whether you are familiar with Lockhart's "Life of Scott." If you are not, by all means make yourselves so. No book has a deeper interest or a better moral. No man was ever more worthy of admiration and sympathy than Scott. We see him rising to the pinnacle of fame, and still retaining his unassuming deportment. The adulation he met with never spoiled the qualities of his heart; and the manful and honourable struggles he made to shake off a crushing load of debt are worthy of all praise. But his life has another lesson—it shows the folly of ambition. He built up his position in order to transmit a name and estate to his children, and to be the founder of a great family. A few years only have since worn on, and the grave has closed over all his children, and his very name in his own line has become extinct. Choose you, like Mary in the Gospel, a better part, and aspire to a surer inheritance. Seek to become of the first-born on high, to lay the foundation of your faith on the rock of Christ, and no changes or chances can ever rob you of the full fruition of your hopes.

Remember me kindly to your father and mother, and believe that I am,

My dear Friends, ever sincerely yours,

JOHN LEYLAND.

To Miss Halton.

Liverpool, January 30th, 1855.

My dear Miss Halton,

Most sincerely do I condole with you in the great loss you have just sustained, which I heard of the other day, through Worsley Battersby. Your mother was, indeed, a woman of no common merit. Earnest in religion, exemplary in the every-day duties of life, humble and patient, she set both her family and others a noble example. The full worth of her character could only be known by long and intimate acquaintance. She was a valued friend of my mother's; and one of the earliest things I recollect being taught was to look upon her with respect. That she was spared in the possession of her faculties, and in tolerable health, to the age allotted to man, must be to you a source of thankfulness. Providence laid on her many trials; but, now they are over, you will derive comfort from knowing that her patience was perfected through suffering. She fought the good fight, and has, I firmly believe, entered into her rest. Death must come. Few—even if they could—would live always. The set time is mercifully hidden in the councils of the Most High. Why it should steal like a thief in the night on some, while to others it approaches step by step, slowly, and in the light of day ; why some fall into the grave like a sheaf of corn, gathered in its season, and others are stricken in the noontide of their strength, or in the flower of early youth, are things we are not now to know.

Human faculties are too weak and imperfect to understand the dealings of Providence. How should the finite comprehend the infinite ? There are wheels within wheels, moving, seemingly, in opposing and contrary directions, and it is only by Revelation that we know there is an eye in the centre, governing all in perfect harmony. Blind and ignorant as we are, we can yet dimly discern that there is profit in trouble. Death takes the good whom we love, and our hearts go with them, and we are insensibly led to follow in their footsteps, in the hopes of a future reunion.

With regards to your brothers and sister,

I remain, my dear Miss Halton, truly yours,

JOHN LEYLAND.

To James Bent, Esq.

Liverpool, March 29th, 1855.

My dear Sir,

Ever since I crossed your threshold in August last I have intended writing to you ; but somehow the month of March has come round, and I am only now putting my intention into execution. I have reflected much on the subject you mentioned at the hasty visit you paid to me in October. If the proposal had come fifteen years ago, I should not have hesitated. When I was growing up, there was nothing I wished for more than to enter the ministry. Efforts to that end I made at home, but they were disregarded, and the current of events carried me to other pursuits. I have often since thought that it would have been a calling in which I should have taken great delight, and in which I might perhaps have made myself useful. But I am got too old now to enter upon a new vocation. Another impediment exists, in my attachment to Hindley, for all my thoughts for the future tend thitherwards. I can hardly tell why. The neighbourhood is not inviting: it is flat, and abounds with unsightly factories and collieries. Yet, spite of all, my destiny seems irrevocably bound up with the place. Thank Mr. Mytton for me, for his offer, for which, however, I know I am principally indebted to your kind and partial opinion.

I often ruminate agreeably on my visit to Baildon. It is no longer as

> "The dusky nation of Cimmeria."

When I think of you now, I can picture you in pretty much the same condition I should be sure of finding you. I enjoy again and again the delicious little peep the plantations allow of the valley stretched before your windows. Your moor I look upon as an old acquaintance; and for the "Aire," wayward as may be its course, brawling or quietly slumbering, I have vowed a lasting friendship.

I am, my dear Sir,
At all times yours and Mrs. Bent's sincere friend,
JOHN LEYLAND.

To Alfred Pennington, Esq.

Liverpool, April 4th, 1855.

My dear Sir,

One subject so completely engrossed our attention in the short time we were together on Saturday, that I quite forgot to speak about the disposal of your second subscription to the Grammar School. If I mistake not, you once expressed a wish that it should be applied to increase the stipend of the master.

I may state, however, what I probably did not at the time you made the observation, that it makes no difference whether the sum be so applied or to the building fund, as the amount of the subscriptions falls considerably short of the cost of the new buildings, and the difference will have to come out of the mine rents, which are ordered to be set apart for the increase of the yearly income; so that if your subscription be added to the building fund a less amount will have to be taken from the mine rents, and if it goes directly to increase the income the mine rents will then be encroached upon in the same proportion. Nevertheless, the trustees would ill appreciate your liberality if they were to appropriate it otherwise than in the precise way you may indicate.

I am, faithfully yours,

JOHN LEYLAND.

To Richard Pennington, Esq.

Liverpool, April 21st, 1855.

My dear Sir,

I have your letter of yesterday, and I am in receipt of one from Mr. Taylor of the same date, in which he says that, not only has the sanction of the Court of Chancery not yet been obtained to the school site, but that there are certain points relative to it on which the Court may need additional information, and which may cause still further delay. This has made me think it desirable to call the trustees together at once, for if two or three months elapse before the various details connected with the application are brought to a conclusion, and our arrangements have then to be made for the building, the season will be too far advanced for it to be proceeded with during the present year.

As time would not allow of my writing for your opinion, I have called a meeting for Wednesday.

I am, truly yours,

JOHN LEYLAND.

To Mr. B. J. Barlow.

Liverpool, May 15th, 1855.

My dear Sir,

The last time I wrote to you was in the summer of 1853, to solicit your aid to the fund for building our new Grammar School at Hindley, a letter you never deigned to acknowledge. I was pleased afterwards to see your name in the subscription list, though I must beg leave to observe it was added through another channel. I hoped that my letter would have at least drawn forth a reply, but I was disappointed, and the conviction gradually settled upon me that I was an illused man. I have tried to make excuses for you. A family man is, I have said, absorbed in the little world of his own household, out of which its anxieties, its hopes, and its enjoyments leave him little leisure to wander. But, granting this, some sympathy is yet due to the larger world without, and especially to old friends and neighbours.

My present object is to awaken you to a consciousness of these duties, and I feel an instinctive persuasion of the success of my efforts. I will only add, then, that I shall have much pleasure in receiving a letter from you, with what news you may have the opportunity of communicating.

I have little to say of myself. When I have told you that I am well, and still at work in Liverpool, I have told everything of a direct personal nature that concerns me. If you continue to take your usual interest in Hindley, you will be pleased to hear that trade is active; that the place is generally prosperous; that since Mr. Hill's death there has been an active and devoted clergyman labouring, with an assistant curate, for its spiritual welfare; that an Operative Reading-room and Library have been established; that the Grammar School has been re-opened lately (in temporary premises), under the superintendence of an able master; and that a Cricket Club has been recently founded, and is in a flourishing condition.

If the township could be formed into a distinct and

independent parish, another important step would be gained. The population at the last census amounted to about 7,000, since which it has considerably increased. The present church has not accommodation for more than 800 people. The influence of another church, with its adjunct of schools, could not be otherwise than beneficial.

Wigan takes away about £300 per annum, in the shape of tithes, to swell the income—already far too large—of the rector, and this sum, both from its amount and the source from whence it is derived, would form a most appropriate endowment for a new church. It is painful to think of the difficulties which stand in the way of such a scheme being carried out.

I must now conclude, and with kind regards to Mrs. Barlow,

I remain, ever faithfully yours,
JOHN LEYLAND.

To Charles Seymour, Esq.

Liverpool, June 1st, 1855.

My dear Sir,

The attempt we made about two years and a half ago to bridge over the silence which had so long separated us, should not be allowed to fail. I never could tell why we were content to let as many years as we did pass away without communicating with each other. Our intercourse at one time was of a very intimate nature, and certainly not more intimate than agreeable, and there was never any cause of quarrel between us. My thoughts often recur to its commencement at school, and to the visits I used to pay in Upper Brook-street, and the peregrinations we were in the habit of making together in the neighbourhood of Hindley. Some of the scenes we have passed through together rise so vividly to my mind, that it is difficult to conceive they are distant as many years as they really are. Whilst I write they crowd upon me, and my fingers itch to transfer them to the paper.

The reply you made to my last letter was most welcome. The long time during which our intercourse was suspended had prepared me to hear of more of the changes every family circle is liable to than, happily, you had to communicate. I rejoiced to find that yours had been so little broken in upon. I had been told, by whom I do not now remember, that you had lost one of your brothers, and was happy to find I had been misinformed. Your mother, I hope, enjoys good health. Pray assure her of my cordial esteem. And Roger; what is he doing? and how is he getting on? I think you told me he was living in London. When a lad he was of a much graver cast than you; nevertheless, no one used to relish more heartily a bit of fun and mischief.

Some months after I got your letter I happened to be called to Manchester on business, and after it was concluded I had just time left to allow me to call at your residence. Unfortunately, you were out, but I daresay you would hear of my visit. I saw your little girl, who seemed to regard me with great apprehension, as she buried her head in her nurse's breast all the time I was with her, so that I could scarcely get even a glimpse of her features. Surely we might plan a meeting somewhere.

My engagements allow of my going little from home, but it would give me great pleasure to see you here at any time.   I am, sincerely yours,

JOHN LEYLAND.

To Richard Pennington, Esq.

Liverpool, June 9th, 1855.

My dear Sir,

The subscriptions paid to the District Bank amount to £409 6s. 8d., and I suppose there will also be about another £100 in Messrs. Woodcock's hands. Abram has contributed no portion of this sum, if we except, what perhaps scarcely ought to be excepted—a single £10 got by me from Mr. Robinson, who certainly owns property in that township, but who lives in the neighbourhood of Liverpool.

The "scheme," you will remember, allows us to use the mine fund to the extent of £800 for the building, and £100 for the site, or £900 in all. The law expenses have also to be paid out of it, and at the present time it stands only at £459 13s. The law expenses, I doubt, will be heavy.

I am, faithfully yours,
JOHN LEYLAND.

To Alfred Pennington, Esq.
Liverpool, June 19th, 1855.

My dear Sir,

A meeting of the Grammar School trustees took me to Hindley on Saturday; but I made no effort to see you, as I supposed, notwithstanding the weather, that you would be away on the journey you told me you had in prospect.

For heavy rain it was a day in a hundred, and the discomfort I experienced in consequence at the meeting was augmented by the misplaced sympathy of your brother. He was sorry the day was so wet, certainly, but it was on account of Mr. Tickle having had to walk so far in it. He was uncomfortable, from the room we met in having no fire, lest Mr. Tickle should suffer. He lamented there were no refreshments, but it was out of fear that Mr. Tickle might famish. Now, if there is one man more than another in the world independent of sympathy, that man is Mr. Tickle. If your brother had grieved for Mr. Gaskell, whose 72 years seem to be weighing now heavily on his shoulders, or for me, who am reduced to the utmost possible verge of tenuity, I could have understood him; but to lament for Mr. Tickle, with his placid brow and rubicund visage, with that happy twinkle of the eye which marks the contented spirit within, that double chin and aldermanic paunch, is, I must say, at variance with all my notions of propriety.

After the meeting was over, I went to Stoneclough, to see Mr. Stott, and returned, late in the evening, to Bolton, with the lower part of my clothes drenched completely through. I took up my quarters at the Swan, and thought it prudent to go straight to bed. My wet clothes I put outside the door of my room, in order that they might be hung before the fire. Next morning I was so long in recovering them—although I plied the bell repeatedly—that I was compelled to leave the hotel without breakfast, in order to catch the train. Observing some blue in the sky, on my way to the station, I suddenly determined to take a ticket to Horwich, instead of to Liverpool. From Horwich station I walked to Rivington village, got breakfast there, and attended morning service in its picturesque and primitive church. On the conclusion of service, I mounted to the top of the Pike, and when I had for some time expatiated on the prospect it commands, descended the other side of the hill to Horwich, where I dined, attended afternoon service in Horwich Church, and returned to Liverpool in the evening. All this, however, is foreign to the object I had in view in writing, which was to tell you that your brother brought a new design for the school to the meeting on Saturday, prepared by a Mr. Marsden, of Bolton. The merit was such that the trustees adopted it at once, although they had previously decided in favour of another.

I am, faithfully yours,
JOHN LEYLAND.

To Alfred Pennington, Esq.

Carlisle, August 3rd, 1855.

My dear Sir,

I am so apt to merge the cotton spinner in the friend, that I am afraid I sometimes occupy an unreasonable portion of your time with my communications. Notwithstanding the effort I have made on the present occasion to follow a more prudent path, inclination has got the better of discretion, and I am scribbling away with no better an excuse than to tell you I am thus far on an excursion to the English Lakes. Happily, letters have not sentient properties, or I should pity the humiliation mine must experience when lying side by side on your desk with your business letters, waiting its turn to be opened. I can imagine a letter sent to negotiate a number of bales of cotton, eyeing it with supercilious disdain, or one come to bargain for twist calling it an "idle baggage," and expressing wonder at its audacity in thrusting itself forward in the company of its betters.

I am afraid I am acquiring roving habits, I enjoy so much an excursion. A sufficient cause, however, exists for my present journey, in the fact, that two of my friends with whom I am in the habit of constantly associating are each engaged in the publication of a book. I can fancy you saying, "I don't quite understand how that can affect you," and I am conscious some explanation will be needed. Know, then, the two books I speak of are remarkable books. They are each (so their authors say) going to produce a revolution in the world. One is on science, the other on philology. The first is to upset the Newtonian theory of gravitation, and to substitute a system of electricity in its place, which shall govern the flux and reflux of the tides, the motions of the planetary bodies, and all other physical phenomena. The latter, through a recent discovery in articulate sounds, is to effect a complete change in the study of languages.

You will at once admit, then, how glad an old Tory must be to escape, for ever so short a time, from such innovating ideas.

The doubts lest the subtle and capricious element of electricity should carry the earth some night out of its usual orbit into the regions of extreme heat or cold, or that, in the perfection of the other system, one may have, at a time of life not pleasant to mention, to learn over again the alphabet on a totally different principle, are enough, as Mrs. Malaprop would say, to give one the "hydrostatics."

If the weather turns out sufficiently favourable to

allow of my seeing the principal lakes in a moderate space of time, I purpose crossing the channel, and visiting Londonderry, the Giant's Causeway, and other objects of interest in the North of Ireland.

I am, faithfully yours,
John Leyland.

To John Wilton, Esq.

Gretna, Scotland, August 7th, 1855.

My dear John,

I can imagine that the address of this letter, to which I invite your attention, if you should happen to have passed it without observation, will surprise you considerably, and that you will be hurrying on, or glancing instantaneously lower down the page, to see what has brought me to a place of such equivocal celebrity. But softly, good sir ; not so fast, if you please. What if I refuse to tell when I came, or how, or for what purpose? If I choose to act so, I shall only obey an impulse which so shrewd an observer as you are must have noticed, however perverse, to be often indulged in by frail humanity.

Men and women receive gratification from torturing their own species, as well as the so-called inferior animals. Lads tie kettles to dogs' tails, and rob birds' nests. Wives scold their husbands, and husbands thwart their wives. If a fellow is unlucky enough to have his hat blown off on a windy day, it causes merriment to the bystanders, instead of exciting their commiseration. The caracolings of the hat are watched with intense enjoyment. It stops, and the owner, breathless and with streaming hair, comes up, stretches forth his hand to grasp it, when lo ! a spiteful gust carries it on with greater velocity than before. Over and over it rolls, "through mud, through mire ;" again it stops, again he reaches it ; he stoops ; it moves on a little gently—a yard or so ; he stretches beyond his power, loses his balance, falls souse full-length in the mire, and his ears are greeted at the same moment with a burst of uproarious laughter.   I am not, observe, defending such practices ; on the contrary, I think them highly reprehensible, and I refer to them only to show that if I was to remain silent as to the object of my journey, I should follow an everyday example.

I will, therefore, explain that I was called here on certain pounds, shillings, and pence business of the Magnetic Telegraph Company, which I hope to conclude to-morrow, when I go on to the English lakes. You have never, I think, visited them, so I shall use my eyes for your benefit as well as my own, in order that we may enjoy the excursion together on my return.

I am, truly yours,
JOHN LEYLAND.

To the Misses Ingham.

Keswick, August 10th, 1855.

My dear Friends,

Probably you have never witnessed the operation of net-fishing ; but if you have not, you may imagine what desperate efforts the poor fish make, when they find they are entangled, to free themselves from the net, and how their efforts only end in being involved further in its meshes. I am like these unhappy and much-to-be-pitied fish, for I am immersed in business, which seems to coil round me the more I struggle for liberty.

Your letter dated some two months ago arrived in due course, and I have only now the leisure to reply. You give your friends an excellent example of diligence. Persevere. The mind is a soil no one cultivates without reaping an abundant harvest. Men and women with well-informed minds not only discharge better the duties devolving upon them, but a wide sphere of enjoyment is opened to them to which others are shut out.   Literally they may be said to

> " Find tongues in trees, books in the running brooks,
> Sermons in stones, and good in everything."

For the last month or two I have been very unwell

and under the doctor's care. I am now on a visit to the lake district, and hope to come back better.

I will not attempt any description of this beautiful country, as I am travelling with a friend who is an inveterate sightseer. When I see you I shall be better able to do it justice than by a letter written, as any letter I now write must necessarily be, in haste.

I am, sincerely yours,
JOHN LEYLAND.

To John Pennington, Esq.

Liverpool, September 4th, 1855.

My dear John,

The "coming of age" of last year was too memorable an event to be effaced speedily from the memory. When the day came round again, I enjoyed the festivities a second time in the recollection. I drank your health, too, in some choice old port, and wished you many returns of the day. I rejoice I can congratulate you also on the gloomy forebodings which filled you, from an unlucky number sitting down at the dinner table on that occasion, being at length dissipated.

No casualty, that I have heard of, has happened during the year to any of the party, without it be to ——, in marrying a widow, and that possibly may not turn out so bad an affair after all.

You will find, my dear friend—if you will allow me to be grave for a moment—that years will begin to pass swiftly with you. In manhood the shuttle in the web of life seems to fly faster than it does in youth. I am nearly twice your age, and yet I dare say it appears to me to be a very little longer time since I attained my majority than it does to you since you attained yours, short as that is, and, possibly, I may be looking upon life much as you are doing.

Youth is precious ; but it is a great mistake to suppose it to be an unmixed good, as great, indeed, as to suppose old age an unmixed evil. Perhaps you will smile at what I say, and think I am making a virtue of a necessity. Be it so. Yet, let me add, that youth should be looked upon with the same sort of feeling we look upon the fruit-blossoms of our gardens. The leaves of these blossoms are arranged with so nice a skill, tinted with such beautiful colours, and breathe such pleasant odours, that we might suppose them destined for a long existence. Yet we never grieve at their speedy decay, as we know it to be a necessary preliminary to the ripening of the fruit. The infirmities of advanced life are, in like manner, the withering of the husk of the soul, which it is soon to escape from, and to stand out of, infinitely more perfect.

I am, faithfully yours,

JOHN LEYLAND.

To Charles Hartley, Esq.

Liverpool, Nov. 17th, 1855.

My dear Hartley,

Just as I was on the point of leaving the office on Monday evening your letter was put into my hand.

After I had been at home and refreshed myself with a cup of tea I turned my steps to Chatham-street, and found that a letter your family had received from you in the morning had not only relieved them from many anxieties, but had placed all of them in a very enviable state of happiness.

This happiness, if it were possible, I augmented by the reading of my letter. I thank you for remembering me so soon after your arrival, and for the interesting details of your journey.

I have no news. The credentials of my letter rest in the date it bears of Liverpool, and I am supposing that to be sufficient to insure its welcome. Zandotti goes on as usual, perpetrating the same bad jokes, and laughing at them as immoderately. He is certainly a most extra-ordinary character. I often think that if he was to come under the observation of some of our best novelists he would be certain to be immortalised. Notwithstanding his many oddities, I confess to a liking for the old man.

I am looking forward to my liberation from business next summer with great pleasure ; so much so, indeed, that I am at times apprehensive of some untoward event arising to hinder it. But sufficient unto the day is the evil thereof. I will hope, spite of any misgivings, that we may meet and expatiate,

"'Midst the chief relics of almighty Rome."

Believe me to remain, sincerely yours,

JOHN LEYLAND.

To the Misses Ingham.

Liverpool, November 28th, 1855.

My dear Friends,

Far from your letters troubling me, they afford me, on the contrary, a very lively pleasure. The oftener therefore you write, the more pleasure I shall have.

I was glad to hear you had been enjoying yourselves in Yorkshire and Derbyshire. The first-named county I know a little of, the latter I have never yet visited. Both, perhaps, possess more than an average share of interest : Yorkshire, from its extent, its commercial importance, its ancient history, and its many ecclesiastical and baronial remains ; and Derbyshire, from its scenery, which, I suppose, may vie with that in any part of the Kingdom.

Your mother proposes a difficult task when she asks me to give an opinion on female education, especially within the limits of a letter. The subject is really so comprehensive, that I hesitate to enter upon it. The disinclination at the present moment I regret the less, as I may be able to talk it over with her in a few days, having business which will call me to Hindley next Saturday, when I will take the opportunity of seeing her. On the subject of education I may say thus much now, that the first thing to be considered is, what will best fit us for discharging the duties of our respective stations in life. It is true, no one can ever have too much of either science or letters ; but the true end of life is not that we may become skilled in this world's knowledge. A person who does nothing but acquire information is like a miser who lives but to hoard money. Home is woman's province, and the qualifications oftenest called into exercise there are unquestionably the most important. Ordinary household duties—sewing, knitting, preserving, pickling—form an essential part. Above everything, it is necessary to cultivate, what indeed carries with it its own recompense—a cheerful temper. Fathers and husbands return home, vexed and wearied with their business in the world, and a comfortable fireside and loving attentions are a far better welcome than a literary or scientific dissertation in a littered parlour. You will see that I am inclined to lay as much stress on the cultivation of the heart as of the head. If this be considered low ground to take, I must urge that there is as much true dignity in discharging humble and everyday duties as there is in fulfilling those which rank higher in the estimation of the world.

I must now conclude, and with kind regards to your father and mother.

I remain, your sincere friend,
JOHN LEYLAND.

To John Allanson, Esq.

Liverpool, December 12th, 1855.

My dear Friend,

You are right; our opinions are continually undergoing change. The intellectual life of man is comprised in a series of cycles. So soon as one is evolved we enter another, and old things are looked upon with changed feelings. The same landscape wears a different aspect as the seasons roll on. Another subject you introduce I must speak upon. I never heard you sneer at religion, nor from others that you did. If such ever was the case, you have acted wisely in abandoning it. You say you doubt. So does every one, at one time or another. The strongest faith has had a weak and trembling origin. There is a growth in grace, as there is a growth of the body. But whatever else you doubt, you cannot, I am sure, doubt the being of a God. Our own wonderful natures (inner and outer), life and death, the earth and its productions, the heavens and their order, all, to our very senses, attest it. And, if there be a God, the lifting-up of the heart to Him for light cannot be in vain. Right thoughts on religion are, beyond all things, important, and I know you well enough to be sure that you will honestly and perseveringly seek to obtain them.

I am, sincerely yours,
JOHN LEYLAND.

To Alfred Pennington, Esq.

Liverpool, January 5th, 1856.

My dear Sir,

I beg to thank you for your two letters, and for your kind invitation. The latter, I am sorry to say, I am unable to accept, owing to pressing office duties. The proposal for a new church at Hindley appears to me to be premature ; not that it is not called for by the state of the neighbourhood, but I consider that efforts should be first directed to obtain the establishment of the township into an independent parish, and the building of the church would then follow as a matter of course. As it is—speaking from the experience I have had in raising funds for the Grammar School—I despair of a sufficient sum being got for the building and the endowment within a reasonable period.

I am, very truly yours,
JOHN LEYLAND.

To James Bent, Esq.

Liverpool, Feb. 5th, 1856.

My dear Sir,

Neither of us write half often enough. I believe I wrote the last, and am willing to take what credit I lawfully may from the circumstance ; but as that letter was written nearly a year ago, it is not much to boast of. I never, however, commit the folly of supposing that if I do not hear from my friends I have lost their regard. When a convenient opportunity presents itself, let me know if there be anything fresh in the Baildon world in which a stranger may claim an interest.

Although I am still living in this busy town, I see nobody and hear nothing. If I had waited for news, I might have kept silence for another twelvemonths.

I rarely come across any of our old acquaintances. —————— I meet oftenest, but he wraps himself in such a mantle of dignity that I always fear my homely "How d'ye do?" will discompose the grandeur of its folds.

I saw from the papers that a son of Mr. Rounthwaite had been distinguished at the Christmas distribution of prizes at the Collegiate Institution, and I occasionally hear through Mr. Kershaw that the Clares keep well.

I am, sincerely yours,

JOHN LEYLAND.

To Charles Hartley, Esq.

Liverpool, Feb. 28th, 1856.

My dear Hartley,

I have been thinking ever so long that every post would bring a letter from you. I received the one you wrote immediately on your arrival at Milan, to which I replied a few days afterwards. I mention this now, in case my letter should have miscarried. I meet your father occasionally, and he tells me he hears regularly from you, so that I have the satisfaction of knowing you are well. By this time you will be able to form some opinion of the people you are living among. Anything you can tell about them or the country will interest me. How do you like the soups our friend Zandotti describes with so much unction?

Here we are just as you left us, with only the difference of being a few months older. For my part, I eat, drink, sleep, and work much as I have been in the habit of doing for years. The weather through the winter has been as mild, with trifling exceptions, as it possibly can have been in Italy. Just before Christmas we had a week of intense frost, accompanied by a wind so exceedingly keen that it seemed to pierce the very joints and marrow, and in one of the earlier months of the winter we had a day or two of extraordinary fog.

The communication with the opposite side of the Mersey was cut off for half a day, and in London, notorious for fogs, it was so unusually dense that the light-fingered gentry seized the opportunity to commit their depredations, and escaped uncaptured.

The business I wish to see brought to an end before I leave Liverpool will, I am afraid, be protracted to a much longer period than I thought likely when we parted. Unless your stay at Milan, therefore, be proportionately lengthened, I must give up the hopes of meeting you there.

Zandotti is well. He complains a good deal at not hearing from you. I am, truly yours,

JOHN LEYLAND.

To James Bent, Esq.

Liverpool, March 4th, 1856.

My dear Sir,

Your reply to my last letter was as prompt as I could desire. I am glad you ask so many questions. If I do not give a full reply to every one, it is because I wish to keep your curiosity alive. First, as to my stay in Liverpool. This I will, and yet I will not, answer. I have so often said "I am going," and continued to stay, that I will not again repeat it. I may yet add that my purpose remains unaltered, but the when and the how rest in the unknown future. My old servant is still with me.

I often visit Hindley, which is making progress in various ways. The present incumbent is a most exemplary man, and his zeal and earnestness will bear fruit in due time.

Our new Grammar School is just completed, and we

are proposing to open it on the first of the coming month.

A proposal to build a new church is now being discussed, which, if not immediately carried into execution, will be, I have little doubt, a few years hence.

The mention you make of snowdrops, crocuses, and other tokens of spring, awoke pleasant memories of garden plots, primrose banks, and shady lanes, and carried my thoughts—I cannot tell where. By-the-bye, did you hear that immediately before the departure of our two right reverend friends—Doctors Barker and Ryan—for their distant dioceses, a special service was held at St. Luke's Church, at which they were present. I mention this not so much to state the fact, if, indeed, you are ignorant of it, as to acquaint you that Dr. Barker surprised many of his old friends by wearing a scarlet robe on the occasion. I feel puzzled to account for the display, as vanity would never venture to creep under the frock of the Bishop. Dr. Ryan contented himself with lawn and unassuming black.

If you come here, as you say you may, I hope you will give me as much of your time as you possibly can.

With sincere regards to Mrs. Bent,

I remain, faithfully yours,

JOHN LEYLAND.

To the Rev. T. Anson.

Liverpool, May 12th, 1856.

Sir,

On instituting inquiries lately respecting a system suitable for the education of boys in a country school, where the ages range from eight to fifteen years, I was recommended to apply to you, as being a competent person to supply the information. The importance of the subject, together with my own earnest desire to render the school as efficient as possible, must plead my excuse for the interruption I make to your laborious avocations. The accompanying document, if you will do me the favour to peruse it, will give you nearly the entire history of the school in question. What may be necessary to add further is, that it is now at work in temporary premises, that the trustees have to appoint a new master after the next midsummer vacation, and that a new school and master's house have already been built in a healthy and agreeable situation. The 'master will have the house rent free, and a salary of £30 per annum. In addition, he is allowed to charge 2s. 6d. per quarter each on thirty free scholars, for instruction in writing and arithmetic, and 10s. per quarter on any additional number the trustees may permit him to teach. The Latin and English Grammars are taught free. From this data you will be able to judge what sort of master is required, and what sort of instruction ought to be supplied. I am myself disposed to have a master of higher attainments than the funds at the disposal of the trustees may warrant. By this means the reputation and utility of the school would be advanced, and it might ultimately become better worth his attention than it is at present.

I am, Sir, your obedient servant,

JOHN LEYLAND.

To the Rev. W. Croston.

Liverpool, May 31st, 1856.

Sir,

The Rev. Mr. Anson, one of Her Majesty's Inspectors of Schools, to whom I had made application, has referred me to you for advice respecting the organisation of a small Grammar School, situate in the village of Hindley, in this county. The resources of the school, along with some other facts relative to its history, are detailed in the enclosed printed document. As the neighbourhood is populous, and in great need of educational establishments, it becomes of more than ordinary importance to render the school thoroughly efficient. The school has been temporarily at work since October, 1854. A new school and master's house have been lately erected, and as the present master is leaving at the end of the current quarter, the half-year commencing in July next presents a convenient opportunity for the introduction of a new system. The trustees meet on Saturday, the 14th of June, for the appointment of a master. They have had one or two promising applications, but as the success of the school depends in a great measure on the selection they make, they would be glad of any advice or assistance you can give them, or if you could inform them if you know any person specially adapted for the office.

The emoluments are £30 a year salary, a house rent free, and a charge of 2s. 6d. per quarter each on thirty free scholars, for instruction in writing and arithmetic, and 10s. per quarter each on an additional number not yet fixed, but which the trustees propose to limit to thirty.

I am, Sir, your obedient servant,

JOHN LEYLAND.

To Thomas H. Sanger, Esq.

Liverpool, June 17th, 1856.

My dear Sir,

I am obliged to you for informing me of the recent important addition to your family. If I have been slow in offering my congratulations, it has been from want of opportunity to put pen to paper, and not from any indifference to your fortunes.

The birth of a firstborn child is a great and a happy era in a man's life. Even the cares which are born with it (for in this life good and evil are mingled in all things, no pleasure being unaccompanied by anxiety, and no calamity without consolation) have a salutary influence.

King David tells us that children are like arrows in the hand of a giant, and that the man is happy who has his quiver full of them, so I cannot be wrong in wishing you may live to possess many such blessings.

With compliments to Mrs. Sanger,

I remain, ever sincerely yours,

JOHN LEYLAND.

To the Misses Ingham.   Liverpool, June 25th, 1856.

My dear Friends,

Whenever I have thought of your last letter I have felt disagreeable twitchings of conscience. The pleasure, therefore, I always take in writing to you is increased at the present moment by knowing that I am acquitting myself of a debt which ought long since to have been discharged.

I always admire your industry. Much that people do in the world, either for the good of society or of their families, is by means of industry. More, in my opinion, is effected by it than by genius. Like the tortoise in the fable, its pace may be slow, but it wins the race oftener than its swifter competitor.

I have just finished reading the life of Etty, the distinguished painter. His biographer says he was a hard worker. Although possessed of unquestionable genius, his diligence and perseverance doubtless contributed materially in placing him in the high position he attained. Even after he became a Royal Academician, in fact, until his health failed him, he continued his studies in the schools of the academy as if he had been only a young student.

I have lately had a three days' ramble in Wales. The particular localities I visited were Bangor, Carnarvon, the Pass of Llanberis, the valley of Llanrwst, and the river Conway. Having heard little previously of the valley of Llanrwst, its many beauties came upon me quite by surprise. It is very little, if any, inferior to the more celebrated valley of Llangollen. When I tell you that it contains a noble river, rich fields, luxuriant trees, hills of varied shapes, a curious old town, with an ancient bridge and a church standing on the margin of the river, you will admit that it contains all the elements of a beautiful picture.

I have little room to add anything more. We have arrived at a charming season of the year; as a sweet poetess tells us—

> " The earth is full of radiant things,
>   Of gleaming flowers and glancing wings,
>   Beauty and joy on every side."

Q

May you both live to see many summers, and to enjoy them with health and friends, and contented and thankful hearts.

I remain, sincerely yours,

JOHN LEYLAND.

To Mr. A. McLaughlin.

Liverpool, July 23rd, 1856.

My dear McLaughlin,

I was sorry to hear that your journey to the Far South had not been productive of as much benefit to your health as your friends had been anticipating. I am afraid you hurried about too much. However, think of nothing now but of getting better. At times I know you are, like myself, prone to despond, but whatever you do keep a good heart. Remember, we can do much in that way if we try; and about business make yourself perfectly easy. But one wish, I am sure, pervades every one at the bank, and that is, that you may come back in sound health, however long you may be in attaining it. Williams gave me the particulars of his journey to Bangor the other day.

I am, yours very sincerely,

JOHN LEYLAND.

To Charles Hartley, Esq.

Liverpool, August 11th, 1856.

My dear Hartley,

If you are short of news, as you say you are in your last letter, how am I circumstanced who see nobody and go nowhere? But for news properly so called, I care as little as any person well can; so if you have ever hesitated to write on that account hesitate no longer. The articles on Italian affairs in the public papers are full of plots, conspiracies, marshalling of troops, repairing of fortifications, and such like topics; and if I be curious on these subjects, I can learn enough, and more than enough, from the newspapers. I would rather you would tell me something either of yourself or of Italy, apart from politics or what may be properly called news. I scarcely know what answer to make respecting my proposed journey. If I am ever to undertake it, certainly every day that passes brings it nearer. It is like one of those phantoms which elude the grasp, and when pursued seem distant as ever. It has been a Will-o'-the-Wisp, and has led me dancing over one bottomless resolution or another for some time. Even yet I cannot guess when I may be able to put it in execution.

I gave your compliments to Frazer and Zandotti. The latter is well, and in excellent spirits.

I must tell you of a little joke I took the liberty to play upon him the other day. I told him I had received a letter from you, and as he appeared desirous of hearing what you had to say, I drew it from my pocket and read precisely as you had written up to the point where you begin to speak in praise of Italy; but, instead of reading on, I continued apparently from the letter as follows:—"The weather is now very hot—in fact, disagreeably so. The heat of the sun is intense. Everything is dried up, and vegetation looks as if it was on the point of becoming totally extinct. The English climate is much villified; but if the refreshing greenness of that country be compared with what is seen everywhere here, it will not lose by the comparison. Summer in England is a delightful season. The heat is tempered by healthful breezes; the fleecy clouds, swimming in the blue ether, cast their shadows on the landscape, and deepen the rich colours of the flowers and herbage, which thus serve as a glorious foil to the golden sunshine. In Italy, instead of this, there are the fierce, glaring, intolerable, monotonous, unmitigated rays of a burning sun. And I have been as much disappointed with the women as with the climate. I had heard a great deal said of the fascination of their eyes, but really there can be no greater delusion, for, between you and me, they have the closest resemblance, of all other things, to green gooseberries. Anything more devoid of intelligence, more apathetic, more wanting in the power of expression, I cannot conceive. The same ugliness is observable in their figures, which are modelled more after the heavy Tuscan or Doric column than the graceful Corinthian or Ionic. Then the cookery is execrable. As Denon said of Egypt, there are temples, temples, and nothing but temples; so there is here soup, soup, and nothing but soup. Soup is given for breakfast, soup again' for dinner, and soup in place of tea. And such soup! Of what it is composed the cooks know—I don't. How I long sometimes for a slice of the delicious roast beef of old England. Milan is a dull place to live in for any length of time. There is little society, and less to look at. I thought much of the Cathedral when I first came; but it has since fallen considerably in my estimation. I met with an English architect one day who had been travelling all over Europe, and who had evidently studied the science he professes thoroughly. He pointed out the glaring defects of the building, and showed that the superabundance of its decorations concealed from superficial observers its deficiency in true elegance of design. I have since had no patience with it, and can see that it is no more to be compared with Westminster Abbey or York Minster than an Italian painting to the work of an English artist."

Here I found it necessary to stop. At every fresh charge I brought against Zandotti's idolised country his indignation increased. His murmurings, gentle at first, grew louder as I proceeded. Then he began to vent all sorts of uncharitable epithets against the English, said you knew nothing at all about what you were writing, and was gradually working himself up into a towering passion. At length I undeceived him; but as the elements bear traces of a storm long after its fury is exhausted, so with him—it was a long time before he recovered his composure.

I am, faithfully yours,

JOHN LEYLAND.

To Mr. A. McLaughlin.

Liverpool, August 20th, 1856.

My dear McLaughlin,

The few lines I wrote to you a week or two ago I wrote in great haste, being engaged at the time with some special duties; but I had just heard that your illness was of a very serious nature, and I felt wishful to say at once that I sympathised with you. I had intended asking you not to reply, for fear of it hurrying you; and although I noticed the omission as I was folding up my letter, I had not time to remedy it. The cheerful tone of the kind note you have since favoured me with has alleviated considerably my anxieties, and made me glad I had not prohibited you from writing. You have done well to place yourself entirely under medical treatment. Half measures in urgent cases never do any good. I will hope that the present fine weather, together with good medical advice, and your own care, may soon perfectly restore you. We must yet remember that God directs all things, and means, without His blessing, are useless. Even Apostles can but plant and water—the increase comes from Him alone. I must repeat my caution about business. Divest your mind, I beseech you, of all cares on that score.

Everybody at the Bank knows that you would be at your post if you could, and it would be doing them injustice to suppose they wish you to return before your health is thoroughly re-established.

I have been intending several Saturdays to come over to Beaumaris, and spend the Sunday with you. Unexpected visitors, however, at one time, and calls to Hindley of an urgent nature at another, have so far prevented me, and I am now on the point of setting out on a journey of some weeks' duration, into the Midland Counties. As my visit will therefore be delayed, I trust that when it does take place I may have the satisfaction of finding you almost, if not quite, recovered.

I am, very sincerely yours,

JOHN LEYLAND.

To the Misses Ingham.

Liverpool, August 21st, 1856.

My dear Friends,

As you are generally good enough to give me, at the least, letter for letter, I have been expecting to hear from you now for a short time past, the ball resting with you; and, as I am in want of a little information you have it in your power to supply, I am writing a hasty line to forestall the letter I am expecting. I am collecting particulars relating to the history of the Grammar School at Hindley, and I wish to know if you can give me the dates of your grandfather's appointment as master, and of his resignation, also the names of his predecessor and successor. Old Ince Hall, near to your house, is one of those places in which I have long taken an interest, partly from visiting there frequently when I was a lad, and partly, perhaps, from its antiquity and quaint architecture. Either you or your mother once told me there were several curious stories floating about it in the neighbourhood, which I should much like to know, and if you would write them down you would much oblige me.

I am, sincerely yours,

JOHN LEYLAND.

To J. P. Williams, Esq.

September 2nd, 1856.

My dear Williams,

I am taking mine ease in mine inn, which said inn bears the sign of "The Woolpack," and is situate in the historic city of Warwick. I have said it bears the sign of "The Woolpack," but I should rather have said it is a house known by that name, for the sign consists simply of the word "Woolpack," being printed in gilt and coloured letters on a board with a black ground. The public ought to protest against such apologies for signs. In olden time the signs of a Wheat-sheaf, a Bay Horse, a Red Lion, or a Fox and Goose, were pictorial representations of the things themselves, which, besides being much more significant, afforded at the same time a channel for the development of dawning genius. It is a step backwards in civilisation, and in an age, too, when it is even thought necessary to establish schools of design for the encouragement of art. My rest here must be brief, and will consequently debar me from entering upon the particulars of my journey. I have been singularly favoured in the weather, and have much enjoyed my wanderings among the romantic scenery of Derbyshire, and the rural districts of Stafford-shire and Warwickshire. The only drawback I have had has been the recollection of our poor friend at Beaumaris. The conversation I had with you about him, just before I left home, has kept recurring to my mind, and has afflicted me more than I can express. I feel grieved that I have allowed, what appear to me now to be trivial matters, to hinder me from going over to see him. I am anxious to know how he is, and wish you would write a line to inform me, addressed to the Post-office, Oxford, which place I expect to reach in a few days.

I doubt you will have nothing good to tell; still, whatever it is, let me know it.

I am, faithfully yours,
John Leyland.

To John Wilton, Esq.

Malvern, Sept. 5th, 1856.

My dear John,

I am here on a first, and a very short, visit, and yet, from the many conversations I have had with you about the neighbourhood, I feel perfectly at home. I have visited several interesting places in Derbyshire; among them, Castleton, Bakewell, Matlock, and Dove-dale—the incomparable Dovedale—and explored some of the caverns. Of course, I saw Chatsworth and Haddon. The first-named mansion rivals what we read of oriental splendour. The house and grounds are the perfection of art. The establishment required to keep them up must be enormous; and great as are the owner's revenues, it is said he cannot afford to live there more than three months out of the twelve. Haddon pleased me better even than Chatsworth. I have since been at Lichfield, Coventry, Kenilworth, Warwick, and Stratford-upon-Avon. Finding myself at the latter place, and within a moderate distance of Worcester, I could not resist the desire of seeing its Cathedral. When there, I was further tempted to diverge to Malvern, so here I am. Malvern and the country round merit all the encomiums you have lavished upon them. The prospect from the Beacon Hill is magnificent. England can scarcely have such another, and I am disposed to think it cannot be exceeded, taking it all in all, in any other country. The accessories of an English landscape are to me as interesting as the more salient features. I love to see the busy homesteads of farmers, with their haystacks and cornstacks scattered over the landscape, surrounded by cornfields, and green pastures, and patches of rich arable land, with

> " The distant plough, slow-moving,
> And beside his labouring team, that swerves not from the track,
> The sturdy swain, diminished to a boy."

But travellers, travelling with the expedition I am doing, have not time for disquisitions, so I must at once stop, and subscribe myself,

Your sincere friend,

JOHN LEYLAND.

To Alfred Pennington, Esq.

Oxford, Sept. 8th, 1856.

My dear Sir,

I take pen in hand in obedience to what I may call an inexorable law of nature, and not with an intention of giving you any particulars of my journey. This ancient city affords materials for a letter, as does my journey hither, which has been through the pleasant counties of Derby, Warwick, and Worcester. I visited the principal localities lying in my route, all of them for the first time, and about which I have something to say, but the law I have referred to attracts my thoughts to the village and the people of Hindley. Hindley, indeed, stands to me in much the same relation that the earth did to the heavenly bodies in the system of the ancient astronomers, who believed it to be the great centre round which all things rotated. Notwithstanding the affection I bear to the place, I have yet sometimes thought—I mention it with diffidence—that it does not possess quite as many attractions for dwellers outside as could be wished.

For example, it has never given birth to any person who has attained any very great distinction in the world. Not but that there may have been many worthy of it who have first opened their eyes there to the light. Like other places, it has doubtless had men who " the rod of empire might have swayed," but they have wanted historians. What should we have known of the siege of Troy if it had not been for Homer, or of the retreat of the Ten Thousand but for Xenophon, or of the charms of angling but for Izaak Walton, or of the great Dr. Johnson but for Boswell ? It would have been fortunate if Hindley had ever been the scene of a great historical event, or if there had been anything wonderful or beautiful in its scenery. It is true it possesses a burning well, which Baines, to his immortal honour, makes mention of. Would that so rare a curiosity was as widely esteemed as it merits. Oh ! if a poet would but rise up among us, to sing of the beauties of the Mill Lane, or of the old chapel and its lime trees, or of the parsonage and its rhododendrons, or even of that noted place of good entertainment for man and horse, the " Bird-i'-th'-Hand ! " Subjects for his muse we could find in abundance. We want but a poet, for Borsden Brook to rival in renown the Doon or the Ouse at Olney ; and even the Dog Pool might then, like Clarty Hole, change its appellation for one as mellifluous as Abbotsford.

When I look round in this city I cannot help but think that the good things of this world are very unequally distributed. If Hindley contained only one of the places of note here so numerous it would be the making of its reputation, and Oxford would be Oxford still. If a single college were placed at the Three Lane Ends, instead of where it is, Hindley would become an object of envy to the whole county. Lamentations for what is not, and what cannot be, are however vain. I can only wish our native village a more distinguished future; in which, I am sure, you will heartily join   Your old friend,

JOHN LEYLAND.

To Alfred Pennington, Esq.

Liverpool, October 31st, 1856.

My dear Sir,

At the present moment I cannot call to mind what church your note refers to, but it may occur to me on reflection. I am going up to London either to-morrow or Monday on business, which may interfere with my inquiries. I will, however, do everything I can to obtain the information you want before I go. If you hear nothing from me, conclude I have nothing to tell. I trust the committee will earn the gratitude of posterity by selecting a beautiful design for the new church. They have noble examples in the builders of our old parish churches and cathedrals. The money view of the question certainly cannot be overlooked; but, for my part, I would have a handsome structure, even if the subscriptions prove insufficient to do more than build a portion of it at first. The spire, or an aisle, or even both aisles, had better wait for another outpouring of liberality rather than stint it in size or ornament.   I am, in haste, truly yours,

JOHN LEYLAND.

To Alfred Pennington, Esq.

London, Nov. 3rd, 1856.

My dear Sir,

On inquiry I found that Mr. Arthur Holme was the architect of the church you referred to. I have since called upon him, and he has kindly lent me the designs both for that and for another church he has lately built in the same neighbourhood. I likewise called on a gentleman bearing the distinguished name of Walter Scott, who is also an architect, and he has entrusted me with his whole stock of plans for churches. Both these parcels I sent to you on Saturday, and hope they reached you safely. I promised they should be returned in about ten days' time. The one which was the object of your inquiry I liked least of any. I shall await the selection of the committee with a good deal of anxiety. They will commit an unpardonable fault if they choose injudiciously.

I am, faithfully yours,
JOHN LEYLAND.

To Alfred Pennington, Esq.

London, Nov. 6th, 1856.

My dear Sir,

I have seen the new church at Ambleside. It is very beautiful, and the committee cannot do better than adopt the same design. The Mr. Scott of Liverpool is a perfect stranger to me. I cannot say whether he has already built a church or not, but I should say it is most likely that he has. His name I have seen frequently in print in connection with the building of either public or private edifices.

Faithfully yours,
JOHN LEYLAND.

To Alfred Pennington, Esq.

Liverpool, Nov. 21st, 1856.

My dear Sir,

The more I consider the plan of placing the new church behind the pile of buildings at the corner of the road, the less I like it. If it be built there, I feel certain that the buildings will be removed in somebody's days, and then the church will neither stand square with the road, nor will the design be adapted to its new surroundings. It would not cost a great deal of money to pull down the buildings and rebuild them in Stony Lane. The committee, I take it, would be warranted in giving the additional sum for the site which would be requisite for effecting this object. I sincerely trust they will consider it fully before they decide to act differently.

I am, faithfully yours,

JOHN LEYLAND.

To the Misses Ingham.

Liverpool, Jan. 6th, 1857.

My dear Friends,

Never apologise again for writing. I assure you I always derive great pleasure from your letters. It cannot but be pleasant to find absent friends bearing one in mind.

The lectures you speak of must have been well worth hearing. Judea and the neighbouring countries possess an interest for old or young in every station of life.

I was at Oxford when I received your former letter, and I am proposing to give you a short account of that city, thinking it may interest you as much as anything I can write upon.

Before commencing, however, let me thank you for the information you sent me about Ince Hall. If you should hear anything more at any time, be good enough to preserve it for me.

Oxford is a beautiful city—perhaps the most beautiful in the three kingdoms. " A city of palaces " is a superlative phrase used sometimes to describe a handsome city. To Oxford it bears a literal application. Buildings of stately architecture abound in every street. Some have ornamental grounds attached to them, containing noble trees, which add greatly to the general beauty.

Nothing, in my opinion, can be finer than the view from Magdalen Bridge—the entrance to the city from the London Road. Domes and spires rise proudly before the eye from embosoming trees or piles of ancient buildings. On the left is the Botanic Garden; on the right, the tower, centuries old, of Magdalen College. The bridge is worthy of its situation, and the river which it spans wanders on the one hand among meadows in the sweet way nature teaches, and loses itself on the other "amid shadowy elms." The antiquity of the place touches the mind forcibly. The noble institutions of buried generations—memorials of their piety and benevolence—meet one at every step.

> "The actions of the just smell sweet,
> And blossom in the dust."

But if the good a man does lives after him, let it be remembered that his evil deeds live also. The influence of the humblest life extends inevitably beyond the limits of its own existence. Careless words even bear fruit we little wot of. Hence the reasonableness of the Scripture : "For every idle word man speaks he shall be judged." Hence, too, the reasonableness of the period of the general judgment at the end of time, for then only can the full measure of good or evil men work in their day and generation be known.

Before visiting Oxford I had been through Derbyshire, Warwickshire, and Worcestershire. I had seen two of our grand cathedrals (Lichfield and Worcester), and done homage at the shrine of our great national poet at Stratford-upon-Avon.

And now I have only room left to say that
I remain, ever yours truly,
JOHN LEYLAND.

To Charles Hartley, Esq.
Liverpool, Feb. 24th, 1857.
My dear Hartley,
After a number of vain resolutions, I am at last fairly at work on a letter to you.

More than four months have passed without my thanking you, which I now beg to do, for your letter of the 7th of October last. I have been well all the time, but, as usual, extremely busy. Few people exist happily who cannot appreciate the minor and unimportant affairs which continually interpose to put off tasks of this nature, and to me, who write slowly and with difficulty, a letter is always a task, although often a pleasant one.

I was in hopes I should have been able to tell you about now that I was on the point of bending my steps towards Italy. For some months I have been looking forward to the spring to realise my long-cherished project. I had bought trunks, and made other preparations for the journey; all of which have proved works of supererogation, as I have buckled myself for another term to the oar.

Poor Zandotti, I doubt, is scarcely as prosperous as when you left, and then he had not much to boast of. His pupils are falling away, and in a great measure through his own remissness. Long as he has lived in the country, he cannot accustom himself to English punctuality. No doubt you recollect his appearance out of doors—his slow and hesitating gait, his seeming obliviousness of everything passing round him, and when in company with any person, his spasmodic bursts of laughter. He looks the very man for sharpers to practise on, and he has accordingly been their victim on a small scale twice recently. One day he was coming out of a shop holding a small parcel of groceries in his hand, when some person ran against him, and whilst he was receiving his apologies, a confederate snatched the parcel and made off with it. I can imagine his bewilderment, and how it would totally incapacitate him from using any means to stop the thief until it was too late. His other loss was a handkerchief stolen from his great-coat pocket in the street, which, if the truth could be known, was probably dangling halfway out. He happened to be lamenting this loss to a friend, who kindly sent him a bran-new one in its place.

When he next met him he said, with a laugh, that he hoped he should soon be robbed of another. Heaven often sends a light heart with a light purse. If Zandotti had not a sous, I verily believe he would be as merry, as laughter-loving, as free from care, as he is now.

I rejoice to have to congratulate you on the state of your health and professional prospects, both of which, I hear, are excellent. With sincere wishes for their continuance,

I remain, faithfully yours,
JOHN LEYLAND.

To Mr. B. J. Barlow.

Liverpool, March 14th, 1857.

I enclose a printed prospectus, which contains all the information you are in want of relating to the Collegiate Institution. I can only reiterate what I said to you in Liverpool, that next after the great public schools I should choose this, if I had a son, for the place of his education.

Several of the lads who have been educated here have passed the Universities with credit. The principal, the Rev. Mr. Howson, is, I am constantly told, eminently adapted for his office.

I hope you got safe home, and that you continue well after your journey.

I am, faithfully yours,
JOHN LEYLAND.

To James Bent, Esq.

Liverpool, April 6th, 1857.

My dear Sir,

Ever since we last met I have been supposing you were well; but as a year, or almost a year, has passed in the interim, I am not unreasonable in asking you to tell me that you are so.

Are you likely to pay another visit here soon? The gardening operations of spring-time, the delving, planting, and sowing must be now nearly over. I have often been gratified on returning to a garden after a brief absence to find the progress which has been made in the unfolding of the leaves, the development of the flowers, and the lengthening of the young and tender shoots. The gratification you would receive from these sources on returning home would be cheaply purchased by a journey to Liverpool, and then you would see your friends, and your friends would see you into the bargain. Therefore I say come, and come quickly.

The Art Exhibition in Manchester will, I daresay, bring you among us some time during the ensuing summer. The opening ceremonial is fixed, I see, for the 5th of May, but it would be well to delay a visit until afterwards. It is too much to expect arrangements of such magnitude to be perfect in every part on the opening day. The London Exhibition of 1851 and the Paris Exhibition of 1855 were neither of them seen to advantage for some weeks at first.

I suppose you have been, like all the rest of Her Majesty's faithful lieges, a good deal engrossed with the recent elections. If I did not well know how capricious public opinion is, I should wonder at the general popularity of Lord Palmerston. Lord John Russell has been a great favourite with the Liberal party, as they call themselves, for a long time ; but they have at last opened their eyes to the fact that the idol they have been worshipping is not of gold, but of common clay. We could have told them that a quarter of a century ago.

I have difficulty in believing Lord Palmerston to be the great man it is the fashion to say he is. His partisans are continually calling on the nation to show its gratitude for his services in bringing the late war to a successful issue, while, in truth, no more credit is due to him than to any other member of Parliament. He was one of a Government to whose culpable negligence the sufferings of the Crimean army were owing ; yet this fact is ignored ; and when the public voice in and out of Parliament compelled the Government he subsequently formed to adopt energetic measures, he carries away, forsooth, the merit !

Present my cordial regards to Mrs. Bent, and say that, although I so rarely see her, I hope she allows me to retain a place in her recollection.

I am, very truly yours,

JOHN LEYLAND.

To James Bent, Esq.

Liverpool, May 4th, 1857.

My dear Sir,

It goes some way to make one a convert to the new doctrine of spiritual communication to learn that you were really within a few yards of me at the very time I was writing my last letter. Who kidnapped you on my threshold you do not say; but it could certainly be no good friend.

I was glad to hear that you were well, and Mrs. Bent and your little boy also. Time flies so quickly, that I was scarcely surprised to hear that the latter had completed his first lustre. I trust his life may be spared for his parents' sake, and for his country's, too, for I know you will instil good principles into his mind, which, with God's blessing, will lead him to grow up in His fear and knowledge. Godly men are the salt of a nation; and for God's Word to have its full influence on the character, the Holy Scriptures must, as with Timothy, be known from childhood.

I was as much disappointed as you were with the result of the Liverpool election. I was at the Conservative committee-room the evening before, and the canvassers spoke in the most confident terms of success, so that even the best informed on the subject were taken by surprise.

I live in hopes to visit you again. Rest assured I shall seize the opportunity whenever it presents itself.

I am, ever yours truly,

JOHN LEYLAND.

R

To Mr. William Taylor.

Liverpool, May 16th, 1857.

My dear Taylor,

Mr. Muirhead has just showed me a letter he has received from you, in which you have been good enough to make kind mention of me. I was glad to learn you were well; and, as several months have elapsed since you left us, I was hoping to hear that you had settled down to some business or profession, when, to my surprise, I read that you had been following the hounds, and at the death of no fewer than ten foxes. I must claim the privilege of a friend to find fault with you for this waste of time, if for nothing more.

My opinion on hunting and such like sports is, that they are cruel, and, because cruel, unlawful. Man has no right to amuse himself with the torture of other beings. If it be the aim of a gentleman in society to wound neither by word nor deed the feelings of another, so it should be equally repugnant to a gentle spirit to inflict pain wantonly on the humblest of God's creatures. It is not, however, to charge you with inhumanity that I took up my pen—for I know these pursuits are indulged in from custom by many estimable men—but to say what I thought our former connection warranted, that a young man who has attained his majority should think of something else than hunting foxes. A man's whole life, believe me, often depends on the start he makes at the outset. The first step certainly should not be taken hastily, but after due consideration has been given to it and a decision arrived at, no time should be lost in idle delays. If a young man was to go to either of the Universities without having gone through the preparatory studies, he would feel himself in an awkward position. There would be books of which he had not the key, tutors and lecturers to aid him in mastering the difficulties of sciences of which he knew not the elements. And it is likewise necessary for a young man to qualify himself for the place he has to fill in the greater university of the world. He must expect to cut a sorry figure if he lets time pass over hesitating what to do, or neglecting the needful preparation. If he does not aspire to honours, he should at least, for his own and his friends' sake, seek to graduate respectably.

Have I spoken too freely? Unless you write a few lines to the contrary, I shall almost fear it. I wished to thank you for remembering me; and when I sat down to write, I could not help speaking as I have done.

With sincere wishes for your welfare.

I remain, truly yours,

JOHN LEYLAND.

To Mr. A. McLaughlin.

Liverpool, June 15th, 1857.

My dear McLaughlin,

I should not have ventured to disturb you with a letter if it had not been for our friend Williams telling me he had written to you, and heard from you in reply. But if I follow his example, I am far from wishing you to follow your own, and reply to this, unless you desire it, and feel perfectly able. Your friends here often think and speak of you, and would be rejoiced to receive a better account of your health than they have lately had.

Nothing to me is more offensive than cant in religion, and I involuntarily suspect a man's sincerity when he obtrudes it at an unseasonable time. If I touch upon the subject, then, for a moment, believe me, I do it with a deep sense of my own unworthiness. I feel I should be wanting in friendship if I were not to remind you that life, even with the strong and healthy, is held by a frail tenure; how much more uncertain, then by one suffering from a serious illness like yours. If God is not yet with you, what He should be to us all, "inexpressibly dear, the chief among ten thousand, and altogether lovely," make Him so, my dear friend, at once. Seek Him with your whole heart, and you will as surely find Him. Invitation is the language of

Scripture, from beginning to end: "Ho, every one that thirsteth, come ye to the waters, and he that hath no money; come ye, buy, and eat; yea, come, buy wine and milk without money and without price." "Therefore will the Lord wait that he may be gracious unto you, and therefore will he be exalted, that he may have mercy upon you." "Come unto me, all ye that are weary and heavy laden, and I will refresh you." And the promises of pardon are equally clear and full: "Come now and let us reason together, saith the Lord: though your sins be as scarlet, they shall be white as snow; though they be red like crimson, they shall be as wool." How He can so freely forgive; how He could so fully redeem; how the Godhead could be veiled in the flesh, suffer and die for the justification and reconciliation of sinners, are mysteries, but are nevertheless true. "As the heavens are higher than the earth, so are my ways higher than your ways, and my thoughts than your thoughts, saith the Lord."

I am, my dear McLaughlin, affectionately yours,

JOHN LEYLAND.

To Charles Hartley, Esq.

Liverpool, July 11th, 1857.

My dear Hartley,

I write to acquaint you that I am alive and in good health—facts which your long silence might dispose me to think you were indifferent to. I would hunt up the date of your last letter, parade it before you, and abuse you well into the bargain, if I did not think the sight of my handwriting sufficient to awaken contrition for your taciturnity.

Make I pray you, what amends lie in your power, and tell me speedily what you are doing and where you are living, if you are become an epicure and growing fat, or turning devotee, or falling in love, as they do sometimes in Italy, or, having fallen in love, about to marry. I have not heard a single word of you for weeks. I do not even know your address; but I suppose, if you are to read these lines, it will be necessary for me to obtain it.   I am ignorant, also, of our friend Zandotti's movements. The last time I saw him was on the evening of the day of the Liverpool election, which occurred about the end of March, when he paid me a short visit, and fired off a volley of puns on poor Charles Turner having lost his election.   Such is the sympathy the world extends to the unfortunate!

The most wonderful thing here is that we have found a Solon of a Prime Minister in Lord Palmerston. And, what is still more wonderful, it is become treason against the majesty of the sovereign people to doubt it.   *He* is the man, and the only man, to rule a great nation.   Therefore, huzza! for the noble lord and the discriminating English public.

I am setting out shortly on a journey down the Wye, and to Bristol, Gloucester, Exeter, and that part of the kingdom.   If you should feel any curiosity respecting my travels, and think it worth while to say so, you shall have full details on my return, but not otherwise.

I am, faithfully yours,
JOHN LEYLAND.

To the Misses Ingham.

Liverpool, July 25th, 1857.

My dear Friends,

I am concerned to hear of your mother's illness. The journey you contemplate to the sea-side will, I hope, not only re-establish her health, but contribute to maintain it for a long time to come.

I suppose you are about finishing the labours of the hay harvest.   Owing to the frequent rains in May and June, the crop has been heavy throughout the kingdom, and you are, no doubt, sharing in the general abundance.   I have many pleasant recollections of the season. When a lad I used to take great delight in throwing about the newly-cut grass, in turning and raking, and tumbling on the haymow.   What blistered hands I used to have, to be sure, with the abominably hard handles of the rakes and pikels! Then at times I filled, with no little importance and self-complacency, the office of butler, the duties of which were to distribute wedges of bread and cheese of unmistakable solidity, and the conte₁t₁ of a huge ston₃ bottle, to my father's haymakers. What with the physical exertion, the hot sun, and possibly the love of the beer itself, it was no easy task to satisfy the thirst of the good people. The repeated applications to the stone bottle form a standing rebuke to the assertions of political economists that demand always regulates supply. Rural occupations are certainly pleasant, and minister as much to the health of the body as they do to the purity of the mind.

The tastes and habits of the nation are changing. Luxury is eating into its very vitals, and putting to shame the simple manners of our fathers and the rational pleasures of the country. The stereotyped phrase is that the age is progressive, yet every day brings records of the most shameful frauds and the grossest immorality. We grow rich; but

> "Poison still is poison, though drunk in gold."

The Exhibition you cannot help being pleased with. So far I have only seen it once, and from a single visit a just conception of its multifarious contents cannot possibly be obtained.

I remain, truly yours,
JOHN LEYLAND.

To Alfred Pennington, Esq.

Liverpool, August 7th, 1857.

My dear Sir,

I was at Hindley the other day, and was told by John Turton that all the ash trees in the neighbourhood are dying. Upon this I commenced an examination of those on my own land, and found his report to be true, and not only that, but that other kinds of trees are dying as well. The first thing which occurred to me on making this discovery was that there must surely be an epidemic raging among trees, and I hastened to Thomas Gaskell, who I look upon as an authority in such matters, to see if he could throw any light on the subject. He told me that numbers of his own trees are in the same condition, and that the cause is in the vapour emitted by the Ince Chemical Works. Now is it not a grievous wrong that a whole neighbourhood should suffer for the sake of one individual; and, moreover, for there to be no remedy except through the risks and anxieties of a law suit? The appearance of the country round Hindley is quite bad enough without making it worse by despoiling it of trees.

I am, faithfully yours,

JOHN LEYLAND.

To Charles Hartley, Esq.

Liverpool, August 22nd, 1857.

My dear Hartley,

The virtuous resolutions which are animating you will condone for all your silence, provided they are steadfastly carried out. I have not yet started on the journey I mentioned to you, but I go in a day or two; and as I may be unable to find time to write immediately on my return, I am seizing the present opportunity, lest I should be utterly cast into the shade by your proposed punctuality. You have my best wishes for success in your recent engagement, which, I trust, will in every sense answer your expectations.

It may perhaps interest you to hear that there have been some remarkable letters published lately in one of the local papers, entitled "Liverpool Life," which describe the amusements of merchants' clerks, shop-keepers' assistants, and young men of that class generally. They reveal a fearful amount of depravity, much of which, in the opinion of the writer, results from the frequenting of music saloons, dancing assemblies, betting-houses, and such like places.

Society was never surely wickeder than now. I see

much that is evil with my own eyes, for in a huge mass of people like there is in Liverpool, a man, if he goes abroad ever so little, must be blind not to see how rife vice is. The population increases so fast throughout the country, that the efforts of the good cannot keep pace in providing counteracting influences.

An acquaintance of mine with whom I was conversing lately expressed his opinion that the millennium was fast approaching. I asked him upon what grounds he based his opinion, when he replied from the general spread of Christianity in the world, and the advancement of religion and morality at home. How men are deceived, to be sure! When a favourite crotchet has to be supported they hoodwink themselves, and stop every avenue of intelligence, lest their theories should be upset. A good man, a member of a religious household, mixing with friends as good as himself, going regularly to church, supporting charitable institutions, attending meetings of philanthropic societies, and listening to eloquent speeches on their utility and success, may be deceived and led to think the world is growing better; but if he will step out of his own charmed circle, and form his opinions as a sensible man ought from actual observation, he will be convinced that we are yet a great way off the millennium.

I am, faithfully yours,
JOHN LEYLAND.

To Mr. W. R. Fitzpatrick.

Bristol, Sept. 1st, 1857.

My dear Fitzpatrick,

In fulfilling the promise I made to write to you during my journey, I must plead the hurry and bustle necessarily incident upon rapid locomotion as an excuse for performing it in a brief and hasty manner.

I scarcely need say that I have had without interruption what is a primary requisite for enjoyment in travelling—good weather—as I believe it has been fine everywhere. The two great landmarks of my journey are visits to Hereford and Gloucester cathedrals. Both of these edifices are incomparable works of art. Cathedrals have necessarily a certain form and design common alike to all, but the individual styles of their architecture and position form a strong line of demarcation between one and another. They are all fitting temples for the worship of the Divine Being. Their vast size harmonises with our ideas of the Great Infinite; and their antiquity, stretching into the dim and distant past, bears testimony that He is the same from generation to generation—yesterday, to-day, and for ever.

I walked the whole distance between Ross and Chepstow, the greater part of the way on the very banks of the Wye, and always within sight of the stream. The scenery forms a succession of pictures of sylvan beauty. Sometimes the river flows through highly-cultivated valleys, interspersed with farmhouses and cottages; sometimes through solitary hills, wooded to their summits—here rising directly from the edge of the water, there receding so as to leave patches of rich meadow land, studded with giant elms or oaks.

I stopped a night at Tintern, and so had an excellent opportunity of examining the ruins of its famous abbey. I never visit any of these monastic remains without getting brimful of indignation at the authors of the work of spoliation. Art for centuries received its only development through religion, and by the destruction of the monasteries many of its choicest productions were consigned to ruin. Retribution ever follows wrong. England has in consequence since been behind other nations in the love and knowledge of art.

Yesterday I crossed from Chepstow hither.

I am, faithfully yours,

JOHN LEYLAND.

To John Pennington, Esq.

Exeter, Sept. 3rd, 1857.

My dear John,

When the 31st day of August comes round, it naturally recalls your birthday to my mind, and, what is also something to reflect upon, that you are become a year older. I was somewhere in the south of England last year at this time, and I remember beginning a letter to you which the hurry of travelling never allowed me to finish.

This year, though again from home, I hope to be more fortunate, and bring my sayings, such as they are, to a conclusion. Let me remind you that you are getting on in life. Another year, and you will actually be a quarter of a century old. Really, twenty-four years is a long space of time to live! You are abstemious, or the infirmities of age, rheums, rotten teeth, and gastronomic feebleness would be telling upon you. Twenty-four years may possibly appear to you now comparative youth, though I am sure there has been a time when you have thought such an age a mature period. Oh! the cheats these hearts of ours put upon us! As we journey on, the cottage behind, and the church spire before, seem to be the points from which spring the arch of the concave heavens, and we ourselves to be standing in the centre; but when we reach the spire we think it points upwards still to the centre, and the heavens to rise further away. However, I must give you the ha'-porth of bread to all this sack, and wish you sincerely many happy returns of the day; and I would also wish you to possess the something that even a Falstaff must be conscious he needs, when, as Dame Quickly says, he comes to "fumble with the sheets, play with flowers, smile on his finger-ends, and babble of green fields."

I am, very truly yours,
JOHN LEYLAND.

To John Wilton, Esq.

London, September 8th, 1857.

My dear John,

By the merest accident I have just heard that you have located yourself in an out-of-the way place, without letting me know a word about it, and I am presuming your other friends have been treated with similar courtesy.   Well, I suppose you will allow us to wish you enjoyment, if you refuse to have our society. I am taking a holiday, and, as you will see from the date of my letter, am got as far as London.

I think I have not seen you since I made the discovery that some recently-erected chemical works in Ince are destroying all my trees at Hindley.   It has grieved me beyond measure, and produced a perfect revolution in my feelings towards the place.   I feel as if I could never live there again.   How can men respond to virtuous influences, when they live in places where the face of nature is laid waste?   Can they even be human?   I tell you they will fall into a more abject state than they ever have been at any period of our country's history since it became Christian.   Call this progress if you will, but do not call it civilisation.

Sincerely yours,
JOHN LEYLAND.

To Mr. Frank Corless.

Liverpool, October 12th, 1857.

My dear Corless,

A few weeks ago I made an expedition into the South of England, and, among other places, visited Salisbury.   After I had made myself acquainted, more or less, with the principal points of interest in the city, I made inquiries how I could get to Salisbury Plain and Stonehenge, and received for answer that a coach left for Amesbury—a village not far distant from Stonehenge—at a stated hour, which would cross the plain by the way.   Consequently I secured a place, and when the coach came to start I had a fellow-passenger so very like you, that I had to look at him well, to be sure he was a stranger.   He had the same form and expression of countenance, the same colour of hair, the same fiery whiskers—in fact, your *alter ego*.   I then fancied you had told me that your family resided in Salisbury, and I felt sure the stranger must be one of your brothers.   As we drew near the end of our journey, I asked him if his name was Corless, to which he replied in the affirmative, looking at me at the same time with a good deal of surprise. I then said, "I am gifted with prophetic instinct, for I never saw you before, and you never saw me." To dispel the awe this revelation might occasion, I added, after a little pause, "I am acquainted with a brother of yours, who lives at Londonderry, and I knew you from the strong resemblance you bear to him." Upon this we immediately became friends. He took me with him to your house, which I found was at Amesbury—not Salisbury—and introduced me to several members of your family. After half-an-hour's chat I rose to leave, when two of your brothers offered to accompany me to Stonehenge. By this time it had got to the middle of the afternoon, and as I had arranged to be in Winchester the same night, I was obliged to return to Salisbury at once. I had no alternative, therefore, than to decline the offer; but I have never since ceased to regret that I did so, as Stonehenge is one of those places I so much wish to see. Pray how are you coming on? Write and tell me what you are doing, and what news there is stirring in Londonderry.

I am, faithfully yours,

JOHN LEYLAND.

To Mr. Thomas Gaskell.

Liverpool, December 16th, 1857.

My dear Sir,

Mr. ———, of the Ince Chemical Works, called upon me on Saturday, and I had a long conversation with him respecting the mischief his works are doing to the vegetation of the neighbourhood. The conversation was productive of no satisfactory result, as he persisted in affirming that all the deleterious gases in his manufactory were either condensed or consumed, and that what were liberated were perfectly innoxious. I asked him to explain the reason of the trees dying all round his works, and he said it must be attributed to other causes. I mentioned you and Mr. Walmesley as being sufferers, as well as myself, and he purposes seeing both of you soon. Pray let him understand that we are not to be talked over in this sort of way, and that we may take legal means of procuring redress. It is a nuisance which every man, whether he owns property or not, ought to join in suppressing. The law justly punishes those who mutilate the human body and brute beasts, and the disfiguring of trees is, in my opinion, a very little less sin. Politically it is pernicious, for the population, growing up in a district despoiled of vegetation, must of necessity be impenetrable to every civilising agency. I am, faithfully yours,

JOHN LEYLAND.

To Charles T. Bright, Esq.

Liverpool, Dec. 23rd, 1857.

My dear Sir,

I take the opportunity of the accompanying business communication to wish you, and the circle at the Cedars, " A Merry Christmas and a Happy New Year ; " and, if it be not irreverent to alter a word or two in a verse of one of our old poets, I would add—

> " Without appearing old,
>   An hundred times may you,
>   With health as good as now,
> These joyous days behold."

Your brother would probably give you a description of our adventures after we left your dinner table the other day. Our object, you will remember, was to have a look at Harrow, but before we got there evening came on, and an evening so dark that we had difficulty in keeping on the broad highway. At one time we were in the hedge, at another in the ditch, and never out of the mire. With much painstaking and perseverance, we found the school, absolutely touched it, yet could not see it. Albert Smith, in his " Ascent of Mont Blanc," describes a *rencontre* he had with a photographic artist who had the whim to take Strasburg Cathedral by night. The result of his experiment was a large patch of black on the paper, which the artist ingeniously said contained the view of the Cathedral, although it could not be seen. So Harrow School, and the chapel and the town, and the prospect from the hill, were before us, only we could not see them. I am, faithfully yours,

JOHN LEYLAND.

To Mr. B. J. Barlow.

Liverpool, December 30th, 1857.

My dear Sir,

I found your letter of the 14th of September waiting on my arrival at home. Believe me, I was not a little sorry to have to pass through Bishop's Stortford without seeing you, especially as, in all probability, it may be long before I am in the neighbourhood again. I halted at Cambridge, Ely, Peterborough, and Lincoln, in my after journey, to view the architectural treasures of these cities, and I daresay I should amuse you if I was to describe the gratification I received. The counties through which my route lay present a totally different aspect to other parts of the kingdom. The level plains, intersected by the long straight sluices of water, are curious sights to a Lancashire man. It happened to be market day when I arrived at Peterborough, and, for the first time in my life, I dined at a farmer's ordinary, and a more intelligent, pleasanter, heartier set of fellows, I was never among. I had an excellent dinner, and I began to suspect that farmers are as good judges in the culinary art as in the qualities of cattle and corn.

I must dissent from your opinion that clergymen are unsuitable persons to be teachers of youth. Their education, their daily reading—essential to their profession, if their preaching is to have any weight with men who mix constantly with the world—and their not being engaged in trade, are so many arguments, to my mind, of their special fitness. The science of money-getting, need surely form no part of education ; it will be acquired soon enough in these days of mammon-worship. A lad should be trained to act his part in life honourably, without reference, or at least, undue reference, to the acquisition of money.

Do not, I beseech you, let your son grow up a Radical. If he does, take my word for it, he will become ill-humoured and discontented, at war with everything and everybody, and himself to boot, doubtful if there be any truth or virtue in the world, and end a miserable life, without gaining the respect or esteem of a single good man.

I am, faithfully yours,
JOHN LEYLAND.

To Frank Corless, Esq.

Liverpool, Feb. 27th, 1858.

My dear Corless,

I was grieved to receive your letter containing the account of your mother's dangerous illness, and I have been further grieved to hear, through Tom Moseley, of its fatal termination. I beg to express my unfeigned sympathy in your great loss, which must have pressed the heavier upon you from your being so long a distance from home, and unable to pay the last sad duties it demanded. One ground of comfort on these separations arises from the consideration that they are not eternal. Night swiftly follows morning and morning night, and every night and every morning lessen the interval between the present hour and another meeting. Further consolation is derived from remembering that our departed friends are at rest and peace.

The past year has been marked by more than ordinary calamity. The mutiny in India has brought sorrow to many a home, and the commercial troubles have been in extent and severity without a parallel.

God grant that we may be spared further affliction, and that the welfare of our souls may have been promoted by those we have already passed through.

I am, very faithfully yours,

JOHN LEYLAND.

To Mrs. Charles Seymour.

Liverpool, March 6th, 1858.

My dear Mrs. Seymour,

It was with very sincere sorrow that I heard of the death of your husband. A dear companion he was of my early days, and early friends have a hold upon the affections rarely or never acquired by those formed in after-life. It has often been a source of regret that I have seen so little of him and his brother of late years, and now they are both gone. I little thought the short meeting we had last September was to be the last. Your own grief will be very great; and this second blow to his poor mother, in her advancing years, will be hard to bear. Pray make known to her my sympathy, and believe me to remain,

My dear madam, yours very truly,

JOHN LEYLAND.

To John Wilton, Esq.

Liverpool, March 11th, 1858.

My dear John,

You might well think I should be surprised when you had to tell that, instead of being seated quietly at home, you were jaunting away at the extremity of the kingdom.

By-the-bye we are unfortunate in our visits to each other. I was out the last time you called on me, and you were out when I called on you shortly before.

Your route lay through so distant a part of the country that I had to consult a map in order to freshen it up in my recollection. Travelling outside a stage coach is glorious work in fine weather. The galloping of the horses through the bracing air, the excellent view obtained of the country, the coachman's ready wit and marvellous knowledge, the old-fashioned inn, the smiling hostess and her welcoming courtesy, the keen appetite generated, and the relish of the savoury viands, set at nought the pleasure derived from the more general mode of modern travel.

Faithfully yours,

JOHN LEYLAND.

To Mr. Frank Corless.

Liverpool, April 13th, 1858.

My dear Corless,

I am obliged to you and your father for your kind invitation, which I am afraid I must defer the pleasure of accepting until another year. Besides Stonehenge, there are several places in the surrounding country I should like to see, and to have you for a cicerone would give me an additional gratification.

For the present year I have planned a Scottish tour. I think of visiting Aberdeen, the Vale of Glencoe, and Staffa and Iona. What say you to joining me? Even if you have seen these places before, you could scarcely fail to enjoy a second visit. Glasgow would be a convenient meeting place; and if you don't like to go the whole round, you can stop short whenever and wherever you like. I live so much at home that the few journeys I take yield me the more hearty enjoyment.

Scott tells us in "Old Mortality" that Ailie Wilson found constant occupation in the yearly visit of Henry Morton and his wife—one half the year in preparation, the other half in putting away the carpet, the huge brass candlestick, and the other articles of state used in the oak parlour on the memorable occasion. My travels serve the same end. I enjoy the anticipation and retrospection as much almost as the journey itself. Think over my proposal, and send me a favourable answer. Your sincere friend,

JOHN LEYLAND.

To the Misses Ingham.

Liverpool, April 20th, 1858.

My dear Friends,

"Madame de Sevigne's Letters" are waiting for you at Harrison's, wrapped in brown paper, addressed to your father.

On my visit of the 20th of March I did not go to Hindley direct, which prevented me from bringing them with me, as I promised. You may not yet, perhaps, admire them. I remember when I was your age reading the "Spectator," and thinking it dry reading; and if you should now think the same of "Madame de Sevigne's Letters," I can only say, keep them by you, for the time will come when you will enjoy them as much as I do now Steele's and Addison's essays.

I was sorry to find you a teacher in a Sunday school connected with a Dissenting place of worship. Do not, however, misunderstand me. To be a Sunday-school teacher is an important, nay, for those who have the opportunity, an imperative, duty. The attachment I have for the Church of England is, I trust, wholly unaccompanied by uncharitableness towards other forms of religion; and when I say I regret that you are teaching in a Dissenting school, it is from the conviction that, as a daughter of Church parents, any help you can give in that way should be given to the Church. The form of public worship of Dissenters never approved itself to my mind. It always appears like family prayer—good as far as it goes, but wanting in that dignity and solemnity which befits the public worship of Almighty God. The minister trips up the steps of the pulpit without vestments, as if he was about to deliver a scientific lecture; and I have seen dissenting congregations conduct themselves as if they were listening to such a discourse. I love a liturgy: as an old divine well puts it,—" If I must pray, let it be in words which have been on many a saint's lip, which have been often up at the throne of grace, and brought down thence many a blessing." I love to hear it, too, in our grand cathedrals, the very stones of which draw the soul heavenwards. The mysterious beauty of these glorious piles kindles emotions of awe and veneration : the heart involuntarily, utters—"Lord, I love the habitation of Thy house, and the place where Thine honour dwelleth." And when I cannot have these, I love to hear the scriptural and comprehensive prayers of our Church offered up in a building, if humbler, of the same type, and with a like ceremonial.

I am, sincerely yours,
JOHN LEYLAND.

To John Blackburn, Esq.

Liverpool, May 3rd, 1858.

My dear Sir,

I have received your reply to my telegram of this morning, and will write to Andrews on the subject. When you come next week, I shall have a long story to tell of a very pretty quarrel which is raging between the secretary and the auditor. We are as full of it as the great Twamley, the inventor of the floodgate iron, was of self-importance. India bills, agricultural statistics, the capture of Lucknow, and other topics of the newspapers, sink into insignificance by the side of it. Both combatants have Attic courage, so we may expect a desperate fight.

Faithfully yours,
JOHN LEYLAND.

To Alfred Pennington, Esq.

Liverpool, May 29th, 1858.

My dear Sir,

I must apologise for being so long in acknowledging your note of the 22nd inst., which John Turton duly handed to me, along with Poole's sovereign.

The pleasure of visiting Bolton Hall I must forego, I am afraid, until another summer, as I am engaged with a friend to visit Harrogate, Ripon, and Bolton and Fountains Abbeys, early in June. Then I have arranged to spend a day or two in Wales, with another friend, shortly after; and towards August I go into

Scotland: so that I really must not engage in any more jaunting expeditions.

Believe me to be, faithfully yours,

JOHN LEYLAND.

———

To the Misses Ingham.

Liverpool, June 17th, 1858.

My dear Friends,

Anyone who has observed the operative classes in this part of the country with the close attention I have done will be thankful for Sunday schools, and for any other institutions likely to exercise on them a Christianising influence. I would not, therefore, have any misconception exist as to my views of their utility. The best of motives, I am sure, led you to undertake the duties of a teacher. The amount of depravity which exists in the world you have no conception of, and I trust never may. We are in the world, but we are not to be of it. We owe it duties in setting an example of godly conversation, and in performing acts of mercy and charity. The training of the young in religious duties in a Sunday school is one way of discharging these duties.

Devonshire, I have no doubt, will highly delight you. Your principal resting-place, I suppose, will be in Mr. Spry's neighbourhood. I wish to know when Mr. Heywood left the Wigan Grammar School, and what was his ultimate fate. Mr. Spry, if you see him, will give you the information, if you will kindly ask him for me.　　I am, sincerely yours,

JOHN LEYLAND.

———

To John Blackburn, Esq.

Liverpool, July 2nd, 1858.

My dear Sir,

My first impulse in acknowledging your note of yesterday was to say a word or two to express my regret at the loss of your proposed holiday, but further consideration inclines me to think I ought rather to congratulate you on the extension of business which has been the cause of the loss. Both of us have the consolation of knowing that if our journey be postponed a few months the hills and valleys of Yorkshire will be there much as they are now, the rivers will still run in their accustomed channels, and even Fountains and Bolton Abbeys cannot in the interim moulder into much deeper ruin. I am, faithfully yours,

JOHN LEYLAND.

To Thomas H. Sanger, Esq.

Liverpool, July 13th, 1858.

My dear Sanger,

I am taking the opportunity of being at home a day from business, through a slight indisposition, to thank you for your letter. In the six years I have been connected with the company I have only been absent on account of illness a single half-day before to-day, so that I have enjoyed a full measure of health during these years.

I was glad you spoke a word on behalf of our friend at Londonderry. I had myself done the same once or twice previous to receiving your letter, and I am sure you will be pleased to hear that his claim has at last been acknowledged. I am obliged by your kind offer, in the event of my going to Ireland. Notwithstanding the wish I cherish to see once again the land of potatoes, I have fixed to go this year to the "land o' cakes."

Before I had been in either Scotland or Ireland, I was prepossessed in favour of the Scotch, and against the Irish. After I had visited the two countries, my opinions underwent a complete change. The frank and courteous manners of the Irish, their readiness to oblige, their good temper, and, if you will, their blarney, contrast favourably with the cold and distant treatment—approaching to absolute discourtesy—a traveller meets with from the Scotch.

I am, sincerely yours,

JOHN LEYLAND.

To Mr. Frank Corless.

Liverpool, August 20th, 1858.

My dear Corless,

The excuse you give for not joining me in Scotland, I doubt if I ought to admit. I shall be sincerely sorry to lose your company, and if I thought it would be of any avail, I would ask you, even now, at the eleventh hour, to reconsider your determination. Sanger, you say, told you I was unwell, which is quite true, though my illness has not been of a serious character. I am now considerably better, the treatment of my medical man having been so far successful as to lead me to hope there remains only the change of air which a journey will afford to complete my recovery.

The British Archæological Association, I see, has been holding its annual meeting at Salisbury. I read with more than ordinary interest the accounts of their proceedings from having recently been at some of the places the members have been investigating. I was a lover of archæology long before the science became popular, and I often regret that my avocations are of such a nature as to preclude me from taking part in the deliberations of one or other of these societies. With sincere wishes for your health and prosperity,

I remain, sincerely yours,

JOHN LEYLAND.

To Mr. Wm. R. Fitzpatrick.

Edinburgh, Sept. 9th, 1858.

My dear Fitzpatrick,

Owing to circumstances which I will narrate when I see you, I changed the plan of my route at the last moment, and in consequence only arrived in Glasgow late on Monday evening.

I am seizing the first pause which has occurred in my movements to thank you for your letter, which I found waiting for me there, and for the calls you have been good enough to make in Brunswick View. There has been the same sort of weather in Scotland which you describe having had in Liverpool, rain having fallen nearly every day.

I will not say a word about my journey, as I know you would prefer waiting for *viva voce* details, which I will enter into as fully as you like on my return.

I am, truly yours,

JOHN LEYLAND.

To J. P. Williams, Esq.

Durham, Sept. 13th, 1858.

My dear Williams,

You must be growing particularly particular to change your lodgings twice in one fortnight. Some little time ago a gentleman, many years a widower, began to bore his friends by telling them how he was worried to death by servants and with the cares of housekeeping. It came out presently that he was on the point of marrying again, and took this method of breaking the ice. What the secret of your restlessness may be I cannot even imagine. With prelacy in front and popery in the rear, I should say your present abode is sufficiently perilous.

I noticed your pleasantry of being ill able to afford frequent removals, which to me is a proof, though an unnecessary one, that your worldly goods are increasing. Such statements always mean the reverse of what they say. If a man makes a loud profession of religion, be sure there is a hole somewhere in his moral coat. Observe, *I* don't complain of poverty. On the other hand, I am ready to proclaim on the house top that I am growing rich. How I am beginning to hate those inveterate plagues—poor people! Why don't they work, get money, and hoard? One should never then be afraid of lending or of payments not being met at the precise moment they fall due.

I have been breathing fresh air among the hills of Scotland, and am thus far on my homeward route. The Scotch are no favourites of mine. You will have read the recent articles in the public papers on their drinking propensities, which show from authentic documents that for every man, woman, and child in the country, three gallons of whisky are consumed annually, and that they spend from seven to eight millions of pounds sterling every year in that beverage alone. Although whisky is their principal drink, other kinds of spirits, malt liquor, and wine must be consumed in addition. And the *Lancet* not long since gave statistics, proving how much worse they are, compared with either England or Ireland, in another and a grosser immorality ; and yet they have the effrontery to say they are the most religious people on the face of the earth !

I shall have to forward this letter to your works, as I have not got your note with me, and I have forgotten the address it bore, which does not, however, matter much, as it may have been changed once more by this time. If you will keep me informed of your movements, I will find you out when I get back to Liverpool.

I remain, faithfully yours,
JOHN LEYLAND.

To Frank Corless, Esq.

Liverpool, Oct. 30th, 1858.

My dear Corless,

I could have foretold your boils if I had known of your journey into Wiltshire. If we exceed the simple fare nature prescribes, we must pay the penalty in one form or another. You would have been spared the annoyance of this visitation if you had accompanied me into Scotland.

If you have any curiosity respecting my journey I will gratify you. First I went to Edinburgh, then by sea to Aberdeen, and crossed the country to the western coast, saw Staffa and Iona, and after calling at Glasgow, returned to Edinburgh by way of Loch Lomond, Loch Katrine, and Stirling. An adventure I had will amuse you. I must premise that I travelled in company with a friend from Liverpool, and at Braemar we had a discussion as to our further route, which we settled by determining to go through Glen Tilt to Atholl. The distance between the two places is thirty miles, and there are good carriage roads for the thirteen miles nearest Braemar and the eight miles nearest Atholl. The intermediate nine miles is a difficult road, and can only be traversed on foot. As the weather was unpromising, we were advised to take another route; but although my companion needed even more than myself the experience of travel in a wild and desolate country, we adhered to our resolution, engaged a carriage which took us as far as the carriage-way extended—nearly to the entrance of the glen—and then continued our journey on foot. Glen Tilt is a narrow ravine, not much unlike a deep railway cutting, with the river Tilt instead of the rails running at the bottom, the pathway being on the right bank at a considerable elevation above the stream. The walk was pleasant enough until we came to the river Tarf, which falls into the Tilt down a ledge of rocks directly across the footpath. The usual body of water passing down the river was swollen by recent rains, and we were wrapt in admiration as we gazed at it foaming and thundering down. But our admiration speedily gave way to perplexity on recollecting that we had to cross. Although we had been told the streams might be full, neither of us anticipated so fierce a current. Imagine our situation; not a house nor a human being near, rain beginning to fall, a walk behind us of at least sixteen miles, and an impetuous river in front. A dilemma sufficiently disagreeable, I am sure, you will admit. After some consideration, it seemed the most desirable course to go straight on; so I stripped off my nether garments, and as the Tarf in front of the footpath boiled and whirled and looked very deep, crossed the Tilt, which scarcely reached the knee, to the opposite bank, thinking it would be better crossing back again to the footpath lower down the stream. While crossing, and for some time afterwards, my companion stood irresolute on the brink; I called to him to follow, but he remained motionless, gazing on the water. At last, however, he waded leisurely across. An idea then seized him that there must be a footpath on the left bank, and he commenced scaling a steep cliff, which rose from the river near where we were standing, to ascertain. Meanwhile I became apprehensive of taking cold, as I had been partially disrobed for a full hour, and I called to my companion at the top of my voice that I must at once make an attempt to cross back again. The river below the confluence contained, of course, the united waters of the Tarf and the Tilt, and the task was difficult, if not dangerous. I chose a spot where some huge stones lay in the bed of the river, one of considerably larger size than the rest lying in the centre. To this stone I got easily, as the bulk of the water ran between it and the opposite bank ; and even the more difficult portion I got through quite as well as I expected, although I had no idea of the strength of the current until I was in the very middle. My companion, seeing my success, prepared to follow, and got safe to the big stone I have mentioned. The next step he made he slipped, and down he went up to the very neck in the water. Wicked as it seems, I can never think of his mishap without laughing. His head, crowned by a broad-brimmed hat, was alone visible, and as he has a good round face, presented a comical sight. His wet clothes became a serious incumbrance, and he rested on the stone to detach himself from a portion of them—an operation of considerable difficulty. The roar of the water prevented me from hearing him call—as he told me afterwards he did repeatedly—that he should never be able to get across. The next effort he made, however, brought him safe over, but the pallor of his countenance indicated how trying the task had been. Luckily, I had a flask of whisky in my pocket, which helped to restore him, and was of essential service to us both.

The rivers I met with afterwards I viewed in a new aspect—looking at them entirely as to their capability of being forded. Streams scarcely covering the pebbles at the bottom, however picturesque, I sneered at ; the deeper and fiercer currents I respected as worthy antagonists.

This story has spun out to so great a length that I must at once conclude, and say in the usual form—though, believe me, not in mere form—that

I remain, sincerely yours,

JOHN LEYLAND.

To Charles Hartley, Esq.

Liverpool, Nov. 27th, 1858.

My dear Hartley,

It seems I am to depend on accident to learn anything of you. I see your name mentioned from time to time in the papers, and conclude that you are making good way in the world, which I very sincerely congratulate you upon. I have not been in London since we met last December, but I hope to be there, God willing, in the course of next summer. I have a strong love for the country, yet, if I must lead a town life, I should choose London, a world in itself, before any other. Smoke and noxious vapours are doing what they can to wean me from my native place. They may succeed ; I don't know.

You would, of course, read the published accounts of the meeting of the Society for the Promotion of Social Science held here a few weeks ago. I heard the old president of the society, Lord Brougham, and his successor, Lord John Russell, with most of the other leading public men who honoured the society with their presence, speak one evening at the Liverpool Institute. There are about Lord Brougham unmistakable indications of a man of genius. Lord John Russell, on the other hand, looked the very personification of mediocrity. He made the most commonplace observations in the most commonplace manner. And his whole career bears evidence that his abilities are of a very ordinary character. A scion of an influential Whig family could not be otherwise than a welcome adherent to the Reform party at the commencement of

the Reform Bill agitation, nor receive other than an office
as he did in the foremost ranks.   The public grew accustomed to his name, and fancied he must be qualified for
a leader, filling, as he did, a leader's place.   His ultimate fall, therefore, was inevitable.   Moreover, the
miserable intrigues he invariably enters into when out
of power, a truly great mind would instinctively shrink
from.   Palmerston is the abler and the honester poli-
tician, and his judgment less warped by the spirit of
party.

I am, faithfully yours,
JOHN LEYLAND.

To the Misses Ingham.

Liverpool, Dec. 18th, 1858.

My dear Friends,

I have just referred to your last letter, and
noted two things—first, that it is dated four months
ago ; and, secondly, that I have never thanked you for
the information you procured for me respecting Mr.
Heywood.

The pleasure you take in rendering services to your
friends will, I know, be a sufficient recompense, yet it
is fitting I should thank you, as I now beg to do, for
your inquiries.

What you had to tell did not much surprise me.   For
five years I was a scholar under Mr. Heywood, and was
so grossly neglected that I feel less sympathy for his
misfortunes than I should otherwise have done.   It
may be severe to say that his dismissal from the school
and the poverty he afterwards fell into is an instance of
what is continually occurring even in this life—just
retribution ; but his faults certainly were many and
grave.   I remember our Saviour's admonition on judgment.   Those upon whom the tower of Siloam fell were
not sinners above the rest of Galileans; therefore, I will
say no more.   Afflictions, I know, come alike to all.   The
moral government of the world is wonderful, and as
profitable for consideration as the laws we can better

understand of the physical universe. Many of the
operations of nature stand revealed as an open book.
We can see how frost mellows the earth for the seed
we cast in her bosom, how the clouds let fall their
showers to quicken the seed into life, and how the sun
shines forth to mature and ripen it. So in the moral
world: trials hold us subject to their dominion at one
time, anxieties cloud around us at another, prosperity
in its turn warms with its welcome beams; and all
that our moral and spiritual growth may be promoted.
Thus much is evident, and faith requires us to believe
that everything works together for our good.

I felt sure you would enjoy your Devonshire journey.
You travel so leisurely that you can see the country
well. On the contrary, I hurry through quicker—not
from inclination, but from a wish to see as much as
possible in the time I can spare for the purpose.

I am, sincerely yours,

JOHN LEYLAND.

To Richard Pennington, Esq.

Liverpool, Jan. 5th, 1859.

My dear Sir,

January, you will remember, is the month
appointed for holding the annual meeting of the
trustees of the Grammar School. I remind you of
it thus early in order that it may be fixed at a time
when you are likely to be in the neighbourhood, and
that I may have a sufficient time previously to issue
the usual notices. Wednesdays and Thursdays are
inconvenient days to me; if any other would suit you
equally well, they would suit me better. Your brother
tells me he spent a pleasant Christmas at Westfield.
The weather, I find, was as bad with you as it was in
Liverpool. Unfortunately I was laid up with a severe
cold, which prevented me from even going to church.
Wishing you and your family a happy new year,

I remain, faithfully yours,

JOHN LEYLAND.

To Alfred Pennington, Esq.

Liverpool, Jan. 6th, 1859.

My dear Sir,

Estimates for lithographing five hundred copies of the design for the new church are enclosed. There is a great difference, you will observe, in the prices ; and possibly there may be as great a difference in the quality of the workmanship, but of that I cannot speak. The accompanying view of Ackworth chapel and schools is a specimen of Maclures work. Marple and Mawdsley have not furnished specimens. Maclures desire me to say that whatever they undertake they do well. Mawdsley's price may have been fixed lower than the ordinary rate, as he is a friend of mine. I shall be happy to do anything more that may be needed. Perhaps it would be desirable for you to inquire Manchester prices.   I am, faithfully yours,

JOHN LEYLAND.

To the Rev. P. Jones.

Liverpool, Jan. 13th, 1859.

My dear Sir,

Shortly after I last saw you it occurred to me that, if there were to be any changes in the administration of Mather's Charity, it would be desirable for them to be considered before the annual meeting, in order that they might then be formally passed. I therefore put myself in communication with Richard—through James Eatock, his acting trustee—who has since been over here to advise with me on the subject. Little progress has been made, I am sorry to say, as Richard is a difficult person to deal with. His present views do not seem to be altogether in harmony with the directions in his deed of gift, which places the trustees in a difficult position. Although the strict letter of the deed is doubtless binding on the trustees, yet I hold it to be their duty to defer as much as possible to his wishes. So far he has consented for the appointment of one mistress only. I will do all I can to make the arrangement you desire; but, if I succeed, it cannot be finally effected for some weeks to come. Your proposal to guarantee a small sum in addition to the mistress's endowment is kind. I will see you before the meeting, and acquaint you if anything be decided upon previously. The £1 due to the trustees of the Grammar School from the Mobberley estate be good enough to hold over until I see you. I am, faithfully yours,

JOHN LEYLAND.

To Richard Pennington, Esq.

Liverpool, February 10th, 1859.

My dear Sir,

For some time after the hour appointed the trustees were represented the other day only by Thomas Gaskell and myself, when at last an addition came, in the no less important individual than the Rev. John Jones Dixon. Delightful it was to hear how favourably the reverend gentleman regards us. Mr. Hallas is an excellent master; and the boys so remarkably clever that they can execute with facility sums in arithmetic that would puzzle even him, a justice of the peace! And in proof that his expressions of interest and admiration were not mere idle words, he promised to give £5 in prizes at the next Christmas examination. Whence is this new-born zeal? For more than four years — the most critical period in the history of the school—he has not attended a single meeting of the trustees, and has been apparently unconscious of any connection with them, or of any responsibility resting upon him by virtue of the trust. Some of us have been struggling with difficulties all the time, obtaining governing powers from the Court of Chancery, paying lawyers' bills, husbanding resources, collecting subscriptions for new buildings, and establishing the machinery of the school. During this period we have often needed counsel, and the oracle has been dumb; we have been houseless, and the priest has passed by on the other side. Now that we have gotten a fair roof above our heads, and gone some way towards extricating ourselves from debt, we are greeted with patronising smiles.

I am, faithfully yours,

JOHN LEYLAND.

To James Bent, Esq.

Liverpool, Feb. 26th, 1859.

My dear Sir,

You have been to Liverpool I hear, and never called on me. It is difficult to become possessed of such a piece of news, and to preserve at the same time one's equanimity; yet the idea of being forgotten is so unpleasant, that I persuade myself there must have been some good hindrance or other, or I should once more have shaken you by the hand. Nearly a year and a half has passed since we met. Time is something like Sancho Panza's doctor in the Island of Barataria, for days and weeks no sooner dawn than he touches them with his wand, and they vanish.

Neither of us anticipated then that the Tory party would be so soon installed into office. Of all surprising things, the dissolution of Lord Palmerston's Government is the most surprising. His personal popularity for the two or three preceding years exceeded that of any other minister of the present generation. The country elected a parliament expressly to support him, and the press spoke generally and heartily in his favour. Yet his prestige—and more from mistakes than faults—has as suddenly collapsed as one of those bodies we read of in the Etruscan tombs, which presents, when the tomb is opened, an apparently real form and substance for a moment, and dissolves the next into a handful of dust.

I look with apprehension on this new Reform agitation. If left to their own instincts, Lord Derby's Government would deal wisely with that and every other question. Lord John Russell, to serve his own ends, set the ball in motion; and John Bright, prompted, like Milton's

Satan, by hate and ambition, his chief characteristics, has done all he could to keep it rolling.

I am, ever sincerely yours,
JOHN LEYLAND.

To Mr. Thomas Brereton.

Liverpool, April 16th, 1859.

My dear Sir,

Something like seven years have passed since I heard anything of you. In the early part of this long period I wrote to you once or twice, and subsequently, when in town, inquired personally both at the house you were living in when I last saw you and at the Royal Academy, but without receiving tidings from either place. During the first two or three years I concluded you were gone where all painters go at one time or other of their lives—to study in Italy; and when more years passed and I still heard nothing, and never saw your name in any list of artists, all of which I searched that I could lay hands upon, I confess I began to think we should never meet again in this world. It was only on the last day of the last Liverpool Exhibition that I became aware I had been entombing you too soon. About the very hour of closing I was at home putting away my catalogue, when I remembered I had never looked carefully over the artists' names; and on turning the pages, to my great surprise, saw yours attached to two pictures, neither of which I had observed in the single visit I had paid to the Exhibition two days previously. I need not say I was rejoiced at the sight; and if I had known your address, which I was only able to procure a day or two ago, you would have heard from me sooner. I hope you will speedily satisfy my desire to know how the world has gone with you all these years. Are your father and mother still alive? If so, present to them my kind remembrance. I have spent the seven years altogether at business. Every now and then I have formed resolutions of breaking away, but

T

it is still, and likely to be for at least a little time to come, my occupation. I feel as young and look upon life as brightly as ever. I have never climbed, and I have never fallen. If I had been ambitious, and even, as the world calls it, successful, I might have had disappointments I am now free from to mourn over, and a soured temper to embitter the remainder of my days. Mercies without number I have received from the hands of God. Truly " the world is full of His goodness, and of the wonders that He doeth for the children of men."   I am, ever yours truly,

JOHN LEYLAND.

To the Misses Ingham.

Liverpool, May 14th, 1859.

My dear friends,

The account of your Christmas visit, and the other news contained in your last letter, much interested me. Large towns like Manchester unquestionably possess the advantages you speak of; but in times like the present, when it is sought to endow them with an unfair portion of political power, it becomes necessary to look upon the other side of the picture as well. The much-maligned lower classes of the rural districts are, I believe, as intelligent, apart from book knowledge, and as competent to form a true judgment on public men and measures, as their equals in towns. In the important point of morals they rank higher; for even John Bright, with all his bitter prejudices, must admit that the temptations to vice, and the opportunities of indulging in it secretly, are necessarily greater in places where large numbers of people congregate. It is obvious, also, that vicious habits impair the judgment, and render a man less capable, whatever order of intellect he may possess, of discharging his duties as a citizen. Small towns and counties serve one special object—they act as breakwaters in our political system against the restless waves of thought of populous communities.

I do not approve of such lectures as you tell me have recently been delivered at St. Catherine's Church. Controversial discourses of this character, in my opinion, do a great deal more harm than good : they certainly never make converts to Protestantism, and as certainly stir up bitter and uncharitable feelings between the different churches. The commandment given to us by our blessed Lord, to love one another, condemns all such one-sided views of religion. Melancthon, when dying, rejoiced that he was going where he should be free from the hatred of divines ; and if the spirit which animated him in his last hours was more generally diffused among a certain class of our clergy, gospel truth would be received the more readily by their hearers. There is enough of infidelity and immorality in the world with which the various Christian bodies may wage war, without turning their weapons one against the other. Any religion is better than none, the most debased inculcating more or less faith in an overruling Deity, restraint of passion, and the exercise of self-denial. Doubtless every Christian ought to think his own form best, or join the communion he prefers. And this reminds me of what I have more than once said, that I cannot altogether justify you, as members of the Church of England, teaching in a dissenting school. Our own church has a stronger claim for help than any other, and so great a responsibility rests upon her at the present day, that it behoves her members to support her by every means in their power.   I remain, faithfully yours,

JOHN LEYLAND.

To Charles Hartley, Esq.

Liverpool, May 30th, 1859.

My dear Sir,

A paragraph in one of the papers not long since gave me the first intimation that you were about "settling in life," as it is called, and I have since heard that the event has already taken place. I have, therefore, much pleasure in offering, according to established custom on such occasions, my congratulations, and in expressing my sincere wishes for your happiness.

The war which has opened upon us has caused the general election to pass over with comparatively little interest. Whatever measures the new Parliament may pass, it will, I think, preserve us from organic change. But the tendency of public opinion appears to me to be setting in the direction of democracy ; and I should not be surprised if in the next quarter of a century household suffrage, the ballot, and other radical measures were to become law. They have active and unscrupulous supporters, and there is always some demagogue ready to agitate and mislead the people. Changes in laws produce corresponding changes in the character of a people ; and if these and like measures are adopted, the country will fall into a state of degradation (not at once, nor in a short period, but gradually and surely), which not even the most apprehensive among us at present contemplates.

I am, faithfully yours,
JOHN LEYLAND.

To John Blackburn, Esq.

Liverpool, June 3rd, 1859.

My dear Sir,

The business we were talking about when you were last in Liverpool has been brought, like the working of the Atlantic cable, to a premature end; and whether anything will finally come either of one or the other, time only can show. Judging from present appearances, it would seem to be unlikely. If the weather has been with you in Yorkshire as it has been with us for some weeks past, you will be rejoicing at the recent rains. The drought here had become intense, and vegetation was at a complete standstill. I often think how exactly and beautifully the Psalms describe such changes as we have just witnessed. What language could be more appropriate at the present moment than this? "Thou, O God, sentest a gracious rain upon thine inheritance, and refreshedst it when it was weary." And again: "Sing praises unto God, who covereth the heaven with clouds and prepareth rain for the earth, and maketh the grass to grow upon the mountains, and herb for the use of man."

I am, faithfully yours,
JOHN LEYLAND.

To James Bent, Esq.

Liverpool, July 4th, 1859.

My dear Sir,

Before I received your explanation I felt sure there must have been a good reason to prevent you from calling upon me when you were in Liverpool, and I did not for a moment wrong your friendship in believing that you were able to call and would not. I was glad to hear that you, Mrs. Bent, and your little boy, were well in every respect, and I pray that these conditions may be of long continuance.

It is so difficult for me to leave business that I cannot at present accept your kind invitation. About a year since I made an engagement with a friend to go for a day or two into Yorkshire, in order to see Harrogate, Fountains Abbey, and one or two other places. After holding myself in readiness for several weeks to start at a minute's warning, unforeseen circumstances arose to prevent him from going. The engagement has been renewed for this year, and, if all keeps well, I hope, towards the end of August or the beginning of September, to be as near to you as the places I have named, and to run over from some point, before leaving the neighbourhood, for a few hours' talk. More than this I cannot see my way to.

I anticipated a different issue of the late election contest in the West Riding. If that constituency and one or two others had followed the example of South Lancashire, we might yet have had a Tory government. I am proud of our county victory for two reasons—first, that such important interests as this division represents should speak in the cause of order and loyalty; and, secondly, that I myself had a share (though, in truth, a very humble one) in bringing it to pass. It is a wonder that a man with Mr. Crossley's stake in the country should hold such extreme opinions. But business men are so accustomed to view everything in its relation to pounds, shillings, and pence, that it narrows their political understandings, and prejudices them against every other than their own class interests.

I am, sincerely yours,

JOHN LEYLAND.

To John Pennington, Esq.

Liverpool, July 14th, 1859.

My dear John,

You may possibly call to mind a conversation I had with your uncle Alfred, when I was at Alderley in December last, respecting the Hindley Grammar School, in which I expressed a wish to raise a sum of money for its benefit. The desirability of an addition to the funds of the trust I could make evident if I was to enter into the subject; but, as it is an everyday want in charities, I have no doubt you will take it for granted without further explanation. The *modus operandi* is not easy to devise. I have considered and rejected all sorts of schemes. A bazaar would perhaps be the most appropriate form; but, unfortunately, there are not a sufficient number of respectable families in the neighbourhood to carry one to a successful issue. A concert or a soiree would not pay expenses, and the only feasible thing appears to me to be a ball, to be held somewhere about next Christmas. If you and Egerton Wright would lend your zealous aid, such a scheme might raise the money we want. As for the place, the school, the Bird-i'th'-Hand, and the Wigan Assembly Rooms, have each their several advantages, the relative merits of which you will be able to judge of better than me. I think even I could dispose of a fair number of tickets, and our friends at Hindley and elsewhere would, no doubt, exert themselves to better purpose. May I reckon upon your help to the project?

I am, very truly yours,
JOHN LEYLAND.

To Frank Corless, Esq.

Liverpool, July 20th, 1859.

My dear Corless,

I feel much honoured by your father's kind invitation. I had not forgotten our engagement; but, no mention having been made of it for some time, I had arranged otherwise for my holiday. As my plans, however, provide for a week's stay in London, I shall have much pleasure in altering them so far as to spend a portion of the week in Wiltshire. I should like to fix my journey at the same time with yours, whenever that may be, as half my enjoyment will be lost if you are not there. At the present moment I cannot speak with any greater certainty of the time than that I am proposing to be in London about the second week in September.

Accept my best wishes for your welfare and that of your family.

I am, ever yours sincerely,
JOHN LEYLAND.

To John Wilton, Esq.

Liverpool, August 2nd, 1859.

My dear John,

I have been driven, from one cause or another, to write at the last hour, as post time is drawing near, and you land at Aberdeen to-morrow; I must, therefore, confine my observations strictly to the task you assigned me when setting out on your journey. Before you leave Aberdeen visit its two colleges, especially

King's College, the older foundation, which contains several interesting antiquarian remains.

The bigotry of the Scotch has allowed all their old cathedrals, with the single exception of Glasgow, to fall wholly or partially into ruin. Their own houses are ceiled with cedar and painted with vermillion; the temples of Almighty God in the land are, for the most part, no better than barns, and their piety is contented therewith. Of Aberdeen Cathedral the nave is the only existing portion, yet your reputation as a traveller would suffer if you were to leave the neighbourhood without seeing it, as well as the Bridge of Don, which is a mile or two further on in the same line of road. From Aberdeen go by rail to Banchory, where coaches will be in waiting to carry you to Ballater. In this stage you will be introduced to a celebrated beauty of these parts, whose charms I predict will make a lasting impression on you. Do not put yourself in a flutter— I am speaking of the river Dee, not of a young lady. Balmoral Castle stands nine miles beyond Ballater, to see which it will be necessary to obtain an order beforehand from a servant of Her Majesty who lives at Braemar. Your next resting-place will be Braemar, and if you take up your quarters at the Fyfe Arms you will find in the landlord a person able to give every information respecting Glen Tilt. If the weather be favourable, I should certainly recommend that route. Stay a day or two at the Atholl Arms, at the opposite extremity of the glen. I have not forgotten the attention I received there after my memorable fording of the Tilt last year, and I should be glad once more to offer my acknowledgments to the proprietor for the attention I received when I arrived at his house on that occasion, wet and weary. Coaches run from Blair Atholl to Dunkeld, and from Dunkeld (through Kenmore, Killin, Crianlarich) to Loch Lomond. I would recommend you to sail down Loch Lomond and back to Inversnaid, cross Loch Katrine to the Trossachs, take the coach to Callender, walk by way of Crief to Perth, take the rail to Stirling, and sail down the Forth to Edinburgh.

Any guide-book will inform you of the particular objects
of interest of each locality on the route.

I am, faithfully yours,

JOHN LEYLAND.

To Mr. Thomas Brereton.

Liverpool, Aug. 10th, 1859.

My dear Sir,

Your letter gave me a good deal of pain. I was
sorry to hear of the anxieties you are subject to, and
sorry, too, to think that you have become weaned, as
you term it, of painting. Pardon me if I say it appears
to me a great mistake to suppose that religion should
hinder us from persevering in, or performing with efficiency, the duties of this life. Certainly the whole
heart and life should be consecrated to God's service;
but then we serve God in discharging such duties
honestly as much as we do in the duties of prayer and
praise. Whatever may be said of painting, I look upon
it as a noble art, and worthy of careful study and cultivation. What is an artist but one who has a keener
perception than another of the beauties of Nature, and
the power to embody the conceptions she originates in
a material form? The influence of a work of art upon
the mind of the beholder is for good. Salutary emotions
are excited, and the innate love of beauty implanted by
our Creator is gratified and nourished. I cannot imagine
it possible for a man to scoff at holy things in one of
our grand cathedrals, or to indulge in mean and grovelling thoughts while gazing on the productions of the
great masters in painting.

In the course of a few weeks I hope to be in London,
when we can talk over these things at leisure. I congratulate you on your father and mother being spared
to you so long.

I am, very truly yours,

JOHN LEYLAND.

To the Misses Ingham.

Liverpool, Aug. 15th, 1859.

My dear Friends,

Far from thinking you gadabouts because you follow up a journey into Derbyshire by one to Lytham, I consider you are enjoying rational amusement.

I am about taking a holiday myself, the first portion of which I propose to spend in visiting Harrogate and some neighbouring places ; to go thence through Norfolk and Suffolk to London, and afterwards to Wiltshire. Not having been well for some little time past, I am looking forward to my journey not only for enjoyment, but also to put me in a fresh stock of health.

It is surprising what a benefit change of air and scene produces. To me they have always proved of essential service, although in some of my journeys I have gone through an amount of exertion and fatigue that would have laid me up if I had done it at home. Excursionists of the lower classes visiting Liverpool often amuse me. In the hottest days of summer the women are wrapped up in thick woollen shawls, with furs round their necks, and loaded with big baskets and umbrellas. If the men are less oppressed in attire, you see them turning out of the various public-houses wiping their lips, indicating that they are equally bent on attaining discomfort in another form. John Turton, who works for me at Hindley, came with two of his daughters to Liverpool by an excursion train a few weeks ago. One of the girls had been up all the preceding night through the excitement of the journey, and she was so drowsy in consequence that whenever she sat down she fell asleep. They called upon me in the afternoon, and they all said they were thoroughly wearied and anxious to be back again at home. However, spite of fatiguing accompaniments, such journeys are no doubt pleasant to think upon afterwards.

I am, truly yours,

JOHN LEYLAND.

To Mr. Frank Corless.

Liverpool, August 23rd, 1859.

My dear Corless,

I am afraid I must again postpone my journey into Wiltshire. My health, never strong, has been for several years past more delicate during the summer months than at other periods of the year, and at the present time I am so much worse than usual that it is absolutely necessary I should keep quiet, and take only gentle exercise in my approaching holiday. If I am sufficiently recovered, after the customary period, to be able to return to business, I shall be grateful. Will you kindly say all this to your father for me, and express further the disappointment I feel at being obliged to decline a visit I had been anticipating with so much pleasure. I am, faithfully yours,

JOHN LEYLAND.

To John Blackburn, Esq.

Liverpool, August 25th, 1859.

My dear Sir,

I was glad to hear that you had brought your labours at Kirkstall to a close. I leave here, God willing, on Saturday, by the 3.50 p.m. train, and will stop at Stanningley station.

If the present beautiful weather continues, it will enable us to make the round we have planned on Monday and Tuesday, and I can then start for Hull on Wednesday. My health is much as it was when you were in Liverpool—not better. I am looking anxiously forward to this journey as a means, with God's blessing, of restoring it.

I am, truly yours,

JOHN LEYLAND.

To the Rev. P. Jones.

Liverpool, August 25th, 1859.

My dear Sir,

I lost no time in placing the appeal on behalf of our new church in Mr. Mawdsley's hands immediately on his return home, and I hoped to have been able to have forwarded to you a proof of it before now. The delay has been occasioned by the artist, in transferring the drawing to the stone, but Mr. Mawdsley promises to have it ready by Saturday. As I am leaving home for a few weeks, I have requested the proof to be forwarded direct to you at Rocester. Any alterations it may require Mr. Mawdsley will attend to, and you will perhaps kindly instruct him how to dispose of the sheets when completed.

I am, faithfully yours,

JOHN LEYLAND.

To John Blackburn, Esq.

Sept. 9th, 1859.

My dear Sir,

After many stoppings and much winding about, I got housed safe last night in London. The fresh air has done me good. I feel stronger and in better spirits, but I am not yet what I should like to be. The weather turning out squally, I did not go by sea from Hull, as I had intended the day after I parted with you, but went to Norwich instead, through Lincoln, Boston, Peterborough, and Ely. I have had several glimpses of the scenery I love so much in Norfolk and Suffolk: rivers, pure as the Creator destined them to be, flowing through green pastures and meadows; cottages and farmhouses embosomed in their gardens and orchards; and church towers and spires peeping from among masses of rich foliage. Our next meeting, I suppose, will be in the middle of October, when I can give you as little or as much of the details of my journey as you may care to hear. I am, very truly yours,

JOHN LEYLAND.

To the Editor of the *Times*.

Oct. 19th, 1859.

Sir,

A recent visit to Peterborough furnished me with an opportunity I had long desired for a visit to

the ruins of Croyland Abbey.   I was sorry to find that
a part of the west front of the church had fallen a
short time previously, and that a much larger portion,
if not the entire arch of the great window, is likely to
follow.

I write these lines, trusting you will allow me through
the medium of your columns to call the attention of
some of our archæological societies to the circumstance,
in the hopes they may be able to devise some means to
preserve what yet remains of this ancient edifice.   The
church, with the exception of the north aisle of the
nave, which is still used for divine worship, is in ruins.
The pillars, however, dividing the nave from the north
aisle are standing, and apparently as strong as when
they were first reared, as are also some of those of the
south aisle, so that, if funds were forthcoming, the
entire building might easily be restored to the former
purpose.   One of our great noblemen owns a large and
valuable property in the district.   Is he, or are the
other wealthy families of Lincolnshire, so little interested
in the remains of an institution which did so much for
the early civilisation of their county, as to let them
crumble away atom by atom without an effort to stay
the progress of decay?   The dimensions of the church
are not too large for a town which numbers, as Croyland
does, 4,000 inhabitants.   I may also mention that I
observed the pavement broken up for something like a
yard square on the summit of the famous triangular
bridge, which must render the arches very liable to
destruction.

I am, sir, your obedient servant,

SPECTATOR.

To John Pennington, Esq.

Liverpool, Nov. 8th, 1859.

My dear John,

Permit me to remind you of the promise you
made two or three months ago to superintend a ball
sometime in the coming winter in aid of the funds of

the Grammar School. As this seems the only practicable scheme for raising money for the school, and as with your co-operation it carries with it the promise of success, we must not let it fall to the ground. Have you spoken yet to Egerton Wright? If not, I should think all you have to say to him can be as well said by letter as in an interview. When I first mooted the subject, I thought it might be with a ball as with fruit—that the first gathering would be the best—and was therefore wishful to fix it early in the season ; but as we are now in November, that cannot be. A long notice I apprehend to be essential to success.

I am, sincerely yours,

JOHN LEYLAND.

To John Blackburn, Esq.

Liverpool, Nov. 25th, 1859.

My dear Sir,

No progress has been made yet in the affair you inquire about in your letter of yesterday ; but as the consideration of it is to be resumed at an early day, the result may perhaps be arrived at in time to allow us to discuss its provisions on your next journey to Liverpool. I was surprised to find you already acquainted with the great military organisation going on among us. Mr. Bright has succeeded in enlisting nearly the whole of the staff capable of bearing arms. Even that man of peace, Mr. Riley, forms no exception to the number. I must, however, do the gentleman the justice to state that he exhibited a discreet hesitation and reticence in giving his consent when the proposal was laid before him. Possibly he might be thinking if his better half (who, if what is said of her be true, rules at home with commendable and salutary vigour) would sanction the step. Mr. Bright will be Captain Bright henceforward, if you please ; and before your next journey I would recommend you to furbish up your military knowledge, to rub the rust off your sword, clean the lock of your gun, pipeclay your regimentals, and study your positions, or you will never be able to understand our conversation. The words "right," "left," "march," "halt," "present arms," "fire," will be interlarded in our ordinary discourse. In the midst of all this martial ardour, I, unfortunately, am condemned to inglorious inaction through my shortsightedness. An object must be as large as the dome of St. Paul's for me to trace even its dim outline at rifle distance, and I might as reasonably hope to take the command of the Channel fleet as to hit so far off a mark of the dimensions of an ordinary mortal. But, useless as I am for such purposes, I can still subscribe myself

Your sincere friend,
JOHN LEYLAND.

To Alfred Pennington, Esq.

Liverpool, Dec. 5th, 1859.

My dear Sir,

A meeting has been arranged for next Monday, the 12th instant, at five o'clock in the afternoon, at the Eagle and Child Inn, in Wigan, to take into consideration the Hindley Grammar School question, at which I hope you will be able to be present; and as it would be desirable to secure the attendance of a respectable number, perhaps you will be good enough to ask anyone likely to feel an interest in the proceedings to accompany you.   I am, faithfully yours,

JOHN LEYLAND.

To John Blackburn, Esq.

Liverpool, Dec. 8th, 1859.

Would you believe it, my dear sir, jealousies are already peeping forth in our new rifle corps. That such ill weeds should spring in any soil is bad enough; but it is worse when they show themselves, even ever so gently, in a body originated purely from patriotic motives. Presuming you to be as ignorant in military affairs as I once was, I will state that for the efficient government of a company a captain, a lieutenant, and an ensign are indispensable. To the first-named office Mr. Bright was raised by general acclamation. The second is filled by a Mr. Burgess ; who, if he brought a contingent of twelve men on the express condition of gaining the appointment, did it, doubtless, from the overwhelming conviction that nature had so eminently fitted him for the duties, that it would be treason to a glorious cause not to make the stipulation. However, it is to the ensigncy that my introductory remarks have reference. This appointment is not yet made, but there are two aspirants for the honour. The palms of Mr. Riley and of Mr. Horton are both itching to grasp the banner of the company. Each thinks himself qualified, and each entitled to bear it. The first act of the captain will be to decide between these rival claimants, and he may perhaps in consequence learn that rank has burthens as well as privileges. What course the un-successful candidate may pursue—whether he will have the magnanimity to forget his disappointment and cheerfully serve under his fortunate competitor, or whether he will retire to his desk as Achilles did to his ship, and sit unmoved at the call to drill, are questions the future alone can unfold. The fact that great epochs are fertile in great men is verified by the finding of military officers in an urgent moment, fully fledged, among those who have devoted their several lives hitherto to the peaceful pursuits of commerce.

I am, faithfully yours,

JOHN LEYLAND.

To Richard Pennington, Esq.

Liverpool, Dec. 17th, 1859.

My dear Sir,

I am about to ask your permission to postpone my visit to Rugby for a few months. Quiet must be essential to Mrs. Pennington in the present delicate state of her health, and I am not myself so strong as to disregard the danger of taking cold in a long journey in the present inclement weather. It will be pleasanter to meet all well, and I sincerely trust the warm spring weather will re-establish Mrs. Pennington's health, if other means fail in effecting it sooner.

Egerton Wright attended the meeting last Monday with two of his friends. On a former occasion he had kindly expressed his willingness to undertake· the management of a ball in aid of the school funds, but both then and at the meeting he said that he was quite sure we should clear nothing by it. As his opinion is conclusive on the point, and money is our sole object, we must necessarily abandon the idea. Nothing remains, therefore, if we are to raise a special fund, but to set on foot a subscription. To this end I am proposing to issue a few circulars according to the enclosed form, if it meets with your approval, and I am in the hopes you may succeed in persuading some of your wealthy friends to put down their names for handsome donations.

Wishing you all a happy Christmas,

I remain, my dear sir, faithfully yours,

JOHN LEYLAND.

To Richard Pennington, Esq.

Liverpool, Dec. 24th, 1859.

My dear Sir,

I have received a letter from Mr. William Lyon, of Hindley, informing me that the coldness of our school was a subject of general complaint at the examination on Tuesday, and that several of the boys are ill in consequence. He suggests that a stove be erected, and if the trustees have not sufficient funds, that a subscription be entered into to meet the expense.

I thought I had better put you in possession of this information at once, as another stimulant to the liberality of your guests, which, applied under the genial influences of Christmas festivities, must prove irresistible.   I am, faithfully yours,

JOHN LEYLAND.

To the Misses Ingham.

Liverpool, Jan. 3rd, 1860.

My dear Friends,

I have waited thus long since receiving your letter for a quiet opportunity of saying that I sincerely hope your "half expectations" of coming to Liverpool this Christmas will be realised.

The journey I took in the autumn to which you allude was the means, through the blessing of Providence, of re-establishing my health. During the whole of the summer I had been more or less ailing, and for some weeks before my journey I became considerably worse. Much as I enjoy travelling, I set out without any anticipation of pleasure. I went simply because I had arranged to go, and moved mechanically from place to place ; yet for all that I begun to improve, grew gradually better, and when I got home I was quite well.

I have seen York twice, and share in all your admiration for the Minster and the ruins of St. Mary's Abbey : the one beautiful in its perfection ; the other scarcely less beautiful in decay. Rare and cultivated intellects could alone conceive and execute such incomparable works. I should like to have lived in the "great ages of faith" in which they were reared. Infidelity has usurped the place of faith in these latter days, and money-worship, frauds in trade, immoralities of so gross a character that if they were not recorded by a credible press would be disbelieved, and demagogues applauded by an ignorant multitude, are the pestilent brood it warms into being. If you or I can do little or nothing to arrest these grievous sins, we can at least refrain from following the multitude to do evil.

I am, faithfully yours,

JOHN LEYLAND.

To Alfred Pennington, Esq.

Liverpool, Jan. 30th, 1860.

My dear Sir,

It is quite impossible to excuse you from filling the office of trustee to the Grammar School. I should as soon think of seeing the play of "Hamlet" with the part of Hamlet left out. So you must bear the infliction as patiently as you can, for there is really no remedy. Pray disabuse everybody of the mischievous notion. that we have plenty of money. The most strenuous exertions will, I doubt, prove insufficient to raise a fund adequate to our various wants. I enclose the corrected proof of a circular I am going to issue, which I wish to have your opinion upon.

I am to have twenty copies of the church appeal sent from the printer's at once.

Faithfully yours,

JOHN LEYLAND.

To Alfred Pennington, Esq.

Liverpool, Feb. 13th, 1860.

Thank you, my dear sir, for consenting to be a trustee to the school. The office of acting trustee is certainly not an enviable post. If I could have foreseen the labour it would have entailed, I question if I should, with all my goodwill for the school, have had the courage to undertake it.

I am, faithfully yours,

JOHN LEYLAND.

To John Blackburn, Esq.

Liverpool, Feb. 27th, 1860.

My dear Sir,

I ought not to allow you to make a hasty promise in favour of any of the charities I am interested in. Your own neighbourhood, I am sure, has numerous claims upon you; therefore, consider your kind offer as not having been made until you come among us again. I sincerely join you in sympathy with Mr. ———— on his loss of the auditorship. The reflection that it is all owing to his own want of discretion will doubtless increase the bitterness of his disappointment.

Our rifle corps begins to fill a larger space in the eyes of the public. The officers have taken a large house in Soho Street, to which they have given the name of "The Barracks." A wall dividing the yard from the adjoining premises is to be removed, so as to form a place of drill in fine weather, and two large rooms of the house are to be laid together for the same purpose when the weather is wet. Apartments are already fitted up with carpets and other luxuries for the commissioned and non-commissioned officers. The feast given by the captain to the corps, at which champagne was so liberally circulated as to cause by far the greater number of the guests to be oblivious of proprieties, took place, if I mistake not, the last night of your stay in Liverpool. Well, there is another grand field-day in contemplation, for, as the captain entertained the corps, the corps are now proposing to entertain the captain. There is also the whisper of a project for holding a grand ball at the Barracks, so that, what with the festivities, the smart uniform which sets off the person so becomingly, and one thing or another, no wonder the service is popular. To lovers of peace like myself it is gratifying to observe that fighting and bloodshed are banished by common consent from the thoughts of the members.

I am, very truly yours,

JOHN LEYLAND.

To John Wilton, Esq.

Liverpool, March 24th, 1860.

My dear John,

It was gratifying to me to receive your cordial expressions of esteem and affection. Believe me, I value our friendship equally with you, and look back on its long continuance with the same feelings of pleasure. It was also gratifying to me to hear that in entering upon new relations your old ties were at the same time striking deeper root. Sometimes I confess I have experienced a feeling of regret when my friends have entered the marriage state—not that I have not rejoiced at their prospect of happiness, nor that I would not have promoted it to the utmost of my power, but because it seemed as if the old confidential intercourse must in some degree either change or cease.

If domestic duties have the first claim on a man's time and thoughts, those of the outer world will with you, I am sure, be also in their turn recognised.

I sincerely wish you a long, happy, and prosperous married life.

I am, ever truly yours,

JOHN LEYLAND.

To John Blackburn, Esq.

Liverpool, April 13th, 1860.

My dear Sir,

We have all been much shocked to-day on hearing of the sudden death of Mr. ———, which occurred the day before yesterday. He has been with us so much for several years past, and his restless temperament has caused him to be so constantly present to our thoughts, that I question if any similar event could have impressed the text, "In the midst of life we are in death," more forcibly upon us. I got home comfortably on Monday, notwithstanding the extreme cold. Mr. William, I believe, is writing by this post to say that we shall not be ready for you until the middle of next week.

I am, faithfully yours,

JOHN LEYLAND.

To the Misses Ingham.

Liverpool, April 17th, 1860.

My dear Friends,

Your visit to Liverpool in January gave me, I assure you, much pleasure. I trust we may all be spared to another Christmas, and that nothing may prevent our meeting again. The older we go, the more pleasure we take in talking over the events of early life. The skies then seem to have been so bright, the breeze so fresh, the flowers so sweet. Now—but let me say even now, and to older persons than your mother and me, life need not be dreary. Singular it is how vividly conversation with an old friend recalls the past. The events we pass through seem to be photographed on the memory, and to need only some special circumstance to give them form and shape, just as the application of cyanide of potassium does the action of light on a collodion preparation. Memory may hereafter be an important instrument in the punishment of the wicked. The evil deeds done in the body, viewed without the false glosses and deceitful excuses of frail humanity, will, I can conceive, be intolerable.

Thank your father, for me, for his subscription to the Grammar School Fund. The call of the trustees upon the public has been so far successful as to place me in a position to hand over the management of the school to the new trustees with its finances in tolerable order. The school is doing a good work in the neighbourhood. The various civilising influences we possess seem yet lost. But what then, are we to sit idle and do nothing? Let the Scriptures give answer: "In the morning sow thy seed, and in the evening withhold not thine hand, for thou knowest not whether shall prosper either this or that, or whether they both shall be alike good."

Ever truly yours,

JOHN LEYLAND.

To Mr. Frank Corless.

Liverpool, May 6th, 1860.

My dear Corless,

The last letter I wrote to you was in August last, when I was on the point of setting out on my usual autumn excursion. Although I was suffering at the time from an accumulation of maladies, it was the turning point to a better state of things, for the change of air and scene was the means, under Providence, of re-establishing my health. I was near seeing you in London. On the evening of the day of my arrival I called in Threadneedle Street, to be told by the porter that you had left only five minutes before. The next day, or the day after, you were summoned, I heard, to some place in the eastern counties, so that our meeting became impossible. I learned with much satisfaction that you had settled at Cambridge. If the *genius loci* exercise over you their wonted influence, you are a man to be envied. Books, good society, robust health, and the wherewithal to keep the wolf from the door, form a respectable aggregate of worldly enjoyments.

What do you think of the two great political questions which have been occupying public attention the last few months—the Reform Bill and the Budget? To me both these measures seem to be of questionable character. I confess I should not be much surprised whatever measure Lord John Russell was to introduce, especially if it bore any relation to Reform, which he seeks to appropriate for his own political ends, without any consideration for the wants of the country. From Gladstone I had hoped better things than a Budget of experiments. The three principal features of the Budget—the reducing of taxation on luxuries instead of necessaries, the undue increase of direct taxation, and the removing of long-established sources of revenue, with a balance on the wrong side of the account—are all objectionable. Years since I remember reading a fable, in which a simpleton, a man of common sense, and a "clever" gentleman were the actors. They were in pursuit of a thief, and soon came to a roadside inn, where the simpleton suggested that the thief might have called, and proposed to search the house. Common sense objected, saying the man would never think of staying so near home, for fear of capture. The "clever" gentleman said the thief would argue that he would never be suspected of remaining in his own neighbourhood, and that very likely he would be found inside. Common sense was overruled, the house was examined, and no thief found—the time lost in the search affording him the opportunity to escape. The "clever" gentleman is no forced type of Gladstone and his arguments.

I am, faithfully yours,

JOHN LEYLAND.

To Mr. Thomas Brereton.

Liverpool, June 14th, 1860.

My dear Sir,

Like myself, I presume you have been following your usual occupations day by day since we met last autumn in London. If neither of us see much variety, we enjoy what both of us believe to be better—quiet and peace.

You will rejoice to see that the proposal for holding an art exhibition in 1862 is likely to be carried out. Evidence of the good effect produced by the great Exhibition of 1851 and the Manchester Exhibition of 1857 is abundantly manifest. The greatest art revival in our days has been in architecture; and although it had its origin before the date of either of the two exhibitions, it received from them, doubtless, an additional impulse. In Liverpool, as in other large towns, buildings for commercial purposes are rising up of great artistic excellence. The increasing wealth of the country furnishes the means, fortunately, for the gratification of this newly-acquired taste, and will in a few more years enable our commercial towns to vie with the old Italian cities.

The constant presence of beautiful objects cannot fail to give a healthy tone to the mind. Why, otherwise, would Providence have clothed the earth with so much beauty ? Its various productions might have possessed all their useful properties without graceful forms and brilliant colours. Even as regards this life purely, and excluding all reference to a future, man cannot live by bread alone.

Of the sculptured leaves and the birds and angels on our old buildings it has been well said, in a recently published poem,

> " And the tendrils will unroll, and teach us
> How to solve the problem of our pain ;
> And the birds' and angels' wings shake downward
> On our hearts a sweet and tender rain."

Yet, after all, we are far from being sufficiently alive to the importance of art. What has been already accomplished is as nothing compared with what remains to be done. In every town an Augean stable has to be cleansed. Manufactories and collieries, both in town and country, should be compelled to consume their smoke, and chemical works be banished to remote places. If trees, and the face of nature generally, are to be disfigured, it is useless to hope to refine men's minds by stone and marble, let them be fashioned ever so cunningly.

I am, very truly yours,

JOHN LEYLAND.

To Mr. S. Wilton.

Liverpool, June 22nd, 1860.

My dear Simeon,

It was only the other day that I was called upon to congratulate your brother John on his wedding, and now a similar duty devolves upon me to you on yours. It is pleasant to see one's friends one after another settling in life, and entering upon duties which, while contributing materially to their happiness, are at the same time incentives to exertion and safeguards against many temptations.   And as it is

> "The common fate of all,
> Into each life some rain to fall,
> Some days to be dark and dreary,"

so it is a prudent part to secure those on whom, when these days come, we can rest assured of sympathy and help, and to whom we can pay back in the same need the same love and duty.

With sincere wishes for your and your wife's happiness,   I remain, ever yours truly,

JOHN LEYLAND.

To Mr. Frank Corless.

Liverpool, August 25th, 1860.

My dear Corless,

I have no hope, I am sorry to say, of being able to get as far as Wiltshire this summer, although my health is better than it was a year since.

I had planned to spend the holiday I am about to take in a ramble in the midland counties, but travelling in the sort of weather we have had all summer, and which seems likely to continue, is unpleasant, besides the risk it involves of taking cold; so that I have decided upon going to the Isle of Man instead.   The air there is pure and bracing, and if I should even have to remain indoors all the time, I can scarcely fail to receive benefit.

Public interest is concentrated just now on Garibaldi's movements.   The effect they may produce on the powers outside of Italy, especially on our neighbour across the channel, lends to them additional gravity. Louis Napoleon is so thoroughly selfish, that it is difficult to speculate upon what he may do.   Many people give him credit for great ability.   It is true he has succeeded, and marvellously; but success is easy of attainment when the conscience is unfettered by scruples.   He swore to maintain the republic; and when opportunity allowed him to grasp the imperial power, he broke his oath without the smallest compunction. In the annexation of Savoy it was the same. The declarations of disinterestedness with which he entered on the Italian war were as clear and precise as it was possible for them to be. A turn in the wheel came which tempted his ambition, and the real interests of a great nation were imperilled by its gratification.

I am, faithfully yours,
JOHN LEYLAND.

To John Blackburn, Esq.

Douglas, Sept. 8th, 1860.

My dear Sir,

You will see from the date of my letter that I decided at last on going to the Isle of Man. I have every reason to be satisfied with the choice I made, and I have had—what you will, perhaps, be surprised to hear—fine weather. The season has not been as wet here as in England, yet fewer strangers have visited the island than in ordinary years, and the fisheries have proved less productive; both of which circumstances have affected the general prosperity. The grain crops are, however, expected to yield an average quantity, if the present weather continues two or three weeks longer. Up to the present time I believed the climate to be cold; I learn, on the contrary, that it is remarkably mild, and the variations in the temperature throughout the year less than in most places in Europe. In proof of the mildness of the atmosphere, I may instance that I see various flowers flourishing in the open gardens which only grow with equal luxuriance under glass in England.

I would have asked you to write and tell me what your movements are if I had been remaining here long enough to receive a letter. In spite of the uncertainty of the weather, I purpose going on Tuesday next to some place in the midland counties.

I am, faithfully yours,
JOHN LEYLAND.

To the Misses Ingham.

Liverpool, Sept. 29th, 1860.

My dear Friends,

August and September are the months English people of the present day migrate from their homes and business to the seaside and other places. You, I suppose, have been taking the journey in Wales you were speaking of, and I am also just returned from an excursion. For the first time in my life I have been to the Isle of Man. The access thither from Liverpool is so easy that I have hitherto avoided going, thinking I could take a run over at any time. I had mapped out a route for the midland counties, but the uncertainty of the weather made me give it up. At the Isle of Man I thought I should at any rate have the certain advantage of the bracing sea air, however unpropitious might be the skies. It is a place well worth seeing. Coast and inland scenery it possesses of great beauty. There are also Druidical remains, and many early Christian crosses. The ruins of Peel Castle and Cathedral, which stand on a rocky island of about five acres in extent, separated only by a narrow channel from the mainland, are perhaps the finest sight in the island. The town of Peel, on the point of land below ; the bay, with the varied outline of its coast ; and a wide expanse of sea, viewed from the ruins, form also a perfect picture.

The visitors are chiefly operatives from the manufacturing districts of Lancashire. Their habits I watched with some interest. Early in the morning they sally out, partly for a walk, but principally to buy herrings for breakfast, which they carry back to their lodgings on a string dangling from their fingers' ends. The men are all armed with walking-sticks, and they handle them as if they had never had such things in their possession before. Eating and drinking seem to be their chief business the whole day long. Excursions in open cars to the different places of note are of everyday occurrence, and the occupants pass more or less uncomplimentary jokes on every person they meet. To those who cannot understand that it is out of the exuberance of their spirits on the rare occasion of a holiday, these jokes are not cordially received.

Fine weather having set in, I returned to Liverpool, and took a circuit in the west of England, which, as my paper is full, I must describe, if you are curious about it, at some other opportunity.

I remain, truly yours,

JOHN LEYLAND.

To the Misses Ingham.

Liverpool, Nov. 16th, 1860.

My dear Friends,

I was scarcely sanguine enough to expect you to come over for the event of the 13th inst. ; but as St. George's Hall is a sight worth seeing at all times, and especially when it is filled with a large assemblage of gaily dressed people, I thought I would give you the option. But I shall be much disappointed if you do not come at Christmas, according to your promise, for at least a quiet visit, if not for the amusement we were talking of last year.

You speak in your letter as if you had some commission you were wishing me to execute. I hope you know me well enough to feel sure that it would give me pleasure to render you any service. If there be anything, therefore, I can do for you, pray let me know what it is at once.

I must give you a few particulars of the second part of my autumn journey. My route lay through a district exceeded by none in the kingdom for fertility, as you will say when I enumerate the places I stopped at, which were, Shrewsbury, Church Stretton, Ludlow, Leominster, Hereford, Ledbury, Malvern, Worcester, Pershore, Evesham, Tewkesbury, Cheltenham, Gloucester, Droitwich, Kidderminster, Hagley, Hales-Owen, and Birmingham. Some of the intermediate stages I made on foot, others by rail. It was the time of the gathering in of the harvest, when the golden sheaves give a richness to the colouring of the landscape and the reapers an animation which it wears at no other season. The district abounds in the growth of fruit, and the trees in the numerous gardens and orchards, and even in the field hedgerows, were bending under their russet, bright yellow, scarlet, and purple clusters. Owing to the abundance of the season, fine magnum bonum plums were selling in Worcester market at two or three pence the dozen; and at Evesham, a place famous for plums, I was told that in 1852 (also an abundant year), 9,000 pots, consisting of five-quarters each, were sent from that neighbourhood to the different markets for sale, and that it was computed the quantity would be exceeded this year.

I stopped at the little station of Hagley, in order to see Lord Lyttelton's seat. The park is noted for its scenery. The name of Milton's Hill is given to an eminence from which a lovely prospect is obtained. The stately mansion lies just below, and the park, varied in its surface, spreads in ample dimensions around, ornamented with clumps and belts of noble timber. The eye embraces a wide tract of country beyond, extending even until it fades into mist in the distance. A seat on the hill is inscribed with the appropriate words from "Paradise Lost":—

> "These are Thy glorious works, Parent of good,
> Almighty, Thine this universal frame,
> Thus wondrous fair: Thyself how wondrous then."

The first Lord Lyttelton was a friend of Pope and Thomson, and raised monuments to their memory in the park, which are still in existence. From Hagley I walked to Hales-Owen, distant about three miles, where I stopped to see the grave of Shenstone, in the churchyard, and I also saw through a portion of the grounds of his old residence, the Leasowes.

I am, truly yours,

JOHN LEYLAND.

To the Rev. William Morton.

> Liverpool, Dec. 18th, 1860.

My dear Sir,

I believe I informed you, about the beginning of the year, that there was a possibility I might visit Oxford in the autumn; but the weather was so wet at the time of my setting out, and there appeared so little prospect of any amendment, that I abandoned the idea at the last moment.

I read your university news with a good deal of interest. Your election I observed with much pleasure, and, although late, I am not the less sincere in offering to you my congratulations. More recently I have noticed, and also with much satisfaction, a statement in some of the public prints that the two universities were more in accord on the question of middle-class examinations. One examination in the year, made alternately by each university, would seem to be amply sufficient; and on this point, as well as in the granting of degrees, a common action is desirable. Some of your influential men, I understand, look with disfavour on these examinations. The cause, I presume, will arise from their jealousy of stamping with official approval what must be, even with the best prepared of the candidates, imperfect scholarship. The movement, in my opinion, however, seems to be well timed, and calculated not only to place middle-class education on a sounder basis, but also to deepen the affection for the universities in the minds of the great body of the people. I am, very faithfully yours,

JOHN LEYLAND.

To Alfred Pennington, Esq.

> Liverpool, Dec. 29th, 1860.

My dear Sir,

Your New Year's Day dinner party offers to me a great temptation, and I am exercising no little self-denial in sending an excuse from joining it; but this severe weather affects me so much that I dare not venture from home while it lasts. I regret it the more as I am anxious to be on friendly and neighbourly terms with all of the guests you are expecting. Wishing you a happy new year,

I remain, very faithfully yours,
JOHN LEYLAND.

To Alfred Pennington, Esq.

Liverpool, New Year's Day, 1861.

My dear Sir,

On the temperature becoming unmistakably warmer yesterday, I had some thoughts of taking you by surprise at your dinner hour to-day, but I ultimately came to the conclusion that you might possibly have filled up the place at your table originally destined for me. If I had received your note of yesterday last night, instead of being seated solitarily at home, as I am at the present moment, I should have been drinking some of your good old wine, and in the company, more-over, of Hindley churchwardens—functionaries whose predecessors used to inspire my boyish mind with something akin to awe at their power and dignity; but your note, coming this morning, was too late to enable me to make the necessary arrangements for a journey.

I have just learnt the uncomfortable news that the frost is setting in again keenly.

I am, very faithfully yours,
JOHN LEYLAND.

To the Rev. P. Jones.

Liverpool, Jan. 4th, 1861.

My dear Sir,

My time is so fully occupied that I cannot, I am sorry to say, help you with a lecture. Our secretary lectures occasionally on the subject you name, and another season I hope to secure his services for Hindley, for at least one evening; but he is so much from home, and has so many engagements, that I do not think there is any prospect of getting him at present.

I saw Mr. Holden this morning on the subject of a subscription to our new church. He said that having no interest in the neighbourhood, except through the Moss Hall Colliery, he could only subscribe through the company, and that Mr. Christopher was the proper person to apply to. However, he appeared well-disposed to the object, and promised to bring it before the notice of Mr. Christopher.

I am, faithfully yours,

JOHN LEYLAND.

To the Rev. William Morton.

Liverpool, Feb. 13th, 1861.

My dear Sir,

The proposed appeal to your university will, I trust, promote the efficiency of middle-class examinations. The good certain to result from the combined and harmonious action of the two universities will prove greater, I apprehend, both directly and indirectly, than the most sanguine among us anticipated. The Liverpool centre has, I see, carried itself well in the last Cambridge examination.

The work of your *Septem Contra Christum* is acquiring an unenviable distinction. I have not read it myself; but, from the opinions expressed in public by men of different parties in the church, its influence, I judge, will be detrimental to religion. And yet, in some of the criticisms which have appeared, the authors are spoken of as men of undoubted piety.

I am, faithfully yours,

JOHN LEYLAND.

To the Misses Ingham.

Liverpool, April 3rd, 1861.

My dear Friends,

Considering the severity of the weather, you were fortunate in escaping any ill-effects from your Christmas journey. For some weeks after you left all

x

the ladies I met were eloquent on the inconveniences resulting from the frost. The want of water, the bursting of pipes, the flooding of parlours and bedrooms, the disfiguring of walls and ceilings, and, what was yet more terrible, apprehensions of the explosions of kitchen boilers. Never was change of weather accorded a heartier welcome than when the thaw set in. Being less dependent on such artificial means for domestic conveniences in the country, you may, perhaps, feel some difficulty in appreciating the magnitude of the evils we have had to undergo.

I was less disposed to attribute the silence between us subsequently to you than to me. That it was high time for it to be broken I knew, but I contented myself with wishing and waiting for an opportunity, for, as you well know, I am closely occupied.

I return you many thanks for the magazines, but I must prohibit you from sending any more : I really cannot feel comfortable to tax your kindness further. It is a pity that the papers on the History of Wigan are not written by a more competent hand. To say nothing of the special claims this particular history has upon our attention, it must, in common with other parishes in the kingdom, have facts interesting to the general reader, if a fitting pen could be found to record them.   I am, sincerely yours,

JOHN LEYLAND.

To the Rev. William Morton.

Liverpool, April 10th, 1861.

My dear Sir,

The change about to be made by Oxford in the examination of the middle-class candidates, respecting their proficiency in Scriptural knowledge, will be beneficial. As the entire scheme is new, and of such vast importance, modifications must inevitably from time to time be needed before it can fully answer the objects of its promoters.

Cambridge has not, I fear, much heart in the movement. She seems to act as if it was a step expected from her position, rather than from a sincere conviction of its utility.

By this time, I suppose, you will be pretty well tired of the controversy upon "Essays and Reviews." The current of public opinion has set in strong against the book. For my part, I can never help feeling sympathy for the object of popular and indiscriminate censure. Justice is sure to be sacrificed; and I should be disposed in this instance to fear—not having read the book—that its authors are suffering some wrong, were it not that the whole of the episcopate, and good and earnest men of almost all sects and parties, have condemned the opinions put forth.

I am, faithfully yours,

JOHN LEYLAND.

To Mr. Thomas Brereton.

Liverpool, June 11th, 1861.

My dear Sir,

Before this time you will have entered upon the two great undertakings your father told me you had in prospect when he was in Liverpool, and the agreeable duty therefore devolves upon me of offering to you my hearty congratulations. So great a prudence has always marked your proceedings, that I can confidently predict success in your new vocation, and happiness in your married life.

I am not contemplating a journey to London this year; but, if life and health be spared, I hope to come up and see the Art Exhibition next year. The Exhibition will, no doubt, as previous exhibitions have done, accomplish a good work. This busy, working age lays such an iron grasp on the time and thoughts of the great bulk of the community, that, if it were not for special instruments, art would have a more uphill struggle than it has. Exhibitions are to art something like what the Sabbath is to religion—the means of impressing the indifferent with its importance, and of revealing the delights which the pursuit of it affords. I am, truly yours,

JOHN LEYLAND.

To the Misses Ingham.

Liverpool, July 8th, 1861.

My dear Friends,

I was sorry to hear of Mr. Spry's death. The friendly terms which have subsisted between your family and him for a long period will cause you to feel his loss severely. My own intercourse with him, I regret to say, ended with my schooldays. A very worthy man I believe him to have been—one of those, indeed, who are content to fill with integrity the station Providence has assigned them, without aspiring to wealth or worldly honours. Many such have passed unknown from among men, to be known and honoured by an assembled world in the great day of account. That he lived to see more than his threescore years and ten, and to enjoy for many years the competency he had so well earned, will mingle pleasant thoughts with the regrets of his friends.

I did not know until I received your letter that you accustomed yourselves to equestrian exercise. Our neighbourhood does not offer any great choice of rides. The one you describe having taken is, perhaps, as agreeable as any you could have selected. The dominion of the steam engine is extending wider and wider in this locality, and rural districts must become in precisely the same degree fewer. Those who love to look on God's works in the fields and trees will be driven to other places. The ties which bind all men, more or less, to their native place, have been with me unusually strong; and it has cost me no little struggle to admit the possibility of finally settling elsewhere. The Ince Chemical Works have done more than anything else to bring about such a result. They do me continual mischief. The garden and orchard at Cheetham House, formerly most productive, have been destroyed. The larger forest trees on the property have died one after another, and now even the young trees are dying.

I am, faithfully yours,

JOHN LEYLAND.

To Mr. Frank Corless.

Liverpool, July 25th, 1861.

My dear Corless,

The object of these lines, I may as well confess at the outset, is to extract a letter from you, although I know you have, like me, few opportunities for writing. If, in so doing, I excite sensations similar to what the subject of a dentist experiences when the instruments of the profession are unfolded before him, remember that when the letter is written you will enjoy a feeling of relief akin to the being quit of a decayed and troublesome tooth.

The long vacation must present a strong contrast to term time to residents of Cambridge. The newspapers described the last term as being unusually gay, in consequence of the presence of the Prince of Wales and his suite. The directors of His Royal Highness's education have taken a questionable course in first sending him to Edinburgh, then to Oxford, and lastly to Cambridge. Their motive has been, doubtless, to free him from sectarian views in religion or politics; but what has been gained in this respect will, I fancy, be at the expense of that exact mental discipline which a single systematic course of study can alone supply.

How continually the prevailing subject of interest changes. At one time it is the war in the Crimea; at another, the rebellion in India, and the battles in Italy. Now, the disruption of the United States is the great event overshadowing all others. A careful consideration of the history of the United States for some time past goes far to show that the struggle was, sooner or later, inevitable. Each section has a different climate and social condition; and their trading interests—so powerful an influence among Americans—run in separate channels. Changes in the minds of men are often effected before they confess openly even to entertaining doubts; and, in like manner, a divergence between North and South must have been long silently growing, otherwise the election of President Lincoln could scarcely have originated the unhappy measures for a final separation. I am, faithfully yours,

JOHN LEYLAND.

To James Bent, Esq.

Liverpool, August 9th, 1861.

My dear Sir,

Retrenchment is said to be more difficult to effect by people deeply in debt than when they are only a little behindhand in the world; just as a long silence between friends is always more difficult to break than a short one. If I carry my illustration a step further, and say that the man who reduces his expenditure, and endeavours to establish an equilibrium between it and his income, deserves to succeed, it is in the hope that you will apply it to my letter, and give me what I am anxious to obtain—an early reply.

It was on the first day of September, 1859—close upon two years ago—that I paid a short visit to you at Baildon, since which not one word have I heard of you. I trust that you and your dear wife and son have been well all the time. Thanks to the Great Giver, I am in the enjoyment of health, and remain in all other respects as when we met. But, if the two years have passed over your household and mine without change, they have been fertile enough in events of public importance. In two sessions of Parliament we have seen the vagaries of a Chancellor of the Exchequer supported by numbers sufficiently large to carry them into law, and his schemes dignified with the name of "finance." Abroad, Louis Napoleon has been acting his strange part—tyrannising in the kingdom of which he is the present head; causing war, devastation, and bloodshed in Italy, and disturbances elsewhere. The Bonapartes are verily a scourge to the human race, and their ascendancy has been over-accompanied by terrible evils.

Of King Victor Emmanuel and his late minister, Count Cavour, can better be spoken? Scripture has pronounced a malediction upon the man who destroys his neighbour's landmarks. Victor Emmanuel and Cavour have done this, and seized, without scruple, upon possessions not their own. The necessities of their position, put forth as an excuse by their admirers, is unworthy of a reply. If that justifies crime, every felon arraigned before a bar of justice might plead it. Wrong thus openly committed leads one to think of the saying of Job, "I would not live always," and to yearn for that kingdom where the King of Righteousness reigneth, and where "there shall in nowise enter anything that defileth."

Ever yours sincerely,

JOHN LEYLAND.

To Alfred Pennington, Esq.

Liverpool, Aug. 26th, 1861.

My dear Sir,

I have received your letters of the 21st and 22nd inst., and I return herewith their respective enclosures. Mr. Doria's plan for founding exhibitions is worth remembering, and I hope a time may come when it will be considered with a view of applying it to our own Grammar School. I once took the liberty of suggesting something of the kind to our friend Thomas Gaskell, who heard me with exemplary patience; but he did not yet permit me to infer that it would influence his conduct. I do not think he is connected with the Gaskells of Clifton and Manchester. His family, I have understood, were settled in Burtonwood before they removed to Hindley.

Towards the end of this week I purpose leaving home

for a holiday, and I wish you, therefore, to keep the papers I left with you until the end of September. I shall have to crowd a good deal of business into the few intervening days between now and the time of my departure.

I am, truly yours,
JOHN LEYLAND.

To the Rev. William Morton.

Mitre Hotel, Oxford, Sept. 12th, 1861.

My dear Sir,

On inquiring this afternoon at your door, I was told, as I expected to be told in the middle of the long vacation, that you were from home. I went over your college, and spent some time in examining the various buildings. The new works are beautiful, and must add largely to the fame of the architect. The college authorities also deserve great praise for undertaking renovations so extensive and costly.

There are several ornaments, I observe, added, or in course of being added, to the city since I was here last, five years ago. Among them I may mention the museum, the church in St. Giles's district, and a something—I cannot make out what—in the street leading from the railway station.

If it be not a heresy to say it, the books of Bodleian have not a sufficiently dignified lodging. Your fine trees I admire as much as your buildings, magnificent though they are. Smoke and certain descriptions of manufactures are fast destroying the trees in my own neighbourhood, which in a few years will be bereft of everything higher than a shrub. I wish the public mind could be impressed with the important truth that a country denuded of the ornaments nature provides will effect hurtfully the moral, if not the mental powers of its inhabitants.

I am, faithfully yours,
JOHN LEYLAND.

To the Misses Ingham.

Liverpool, Feb. 10th, 1862.

My dear Friends,

You have done well in resolving not to let our correspondence cease, and I trust that any irregularity on my part may not cause your resolution to waver. I have made an expedition in your neighbourhood since I saw you. Business having kept me at Hindley one Saturday in November beyond the time of departure of the last train, I walked to Wigan for the night; and, Sunday morning being fine and frosty, instead of returning to Liverpool, I determined to walk to Newburgh Church for morning service by way of Wigan Lane and Standish. In passing through Wigan Lane I observed many changes since I was there last. New buildings and colliery chimneys had risen up in the interval; but the walk is still pleasant. On inquiring the distance from Newburgh Church soon after I passed Wrightington Hall, I was told that Wrightington Church was considerably nearer; and as I had not too much time upon my hands before the hour of service, I went thither. I had never before heard of this church, which, it seems, was erected five or six years ago. It is a small, neat, Gothic edifice, situate on rising ground, at some distance from any houses. After service I got a little dinner at the Dicconson Arms, and after that walked on to Newburgh. The road passes Parbold Hall, a residence evidently at the period of its erection of some note, and which now but wants trees and ornamental grounds to perpetuate its former state. Parbold Beacon, a landmark you are doubtless familiar with, stands not far from the Hall. At this point the valley of the Douglas opens, and presents a scene, for the heart of manufacturing Lancashire, of singular variety and beauty. From Newburgh I returned by rail to Liverpool.

I had seen the account of Mr. ———'s death in the papers before I received your letter, and was much shocked at its suddeness. For a man to be in health one hour, subject to the cares, the interests, and the pleasures of this life, and all these things to have passed away in the next, and a new state of existence entered upon, is a change of awful solemnity. His works did my place great injury, and of such a nature as to be irremediable, but I should be a heathen and not a Christian man if I was to let resentment continue after the grave has closed over him.

With every good wish,

I remain, sincerely yours,

JOHN LEYLAND.

To Mr. Frank Corless.

Liverpool, Feb. 22nd, 1862.

My dear Corless,

I am so thoroughly immersed in my own personal occupations, that I was not aware you had left the service of the company until I received your letter. Although I had been made acquainted with the recent reductions in the staff, and for some time even before they were carried into effect, I had no suspicion they would touch your interests. I must express the sincere regret I feel at losing you as a colleague, and at your services being dispensed with before you had made some engagement for the future. Inactivity to one endowed like you with considerable physical energy, must, I can well understand, be inexpressibly wearisome. Disappointments come to all at one period or another, and fulfil, as all God's providences do, their work of good. A clear sky and a bright sun are pleasanter than clouds and rain, but clouds and rain are equally necessary agents in rendering the earth fruitful. Perfect confidence in God's love is the only sure anchor to rely upon, when, as Cowper says—

> "Day by day some current's thwarting force
> Sets us more distant from a prosperous course."

As your present residence is within an hour's journey

of London, where you may be called frequently to make inquiries, I should recommend you—as you ask for my advice—to stay there for the present. Just now is an unfavourable time for entering upon new undertakings. The civil war in America has caused a depression in almost all branches of trade; and the general opinion is that even peace would not cause things to flow speedily into their old channels. North and South are unlikely again to unite; and when the war is over— if there should even be no changes in the political system—a long time must pass before industrial pursuits can be carried on with their former energy.

I am, faithfully yours,

JOHN LEYLAND.

To the Misses Ingham.

Liverpool, June 13th, 1862.

My dear Friends,

When we last met you told me you were contemplating a visit to Liverpool, for the purpose of purchasing spring dresses; since which, naturally, I have been long and patiently looking for your coming. Will you quite forgive me if I say that this tedious delay suggests uncomfortable doubts of your insensibility to what is passing in the world around us? The snowdrop and crocus heard long since the call of spring in their winter bed, and came forth. Primroses have followed in their train, and gemmed many a copse and many a green lane. Other flowers have bloomed and withered too; and others, again, are now mantling the earth with their beauties. And, in the midst of all this, I have to associate you with the cold and gloom of winter! In this month of June—every field an embroidery of variegated colours, every hedge a mass of verdure, every tree umbrageous, the air soft and warm, full of odours and of harmony—I am picturing you muffled up in furs and woollens, your faces blue with cold, and a shiver now and then creeping over you. Really, this is terrible. Ladies are sometimes accused of an undue love of change in apparel; but, if excess be wrong, will the opposite extreme, think you, be quite free from blame? If my remonstrance should awaken your curiosity as to the prevailing colours in ribbons and the patterns of gowns, may I beg of you to remember that even a fastidious taste may be gratified in the shops of Liverpool, and that I long for an opportunity of giving my advice on such momentous subjects.

I am, very faithfully yours,

JOHN LEYLAND.

To the Rev. P. Jones.

Liverpool, June 21st, 1862.

My dear Sir,

I called yesterday at the Parsonage to have paid my subscription to your schools for the current year, and was sorry to learn you were out. I am so much occupied at present, that I cannot come over again before Saturday, the 5th July. If the afternoon of that day would be convenient for a church meeting (say three o'clock prompt), I shall have much pleasure in attending.

I am, my dear sir, faithfully yours,

JOHN LEYLAND.

To Mr. James Eatock.

Liverpool, July 31st, 1862.

My dear James,

The Trustees of Mather's Charity could not, I think, with propriety, do other than hold a special meeting to consider the letter which has been addressed to them by the Visitor.

I hope to be over next Saturday, but as the time is now too short for the other Trustees to receive notice of a meeting for that day, it had better be deferred. If

Saturday, the 16th of August, will suit you and Mr. Jones, I will (D.V.) attend.

I am, truly yours,

JOHN LEYLAND.

To Mrs. Owen.

Liverpool, Aug. 12th, 1862.

My dear Mrs. Owen,

Not having seen or heard anything of your mother for several years, I have feared that I might one day hear some such news as your card announced. I have no doubt her end would be peace. In the time of my acquaintance with her she always seemed to set death before her, and to live in continual preparation for it.

The appointed law of this life is, as we all well know, that we must sustain, from time to time, these bereavements, and undergo trials of various kinds. But if we have often to sorrow, as often do we find true what St. Paul said to the Corinthians : "God comforteth those that are cast down." If we are born to trouble, there is yet much happiness given. The power, and wisdom, and love of God encompass us on every side, and those who truly know this, as, I believe, your mother did, have peace even while experiencing that ruin, sorrow, and death, came into the world by sin.

Time is short, and revelation opens a future life to our view, where God—seen here in His works and providences something like the fertility of Canaan was seen by the Israelites in the cluster of grapes from Eschol—will be revealed in the fulness of His love and the brightness of His glory. "O how plentiful is God's goodness, which He has laid up for them that fear Him."   I am, my dear Madam,

Very truly yours,

JOHN LEYLAND.

To the Misses Ingham.

Liverpool, Dec. 27th, 1862.

My dear Friends,

I received a remembrance from some unknown friend on Christmas Eve, in the shape of game. No letter came with it, but I learned from the bearer—a railway messenger—that it came from Wigan. Now, as I am naturally wishful to know which of my friends bears me so kindly in remembrance, I shall be glad of your aid in penetrating the mystery ; and, if you succeed (as ladies generally do when they set about anything), pray tender to him, or her, or them, my cordial thanks.

I am working hard just now, and although I shall probably continue much occupied for several months to come, I will endeavour either to write a longer letter, or to pay a visit to you before long.

With the best wishes of the season to all under your roof,

Believe me to be,

Ever yours truly,

JOHN LEYLAND.

To Mr. Frank Corless.

Liverpool, Jany. 31st, 1863.

My dear Corless,

Tom Moseley was in Liverpool for a few hours on Saturday, and surprised me unpleasantly by telling me you had determined upon emigrating to Queensland. The news almost neutralised the pleasure I had in hearing you were well.

I hope you have not made an irrevocable decision, and that before you do you will consider the claims of your family and friends, and old England.

There may not perhaps be much elbowing in a new country, but, depend upon it, there are some ugly scratches to be had. Take a friend's advice, and stay where you are.

Things are going on much as usual in the Magnetic world. We are pursuing the even tenor of our way, prospering on the whole ; and monied men, the great powers of the present day, are beginning to honour us with their smiles. Outside there is gloom enough. The cotton dearth, though less felt in Liverpool than in most parts of South Lancashire, still exercises a depressing influence. It is curious to note the conduct of the two demagogues, Cobden and Bright, in this crisis. For such loquacious gentlemen, they have throughout observed a remarkable silence ; but no wonder, for the institutions they have held up as a model for England to shape herself by are being dragged in the mire. If our own government could have been charged with but a fraction of the tyranny, defiance of law, extravagance, mismanagement, and incapacity, which have been committed by that of the United States, what fierce denunciations we should have had—what agitation and monster meetings—what soirees, and dinners, and talk! These men have done a vast deal of mischief. A love of material prosperity has been the chief—I might, indeed, say the only— thing they have inculcated. As truly as was ever done by Jeroboam in ancient Israel, they have set up a golden calf, and called upon the world to bow down and worship it. "Buy, sell, and grow rich," has been their cry; "and perish patriotism, loyalty, and ancient truth."

I am, faithfully yours,

JOHN LEYLAND.

To the Misses Ingham.

Liverpool, Feb. 13th, 1863.

My dear Friends,

Until the present moment I have never been able to acknowledge your last kind letter. Besides usual and unusual duties, I have been giving up my house here, packing up books and other things for

Hindley, so that I can plead a good excuse for the delay. I cannot advise any investment for your idle money at present, but I will bear your wishes in mind, and you shall soon know if I hear of anything promising. Of the mysterious rites you are practising, what shall I say? Will it be much to be wondered at if they make me fear to visit you? If I ever again venture, I must really have your promise, before I cross the moat round your house, that you will exercise no unlawful spells; as, in all the accounts I have ever read of incantations, doubters like myself are invariably punished when they enter a magic circle.

I am, ever yours truly,

JOHN LEYLAND.

To Alfred Pennington, Esq.

Liverpool, April 5th, 1863.

My dear Sir,

I got the note you wrote at Bolton Hall respecting the wardenship. Mr. Jones had asked me to fill the office previously; but as I have so many engagements on hand, and as it will be the end of June before my duties here terminate, when a fourth of the warden's year will have expired, I have begged to be excused.

I have been so busy with workmen, since my removal to Cheetham, that I have neither had time to call upon my friends, nor been in a fit state to receive them. An accident which befell Robert Marsh has caused me unexpected delay. He was standing one day on a joist over his smithy, when it broke in two, and he fell a height of ten feet to the floor. He was shook a good deal, but is now recovering. I made him laugh heartily one day before his accident. He was fixing a gate for me, the hinges of which were in the shape of the letter L. The iron loops fitting on the perpendicular part of the L were a little tight, and the gate stuck and would not fall down, whereupon he jumped on it, saying the weight of his body, together with his sins, would certainly bring the gate to its proper place. I cried, "Hold! don't put your sins on, or you'll crush it to splinters."

I am, faithfully yours,
JOHN LEYLAND.

To John Blackburn, Esq.

Liverpool, Aug. 18th, 1863.

Dear Mr. Blackburn,

I was sure you would feel all the better for breathing the sea air.

The exactions of business are now so great that holidays have become not merely seasons of recreation, but absolute necessaries for restoring wasted energies and strength. Work is good, and the older we grow the more sensible we are of the fact. The great point is not to permit worldly occupations to encroach too much on other pursuits.

In haste, truly yours,
JOHN LEYLAND.

To John Blackburn, Esq.

Lichfield, Sept. 18th, 1863.

Dear Mr. Blackburn,

On my arrival at Salisbury last Monday I got your note of the 10th inst.

Hampshire, and one or two other counties I have passed through, present many notable things apart from buildings or historical associations. The excellency of the farming is conspicuous. Fields of large size, level almost as a lawn; the green crops—all that are now outstanding—clear of weeds, and trim hedges shooting forth in straight lines, evidence a high state of culture. The trees are beautiful, wide in girth, their huge limbs spreading on all sides, varied in form as the human countenance, and their twisted roots striking into the soil with a grasp to last for centuries. Evidently they are not subject to noxious vapours. A greater

Y

wrong does not exist than that done by chemical works
and manufactures generally, for which it is difficult, if
not impossible, to obtain adequate redress. The property
of an entire neighbourhood may be injured by a single
individual, and, what is worse still, animal life suffers
as well as vegetation, and to an extent difficult to
appreciate.

Strange that our legislators have such tender sympathies for men whose calling injures their neighbours'
property, and destroys the handiwork of the great
Creator, which, in His wisdom and power, He pronounced
to be good.

Faithfully yours,
JOHN LEYLAND.

To Mr. Frank Corless.

Liverpool, Nov. 16th, 1863.

My dear Corless,

Years ago I used to think I had so little leisure
that I could not possibly have less, yet since I have
travelled daily to and from Hindley every portion of
the day has been filled up, and I have not a single
moment unemployed. The railway journey alone
occupies two hours and a half, and, in addition to
business engagements, public meetings and committees
at Hindley have in consequence of my residence there
asserted claims which I could not, and which, indeed,
I had no wish to deny. One great work we have in
hand is the building of a new church, the meetings in
connection with which have been very numerous.

These various engagements have been the occasion of
my long delay in writing, and for the same reason I
must beg of you to accept a few hasty lines in place of
the much longer letter I should, under other circumstances, have written. Immediately on my return
home I spoke to Bright on the subject you and I talked
over, when he told me that Sanger had received
instructions to acquaint our friend with the hopelessness
of his expectations. Disappointments are often followed

by success ; nay, not unfrequently they form its very cause. If no other result follows, a lasting good is acquired, if Patience hath her perfect work.

Your letter relieved me from my apprehensions concerning the dish of Amesbury mushrooms, or I should say rather of fungi, of which you were imprudent enough to partake. Before you venture on a similar experiment take thought of what you are doing. Although I am, I confess, ignorant in that branch of natural history, I yet feel safe in asserting that Lancashire produces the genuine species.

Pray give my regards to your family, and say that I look upon my visit to Amesbury as a red-letter day that will be long noted in my calendar.

Faithfully yours,

JOHN LEYLAND.

To the Rev. P. Jones.

Hindley, Dec. 28th, 1863.

My dear Sir,

I have to thank you for your letter, and for the accompanying report of the Hindley charities. I was glad—as I always shall be—to hear from you ; and if I do not reply as soon or as often as I ought, attribute the delay, I pray you, to its true cause—my very numerous business engagements. On reading your letter I could not help the painful reflection that our intercourse must in future be limited to the exchange of a letter occasionally, instead of the frequent meetings which, in all probability, would have continued, but for what I wish I could look upon in any other light than—will you forgive me if I say it?—the ill-judged step of resigning your incumbency.

You know Hindley too well to expect much news ; yet change in this world sweeps onward with such an irresistible current, that every letter you receive from the neighbourhood may tell of events affecting vitally the persons or the interests of one or other among us.

The new church is making, on the whole, satisfactory progress. The foundations are laid, and the walls just commenced. Nothing further, however, of any moment, will be done until longer days.

I received a notice of the proposed interference of the school property by the new railway, but the company omitted to send the usual form on which I could signify my assent or otherwise to the scheme. If one had been sent I should have signified my approval of it, as I think it cannot injure, and may benefit, the property.

The Reading Room soirée was a great success. As you appear to have seen only the account given by the *Wigan Observer*, I send you by this post a copy of the *Examiner*, which contains a fuller report of the proceedings.

I remain, truly yours,

JOHN LEYLAND.

To Mr. Frank Corless.

Liverpool, Feb. 29th, 1864.

My dear Corless,

Ever so many pleasant pictures filled my mind on receiving a letter, some days ago, bearing the postmark of Amesbury. I thought of its swelling downs, of the wealth of the flocks they sustain, of the big farm homesteads, looking like the capital cities of fertile provinces, with their barns, and granaries, and stables, and cattlesheds, and, not least, their significant cluster of corn and haystacks. Goodly trees unmistakably luxuriant seemed to stretch their leafy arms far and wide before me, and brooks in which fish could live shone like silver in the sunshine, and gave forth pleasant music in their sinuous course.

What different scenes are these from that which presents itself from the window of the office I am writing in. I am sixty steps above the earth, and on a wide space, deep in front, men are excavating the site of a great new building. A brick wall separates the excavations from a confined street, in which noisy vehicles are passing, and crowds of people hurrying backwards and forwards.

Around the opening tall buildings rise, surmounted by slated roofs; and chimneys, difficult to number, shut in the prospect. I have yet something pleasant to look upon, for the lantern spire of St. Nicholas's Church rises in the background, and above all are the heavens : for, thank God! wherever we are, we may look up there if we will.

I opened my letter and found it was from you, and that you are still anxious to exchange the pleasant scenes I have pictured for some such place as lies before me. I do not say you are wrong; but I do say that your present lot is good, that you have a great deal to be thankful for, and that numbers would envy your position.

All men are, doubtless, best with a fixed occupation ; and some sphere of duty will, in God's time, assuredly open to you. Do not emigrate. You are not as young as you have been ; you have always been accustomed to the comforts and luxuries incident to a highly-civilised state of society ; and you would find life in a new country beset with hardships. Let me, therefore, again entreat you to dismiss such thoughts once and for ever from your mind.

You will be sorry to hear that Edward Bright is suffering from a severe attack of illness. He is now out of danger, but he has been within a step of death. Robert John Taylor came over when the news reached him, and remained until the crisis passed.

I am, very truly yours,
JOHN LEYLAND.

To the Rev. P. Jones.

Hindley, June 6th, 1864.

My dear Sir,

If it had not been for the Johnsons, I should

many a time have wondered what had become of you, but every now and then they have told me you were well and still in London. If you have health, therefore, you have that which

"With transport touches all the springs of life."

I am sure you will have pleasure in hearing that things generally are going on well at Hindley. Trade is prosperous. The Penningtons' mills have continued all along in full work; the Castle Hill Mill, which has been standing idle from before Christmas, resumed work a few weeks ago; and the colliers have been regularly employed during the whole of the winter and spring at advanced wages. The building of the new church is rapidly advancing, and the architect and the clerk of the works report favourably of the manner the work is being done. Ince Church, now that it is finished, looks well; but the general opinion is that our own will look better.

The Ecclesiastical Commissioners have granted a perpetual annuity of £33 6s. 8d. for interest on £1,000, part of the £1,300 we promised towards the endowment, the whole of which sum we had to pay on the 1st inst. The contractor is also drawing freely upon our funds, so that we are anxious for the subscriptions to be paid in. Can you say when we may hope to receive the grants made by the Incorporated Church Building Society, and the Diocesan Church Building Society, and who are the persons to communicate with on the subject? The whole, or even a portion of these sums, would now be acceptable.

We are at present enjoying as much of the freshness and beauty of summer as we can hope for with the surrounding manufactories. The swallows are with us, the cuckoo is singing, and the lark and the thrush. I have heard the pleasant cry of the corncrake close to my house for the greater part of the past month, and numbers of yellow wagtails have been disporting themselves for some time about the brook in Adam Lane—a bird I never recollect observing in that locality before. Such of the fruit trees as are left have been covered

with bloom, and lilacs and laburnums have been richer
in flowers than for years past. Unfortunately, there
is a reverse to all this. I could tell of smoke, and
vapours worse than smoke; of trees dying in their
prime, of plants and shrubs shrivelled in a night. If I
were Caliph just for one day I would expose every one
of the originators of such mischief to his own vapour
for twenty-four hours, and if they were all suffocated
their fate would be well merited.

I remain, faithfully yours,
JOHN LEYLAND.

To the Rev. P. Jones.

Hindley, Feb. 9th, 1865.

My dear Sir,

A serious difficulty has arisen relating to the
new church. Mr. Bridgeman, the present Rector of
Wigan, refuses to carry out the promise made by his
predecessor, to endow it with £50 per annum out of the
revenues of the rectory, unless he has the whole and
undivided patronage. The committee are not disposed
to concede the point to him, and if he persists they will
probably have to address themselves to the task of
obtaining funds for an equivalent endowment elsewhere.
The preliminary step, they think, is to secure the district;
and if the Ecclesiastical Commissioners would legally
constitute it, as the case stands at present, a great
hindrance to the success of a public appeal would be
removed. From the correspondence you have had with
them do you think they would be willing to complete
at once the necessary formalities?

I trust you continue well. Although we seldom
exchange letters I hear of you not unfrequently, as you
may also of me through some of our mutual friends.
The parish is not prospering as its friends could wish,
as I have no doubt you are aware.

The more experience I have of the world the more I
see the necessity of confidence in God, not only as
regards our personal concerns, but in the events which

occur in our several localities, as well as in the wider sphere of politics. The Scripture, "Be still and know that I am God," contains one of those great truths which, when comprehended and received, relieves the mind from many anxieties.

I am, very truly yours,

JOHN LEYLAND.

To the Rev. P. Jones.

Hindley, April 17th, 1865.

My dear Sir,

The committee for the building of St. Peter's have been deliberating ever since I last wrote to you about the patronage. Sometimes they have been disposed to yield to the demand of the rector, unjustifiable as they think it; and sometimes they have determined to give the patronage to trustees, according as the difficulties of procuring a suitable endowment have appeared more or less great to them. Although the question is not yet formally settled, the committee have virtually decided that the whole and undivided patronage shall be vested in trustees.

An appointment will, therefore, probably soon be made, and we are all anxious to get a good man for the district. I have reason to believe that the incumbency would be offered to you if you would accept it, and I write for the express purpose of asking you to authorise me to say whether you would, under such circumstances, do so or not. I must pray you to consider that a most important field of labour is thus opened for which you are specially fitted. You have a thorough knowledge of the people and their wants, which years of experience could only give to another. The people would have confidence in you; and if the Church is to retain her legitimate influence, there is no time to lose in experiments. That your duty is to say you will come appears to me to be plain; and may I be allowed to add that, by resigning the living of All Saints', you committed, in my opinion, a wrong to the Church. By accepting that of St. Peter's you would make reparation for the wrong. The motives which led you to act as you did I have never ceased to respect, and I always admired the earnest faithfulness with which you discharged for so many years your important duties.

Believe me, my dear sir, to be
Yours very faithfully,
JOHN LEYLAND.

To the Rev. P. Jones.

Hindley, April 26th, 1865.

My dear Sir,

I received your reply to my letter with unfeigned sorrow. I have been cherishing, I confess, a secret hope ever since you left that those things which were difficulties to you when you were with us might be removed by further consideration, and that when our new church was ready, you too might be ready to be its minister. I am sincerely grieved that my hope has proved vain.

I did not refer to your resignation in an unfriendly spirit. A thought passed through my mind whilst I was writing, which I meant to use as an argument to induce you to accede to our wishes, that others, anxious like yourself for the welfare of the Church, look upon your resignation as tending to bring about a different result from what you do. No doubt my meaning might have been better worded, but the few letters I write I have to write with more or less haste, as I still make my daily journey to Liverpool, and have all the engagements I had two years ago. Believe me I have no feeling towards you but of sincere regard.

I am, very truly yours.
JOHN LEYLAND.

To John Blackburn, Esq.

Liverpool, May 3rd, 1865.

My dear Sir,

I was glad to receive a better account of your health. The air and water of Ilkley will shortly, I have little doubt, with God's blessing, perfect your cure.

I have a vivid recollection of the rich valley of the Wharf, and the extensive prospect there is from the Ilkley side, of farm land, woods, and river. The very recollection is almost enough to make one breathe the freer. Certainly I should like to be with you, but such a thing at the present time is impossible. Bright's marriage comes off to-morrow. We are all busy in preparation.

I did not receive the paper you say you sent.

I am, faithfully yours,
John Leyland.

To the Rev. P. Jones.

Hindley, April 14th, 1866.

My dear Sir,

I rejoice to inform you, and I know you will also rejoice to hear, that our new church is now on the very eve of completion. The pulpit, reading desk, communion table, and font, are only wanting inside, and the levelling of the yard outside, the fence wall being already built, and the entrance gates erected. On all hands it is admitted to be a handsome building. A design often looks better on paper than the building itself; in this instance the building looks quite as well, if not better, than the design.

Since I saw you in London I have been to look at Mr. Eckersley's church at Poolstock. Although a more costly building, it falls short of St. Peter's in symmetry and grace. The architect has, in my opinion, made a mistake in adopting a style partaking both of the middle and later periods of Gothic art. Buildings which have come down to us from past generations are valuable historical records, and doubtless ought to be preserved as nearly as possible in their original form, even if that form be at variance with generally acknowledged rules; but it is a very different thing to erect new buildings in a mixed or transition character. Purity here, according to one or other of the recognised divisions of art, is essential.

The Building Committee of St. Peter's are much in want of funds. The paid subscriptions are exhausted, and a large sum advanced by their bankers in addition, the repayment of which the present four members of the committee have had to guarantee. The grants made by the Incorporated Church Building Society and the Diocesan Church Building Society, will not be paid, I find, until after the consecration, and we are therefore desirous of getting in the outstanding subscriptions. The sum promised by the late Mr. Rowbottom has never been paid. If you would kindly mention this to Mrs. Latham, she would probably bring it before the notice of Mr. Rowbottom's executors.

The arrangements with the Ecclesiastical Commissioners for the district are not yet brought to a final close ; but the communications recently received lead us to expect that the district we applied for will be granted with but little modification.

The incumbent will not be appointed until the whole of the arrangements are complete, as the committee will then know their exact position, and what stipend they can offer. I am, yours very truly,

JOHN LEYLAND.

Messrs. Parry and Gamon.

Hindley, near Wigan, July 13th, 1866.

Gentlemen,

You are probably aware that a new church has been recently erected in this township, to which the name of St. Peter has been given. A district is promised by the Ecclesiastical Commissioners ; but, owing to the Act of Parliament under which we proceed—the Private Patronage Act, I believe—consecration, we are informed, will have to take place before the district can be formally assigned.

The conveyance of the site to the Ecclesiastical Commissioners is now being prepared by the solicitor of the Building Committee, Mr. T. F. Taylor, of Wigan, and the solicitors of the Ecclesiastical Commissioners.

When this is completed, which we hope will be in the course of a week or two from the present time, the building will be ready for consecration. Perhaps you will kindly inform me if there is anything which will require previous preparation. Tables of the Commandments, Creed, and Lord's Prayer, a font, and plate for the holy communion, have yet to be supplied. As we think some of our friends may, in time, present us with these things, we wish to know if it is absolutely necessary they should be provided before the consecration.

I am, Gentlemen, your obedient servant,

JOHN LEYLAND.

To Messrs. Parry and Gamon.

Liverpool, August 7th, 1866.

Gentlemen,

I forward, by book-post of this day, the printed form of queries received with your note of the 14th ult., with answers written opposite to the several questions. Tracings, in duplicate, of the ground-plan of the church, showing the sittings, I also enclose, and the copy of a letter addressed by the secretary of the Ecclesiastical Commissioners to Mr. T. F. Taylor, dated the 14th of June last, which will acquaint you with what is being done by the Commissioners. Since the letter was written the conveyance of the site has been completed. The committee would be grateful for any assistance you can render in hastening the completion of the remaining arrangements.

I am, Gentlemen, your obedient servant,

JOHN LEYLAND.

To Messrs. Parry and Gamon.

Hindley, August 30th, 1866.

Gentlemen,

I handed your last letter to our solicitor, Mr. Taylor, of Wigan, and requested him to communicate with the solicitors of the Ecclesiastical Commissioners respecting the deeds you mention. We hope to have all the church furniture provided by the end of this week, and to forward a certificate to the Commissioners setting this forth.   The committee do not now wish the consecration to take place until after the middle of September.

I am leaving home for a short time, and if you should have occasion to write to the committee before you hear from me again, I should be glad if you would address your letter to Mr. Taylor.

I am, Gentlemen, your obedient servant,

JOHN LEYLAND.

To Alfred Pennington, Esq.
Royal Hotel, Den,
Teignmouth, Sept. 11th, 1866.

My dear Sir,

I have heard nothing about St. Peter's since I left home, but I suppose all the arrangements will now be completed, excepting the actual ceremony of consecration.   I saw Mr. Jones when I was in London, and asked him to draw up an address to prefix to the statement of accounts which the treasurer proposes to issue. This address I enclose.   The paragraph on the second sheet under the letter A, he suggests, should be printed so that it may be detached by a perforated line from the other part of the circular.

I hope to be at home by the end of the week, and if you will call at my place on Sunday evening, all keeping well, you will find me there.

I am, faithfully yours,

JOHN LEYLAND.

To Messrs. Parry and Gamon.
Liverpool, Sept. 24th, 1866.

Gentlemen,

I laid your letter of the 21st inst. before the Building Committee of our new church, at Hindley, on Saturday evening.

The committee request me to ask if the Bishop would

kindly fix some day other than Tuesday or Friday for the consecration, as many of their friends who have helped them with subscriptions, and others from whom they hope to receive help, are engaged in the cotton trade, the markets for which at Manchester are on the days I have named, and they would consequently be prevented from attending.

I am, Gentlemen, your obedient servant,
JOHN LEYLAND.

————————

To Messrs. Parry and Gamon.

Liverpool, Sept. 27th, 1866.

Gentlemen,

I am desired by the Building Committee of St. Peter's Church, Hindley, to express their thanks to the Bishop for meeting their wishes respecting the day of consecration. They understand that Monday, the 15th of October, is the day fixed for the ceremony, and that the hour for the commencement of the service is eleven o'clock in the forenoon.

The committee would be glad to learn the Bishop's wishes respecting the administration of the sacrament, whether it should be immediately after the consecration, or on the Sunday following.

I am, Gentlemen, truly yours,
JOHN LEYLAND.

————————

To the Rev. P. Jones.

Liverpool, July 15th, 1868.

My dear Sir,

I have to thank you for two letters. I am sorry Mr. Loraine cannot come, and as August is so near I am not now sanguine of getting any help during the month.

Your visit to Buckinghamshire will have been to you an agreeable change. I take so much pleasure in the pure country myself that I can well understand how much you will enjoy it. We still continue without rain. The supply of water at Hindley—never good—is now become inconveniently inadequate to the wants of the inhabitants. A day or two ago my eye fell upon a verse in the Psalms: "The rivers are turned into a wilderness, and the water-springs into a dry ground," which is an exact description of our present condition. A few pages further on I read that "it is God who covereth the heaven with clouds, who prepareth rain for the earth." Prayers for help are needed.

I am, faithfully yours,

JOHN LEYLAND.

To Mr. John L. Martlew.

Queen's Hotel, Harrogate, April 25th, 1869.

Dear John,

I only arrived here this morning, and I am afraid there will not now be sufficient time left for me to hear from you, and to reply before you should decide on the question you are considering. Always cultivate economy. It is useful to everybody, but to young men of limited means it is of vital importance. It strengthens their habits of self-denial, keeps them from incurring debt—which leads to the ruin of thousands— and has a salutary influence in a variety of ways. Occasions occur at the same time when it is prudent to take other things into account, as it now does with you. Your expenses may be increased, but then your comfort may also be increased.

Any letters which may come for me be good enough to forward up to, and including, Wednesday in next week (but not after) to the above address.

I am, affectionately yours,

JOHN LEYLAND.

To Mr. John L. Martlew.

Queen's Hotel, Harrogate, April 30th, 1869.

Dear John,

I am glad we both agree as to the propriety of the proposed change.

You say nothing about college, and those intricate problems you were lately busied with.

It is told of Alexander the Great that, when he had subdued all the then known world, he wept because there was nothing more to conquer. I am thinking I may possibly find you on my return similarly affected. Having worked out your two last problems, you may be suffering disappointment at there being no more so difficult to triumph over. Be of good comfort, however; the field of study is wider than you imagine.

I am, sincerely yours,
JOHN LEYLAND.

To Alfred Pennington, Esq.

58, Threadneedle Street, London,
Sept. 3rd, 1869.

My dear Sir,

The specification of the organ for St. Peter's I sent, as you wished, to my friend, Mr. Blackburn. I have just got it back, and return it herewith along with his letter.

From the date of my note you will see that I have arrived in the great city.

In haste, very truly yours,
JOHN LEYLAND.

To John Blackburn, Esq.

58, Threadneedle Street, London,
Sept. 4th, 1869.

My dear Sir,

Your letter respecting the organ I have forwarded to my friend, Alfred Pennington. What has been done lately by the committee I do not know, nor who drew up the specification, but I do not think it was Schulze.

The organist of Leeds Parish Church, who is a friend of one of the committee, is expecting Schulze on a visit, and he has promised to bring him over to look at our church, so that it is quite possible he may be entrusted with the building of the organ.

In haste, very truly yours,

JOHN LEYLAND.

To Mr. H. J. Green.

Liverpool, March 1st, 1870.

Dear Mr. Green,

I was glad to hear of your safe arrival in London. It is trying to part with old friends, and I have no doubt you felt this acutely on Friday.

Mr. Bright is here, and he told me yesterday that he had arranged for Martlew to be in his brother's office, to commence business there on Monday, the 14th inst. He must, therefore, come to town on the previous Saturday (*i.e.*, the 12th inst.), by the London and North-Western Railway ; and I should feel obliged if you could arrange to meet him at Euston Station.

Will you favour me with a line, saying if you can do this ?   I am, truly yours,

JOHN LEYLAND.

To Mr. John L. Martlew.

Liverpool, March 16th, 1870.

Dear John,

I have received your two letters. You say you feel lonely, and let me tell you that I share with you the feeling. For two years I have had the daily care of you, so that I must needs feel your absence. I am in the midst of the exactions of an unusually busy day, and I should have preferred writing when I could have said more than I can say now, but you asked me to write, and I therefore write.

I will come up to town as soon as I am able, which yet, I am afraid, may not be until the middle of May.

I am, affectionately yours,

JOHN LEYLAND.

z

To Mr. John L. Martlew.

Liverpool, March 22nd, 1870.

Dear John,

It gave me great pleasure to think my hasty note of the 16th inst. was welcome. I am sorry you feel lonely, but yet I would rather you should feel so than be insensible to the change. The last people I envy are those who can leave old friends and accustomed places without emotion.

I said much to you in the way of counsel and warning before you left. Almost I feared I wearied you, yet now I feel as if I had said little. If, in this or other letters I may write, I reiterate what I have said, or caution you more than need be, believe me I am actuated only by kindness. Pitfalls and snares are on every hand of youth in London, and, like the apples of Sodom, present a fair and attractive appearance. The paths of right and wrong run at first near together, seemingly, indeed, side by side, but the further they are followed the wider they diverge. Resist the first impulse to wrong. I am sure you will grow daily more reconciled to your new home and duties.

The time of my proposed journey to London will soon be here, and, in the interim, write to me often; it will be a means of occupying and diverting your thoughts.

I am, affectionately yours,

JOHN LEYLAND.

To Mr. John L. Martlew.

Liverpool, March 29th, 1870.

Dear John,

Your letter of the 21st inst. was not delivered until after I had written mine of the following day's date. I have since received one from you dated the 24th inst. I can easily believe that the sight of Greenwich Hospital would fill you with admiration. In my opinion it is one of the grandest of our public edifices.

The style of architecture is well chosen, and admirably adapted for its purpose. The ample space which surrounds it, the stately domes, and the noble Thames rolling in front, are features which few, if any, of our other public buildings can equal.

The fine trees always delight me, as they seem to delight you. How I should rejoice if we had any such at Hindley. I have been planting in a small way ever since I was a lad, but if the trees I put down survive the vapours and smoke of the neighbourhood a few years, they are overpowered at last. I should like you to tell me what you see in your rambles, and to describe the impression the various sights make upon you.

I hope you are living frugally and within your income. The temptations to spend money in London are numerous, and unless you are determined, *very determined*, you will soon be drawn into excess. Pay ready money for everything you get, never buy a single thing until you have money in your pocket to pay for it. Enter your receipts and payments carefully in a book. Unless you see the various items in black and white you will never know how you stand. Your office hours are easy enough. Half-an-hour, I suppose, will be sufficient to carry you from your lodgings to Old Broad Street. You have, therefore, time in the morning and in the evening which you should employ profitably.

I am, sincerely yours,

JOHN LEYLAND.

To Mr. John L. Martlew.

Liverpool, March 30th, 1870.

Dear John,

You are right in seeing what you can of the marvels of the great city. Go alone; don't have companions. Not one out of a vast number but will influence you for evil. Affectionately yours,

JOHN LEYLAND.

To Mr. H. I. Green.

Liverpool, April 2nd, 1870.

My dear Mr. Green,

Some people take a long time to accommodate themselves to new duties. I don't know whether you are one of the number, or if you can fall at once, as the saying is, easy into the saddle. Your old colleagues, Arnold, Jones, and Houghton, will, I have no doubt, prove of great assistance both to you and the post-office, in bringing their department into working order. I trust they are all well, and that they like London. Give to each of them my regards. I should be glad if you would let me know now, and from time to time afterwards, how John Martlew gets on. As he is away from his relatives and friends, I wish you to watch over him carefully. He is singularly careless, I am sorry to say, in money matters; and, with his slender income, if his thoughtlessness is not checked, it may quickly lead him into difficulties, which even subsequent prudence may be long in extricating him from. Extravagance, for such it really should be called, is a vice, and, like all vices, grows with what it feeds upon. The superfluity of to-day becomes the necessity of to-morrow. A good many young men are more careful to clothe their backs than to store their heads. They do not seem to be able to comprehend that smart clothes and prodigality in spending money, in the absence of other qualifications, are but poor passports to respectability. If Martlew goes wrong in any way be sure and let me know at once. It is mistaken kindness to screen a fault. An accidental error, if reproved, may be avoided afterwards; if concealed, and passed over without rebuke, it soon grows into a confirmed habit.

I am, faithfully yours,

JOHN LEYLAND.

To Mr. John L. Martlew.

Liverpool, April 5th, 1870.

Dear John,

I observe you use office paper with printed

heading for your private letters. This paper is not yours, and you should not therefore use it. Be honest strictly and scrupulously in trifles. From my own purse I will glady furnish you with a stock both of paper and envelopes when I am in town.

In haste, sincerely yours,
John Leyland.

To Mr. John L. Martlew.

Liverpool, April 12th, 1870.

Dear John,

My old friend, Thomas Gaskell, is dead. Last Friday Mr. Walmesley was over, and was with me at the Grange for some time. On our way thence to Ince we called upon Mr. Gaskell at about one o'clock at noon, found him sat in his arm-chair, not worse than usual, and had such conversation with him for the space of half-an-hour as he was capable of joining in. We then proceeded to Ince and Wigan, where I parted with Mr. Walmesley. Between six and seven o'clock I returned to the Grange, and soon afterwards a messenger came to tell me he was dead. I went directly to his house, and found him lying just as he died. It appears that after Mr. Walmesley and I left him he continued as usual, partook of tea, and at a little past seven fell from his chair and died almost immediately.

You have told me nothing yet about your cost of living. I sincerely trust you are not exceeding your income. Make a rule, I beseech you, to save something, however little, weekly. If you are able to show me your account book, with all the *pros* and *cons* regularly entered, it will gratify me.

The University Boat Race is a sight I have long wished to see. The bright sunny day of Wednesday must have contributed much to the enjoyment of the spectators, and I do not wonder at your being highly pleased.   Tell me when you next write whether you take your walks alone or in company.

I am, sincerely yours,
JOHN LEYLAND.

To Mr. John L. Martlew.

The Grange, Hindley, April 23rd, 1870.

Dear John,

Your letter, describing your visit to the Crystal Palace, was delivered as I sat at breakfast on Sunday morning.

The incessant mental strain I have had to bear since last Christmas, through the breaking up of the Magnetic Company, causes a complete prostration of the system whenever the necessity for exertion is for the time removed, so that any diversion in these intervals is welcome. Your letter came seasonably, and afforded a lively and pleasant relief. Undoubtedly the Crystal Palace is an interesting place. So vast, and, if I may use the word, so ethereal is it; so abundant and so beautiful are the objects of nature and art within its precincts, that the mind, on a first visit, cannot escape a delightful bewilderment. I well remember the first sight I had of the building in Hyde Park, in 1851. It was a sunny morning, near the end of October. I entered by the central transept, and the first object I saw was a lofty elm, whose branches stretched almost to the very roof. The leaves were of the brightest yellow, and, as they became loosened from the branches, floated downwards, here singly, and there in a gentle shower. The stalls in the body of the nave and the fronts of the galleries displayed hangings of gay and varied colours, and a busy throng of sightseers was moving everywhere. All these elements contributed to form a scene so remarkable that it is yet as vivid on my mind as when my eyes first fell upon it. Knowing you intended to visit the Palace on Good Friday, I read the account of the proceedings in the *Times* of the following day, and I thought the amusements provided for the visitors were liberal even to excess. What with the ordinary and the extraordinary sights, the fine weather, and the large assemblage, you must have seen it under favourable circumstances. Permit me to say here a word for conscience sake. I fear this is not quite the right way to spend Good Friday. However, as you are bound to make good every day in the week at the office, I will not now, though I may hereafter, cavil on that head. You have said nothing in any of your letters about going to church. May I ask you to make it a rule to attend once at least on the Sunday? Going even for form's sake is better than not going at all. It is an acknowledgment—a poor one I admit— but still an acknowledgment of our dependence on God, and of our need of His pardon and care. To go in devout humility, and with an earnest desire to learn God's will, cannot fail to be followed by blessing. Our thoughts, desires, enjoyments, incessantly turn away, as you yourself well know, from what is good and right.

You are now young, and have the world before you. Give way to your appetites, and you may for a time enjoy pleasure, or what goes by the name of pleasure. On the other hand, with God's help—help that often comes by Sunday worship—you may restrain unruly passions, lead a pure, godly, and sober life, and enjoy genuine happiness. And how great will be the satisfaction, should you be spared to middle life, or old age, to look back and to reflect that you have led no brother or sister astray, corrupted none by evil conversation, but, by a good example, won many to virtue.

I am, affectionately yours,

JOHN LEYLAND.

To Mr. John L. Martlew.

Liverpool, May 7th, 1870.

Dear John,

The Globe Parcel Express Company should deliver to you on Monday a packet of stationery, which

I have confided to their care this morning here for carriage. Let me know if they discharge the trust they have undertaken. You will find some postage stamps in the packet, which I send to enable you to frank the letters you write to me. When they are all used tell me.   I am, sincerely yours,

JOHN LEYLAND.

To John Wilton, Esq.,

Liverpool, May 7th, 1870.

My dear John,

I only received your kind letter after ten o'clock last night. How many recollections of past years sprung up at the sight of your handwriting, which I had not seen for ever so long a time! Both of us have made a many stages in our homeward journey in the interval, the hair has thinned or whitened, and the furrows in the face worn deeper. But we have lived poor lives if we have failed in discerning how empty are most of the tempting things life offers, and how precious and abiding are the love and affection of our friends.

The truer interpretation experience gives of God's providences yields also its fruits in a wider sympathy, greater patience, and brighter hopes for hereafter.

I am still in harness for the Magnetic Company, but my duties cease with the present month. The first week in June I am to be occupied, God sparing me, with the business of an estate belonging to a gentleman who lives in the south. After that I shall be at liberty, and will write to arrange for a convenient time to visit you.   I remain, affectionately yours,

JOHN LEYLAND.

To Mr. John L. Martlew.

The Grange, Hindley, Aug. 8th, 1870.

Dear John,

Our great yearly fair was held on Thursday. It passed over in much the same way that preceding fairs have done. There were the club processions in the forenoon, and services in the Old Church; and in the afternoon the school processions and the usual tea parties.

Mr. Southworth opened, as he has done for several years past, a field behind his house for the children of the Old Church Schools to amuse themselves in, between the close of the procession and the time for tea. As I had been victimised in providing a number of prizes to be run for, consisting of dolls for the girls, of balls, foot-balls, nine-pins, and other things for the lads, I repaired thither soon after four o'clock to distribute them. Great fun the races caused, I assure you. At the instigation of Mr. Newbold, the three Misses Mort, Miss Tindall, Mrs. Holcroft, and a Mrs. Oakes went in for the largest doll. The six competitors ran only quietly—for they wore much finery, which a rapid motion might have disarranged—and nearly abreast, but, unluckily, just as they neared the winning-post, they tripped one another up, and down they all fell in a heap. As a veracious chronicler, I am afraid I must record that the first effect of this unfortunate event on the bystanders was a hearty fit of laughter, but as soon as their emotions permitted, assistance was duly rendered, and the prostrate competitors were raised again upon their feet. Miss Tindall's bonnet received damage in the fall, which seemed much to disturb her equanimity. I am afraid she is not a philosopher, but then, perhaps, philosophy could scarcely be expected under such trying circumstances. The race had to be run over again, and Miss Tindall came off the victor. The acquisition of the prize, I hope, would soothe any asperity in the breast of the lady which might be occasioned by the mishap to her bonnet.

When the day was waning I sauntered through the Market Place and Market Street. There were fewer people, I thought, than usual, and fewer attractions. A single show, the great curiosity in which was a fat lady weighing five hundredweight, was tempting the pennies from the pockets of the sightseers.

Oyster stalls, fruit stalls, and gingerbread stalls were numerous. A shooting gallery had its admirers, but the chief attraction centred in a bicycle apparatus. The machine revolved in a circle, and contained from forty to fifty seats for riders, two abreast, who propelled it in the usual manner by the motion of the feet. The proprietor would reap a golden harvest, for no sooner did one set of riders dismount than their places were filled by others.

The drought still continues in this district. With the exception of a slight shower yesterday, we have had no rain since you were here. Many of the shrubs at the Grange are dying for want of moisture, and our stock of water is now reduced to so low an ebb that we dare not use any for gardening purposes. The grass in the fields is burned up, and the leaves are falling from the trees as if it were autumn.

To-morrow I go on a short visit to my old friend, John Wilton. As he lives in Eccleston, within a few miles from Liverpool, I may probably run over there once or twice during my stay.

I am, sincerely yours,
JOHN LEYLAND.

To Mr. John L. Martlew.

The Grange, Hindley, Aug. 16th, 1870.

My dear John,

My sympathies go entirely with yours in favour of the French armies. Prussia's conduct to Denmark was so unjust and rapacious, and to Austria also, that I doubt not the atrocious wickedness she committed will, sooner or later, be punished. If you or I, in our private capacity, had been guilty of like conduct, we should have been arraigned before the bar of justice as felons. France is possibly not much better; but, at any rate, she has not openly of late years defied justice, honesty, and solemn engagements, as Prussia has done.

I am, sincerely yours,
JOHN LEYLAND.

To Mr. John L. Martlew.

> The Grange, August 20, 1870.

My dear John,

You have either more time than I have, or you can use your pen more readily, for, although I try to keep up with your letters, I find myself always in arrear. I do not know how many I have received since I last wrote, but several, and two newspapers to boot. I like seeing the London papers, yet I am far from wishing you to supply me with them. Hindley is not so remote from the civilised world but that they may be picked up here occasionally.

It is very grievous to see the hostile part the *Times*, and one or two other leading journals, are taking in reference to France in this unhappy war. Richard Cobden is not a man I care to quote, but he spoke the truth when he said "the *Times* had an instinct for evil." To turn about as it does, and follow the winning side, to hold up a man or a course of policy for vituperation one day, and to slaver him or it with flattery the next, is as abject a course as any journal can pursue.

> I am, sincerely yours,
>
> JOHN LEYLAND.

To Mr. John L. Martlew.

> Morecambe, Sept. 6th, 1870.

Dear John,

I came here yesterday, and am staying at the North Western Hotel. From what I have seen of the place I do not think I shall stay long, therefore do not write, as I may leave before a letter could arrive. Being so near Cumberland, I may very likely take the opportunity to have another look at the lovely lakes and the grand mountains with which it is enriched.

I am suffering, I am sorry to say, from a great depression of spirits, and without the existence of any special cause. I am, sincerely yours,

> JOHN LEYLAND.

To Mr. John L. Martlew.

King's Arms Hotel, Keswick, Sept. 7th, 1870.
Dear John,

You will see from the date of my letter that I am carrying out the project of visiting the Lake District, which I told you I was entertaining in the short letter I wrote to you from Morecambe. That place did not take my fancy. The air is far less bracing than Blackpool, and ebb tide leaves bare extensive sand banks, and a beach covered partly with pebbles, and partly with mud, between the water and the promenade, which is another drawback. The first halt I made after leaving Morecambe was at Lancaster, a town I had not seen since I was a lad of fifteen, and yet I remembered its chief features distinctly. I next stopped at Penrith, and next at the place whence I am writing. The weather is unsettled, and my stay may consequently only be short. I am somewhat better than I was at the early part of the week.

The events happening in France are so bewildering that one can scarcely estimate their vast importance. The fall of Napoleon inspires me with no regret. The Bonapartes are, and have ever been since they had a name in Europe, a wicked family, trampling upon right, justice, and truth for their own aggrandisement. For the French nation I feel a profound sympathy in this their time of sore trial, and trust they may soon be able to retrieve their fortunes and vindicate their power in the face of Europe. I have still faith that they will be able to do it.

I am, affectionately yours,
. JOHN LEYLAND.

To Mr. John L. Martlew.

Keswick, Sept. 9th, 1870.
Dear John,

From an early hour this morning up to a short time ago the rain was falling heavily, and caused me to fear I might be kept a prisoner in the house all day. Somewhat suddenly the rain ceased, a breeze has sprung up, and I am not without hopes of being able to turn out. Yesterday was most enjoyable ; thick and heavy clouds in the early morning gave place to a blue sky and sunshine in the forenoon.

I accompanied a number of gentlemen in an open carriage along one side of Derwentwater, through Borrowdale to Buttermere, returning to Keswick by the Vale of Newlands. The drive, including the time spent at lunch, occupied from ten o'clock in the forenoon to six in the evening.

All keeping well, I shall be in London now very soon.

Sincerely yours,

JOHN LEYLAND.

To Mr. John L. Martlew.

Lichfield, Sept. 11th, 1870.

My dear John,

The wet and stormy weather I met with in Cumberland determined me to turn my steps southwards at once. I could have reached town to-day, but that I thought I should like once again to worship in the glorious Cathedral of this city. To-morrow I may be there by noon, and if you wish to join me, you can do so when your day's duties are over.

I am, sincerely yours,

JOHN LEYLAND.

To Mr. John L. Martlew.

The Grange, Hindley, Sept. 28th, 1870.

My dear John,

Thanks to a good Providence, I arrived safe at home last night. The beautiful weather yesterday made my homeward journey pleasant. The Great Northern Railway, which I travelled by, runs through an interesting country. The sere and yellow leaves of the trees gave a beauty to the landscape which not even bright, joyous, hopeful spring-time, nor yet summer—

> "In universal bounty shedding herbs,
> And fruits, and flowers"—

can rival. These autumn leaves seemed to present an analogy to man in his decline. The fruits of a chastened spirit, ripened by the discipline of life's labour and trials, are, like their yellow, their gold, and their scarlet, more beautiful far than youth, whose freshness is so often marred by ungovernable passions and grovelling aspirations.

I am, affectionately yours,

JOHN LEYLAND.

To Mr. John L. Martlew.

The Grange, Oct. 11th, 1870.

My dear John,

Our annual Cricket Club supper came off last night. A goodly number assembled to partake of the savoury viands prepared by that excellent caterer, Mr. Jaggar. Speeches, too, there were of an excellence rarely, if ever, surpassed in our local annals. Witness that of one of the vice-presidents, who, when proposing the toast of the magistrates of the county, after some eulogistic remarks, added, " but perhaps the least said about them the better."

I am, sincerely yours,

JOHN LEYLAND.

To Mr. John L. Martlew.

Chester, Oct. 19th, 1870.

My dear John,

In the autumn of last year, you will recollect, I dare say, spending a Sunday with me in this ancient city. I am writing in the coffee room of the same inn we then stayed at, which bears, you may perhaps remember, the good old-fashioned sign of the " Hop

Pole." I am alone. I have read all I care to read in the papers; there are no books lying about save a mutilated Cheshire Directory; so I have betaken myself to scribbling for want of something better to do. I am come here to attend the Diocesan Conference. The subject of consideration to-day has been education, which, important as it is, is not the first question a Church Conference, in my opinion, should address itself to. The meeting was held in a large room in the New Town Hall, as ill adapted for the conveyance of sound as any I was ever in. The consequence was that, having a seat at some distance from the platform, I heard very little of what was said. To-morrow the questions selected for discussion are, " How to augment the income of small livings," for the morning; and "The best means of securing lay help," for the afternoon. I am, sincerely yours,

JOHN LEYLAND.

To Mr. John L. Martlew.

The Grange, Nov. 5th, 1870.

My dear John,

And so this Titanic struggle is ended. Like the poor unfortunate French armies, you have had to capitulate, being fairly vanquished by the superior strategy of the enemy.

Only yesterday the heavens were black with clouds, peals of thunder were rolling, the wind was sweeping wildly along. To-day

" The groan, the burst, the fiery flash is o'er,"

the sun is smiling on the landscape, the mountain peaks glowing in roseate light, the valleys lying in serene beauty, the hum of everything rising in sweet melody to the ear. The change is refreshing.

Seriously, I am pleased that the quarrel has ended as it has. You have behaved well.

I am, sincerely yours,

JOHN LEYLAND.

To Mr. John L. Martlew.

The Grange, Nov. 15th, 1870.

My dear John,

I expected to have received a letter from you this morning, informing me of the result of your interview with Mrs. Smith on Saturday. Deal fairly with her. In money transactions, as indeed in everything else, think, in the first place, what is just and right to do. Afterwards look to consequences. If a man acts thus he will never go far astray, and will escape many a difficulty.

I may very likely come to London for a few days before Christmas.

My old malady—a depression of spirits—is again troubling me. A day or two at Blackpool would, I think, be of service, but I doubt if I can find time to go.

I am, sincerely yours,

JOHN LEYLAND.

To Mr. John L. Martlew.

The Grange, Nov. 22nd, 1870.

My dear John,

A severe cold has been added to my other ailments, and compelled me to be a prisoner in the house. "Hope," which "springs eternal in the human mind," animates me still, so that I am not wholly cast down. Nevertheless, I am grievously unwell.

I was pleased to hear by your note of yesterday that you had satisfied Mrs. Smith's demands. Her moderation is to be commended. Mr. Green will, no doubt, have told you that I met him in Liverpool on Wednesday. It does one good to look at his jolly face and portly figure. He spoke kindly of you. I took the opportunity of my visit to purchase backgammon board and men, chessmen, and playing cards. No doubt you will laugh at my complainings after this.

I am, sincerely yours,

JOHN LEYLAND.

To Mr. John L. Martlew.

The Grange, Nov. 30th, 1870.

My dear John,

If I tell you I have been out of doors again you will suppose that my cold is better, and you will be right. Still my recovery is not yet so advanced as to permit me to dispense with care and wrapping up. I am vexed to tell you I am summoned to serve on the jury at the coming Liverpool assizes, from Monday the 12th to Saturday the 17th of December. This unfortunate engagement will render it impossible for me to visit London before Christmas.

In a recent letter you say something of my teaching you certain games, instruments of which I told you I had been purchasing. I will now give you a first lesson. Use the spade of diligence, and the club of perseverance, keep an honest heart, and hold fast the diamond of purity.

Play these cards as I recommend, and I pledge my word that you will win something worth having.

I am, sincerely yours,

JOHN LEYLAND.

To James Bent, Esq.

The Grange, Hindley, near Wigan,
Dec. 10th, 1870.

My dear Mr. Bent,

My own experience of the difficulty of breaking a long silence, I must say, confirms the generally received opinion. But the effort—if it be right to use the word—is at once repaid in pleasure, and I cannot help wondering, whilst I am writing, how it is I have never attempted what I am now doing long ago. I have often thought of you. Some three years ago, as far as I can recollect, I was in your neighbourhood, and made an attempt to see you. I got by rail as far as Shipley Station, and walked thence about half a mile in the direction of your house, which I expected to arrive at every minute. Not recollecting the road, I made inquiries, when I was told I was still two miles and a half distant. I had an engagement in Bradford at a later hour in the day, and I found time would not allow me to proceed, so that I was unwillingly obliged to turn back.

I am now living here altogether. The transfer of the telegraphs to Government took away my occupation, and my duties in Liverpool ceased with the month of last May. In health, though not quite well, I have much to be thankful for. I suffer from no organic disease, yet I am often complaining. I am paying the penalty, I am afraid, of too close an application for a long period to business. Still, I repeat, I have great cause for thankfulness.

Great changes have come to pass since we first knew each other, and in no year have they been more startling than in the present. Never have men in high places brought more terrible calamities on the human race at any period of the world's history than the wicked ambition of the present King of Prussia, his unscrupulous Chancellor, and the ex-Emperor of France.

Few of our old Edge Hill friends remain. Dr. Barker, I presume, is still alive. I doubt if Rounthwaite be, as the last time I saw him, now more than two years ago, he was but the wreck of his former self. I cannot name another survivor It is a melancholy task to call over the muster roll of one's old associates, and to find so many familiar names lying in the dust.

> "Swift to its close ebbs out life's little day."

I hope to hear soon from you, and that you may be able to say all is well with you and yours.

I am, yours sincerely,

John Leyland.

FINIS.

John Heywood. Excelsior Printing Works, Hulme Hall Road, Manchester.